The Cold War in East As

This textbook provides a survey of East Asia during the Cold War from 1945 to 1991. Focusing on the persistence and flexibility of its culture and tradition when confronted by the West and the US, this book investigates how they intermesh to establish the nations that have entered the modern world.

Through the use of newly declassified Communist sources, the narrative helps students form a better understanding of the origins and development of post-WWII East Asia. The analysis demonstrates how East Asia's position in the Cold War was not peripheral but, in many key senses, central. The active role that East Asia played, ultimately, turned this main Cold War battlefield into a "buffer" between the United States and the Soviet Union. Covering a range of countries, this textbook explores numerous events, which took place in East Asia during the Cold War, including:

- The occupation of Japan,
- Civil war in China and the establishment of Taiwan,
- The Korean War,
- The Vietnam War,
- China's Reforming Movement.

Moving away from Euro-American centric approaches and illuminating the larger themes and patterns in the development of East Asian modernity, *The Cold War in East Asia* is an essential resource for students of Asian History, the Cold War, and World History.

Xiaobing Li is Professor and Chair in the Department of History and Director of the Western Pacific Institute at the University of Central Oklahoma.

The Cold War in East Asia

Xiaobing Li

Routledge
Taylor & Francis Group

LONDON AND NEW YORK

First published 2018
by Routledge
2 Park Square, Milton Park, Abingdon, Oxon OX14 4RN

and by Routledge
711 Third Avenue, New York, NY 10017

Routledge is an imprint of the Taylor & Francis Group, an informa business

© 2018 Xiaobing Li

British Library Cataloguing-in-Publication Data
A catalogue record for this book is available from the British Library

Library of Congress Cataloging-in-Publication Data
Names: Li, Xiaobing, 1954- author.
Title: The Cold War in East Asia / Xiaobing Li.
Description: Abingdon, Oxon ; New York, NY : Routledge, 2017. | Includes bibliographical references and index.
Identifiers: LCCN 2017013023 | ISBN 9781138651791 (hardback) |
ISBN 9781138651807 (pbk.) | ISBN 9781315624600 (ebook)
Subjects: LCSH: East Asia--History--1945- | East Asia--Foreign relations--20th century. | Cold War.
Classification: LCC DS518.1 .L488 2017 | DDC 950.4/2--dc23
LC record available at https://lccn.loc.gov/2017013023

ISBN: 978-1-138-65179-1 (hbk)
ISBN: 978-1-138-65180-7 (pbk)
ISBN: 978-1-315-62460-0 (ebk)

Typeset in Times New Roman
by Taylor & Francis Books

Contents

Maps

Acknowledgments

Many people at the University of Central Oklahoma (UCO), where I have been teaching since 1993, have contributed to the book and deserve recognition. First, I thank President Don Betz, Provost John F. Barthell, Associate Vice President Gary Steward, Dean of the College of Liberal Arts Catherine S. Webster, and Chairperson of the Department of History and Geography Patricia Loughlin. They have been very supportive of the project over the past years. The UCO faculty merit-credit program sponsored by the Office of Academic Affairs, as well as travel funds from the College of Liberal Arts, provided funding for my research and trips to conferences. The UCO Student Research, Creative, and Scholarly Activities (RCSA) Grants sponsored by the Office of High-Impact Practices, made student research assistants available for the project. Several graduate and undergraduate students at UCO contributed to the book, including Shuhao Liu, Liying Sun, and Jiahui Xu. Annamaria Martucci provided secretarial assistance.

Special thanks to Allan R. Millett at the University of New Orleans, Harold M. Tanner at the University of North Texas, Steven I. Levine at the University of Montana, and Stanley Rosen at the University of Southern California, who made important comments on earlier versions of some chapters that were presented as conference papers. Wynn Gadkar-Wilcox at Western Connecticut State University and Yi Sun at San Diego University shared with me some of the information we have put together as co-authors for another writing project over the past four years. Brad Watkins prepared all the maps. Michelle Magnusson and Ann Riley-Adams copy-edited the chapters.

The completion of this volume on such an important subject requires not only strong support from American universities, but also close co-operation with academic institutes in East Asia. I am grateful to the Dean of the College of International Relations Niu Jun at Peking (Beijing) University, Assistant to President Yu Qun at Northeast Normal University in Changchun, Associate Dean Nomura Shigeharu at Osaka University, Director Zhou Wei of the Institute of Social and Economic Studies at China Tibetology Research Center, Yang Dongyu at Shaanxi Normal University, Department Chairperson Vithal Potdar at Seshadripuram College, Shao Xiao at Ji'nan University, Director Sophia Kim at Pusan (Busan) National University, and Dawa Cairen of the Buddhism Research Center at China Academy of Social Sciences (CASS), for their help and advice on my research in China, Japan, Korea, Taiwan, and Vietnam. This volume is also supported by "Fundamental Research Funds for the Central Universities" (Project #15JNYH006), under Zhang Wenzhen at Ji'nan University in Guangzhou, Guangdong.

During the research period over the past years, my wife, Tran, and our two children, Kevin and Christina, shared with me the burden of overseas traveling to East Asia. Their love and support have made this book possible.

Note on transliterations

The *Hanyu pinyin* Romanization system is applied to Chinese names of persons, places, and terms. Transliteration is also used for the titles of Chinese publications. A person's name is written in the Chinese way, the surname first, such as Mao Zedong. Some popular names have traditional Wade-Giles spellings appearing in parentheses after the first use of the *Hanyu pinyin*, such as Zhou Enlai (Chou En-lai), as do popular names of places like Guangzhou (Canton). The Japanese and Korean names of persons, places, and terms are also translated by following the traditional East Asian practice that the surname is usually written first, as in Kim Il-sung and Yoshida Shigeru. Exceptions are made for a few figures whose names are widely known in reverse order, such as Syngman Rhee. If a place has different spellings in Korean and English litera- ture, parentheses are used at its first appearance – for example, Hahwaokri (Hagaru-ri). The Vietnamese names follow the traditional way that the surname is written first, then middle name, and first name, as in Ngo Dinh Diem and Vo Nguyen Giap. Most people in Vietnam are referred to by their given names, therefore President Diem and General Giap. The exceptions are for a very few particularly illustrious persons, such as Ho Chi Minh, who was called President Ho.

Abbreviations

AAA	anti-aircraft artillery
ADIZ	Air Defense Identification Zone (China)
ARVN	Army of the Republic of Vietnam (South Vietnam)
CAMS	China Academy of Military Science
CASS	China Academy of Social Sciences
CCP	Chinese Communist Party
CIA	Central Intelligence Agency (US)
CMAG	Chinese Military Advisory Group (Vietnam)
CMC	Central Military Commission (CCP)
CPPCC	Chinese People's Political Consultative Conference
CPVF	Chinese People's Volunteers Force (the Korean War)
CSSM	China Society for Strategy and Management
DMZ	Demilitarized Zone
DOD	Department of Defense (US)
DPRK	Democratic People's Republic of Korea (North Korea)
DRV	Democratic Republic of Vietnam (North Vietnam)
DSP	Democratic Socialist Party (Japan)
FECOM	Far East Command (US)
FIE	foreign-invested enterprise
GATT	Global Agreement on Tariffs and Trade
GDP	gross domestic product
GMD	Guomindang (or Kuomintang, KMT)
GSD	General Staff Department (PLA)
HKSAR	Hong Kong Special Administrative Region
HPRS	household production responsibility system (China)
HQ	headquarters
IMF	International Monetary Fund
IOC	International Olympic Committee
JCS	Joint Chiefs of Staff (US)
JSDF	Japan Self-Defense Forces
JSP	Japan Socialist Party
KDP	Korean Democratic Party (South Korea)
KMT	Kuomintang (Chinese Nationalist Party, or Guomindang, GMD)
LDP	Liberal Democratic Party (Japan)
NATO	North Atlantic Treaty Organization
NCO	non-commissioned officer

NDU	National Defense University (PLA)
NEFA	North-East Frontier Agency (Chinese-Indian border)
NKPA	North Korean People's Army
NPC	National People's Congress (China)
NPR	National Police Reserve (Japan)
NSA	National Security Agency (US and Japan)
NSC	National Security Council (US)
OPEC	Organization of the Petroleum Exporting Countries
PLA	People's Liberation Army (China)
PLAAF	PLA Air Force
PLAN	PLA Navy
POE	privately owned enterprise
POW	prisoners of war
PRC	People's Republic of China
RMB	*Renminbi* (Chinese currency)
ROC	Republic of China (Taiwan)
ROK	Republic of Korea (South Korea)
SCAP	Supreme Commander for the Allied Powers (Japan)
SEZ	Special Economic Zone (China)
SMAG	Soviet Military Advisory Group (China and North Korea)
SOE	state-owned enterprise
SSE	Shanghai Stock Exchange (China)
SZSE	Shenzhen Stock Exchange (China)
UN	United Nations
UNC	United Nations Command (the Korean War)
UNF	United Nations Force (the Korean War)
US	United States
USSR	Union of Soviet Socialist Republics
WWI	World War I
WWII	World War II

Introduction

Understanding modern East Asia

The rapid economic growth of East Asia (especially Japan, South Korea, Taiwan, and Hong Kong) set the region apart from the rest of the world in the 1980s. China took off during the last decade of the Cold War and in 2011 became the second largest economy in the world only after the United States. As we taught, our students asked some pivotal questions: What happened in East Asia through the Cold War? How did third-world countries like China develop into economic superpowers in less than thirty years? Why does North Korea still threaten the security of the Asian-Pacific region today? What is going on over the disputed islands in South China Sea? Unfortunately, available history textbooks do not provide significant answers to these important questions. Historians have struggled to fully define East Asia's place in the Cold War.

This book places East Asia, including China, Japan, and Koreas, at center stage for exploring the history of the Cold War from 1945 to 1991. Indeed, conventional texts have adopted a Euro-American centric approach, characterizing the Cold War as a confrontation between two post-World War II (WWII) superpowers: the United States and the Soviet Union; as well as two contending camps: the free world and the communists/socialists in Europe. East Asia's position in the Cold War was treated secondarily or peripherally at best due to cultural and linguistic barriers and the lack of readily available sources for Western researchers, among other reasons. After the collapse of the Soviet Union in 1991, Russian government archives partially opened, providing historians with new opportunities and resources for research in the past ten or fifteen years. More scholars in the West began to recognize the importance of East Asia's role in the Cold War in their recent studies.[1] Then, the communist sources became available in recent years. These sources certainly require historians to be more creative in the construction of new analytical frameworks for a more balanced view. Akira Iriye points out that Cold War historiography is no longer an orthodox-revisionist debate, but "requires a different conceptual scheme."[2]

This book functions as a survey text with different interpretations of the origins and development of the Cold War in East Asia. It explores new historiographical, thematic, and topical trends in the history of modern East Asia. Told with an emphasis on Asian views, it explains how these countries, changed and transformed forever, have survived the Cold War and intermeshed to establish the nations that have entered the modern world. One of our primary objectives is to provide a better understanding of today's East Asia. The book applies to both scholarly debate and college pedagogy by establishing important lines for potential research in the Cold War Studies and opening up new areas for Asian Studies courses. Students will find the book's primary sources, many of which were not readily available in English, of great interest, and will study intriguing and important issues that have been previously overlooked.

A new approach to Cold War history

The volume focuses on important events in East Asia through the Cold War and braids together the global power struggle and local revolutions, reforms, and wars, which affected the lives of hundreds of millions of people. Our narrative and analysis elucidates that East Asia's position in the Cold War was not peripheral but, in many key senses, central. After the Korean War broke out in 1950, East Asia became a focal point of the global Cold War, only four years after Soviet leader Josef Stalin (1878–1953) and British Prime Minister Winston Churchill (1874–1965) issued their declarations of Cold War and US President Harry S. Truman (1884–1972) delivered a speech focused on containment in 1946, now referred to as the Truman Doctrine. Then from 1965 to 1973, the Vietnam War also erupted along the Western Pacific rim, which along with the Korean War consisted of the only two "hot wars" that the United States fought during the Cold War.

Moreover, the active role that East Asia played also turned this main Cold War battle-field into a strange "buffer" between Washington and Moscow. With East Asia standing in the middle, it was less likely that the United States and the Soviet Union would become involved in a direct military confrontation or even a nuclear showdown anywhere in the West.[3] Thus, East Asia emerged as a critical component to keep the Cold War "cold" in Europe for forty-six years; what John Lewis Gaddis described as the "long peace."[4]

Furthermore, East Asia contributed directly to the end of the global Cold War. Although the collapse of the Soviet Union and the socialist camp in East Europe did not occur until 1986–1991, several key issues were already on full display in East Asia in the early 1970s. Two key factors in the demise of the Soviet Union were the serious overextension of the Soviet Union's power and the complete loss of confidence in communism "representing the future" by communists and sympathizers throughout the world.[5] China played a crucial role in creating these factors. This process began first and foremost with the Sino-Soviet split in the 1960s and the Sino-American rapprochement in 1972.

In retrospect, few events during the Cold War played a more important role in shaping the orientation and essence of the Cold War than the Sino-Soviet split. Some Western historians agree that the alliance between Beijing and Moscow was the corner-stone of the Communist international alliance system in the 1950s.[6] Yet, beginning in the early 1960s, the Sino-Soviet alliance began to decline because of complicated domestic and international factors. The most important of these was the debate over whether Beijing or Moscow would become the center of the Asian Communist move-ments. The great Sino-Soviet polemic debate in the early and mid-1960s further undermined the ideological foundation of the Sino-Soviet alliance.[7] Eventually, Moscow and Beijing broke up and buried the shared consciousness among communists and communist sympathizers all over Asia. No longer could communism be seen as the solution to the problems created by the worldwide process of modernization. The hostility between China and the Soviet Union reached a new height in 1969, when two bloody clashes occurred on the Sino-Soviet border.[8] Reportedly, Moscow's leaders even considered using a "preemptive nuclear strike" against China.[9]

Threats from the Soviet Union created motive for Beijing to pursue a rapprochement with the United States.[10] Both President Richard Nixon (1913–1994) and Henry Kissinger (1923–), national security advisor at the White House, saw improved relations with China as beneficial to the United States. In the short run, it would help America get out of the Vietnam War, and in the long term, would dramatically enhance the strategic position of the United States in a global confrontation against the Soviet Union.[11] All of this paved the way for Nixon's historic visit to China in February 1972. Nixon's visit to China reshaped the world that had been profoundly divided by the global Cold War. First and foremost, it ended the total confrontation between the United States and China that had lasted for almost a quarter century, thereby opening a thoroughly new chapter in the development of the relations between the world's most powerful country and the most populous one.

In terms of the impact Nixon's trip had upon East Asian politics, the Sino-American rapprochement dramatically shifted the balance of power between the two conflicting superpowers in the Cold War. While policymakers in Washington found it possible to concentrate more of America's resources and strategic attention on dealing with the Soviet Union, Moscow's leaders, having to confront the West and China simulta-neously, now faced a situation in which the Soviet Union's strength and power were seriously overextended. Moreover, Beijing's cooperation with Washington and confronta-tion with Moscow also changed the essence of the Cold War, a conflict between two con-tending ideologies: capitalism vs. communism. As a result, the global Cold War in the 1970s and 1980s continued more in *realpolitik* ways rather than in ideological terms.[12]

Therefore, the Cold War in East Asia was not only an ideological battle between capitalism and communism, but also their respective political, economic, social, and cultural determinations and resolutions. Throughout this historical period, East Asian countries have paved their ways and risen through evolution, adaptation, and transfor-mation. This text introduces the sources, the persistence, and the flexibility of cultures and traditions in China, Japan, and Koreas in the face of new economic, military, and political challenges from the two superpowers in the Cold War. It demonstrates how East Asian countries utilized the global Cold War politics and economy to craft their own particular versions of survival, struggle, and success in decolonization, independence, industrialization, and modernization through the twentieth century.

Two critical themes: Nationalism and modernization

The volume interprets the impact of East Asia's Cold War on broader aspects in con-temporary East Asian history, particularly nation-building and industrialization. The goal is to map out East Asia's process and experience in decolonization, independence, and modernization. It opens up a new avenue in the Cold War study by using international history to explore the dynamics in eastern modernization through the late twentieth century. In a deeper sense, the global Cold War extended far beyond its diplomatic activities, and transformed East Asia. Odd Arne Westad argues that "the most important aspects of the Cold War were neither military nor strategic, nor Europe-centered, but connected to political and social development in the Third World."[13] In this book, we view global Cold War events and East Asian revolutions as an intertwined history, not as isolated or parallel phenomena. Through a diachronic coverage of the wars, revolutions, and international events, it provides a synchronic theme of modernity in East Asia.

Our perspective examines the tremendous changes and identifies a general movement driven by two ideas: nationalism and modernization. Both served as a central agency in the struggle, survival, and success of these countries through the twentieth century. The Cold War to East Asians was not only about international power struggle, but also about independence and modernization. This common pattern informed economic expansion, political reform, social movements, and intellectual responses to globalization, democracy, human rights, and terrorism into the twenty-first century through two generations that faced varied international conditions and made different decisions according to their time and position. The nationalist and modernization pattern situates their Cold War experience in the indigenous context of each of these countries while taking into account their problems, progress, and challenges. From the perspective of a traditional civilization, they acted according to their own consistent logic in the domestic reforms and international affairs.

Nationalism as the first central theme can better explain the East Asian perspectives on the Cold War. Since the end of WWII did not bring independence to their countries, the first generation of the post-war leaders (1950s–1970s) actively engaged in the Cold War to continue their nationalist struggle for independence and national unification. Among others were Yoshida Shigeru (1878–1967; prime minister in 1946–1954) of Japan, Mao Zedong (Mao Tse-tung, 1893–1976; in power 1949–1976) of China, Jiang Jieshi (Chiang Kai-shek, 1887–1975; in office 1950–1975) of Taiwan, Syngman Rhee (1875–1965; in office 1948–1960) of South Korea, and Kim Il-sung (1912–1994; in power 1948–1994) of North Korea. While military confrontations with the two superpowers, along with cultural and economic exchanges, play a considerable role in the independence movement, these developments need to be understood in the context of already existing nationalist movements in these countries before WWII, and in the context of local economic and political exchanges even earlier in the eighteenth and nineteenth centuries. To avoid overgeneralizations, this volume examines why the first post-war generation – nationalist leaders, elected presidents, communist officials, and ordinary people – adopted to the bipolar international system, and how they took the opportunity in the Cold War to rebuild their countries. They engaged in the Cold War in a drastic way through full-scale wars, national reforms, and major social movements, which reveal the persistence and flexibility of their culture and tradition when confronted by the United States and Soviet Union. When US technology and Russian aid became more involved in East Asia, their assistance was linked by the first generation of the leadership to their didactic attempts at getting adherents for their own independence and nation-building process.

Modernization even sets a broader framework or an analytic guide not only for the evolution of common pre-modern institutions, but also for the recent development of East Asia. The second generation of the Cold War East Asian leaders (1970s–1990s) modernized their countries through a revival or further development of the original Eastern civilizations. Among others were Deng Xiaoping (Deng Hsiao-ping, 1904–1997; in power 1978–1989) of China, Lee Teng-hui (1923–; in power 1988–2000) of Taiwan, and Chun Doo-hwan (1931–; in power 1980–1988) of South Korea. They were dynamic actors in East Asia's modernization rather than passive followers or merely victims of the global Cold War. Conventional Cold War history texts interpret the East Asian modernization either primarily as a story of US foreign policy bringing a stable and unchanging East Asia abruptly into a modern world, or as a story of Soviet communism which inspired and radicalized the uneducated masses. In these narratives, communist or capitalist ideologies led to modernization in East Asia, and their leaders mobilized the masses for the long and often violent anti-Soviet or anti-American resistance that gained popular support. The flaw in these narratives is that they view external actions and influence as the motivating force in East Asian modernity. In retrospect, East Asia's countries and peoples participated in the global Cold War for their own historical reasons in some specific ways, which served their own political agenda, met their economic programs and security needs, and created their own development models.

The two central themes reveal the role of differing ideas about political parties, economic leaders, and social organizations for individuals involved in the bid for modernization. They align all the chapters together through the entire book and provide a new East Asian perspective. Each chapter studies patterns of decision-making indigenous to particular East Asian countries, which are treated as major players rather than as minute, passive spectators or lessor adjuncts in Cold War politics – the treatment given to them in many other works. Political and social elites of East Asia acted according to their own tradition and incorporated Western concepts and technologies. Because their interactions with the superpowers were influenced by the demands of domestic politics, the results often changed the direction of East Asian countries while having a strong impact on their politics and society. Some Western historians have overlooked the complex nature of the tremendous changes in East Asia from the first generation to the next. In retrospect, the Cold War may decenter Europe as the main reason for Eastern industrialization and economic globalization.

This volume endeavors to understand relations among East Asian countries, particularly between North and South Korea, and between China and Taiwan in a specific historical context, while simultaneously trying to elucidate certain common patterns. Above all, it recognizes that "East Asia" is in many ways a modern construction, since it refers to a clear geographic body and can be used only vaguely to refer to a set of ideas. It should not be surprising that in ancient times, the civilizations in territory we now consider "East Asia" followed their own unique development. The East Asian countries in this volume have highly specific experiences with the military, financial, and cultural influences of the United States, Europe, and the former Soviet Union. Some are still communist-controlled states while others are not, resulting in vastly different experience and relationships.

Three text organization features

The book provides a comprehensive source on the Cold War in East Asia and includes general coverage of ideologies from classic Confucianism in 2500 BC to current communism and nationalism. It addresses critical views of on-going issues, such as energy crisis, nuclear threats, poverty, human rights, and environmental protection. All the progress and problems are placed within a broad sociopolitical and socioeconomic contextual framework, exploring East Asian approaches to modernization. A cross-cultural interpretation of this sort involves some challenges for all interested readers. The text, therefore, organizes its overview of historical narrative to a modern East Asian history through three analytical methods.

The first method involves asking about general patterns at key points. The patterns as we have mentioned earlier can be tested as a way of finding meaning and even predictive power in East Asia. They offer a better understanding of complicated policies and identify several unique features in Eastern Asian modernization. By studying the traditional countries, students will understand the key concepts and world views of the Eastern civilizations. The second method, the comparative approach, is vital in our analysis. The book format and organization allows students to compare East Asian with Western and American views and find out when traditional structures and values in the Eastern civilizations confront and share some common issues with other civilizations. They may develop the potential for dialogue between "East and West" and understand the great issues about this region and some common issues with the rest of the world. The third method suggests breaking down the civilization into political, economic, social, and cultural categories. Each of these categories, and also their interrelationships in forming the whole civilization, can be compared across space and time. The text also explores the factor of change over different time periods through the third approach. The division into principal concern involves the great issues of change between the two generations of the Cold War. Students will develop new reading and analysis skills, as well as better writing skills in this new field.

The work has employed primary documents, government papers, and personal interviews in China, Hong Kong, South Korea, and Taiwan. As a textbook, however, it does not include all the primary sources in the endnotes and no foreign-language text in selected bibliography. The bibliography provides useful reference tools and available resources for the further reading of undergraduate and graduate students, high school teachers, public officials, and general audience on this topic, and for those who may be interested in East Asian history during the Cold War and doing some research in American and Western libraries.

The book divides the Cold War in East Asia into three sections and thirteen chapters. The first section, "War and Revolution," includes five chapters as a general coverage from pre-WWII East Asia, to the origin of the Cold War, and the Communist victory in China. Chapter one offers a pre-WWII historical background by exploring when traditional tributary relations were replaced by a European colonial system in the nineteenth century, and how Japan became industrialized with military power in the early twentieth century. Chapter two details Japan's war in the Asia-Pacific region from 1937 to 1945, including major events such as the Japanese attack on Pearl Harbor and Asian peoples' anti-Japanese resistance. Chapter three discusses the American occupation of Japan in 1945–1952 with an emphasis on Japan's reforming efforts. Chapter four provides an overview of the Chinese Civil War between the Communist and Nationalist forces in 1946–1949. Chapter five examines China's domestic and foreign policies in 1949–1957 after the founding of the People's Republic of China (PRC), and the conflicts between the mainland China and Taiwan in the mid-1950s.

The second section, "The East vs. the West," includes four chapters and explains why East Asia became the hot spot of the Cold War in the 1950s–1970s. Chapter six covers the military conflict between China and the United States in the Korean War of 1950–1953. Chapter seven continues the discussion of hot conflict in Southeast Asia by examining China's involvement in the French Indochina War of 1946–1954. Chapter eight analyzes Japan's economic miracle in the 1960s–1970s while exploring the economic and social problems during that time. Chapter nine interprets the reasons and consequences of the Sino-Soviet split in the 1960s and China's armed conflicts with Taiwan in 1958 and with India in 1962.

The third section, "From Bi-polar, Triangle, to Global," includes four chapters examining how the East Asian countries were transformed into modern states before the Cold War ended in 1991. Chapter ten provides a general coverage of the Chinese Cultural Revolution in 1966–1976 and the details of the Sino-US rapprochement in the early 1970s. Chapter eleven discusses Deng's return as the second generation of the CCP leadership and his reform movement in China between 1978 and 1989. Chapter twelve focuses on reforms, changes, and resistance that occurred in both South and North Koreas from 1972 to 1994. Chapter thirteen explains how China survived the Cold War when the Soviet Union and communist system collapsed in Eastern Europe in 1991 with a focus on China's evolution from a third-world country to a world economic power in less than twenty-five years. The conclusion points out new challenges and opportunities faced by East Asia and the United States in the twenty-first century.

Even though it has the world's highest economic growth rate, East Asia is not yet a region with democracy, liberties, and freedom. These countries must address their own problems consisting of, but not limited to, interference from authoritarian governments, arms race (including nuclear bombs) and military buildup, political corruptions, human rights violations, and inconsistency in legal practices. These factors slow down their democratization and impede the improvement of the relations with the West in general, and with the United States particularly. The US government and public must understand these factors and work with East Asian countries on developing shared objectives, interests, and values and thereby draw all of these countries into the international system. China and North Korea, in turn, must live up to their international obligations and global standards.

East Asia has developed patterns of social values, political sensibilities, institutional procedures, diplomatic strategies, and cultural behaviors, and the region shares some common heritage. Globalization has done more than merely narrow the gap between the United States and East Asia. Today, it is impossible to understand domestic politics in the United States without reference to economic and cultural changes in Asia. From defense to finance to technology and the environment, major policy issues in the United States are incomprehensible without reference to developments in East Asia. American college students have both academic and professional reasons to study East Asia, since knowledge of this area of the world will be an indispensable asset for major employers in the future. Sensing this change, this generation's students grasp the need to understand economic and technological changes in East Asia through the twentieth century as an inseparable part of the broader history of the modern world.

Notes

1 For publications on this topic in recent years, see: Leslie James and Elisabeth Leake, eds., *Decolonization and the Cold War: Negotiating Independence* (London, UK: Bloomsbury Academic, 2015); Tsuyoshi Hasegawa, ed., *The Cold War in East Asia 1945–1991* (Stanford, CA: Stanford University Press, 2011); Odd Arne Westad, *The Global Cold War: Third World Interventions and the Making of Our Times* (New York: Cambridge University Press, 2005); John Lewis Gaddis, *We Now Know: Rethinking Cold War History* (New York: Oxford University Press, 1997); Vladislav Zubok and Constantine Pleshakov, *Inside the Kremlin's Cold War: From Stalin to Khrushchev* (Cambridge, MA: Harvard University Press, 1996).
2 Akira Iriye, "Review on Hasegawa's Book, *The Cold War in East Asia, 1945*–1991," in *American Historical Review* 117, no. 1 (February 2012): 175.
3 Xiaobing Li, *China's Battle for Korea: The 1951 Spring Offensive* (Bloomington: Indiana University Press, 2014), 239.
4 John Lewis Gaddis, *The Long Peace: Inquiries into the History of the Cold War* (New York: Oxford University Press, 1987), 6–8, 22.

5 During and after the early 1970s, the "Communist bloc" – and the Soviet Union in particular – faced, among other problems, the declining economy of the Soviet Union, the stagnation of Soviet politics and society under the reign of an increasingly ailing Leonid Brezhnev, the economic crises and, related to them, an energy crunch in East European countries, and the inability of the "Communist bloc" to identify the discourse of decolonization with that of a communist "world revolution." Consequently, as Walter LaFeber points out, "Few people still shared the old hope that other revolutions would follow the Soviet model" at that moment. LaFeber, *America, Russia, and the Cold War, 1945–2006*, 10th ed. (Boston, MA: McGraw Hill, 2008), 309.

6 For the importance of the Sino-Soviet alliance, see: Lorenz M. Lüthi, ed., *The Regional Cold Wars in Europe, East Asia, and the Middle East: Crucial Periods and Turning Points* (Stanford, CA: Stanford University Press, 2015); Zhihua Shen and Yafeng Xia, *Mao and the Sino-Soviet Partnership, 1945–1959: A New History* (Lanham, MD: Lexington Books, 2015); Nicholas Khoo, *Collateral Damage: Sino-Soviet Rivalry and the Termination of the Sino-Vietnamese Alliance* (New York: Columbia University Press, 2011); Thomas P. Bernstein and Hua-Yu Li, eds., *China Learns from the Soviet Union, 1949–Present* (Lanham, MD: Lexington Books, 2011); Lüthi, *The Sino-Soviet Split: Cold War in the Communist World* (Princeton, NJ: Princeton University Press, 2008); Westad, *Brothers in Arms: The Rise and Fall of the Sino-Soviet Alliance, 1945–1963* (Stanford, CA: Stanford University Press, 1998).

7 For a chronological development of the Sino-Soviet split, see: Chen Jian, *Mao's China and the Cold War* (Chapel Hill: University of North Carolina Press, 2001), chapter 3.

8 Thomas Robinson, "The Sino-Soviet Border Conflicts of 1969: New Evidence Three Decades Later," in *Chinese Warfighting: The PLA Experience since 1949*, eds. Mark A. Ryan, David M. Finkelstein, and Michael A. McDevitt (Armonk, NY: M. E. Sharpe, 2003), 198–216.

9 For example, Henry Kissinger recorded in his memoir that in August 1969, a Soviet diplomat in Washington inquired about "what the U.S. reaction would be to a Soviet attack on Chinese nuclear facilities." Kissinger, *White House Years* (New York: Little, Brown, 1978), 183.

10 Chen, *Mao's China and the Cold War*, 7–10, 241–242.

11 Richard Nixon, *The Memoirs of Richard Nixon* (New York: Grosset & Dunlap, 1978), 390; Gaddis, *Strategies of Containment: A Critical Appraisal of American National Security Policy during the Cold War*, revised and expanded ed. (New York: Oxford University Press, 2005), 277–281.

12 Chen Jian and Xiaobing Li, "China and the End of the Global Cold War," in *From Détente to the Soviet Collapse: The Cold War from 1975 to 1991*, ed. Malcolm Muir, Jr. (Lexington: Virginia Military Institute Press, 2006), 122.

13 Westad, *The Global Cold War*, 396.

Part I
War and revolution

1 Imperial powers and pre-WWII Japan

Since "East Asia" is in many ways a modern construction, it should not be surprising that in ancient time the areas we now consider a part of East Asia followed their own unique development trajectories. Wynn Gadkar-Wilcox points out that beginning around two millennia ago, a series of attempts at expansion and conquest from rulers in the North China Plain led to the diffusion of economic ideas, and these disparate places slowly began to share a common heritage.[1] Throughout this area, over the course of many hundreds of years, East Asians in what are now China, Japan, and Korea developed patterns of social values, political sensibilities, institutional procedures, religious institutions, military strategies, and diplomatic behaviors which arose through centuries of change, revolution, war, and reform.[2]

These patterns include commonalities in centralized political institutions, the dissemination of works describing the values and political theories of the Confucian-Mencian paradigm, the spread of Buddhism, and a system of uniquely East Asian diplomatic relations which emerged from that paradigm. These civilizational patterns set a framework not only for the development and evolution of common pre-modern institutions but also for the modern development of East Asia. These common patterns informed economic expansion and reform efforts in the seventeenth and eighteenth centuries and intellectual responses to Christianity, global trade, and European gunboats from the sixteenth century through to the twentieth century.

This chapter begins with the major development of the principal civilizations and political institutions of East Asia from the ancient time to the pre-modern period about 1500. Then, it examines relations between East Asia and Europe from about 1600 to 1800. The Europeans rushed to East Asia with a spirit of adventure, fed primarily by the search for lucrative trading opportunities. To a lesser extent, they were also motivated by the evangelical zeal to spread Christianity to the "heathen" world.[3] Thus, Western countries and merchants were often able to use Christian conversion to cover their true intention of commercial profit. Because of its complexity and international dimension, the European commercial and evangelical pursuit became an ultimate political test for all the East Asian countries.

In the seventeenth century, however, the Europeans were considered uncivilized since they did not know the classic texts, and were treated as other "barbarians" like some ethnic minorities. Then, the emergence of the French and British colonial empires in Asia in the eighteenth century brought the universality of East Asian classical civilization into question. East Asians began to see the French and British as possessing a separate civilization, rather than merely being uncivilized. The urgency of the military and commercial problems wrought by Europeans and Americans greatly accelerated

East Asian efforts at political, economic, and technology reform. By the mid-nineteenth century, educational curriculum of Confucianism, political loyalty to the emperor, and native religions like Buddhism and Daoism (Taoism) came to be understood as part of Eastern tradition, and the alternative to them came to be seen as "Western modernity." This particularistic world view gave rise to proto-nationalistic discourses throughout East Asia. This shift coincided with efforts at reform and social change in East Asian countries.

The second half of the chapter situates Japan's experiences with industrialization in the indigenous context of the late nineteenth century while taking into account its progress, challenges, and problems. It reveals that the classic civilizations set a framework not only for the development and evolution of common pre-modern institutions but also for the modern development of East Asia. But it also explains why Japan's economic success had soon turned the country into a militarist, aggressive East Asian power, and how Tokyo colonized Korea and Manchuria in the early twentieth century.

Classic civilizations and tributary system (from ancient time to 1500)

Through traditional institutions such as the civil service examination system (in China and Korea) and the samurai institution (in Japan), East Asian elites relied on universalistic systems of thought. What determined whether a people or culture was civilized was whether they knew certain canonical classic texts; whether they could read the works of Confucius (551–479 BCE) or Mencius (Men-tzu) (372–289 BCE) or key passages from the *Classic of Ritual* in classical Chinese, and whether they could make decisions about present circumstances based on consulting Chinese dynastic histories. The Confucian-Mencian paradigm is a complex system of moral, social, political, philosophical, and quasi-religious thought.[4] During the Han dynasty (206 BCE–220 CE), the Confucian-Mencian paradigm was adapted as ruling ideology, and Confucius' four books became classics. Confucian ideas of meritocracy in part resulted in the introduction of the imperial examination system into traditional China. The imperial examination system evolved gradually from its origins in 165 BCE. At that time, when the Han emperor called candidates for public office to the capital for an examination of their knowledge of the classics, the examination was an irregular system of gaining office and an alternative to the usual system of appointment and recommendation of officials.

However, by the time of the Sui dynasty (581–618), Confucianism became more firmly re-established and operated as an ideology alongside Buddhism.[5] The national examination had been established as a civil service system to test knowledge of Confucianism. Although the Sui emperors reunified the country, they squandered the treasury to build palaces for their own comfort and vanity. They attempted to re-conquer Korea three times, and several million peasant draftees served as soldiers and laborers for the military expeditions. As a result, the peasants were exhausted and the Sui treasury nearly empty. The burdens on farmers had become unbearable. They rebelled, dealing a fatal blow to the Sui regime. Li Yuan (566–635), one of the rebel leaders, assumed the imperial title at Chang'an and called his new regime the Tang dynasty (618–907).

Confucianism was revived by Zhu Xi (1130–1200), the greatest Confucian master of the Song dynasty (960–1279), in a doctrine that combined commentaries on classical Confucian texts with sensibilities and insights that may have been borrowed from Buddhism and Daoism.[6] He developed methods and paths to reach goodness or become a "gentleman"; a concept Confucius and Mencius summarized in the Four Books. This focus on cultivating virtue helped students prepare for their civil service examination. The imperial examination system based on the Confucian-Mencian paradigm had been well established by the Song dynasty and continued until it was abolished in 1905. Under this system, almost anyone who wished to become an official would have an opportunity to become an officer, a position which would bring wealth and honor to the whole family, if he proved his worth by passing written government examinations. The domination of the civilian bureaucracy in military affairs contributed to the Song army's defeats against the Mongol invading troops. In 1279, the Mongols destroyed the Chinese army, ended the Song dynasty, and established the Yuan dynasty (1279–1368). Nevertheless, the Mongol emperors of the Yuan court adopted Zhu Xi's commentaries on the Four Books for the civil service examinations in 1315.[7]

The Confucian-Mencian paradigm influenced not only China, but also Korea, Japan, and Vietnam during their classic and middle ages through international trade, travel, and cultural exchanges in East Asia. During the Yamato Period (350–710) in Japan, several kings sent missions to China to gain Chinese confirmation of their dominance. When they returned, they brought back knowledge of Confucianism, Buddhism, and the Chinese administrative system. After Silla conquered the other kingdoms in Korea, many war refugees refused to accept the unified Silla government and fled to Japan. Among them were many learned officials and highly-educated scholars who brought the Confucian philosophy and imperial administrative experience to Japan.[8]

One advantage of this universalistic focus was that one did not have to be ethnically Han to be considered civilized. Indeed, Korean elites saw the classic texts and histories as very much a part of their own civilization, and not as something "foreign" or "Chinese." Moreover, non-Han peoples, including ethnically Vietnamese subjects of the empire, could pass the exams in China. The flexibility of this system allowed non-Han rulers such as the Qing to adapt to this system. Mark Elliot, for example, describes the Manchu-Han relations during the Qing dynasty (1644–1911) as "ethnic sovereignty" which offered legitimacy for a dynastic central government to run multiple ethnicities in China.[9]

Before the European expansion in the 1500s, East Asian countries had established centralized dynasties to control their territories, maintained certain social orders, and developed domestic and international trade. Territoriality played an important role for the monarchical governments in the 1500s–1800s, including the Qing dynasty in China, Tokugawa Bakufu (1603–1868), and Choson Korea (1392–1910), allowing them to prove their legitimacy and authority, and to justify their military expansion and social control. According to Charles S. Maier, the term "territoriality" can be defined historically as bordered space (and the properties) under certain political control.[10] In the modern European system of nation-states, "territoriality was the basis of establishing national identity, demarcating state boundaries, and conducting international relations." Yet, Xiaoyuan Liu states that "territoriality did not start in modern time and was not a European specialty."[11]

In pre-modern East Asian history, before the full-scale incursion of Western powers, according to Liu, all East Asian states inside the Sino-centric tributary system possessed territoriality, even though such territoriality differed drastically from the modern/European type. To cope with the international relations in East Asia, a tribute

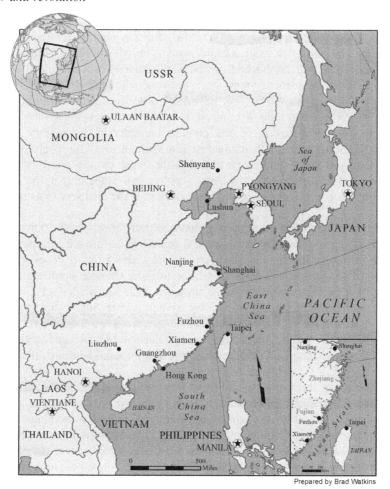

Map 1.1 East Asia

system was formed for conducting diplomatic and trade relations between China and other countries and steppe kingdoms such Xiongnu from the third through eighteenth centuries.[12] Under this system exchanges of gifts between foreign rulers and the Chinese emperor were carried out. Foreign rulers including the Japanese, Koreans, and Vietnamese saw advantages to seeking a mutual relationship with the Chinese empire. They sent their representatives to the Chinese capital to present their tributes (exotic luxury goods, local special products, or people) to the Chinese emperor, and in return, they were rewarded with promises and gifts from the Chinese emperor, such as political recognition, non-aggression agreements, and gifts like porcelain and silk.[13]

The symbolism of the tribute system ensured that the Chinese emperor and the Middle Kingdom would be regarded as superior to their trading partners. Under this system, the Chinese emperor recognized the authority and sovereignty of foreign monarchs. He conferred upon them the trappings of legitimacy. In exchange, rulers from foreign lands, adopting a posture of subjugation, recognized the supremacy of the Chinese emperor and the legitimacy of universal civilization as understood within the

Confucian-Mencian paradigm. This suzerainty over neighboring lands afforded exclusive trading conditions between East Asian countries and also implied Chinese military protection to the subordinate states. Therefore, all diplomatic and trade missions were construed in the context of a tribute relationship. Under such a system, there were asymmetrical power relations between China as the Middle Kingdom and its surrounding subordinate states. In this system, power diminished with the cultural and geographical distance from the Middle Kingdom, so that Korea was placed higher than others, including Japan, the Ryukyus, and other Indochinese kingdoms that also gave tribute.[14]

Under the Ming dynasty (1368–1644), countries that attempted to establish political, economic, and cultural relationships with the powerful Chinese empire had to enter the tribute system. To keep it official, for a short period, the tribute was actually the only existing element of foreign trade for China. Hongwu (reigned 1368–1398), the first Ming emperor, prohibited any private foreign trade in 1371. To increase the number of tribute states, the Yongle Emperor (r. 1402–1424), expanded the tribute system by dispatching massive overseas missions to the South Seas in the early fifteenth century. The overseas expeditions of Zheng He (1371–1435) carried goods to build tribute relationships between the Ming dynasty and newly discovered kingdoms in Southeast Asia, South Asia, and Eastern Africa is an example of the success of this philosophy.[15]

The tribute system had been challenged and interrupted from time to time. During the Han dynasty, for example, Xiongnu came to regard the system as a fraudulent and empty agreement, and chose to utilize the act of tribute with such frequency that it reaped enormous rewards for the subsidiary state. China recognized the disingenuous attitude on the part of Xiongnu and suspended the tribute relationship. In another situation, when there was a war between two tribute states, China was held to its own end of the bargain. The Japanese invasion of Korea in the 1500s is an example of this. Upon the landing of Japanese militants throughout Southeast Korea, the vassal state requested prompt intervention on the part of Ming China in recognition of the binding tradition between the two. Korea had long been most faithful to the Chinese in the tribute system. The two countries had been closely connected since Korea became independent during the disunity of the third through fifth centuries, and China realized that the time had come to uphold its agreement.[16]

The Chinese tribute system, with its burdensome, ritualistic mannerisms, continued until the Qing dynasty when European merchants began arriving. Because Confucian culture placed a greater reward on non-economic functions rather than extra profit, the Chinese preferred to continue tribute customs even when Western merchants began to arrive at the Chinese coast to trade with China. The Chinese were willing and able to extend to Westerners, as "men from afar," a number of concessions and a certain amount of flexibility in meeting Qing requirements.[17] Since Westerners were used to the free market and free trade system, and the Imperial Chinese customs to control trade were not productive and non-economic, the Europeans complained that they could not trade with Chinese merchants in such a way. The Europeans were not pleased with the tribute system, and the Chinese government refused to compromise with the Europeans because the Qing dynasty did not see any clear advantage to establishing special relations with Europeans outside of the tribute system. Thus, Sino-Western trade was limited in the nineteenth century. Finally, the Europeans used military means to force the Qing government to open China's door to trade with the West, resulting in the First Opium War of 1839–1842. After the mid-nineteenth century, Western powers achieved predominance in East Asia and thus an "era of negotiations" began, in which Western international relations culture coexisted with, penetrated, oppressed, and eventually superseded the tributary system of East Asia.[18]

East Asia's response to European expansion (1600–1800)

Above all, "the West" is a problematic label, since it refers to an unclear geographic body and can be used only vaguely to refer to a set of ideas. For example, the imperial and financial strategies of the Dutch, English, Portuguese, French, and Spanish in East Asia were not identical, nor were the missionizing efforts of Jesuits, Dominicans, Franciscans, Foreign Mission Society, or Protestant priests. Similarly, the East Asian countries have highly specific experiences with the military, financial, and cultural influences of Europe. Some were formally colonized to one extent or another, while others were not, resulting in vastly different relationships. Moreover, the notion that Western traders and missionaries from the seventeenth century onwards suddenly and fundamentally changed a hopelessly traditional East Asia is another problematic narrative. From the Silk Road to Mongol contacts to Marco Polo (1254–1324), East Asians had interacted with Europeans for centuries.[19] The modern encounter with the West was not new. Likewise, the Western missionaries and traders who encountered East Asian civilizations in the seventeenth century did not find a closed, hermetic East Asia permanently fixed to unchanging traditional values. The innovations of the Song dynasty, including gunpowder, the printing press, and paper-based currency, show the dynamic nature of these civilizations in pre-modern times. In order to avoid problematic overgeneralizations, this volume explores the experience of peoples throughout East Asia in all of their unique specificity.

Nevertheless, these caveats notwithstanding, it is possible to notice patterns in the history of relations between East Asian countries and the West. Though contact with Europe had persisted since ancient times, the economics of global maritime empires in the sixteenth and seventeenth centuries fundamentally changed the character of these interactions. Though each missionary group had their own unique features, the cultural encounter with missionaries – encompassing not just Christianity but also features of Western art, literature, and astronomy – shared common features in Korea, Japan, and China.

That the Western powers' arrival at the Chinese shores coincided with the Ming dynasty's fatal decline was history's worst irony. In spite of its long and enduring cultural heritage, the Ming dynasty in the end failed to escape in time from its own entangled and outmoded political system. When the Europeans arrived demanding open relations, the Central Kingdom was not only unprepared for the encroachment of the "barbarian" Westerners, but was unable to fully comprehend the gravity of the development. The Ming government had yet to realize the fact that the intruders were decades, if not a century, ahead of China in science and technology.

The Western intrusion into China was spearheaded by Portugal, a major maritime power of the time – in 1535 it extracted from the Ming court a legal sanction to reside and trade in Macao. Spain quickly emulated the Portuguese venture by winning in 1575 a Ming concession to trade along the southern Chinese coast. Shortly afterwards, other European powers followed suit. The Dutch, who established a limited trading operation with Japan in the late sixteenth century, organized a China post by 1656.[20] With its extensive commercial interests in India entrenched in the early seventeenth century, England was the most aggressive European power in Asia during that period.

Naturally, it was eager to expand trade with China, following other maritime powers' East Asian ventures by establishing a Chinese commercial outpost in 1690. France did the same in 1728. By the first half of the eighteenth century, most major European powers had managed to establish commercial outposts in China. Nevertheless, as Ray Huang concludes, the growth of foreign trade did not promote the Ming economy and early industry since the government opposed imbalanced growth among the different regions in China. Such disparity "in turn would threaten the empire's political unity."[21]

Soon after securing the Chinese court's legal sanction to trade, the European powers pursued the systematic exploitation of China by employing their seasoned mercantile techniques. They hardly concealed their imperial ambition from the outset, fully taking advantage of the declining empire's political ineptitude. Since the West's early commercial activities did not overly disturb the giant Middle Kingdom, the Ming court did not regard the West's token presence on its soil a major risk. Nevertheless, Ming leaders remained contemptuous of European commercialism, seeing it as merely an unpleasant irritation for the court and the wider society that sill harbored strong anti-commercial sentiment inherent in the Confucian doctrine. The Chinese government was not alarmed, the Western activities at the time presented only a negligible effect on the giant empire. Nor did the Christianity brought by the Western powers impress the court. Ming mediocre political leadership and cumbersome bureaucracy proved grossly inadequate in dealing with the West's concerted exploitation maneuvers.[22]

After the Ming collapsed in 1644, the Manchus established the Qing dynasty. Unfortunately, the Qing court inherited the Ming's shortcomings and countermeasures to combat Western attempts to dominate commerce were equally ineffective. The Qing government took realistic views toward individual missionaries but more unfriendly attitudes toward Christianity, treating the missionaries more as intellectuals than bearers of new religious canon. Therefore, missionaries were quite well accepted; some even won high government positions. But the Manchu rulers were noncommittal about Christianity, anticipating that fundamental and irreconcilable conflicts would eventually develop between the Confucian doctrines and monotheistic Christianity, and remaining skeptical of the constructive role of Christianity in Confucian China. In spite of its apparent willingness to maintain contacts with some missionaries, the court was vigilant about Christian evangelical work.[23]

While the European attention was primarily focused on China and India, other East Asian countries such as Japan and Korea attracted only secondary interest. The "Hermit Kingdom of Choson" was even out of the Western customary commercial interests.[24] Its remote location and Chinese-oriented foreign relations had effectively deterred the small kingdom from establishing contacts with nations beyond its immediate neighbors. There had been no direct trade or diplomatic relations between Korea and Western nations prior to the dawn of the nineteenth century. Choson Korea, still known in the West as a Chinese dependency, remained hidden from the views of the European powers even when their adventure in China had much progressed.[25]

As the Westerners made their presence in China more strongly felt, the Choson court had become vaguely aware of the nature of the highly advanced Western world. The knowledge brought home by Korean officials who made contacts with European missionaries in Beijing included some fragmentary information about Western science and the world outside of East Asia. Although far from comprehensive, this information trickling in was enough to shake some officials from their long-standing conviction that the Central Kingdom was the only civilized society in the world. Christianity aroused some interests of Korean officials and the traditional Choson society could have accepted or even embraced it. Unfortunately, the Choson court had received only unfavorable reports on the West from its trusted neighbor, the Qing rulers in China, whose troubled encounters with the Western powers effectively precluded the Choson court from viewing Christianity objectively.

In 1627, several Dutch sailors ended up staying in Korea and made guns for the locals after their ship was destroyed by a storm. In 1653, thirty-six more Dutch sailors joined them and worked for the Korean military for the same reason. Michael J. Seth states that "Few Koreans seemed to take the Europeans very seriously as bearers of a great tradition, rather seeing them as just clever barbarians."[26] Officially, Christianity landed in Korea in 1784. However, unofficial contact goes back further, as some publications of Matteo Ricci, the leading missionary during the late Ming dynasty, were introduced into Korea in the early seventeenth century. Unlike the Chinese, Koreans had to import the new religion piecemeal from Ricci's work and recreate it through a long self-study process. As reflected by the time-consuming transfer process that went on undetected for a long time, the Choson court was little concerned with Christianity during its infancy. When Father Pierre Philibert Maubant managed to enter Korea covertly to assume the post of Bishop of Seoul in 1836, the Korean Catholic community had grown to some 9,000 followers. According to Fairbank, Reischauer, and Craig, "Their egalitarian tendencies, their interest in science and technology, and their advocacy of daring innovations may have helped prepare the way for the great changes in store for Korea in more recent time."[27]

As a result, the emergence of the French and British colonial empires in Asia in the nineteenth century brought the universality of East Asian classical civilization into question. East Asians began to see the French and British as possessing a separate civilization, rather than merely being uncivilized. This shift in mentality gave rise to a particularistic point of view, in which Confucianism came to be understood as part of Chinese tradition, and the alternative to Confucianism came to be seen as "Western modernity." In this divided worldview, civilizations were associated with specific ethnicities or cultures. By the mid-nineteenth century, this view gave rise to proto-nationalistic discourses throughout East Asia. Liu concludes that "Such an ethnic essence of Chinese nationalism would become further solidified in China's domestic ethno-politics and foreign crises in the years to come."[28]

China fought five foreign wars from 1839 to 1900 against the European powers, America, and Japan over trade, opium trafficking, and foreign intervention in neighboring Korea and Vietnam. The Qing government was defeated by Britain in the First Opium War of 1839–1842 and by Britain and France in the Second Opium War of 1857–1858. Qing signed several treaties which opened China to British and French trade. Other Western powers followed suit and signed similar treaties in which China lost its rights as a sovereign nation. The Opium Wars, which changed the country forever, were among the most significant events in the history of modern China. After these two wars, China was open to Western commercial influence and imperialist exploitation. The inflow of foreign goods into China without restriction caused the slow but sure disintegration of the domestic economy. Thereafter, step by step, China was transformed from an independent society into a semi-colonial country. R. Keith Schoppa points out that "The Opium War was the opening salvo of a century of aggression by Western nations against China, a century of conflict between very different cultures with sharply differing values; yet each clash would have its own particulars and realities."[29]

In Korea, the fiery anti-Western disposition King Taewongun maintained throughout his rule originated from his intense seclusion policy as his deliberate choice to protect the antiquated kingdom and nationalism. His view of the West was not firmly established when he came to power through the regency. The events that were mostly initiated by the Western powers from his very first year of rule, however, gradually drove him to extreme anti-Western seclusion. Contrary to the general characterization that he was a natural anti-Western, nationalist leader, to a great extent he was forced to take such an extreme foreign policy in order to safeguard the kingdom. For a man of profound nationalistic pride but of little practical knowledge of the non-Chinese world, the hostile and short-sighted reaction to Western incursion was even predictable under the confusing circumstances of the time.

The isolationist policy, however, failed to stop or even to slow down Western expansion in East Asia through the nineteenth century. European trade, Christian missionaries, new technologies, and intellectual exchanges continuing since the seventeenth century undermined the Eastern monarchies and made Westerners the major players in East Asia. The Eastern tradition came to the end in totally different ways, ranging from learning from the West or losing wars to the European powers. This was especially true in the great Chinese empire, which had slipped into the downward phase of a dynastic cycle just as the Western powers began to beat upon the gates.

During the first decade of the twentieth century, the Qing dynasty's political order and economic system crumbled under Western invasions and increasing dissatisfaction, rapidly eroding Manchu authority in Beijing. The anti-Manchu movement founded its revolutionary center overseas. In 1905, Sun Yat-sen, the founding father of Republican China, organized the *Tongmenghui* (or *T'ung-meng Hui*, the United League) in Japan. Among the 1,000 early members were liberal students, Christian merchants, and patriotic young officers trained in Japan.[30] Sun and his secret society spread their revolutionary ideas and organization from Japan to the world by establishing offices in San Francisco, Honolulu, Brussels, Singapore, and many branches in seventeen of the twenty-four provinces of China. Thousands and thousands of Chinese, including many New Army officers, joined the *Tongmenghui* by participating in multiple anti-Manchu activities and accepting Sun's *Sanmin zhuyi* (Three Principles of the People), including "nationalism" (both anti-Manchu and anti-imperialism), "democracy" (a constitution with people's rights), and "people's livelihood" (a classic term for social equality). These three principles "summed up much of the ferment of the age."[31]

On October 10, 1911, amidst an anti-Qing plot in Wuchang, the city of Hubei, some New Army officers revolted (October 10, or "Double Tens," became the National Day for the Republic of China). The success of the Wuchang uprising led many officers to join the revolution. In next two months, fifteen provinces proclaimed their independence from the Qing Empire. The rebellious provinces and *Tongmenghui* joined forces, setting up a provisional government at Nanjing. The provisional government elected Sun as president of the Republic of China (ROC) and he was inaugurated on January 1, 1912, at Nanjing.[32] As a great breakthrough in the Chinese history, it ended 2,000 years of monarchy and built the first republic in Asian history. Sun, however, overlooked the significance of economic issue in a movement to overthrow the traditional social order. Without a far-reaching industrial program, no revolution could succeed in an agrarian society such as China.

Meiji Restoration (1868–1912) and Japan's aggression

In contrast, in less than half a century the Meiji leaders achieved their goals, creating a relatively sound and modernized economy which formed the foundation on which Japan was able to gain national security and economic equivalence with the West. Though Japan shared much culturally with China, Vietnam, and Korea, it began to contrast sharply with them in social and political structure. Significantly, many of the differences between Japan and the other members of East Asian civilization turn out to be points of resemblance between Japan and the West. Feudalism is an outstanding example. So also is Japan's more rapid modernization during the past century, which has produced closer parallels to the West than can be found in China or anywhere else in Asia.

Japan's geographic setting, together with the nature of the Japanese ruling class and the high levels of political administration, meant that Japan was far more capable than China of carrying out a unified and effective response to the West. The decentralization and diversity of the Japanese political situation and social system also allowed a greater variety of responses than what appeared in China. Out of the diversity, some responses to European trade and the introduction of Christianity proved successful.

Japan remained more of a vacillating amalgamation of small feuding military states than a unified country until 1603, when the Tokugawa Shogunate emerged as the central authority. The rule of the Tokugawa Shogunate lasted for over 250 years until the imperial authority was restored in 1868. During this period, Japan's feudal culture smacked of aggressive and audacious nationalism, a unique characteristic that set Japan apart from its more literati-oriented neighbors like China and Korea. Like its continental neighbors, Japan operated as a "rice economy" at the outset of the Tokugawa period.[33] Although farming remained profoundly important to feudal rulers, farmers themselves were not highly regarded as much as in China and Korea.

Unlike its two neighbors where a literati class dominated national politics, Japan was ruled by powerful warlords, shoguns or daimyo, and their followers, the samurai. As a learned and highly motivated group, the samurai played a crucial role not only in the warring period, but also in more peaceful times, remaining the cornerstone of Japan's strong military apparatus.[34] The samurai institution, a Japanese invention, sustained its political leverage until the late Tokugawa period when the shoguns became increasingly interested in European firearms and modern army. The ethical code of samurai, or *Bushido*, had been an active force in Japanese society since the twelfth century. Even though samurai as a social class eventually disappeared – the victim of Japan's industrialization – they had made a significant contribution to the birth of modern Japan. Samurai spirit and ethical code on loyalty, bravery, stoicism, and martial arts of early feudalism all survived until recent times.

After European merchants arrived in Japan during the early sixteenth century, local shoguns and daimyo benefitted from the trade by importing Western medicine and firearms. After all, it was the introduction of European gun technology to Japan in the mid-sixteenth century that gave the victory to the Tokugawa Shogunate (1603–1868) over its other rivals. As a warrior class, samurai also showed a much keener appreciation of the superior military power of the West than did the Chinese civil bureaucrats. With the passage of time, some became more curious about the outside world and interested in opening up their country. A relatively light external impetus set Japan in motion in a way that much heavier thrusts could not bring about in a far more stable China ruled by Confucian elites. As a result, Japan adjusted to the early modern global climate more quickly than China, and this in turn gave it a decisive advantage during the following century.

When many shoguns, daimyo, and samurai complained about the Tokugawa Bakufu and were ready for changes, the US government dispatched a naval squadron to Japan. The expedition force, commanded by Commodore Matthew Perry, entered Yokohama Bay in July 1853 and demanded the Tokugawa government an immediate acceptance of its "open-door" request. Due to the imposing naval intimidation, even though the Shogunate did not immediately agree to America's request, the Edo government was ready to enter into a treaty relationship. When he returned the following February, the Tokugawa leaders signed the so-called Kanagawa Treaty of Friendship with Perry on March 31, 1854. Under the treaty, Japan granted the US two open ports, the right to appoint a consul, the protection of shipwrecked sailors, and the most-favored-nation treatment.[35] Other Western powers quickly took advantage of the success of Perry's mission and extracted similar concessions from Japan: England in 1854, Russia in 1855, and the Netherlands in 1857.

The opening of its door to the Western powers accentuated Japan's internal turmoil. Powerful feudal lords began to defy the Tokugawa Shogunate rule when the signing of treaties with the West shattered the country's existing order. The whole shogun system had depended on mutual antagonism among the domains; however, now many daimyo realized that alliance with one another under the emperor in Kyoto would be a better system than strengthening the Tokugawa control. John K. Fairbank, Edwin O. Reischauer, and Albert M. Craig state that when Japanese feudal lords were "menaced by the West, they did not react with disdain but rather with that combination of fear, resentment, and narrow pride that one associates with nationalism. In fact, their reaction proved extremely nationalistic. Despite the intensity of rivalries among the various domains, most Japanese leaders in the face of the foreign menace seem to have placed national interests ahead of old feudal loyalties."[36]

In 1864, the civil war broke out when the Choshu shoguns and samurai attacked Kyoto and occupied it.[37] The revolting shoguns and reforming samurai insisted on "honoring the Emperor" and returning power to Emperor Kōmei (r. 1831–1866). After Kōmei died during the civil war, his son, Mutsuhito (1852–1912), then only fourteen years old, succeeded the throne in 1868. He adopted the title of Meiji, meaning "Enlightened Rule." In fact, a group of reform-minded samurai, who were the ones primarily responsible for overthrowing the Tokugawa government, would subsequently engineer the national transformation in the name of the emperor. In 1868, the imperial army marched on Edo, and crushed the shogunate troops in November. The civil war was over with a victory of the Meiji Emperor (r. 1867–1912).

The emperor's army helped the imperial court to quickly consolidate its central authority in firm control. The era of the remarkable Meiji Restoration thus began. On April 8, 1868, Emperor Meiji issued the "Charter Oath" (or the Charter Oath of Five Articles) to abolish all feudal domains, privileges, and titles. It removed feudal social limitation by ending class restrictions on professional fields of activity in 1869.[38] Although most of the samurai disappeared as a class, some of their spirit and ethical code such as loyalty, self-discipline, and hard work re-emerged as part of a new nationalistic consciousness. While some others such as *Bushido*, including suicidal attack (or *kamikaze*) and suicide in defeat (or *seppuku*), had survived in the Japanese military until WWII. In May 1869, many shoguns and daimyo began to return their domains to the emperor. By 1870 the new regime obtained major clan members' consent for total abolition of the feudal system.

The end of feudalism was an auspicious beginning for the new central government, which established three metropolitan prefectures (*fu*) and seventy-two other prefectures (*ken*). The central governing Council was divided into three chambers in charge of legislative, administrative, and judicial functions, respectively. In 1872, the Meiji government established the army and navy departments. During the following years, it issued the conscription law, requiring all men, regardless of social background, to serve three years of active military service. It was a revolutionary step that made commoners the foundation of a centralized and modernized military institution. For centuries, commoners had been denied the right to even possess swords. The whole feudal system had depended on the functional division between the commoners and samurai and the deeply entrenched social stratification. After the domains were abolished, samurai lost their professional and social status. The Japanese military was turned from a closed class profession into a mass conscript system.

In the late 1870s, Emperor Meiji appointed Itō Hirobumi, Minister of Finance, to prepare a national assembly and draft a constitution. In 1882, Ito led a group to visit European capitals to study Western political systems. After his return in the following year, Itō chaired a special commission to draft the constitution. Six years later, on February 11, 1889, the Meiji government promulgated a new constitution that embraced a mixture of new Western concepts and traditional feudal ideas.[39] Under its provisions, the emperor was both the sole source and dispenser of all power. Itō and his commission made sure that the emperor remained the political center, controlling the entire governing apparatus. The Constitution also made clear that "the supreme command" of the army and navy was in the hands of the emperor. The Meiji leaders had safeguarded a "constitutional monarchy" system by protecting the imperial power. Japan's new government was fully operational in 1890 with the convocation of its first national assembly, the Diet. The nation eagerly experimented with Western ideas and practices in a selective manner. The governmental reforms assured internal stability, and created a political mechanism for developing a "rich country with a strong military."

The Meiji Restoration industrialized and partially westernized Japan by learning Western political, economic, and military institutions, and importing European technology. The Meiji court's priority was building the nation's commercial infrastructure; railroads and improved roads in which the reform-minded government had heavily invested became responsible for the early blossoming of commerce. The Meiji government played an important role in Japan's economic development during the late nineteenth and early twentieth centuries. It provided a favorable business environment for industrial growth by removing feudal restrictions and an isolationist policy on trade. Some of the political leaders even played a dual role in politics and business. A number of Western nationals were hired into government service as advisers, engineers, and military instructors until the foreign-trained Japanese experts were able to replace them. Mikiso Hane and Louis G. Perez state that "This period thus was characterized by the coexistence of the traditional and the modern forms of the economy, plus a composite sector that combined aspects of both."[40]

In 1871, the government began its financial reform by establishing a national banking system under the newly founded Bank of Japan, following the model of the American banking system. It helped assemble the needed capital, forced weak companies to merge into stronger corporations, and provided the private sector with financial aid and privileges. In 1873, a new land tax system was introduced, replacing the agricultural tax, which depended on individual farmers' annual yields or income, and changed from an unpredictable and uncontrollable tax revenue to a fixed one, based on land size and values.[41] The land tax set the rate at 3 percent of the assessed land value in 1873, and then was reduced to 2.5 percent three years later. Soon the land tax became the chief source of the government's revenues. By the end of the 1870s, the Meiji government finance had developed a sound foundation for the new industries.

Japan's economy began booming in 1905 in the wake of its 1904 victory in the Russo-Japanese War. The military victory over the Russians, and the peace treaty thereafter expanded Japan's colonial empire and made more raw materials, larger international markets, and overseas investment opportunities available. After Meiji died in 1912, the new emperor Taishō (r. 1912–1926) continued Meiji's reform policies.

The new leaders in Tokyo established a Japan-centered economy through colonizing Korea and Taiwan. For this new Japan, the 1900s–1920s were a golden age. Rapid technological progress continued, the military continued to expand, and the infrastructure and the institutions of government continued to modernize. In the 1920s, however, Japan suffered a serious depression. The boom produced by World War I (WWI) came to an end by 1921, resulting in substantial labor unrest in the industrial sector. Protectionism and tariffs introduced by the United States to protect its own industry placed high barriers on Japanese trade. High unemployment, overpopulation, and acute shortages of raw materials all plagued the Japanese economy. The disparity between the rich (especially those who had profited from the war) and the poor caused popular resentment. The price of rice had also increased dramatically during the war, leading to the Rice Riots of 1918, in which tens of thousands of people angry at the inflated price of rice attacked government offices and police stations across the country. Added to this was the Great Kanto Earthquake of 1923 and the subsequent fires that destroyed Yokohama and half of Tokyo, killing as many as 100,000 people and leaving three million homeless. Finally, in 1927 there was a crisis in the banking sector in which 25 percent of Japanese banks failed.

Colonial Korea and Manchuria (1910–1937)

In order to solve these economic and political problems, voices for a campaign to further exploit colonies like Korea and Taiwan and win new territories such as Manchuria in China grew in popularity in Japan. Supporters included political rightists, and the leadership of the Japanese Army in particular. As a counterweight to the modernization of Japan, the military, the repository of conservative influence, had now expanded to include conscripts from relatively poor rural areas. They were receptive to the nationalistic narrative being fostered at the time, in part through the basic education they were provided with in the military.

The instability of the political system, as different groups competed for power, led to the emperor becoming a much stronger symbol. The new emperor, Hirohito (1901–1989), who acceded to the throne in 1926, gave his reign the title "Showa" (r. 1926–1989), or "Enlightened Peace," and remained a symbol of stability and continuity. Emperor worship reached its apex during the Hirohito regime. Japanese people were told that the head of state was divine and the life goal of every Japanese citizen should be utter devotion to, and self-sacrifice for, the nation. This was reinforced by state sponsorship of Shinto, which in turn reinforced the idea of the divinity of the Japanese islands as well as that of the emperor. In short, the nationalism of the time included a spirit of religious, even proselytizing, fervor. At that moment, the Japanese people needed a stronger government which could protect their achievement of modernization and save their livelihood. At the same time the hawks in the upper echelons of the armed forces were pressing for a greater regional role for Japan, especially in Korea and China. Moderates in the military risked assassination by extremist groups.

Japan had colonized Korea since August 22, 1910, when Korea was officially annexed to Japan as the "Province of Choson," and became part of the Empire of the Rising Sun. From the beginning Japan's colonial administration in Korea was sustained by its large-scale military and police forces. Imperial Japan solidified its rule by suppressing the Nationalists and gaining control of the land system, and enforcing rigid administrative changes. Japan then attempted to extort not only political control but also total control of Korea. Along with political colonization, Japan appropriated a variety of economic interests with no less passion. Japanese capital was not only allowed to enter Korea but encouraged to overwhelm the backward Korean economy. As a result, the overwhelming majority of large firms in Korea were now owned and operated by the Japanese. Many of Japan's major banks, utility companies, and industrial giants established their Korean operations, securely protected by the colonial administration. Most non-menial jobs, including even machine operators and engine drivers, were filled by Japanese, while Koreans labored as near-slaves. Even though Japanese built manufacturing factories, modern mines, railways, and postal service for the first time, most of the coal, iron, and food crops (including over half of the rice) were shipped to Japan.

Efforts aimed at cultural assimilation included such draconian measures as the outlawing of the Korean language and even of Korean family names. To imperial Japan, the public education system in Korea became solely another colonial tool devised to teach Japanese values and mores, another step toward molding the children into the emperor's subjects. By 1929, only Japanese textbooks and the Japanese language could be used in schools. By 1932, Koreans were obliged to take Japanese names. The Japanese claimed that they and the Koreans had the same origins and that the takeover by Japan was thus a natural development. By 1945, when the Japanese colonization was over, there were too few Koreans with the education or administrative experience to form a viable government. Japan's colonial rule of Korea lasted for thirty-six years. Throughout the harsh colonial rule Koreans jealously guarded their heritage and resisted Japanization with their lives. They effectively frustrated Japan's concerted attempts for cultural assimilation. By enduring long and cruel mistreatment, Koreans rejected Japan's overtures to make them second class citizens. They remained resolutely nationalistic until the end of the ordeal. The legacy of Japan's colonial occupation was no less tragic in Korea; it provided a direct cause for the nation's division even before it recovered its lost sovereignty.

After colonizing Korea, Japan's next target was Manchuria in northeastern China. With its rich minerals, fertile soil, and nearly 200,000 square kilometers of land, Manchuria seemed to be an ideal target. The Great Depression, which began with the stock-market crash in 1929, hit Japan hard, and there was a subsequent loss of prestige for the pro-business parties in the government. Extremists began to emerge as "champions of the people" against big business, or *zaibatsu* (financial clique), like Mitsui, Mitsubishi, Sumitoma, and Yasuda. These giant corporations had strong influence on the Japanese government by establishing the administration under their control, such as the "Mitsui cabinet" in 1927–1929 and "Mitsubishi cabinet" in 1930–1931. All of them could not solve the problems in the Great Depression. Hane and Perez point out that "The flames of nationalism, militarism, and imperialism were stoked by the economic and social frustrations felt by the masses as the depression brought them to the very brink of starvation."[42]

Japanese people blamed the economic failure on the selfish, profit-driven business leaders and questioned capitalist free market economy as the only choice for the nation's modernization. While the most difficult period was the early 1930s, a new hope in the "planning economy under the state" seemed to provide an alternative, if not a solution, to the Great Depression. They saw the Soviet Union survive the depression with Stalin's centralized, planned economy in the early 1930s; then, Germany walked out of the European depression in two years after Adolf Hitler's implementation of his national socialist economy plans. All of a sudden, authoritarian forms of government, including the Soviet Communist state, the German state socialist system, or the Italian model of fascist dictatorship, became discussion topics among the ultranationalists and militarists in Japan.

Some of the military ultranationalist groups took matters into their own hands, including assassinating civilian officials, attacking political party headquarters, and plotting by field officers in Manchuria. On September 18, 1931, an unknown explosion on a section of the Japanese-held rail line at Shenyang (Mukden) gave the Japanese army the pretext it sought to charge the local Chinese with sabotage and to launch an attack on Manchuria. This was the Mukden Incident, also known as the 9-18 Incident. Within a few months, the Japanese armed forces occupied the entirety of Manchuria, including Liaoning, Jilin, and Heilongjiang provinces. This aggression was later considered to be the first step on the path to the Japanese occupation of large portions of the Republic of China (ROC) between 1937 and 1945. On March 9, 1932, Japan created the puppet state of Manchukuo (State of Manchuria), and invited the last Qing Emperor Henry Puyi (1906–1967), or Xuantong (r. 1909–1912), to serve as the head of the state (r. 1934–1945). In that August, Tokyo formally recognized Manchukuo as an independent country.

The power of Japanese military came from the fact that the army and navy had never been fully subordinated to civil control. When the militarists controlled the government, they extended their power, and established a militaristic country. The greatest coup was the armed rebellion of the First Infantry Division of the Imperial Army on February 26, 1936. Extremist officers led 1,400 troops into the streets of Tokyo, attacking government offices, murdering Prime Minister Okada, killing cabinet ministers, members of the Diet, and their families.[43] For three days, the political center of the country was in a state of siege.

In these circumstances, Konoe Fumimaro (1891–1945) became the next prime minister in 1937–1939 and served again in 1940. Hane and Perez argue that "Konoe was hardly more than a tool of the military."[44] The prime minister had his own political reform agenda, even though it was an authoritarian one, including a wartime economic system under the government control and dismantling all the political parties. Konoe tried to empower the cabinet by promoting absolute obedience by all subordinates to their superiors in the structure of a pyramid. The political centralization and economic nationalization during the Konoe administration received military support for preparing the forthcoming war in the Pacific. The administration began to plan the nation's economy, decide on production and consumption, and fix the prices and salaries.

While the Konoe cabinet reorganized the nation's economy, it also called into question the validity of the European-centered economic order. This in turn sped up Japan's expansions into the Asian continent and Pacific islands. In 1937, the Japanese forces launched a total war on China. Although the Konoe system, a state-controlled capitalist economy, did not win Japan's victory in the Pacific War in 1937–1945, it did set up a successful course for the state-controlled economic recovery after the war in 1945–1951.

Notes

1 Wynn Gadkar-Wilcox, writing sections in "East Asia and the West," by Xiaobing Li, Yi Sun, and Gadkar-Wilcox (unpublished manuscript), introduction.
2 Iriye considers these countries as "Pacific nations." Iriye, "Book Review," 176.
3 Immanuel C. Y. Hsu, *The Rise of Modern China*, 6th ed. (Oxford, UK: Oxford University Press, 2000), 122.
4 For more information on the Confucian-Mencian paradigm, see: Daniel K. Gardner, *Confucianism: A Very Short Introduction* (Oxford, UK: Oxford University Press, 2014); Anna Sun, *Confucianism as a World Religion: Contested Histories and Contemporary Realities* (Princeton, NJ: Princeton University Press, 2013).
5 For more information on the Buddhism, see: John Kieschnick, *The Impact of Buddhism on Chinese Material Culture* (Princeton, NJ: Princeton University Press, 2003); Jacques Gernet, *Buddhism in Chinese Society* (New York: Columbia University Press, 1998).
6 For more information on the Daoism (Taoism), see: Fabrizio Pregadio, *Great Clarity: Daoism and Alchemy in Early Medieval China* (Stanford, CA: Stanford University Press, 2006); Zhang Dainian and Edmund Ryden, *Key Concepts in Chinese Philosophy* (New Haven, CT: Yale University Press, 2000).
7 Patricia Ebrey and Anne Walthall, *Pre-Modern East Asia: To 1800*, 3rd ed. (Boston, MA: Wadsworth, 2014), 140–141.
8 Conrad Totman, *Japan before Perry: A Short History* (Berkeley: University of California Press, 1981), 32–33.
9 Mark C. Elliott, *The Manchu Way: The Eight Banners and Ethnic Identity in Late Imperial China* (Stanford, CA: Stanford University Press, 2001).
10 Charles S. Maier, "Consigning the Twentieth Century to History: Alternatives for the Modern Era," in *American Historical Review* 105, no. 3 (June 2000): 807–831.
11 Xiaoyuan Liu, "From Five 'Imperial Domains' to a 'Chinese Nation': A Perceptual and Political Transformation in Recent History," in *Ethnic China: Identity, Assimilation, and Resistance*, eds. Xiaobing Li and Patrick Fuliang Shan (Lanham, MD: Lexington Books, 2015), 4.
12 Guangqiu Xu, "Tributary System," in *China at War*, ed. Xiaobing Li (Santa Barbara, CA: ABC-CLIO, 2014), 463–465.
13 David C. Kang, *East Asia before the West: Five Centuries of Trade and Tribute* (New York: Columbia University Press, 2012), chapters 1 and 2.
14 Curtis Andressen, *A Short History of Japan: From Samurai to Sony* (Canberra, Australia: Allen and Unwin, 2002), 62–63.
15 Xiaobing Li, *Modern China: Understanding Modern Nations* (Santa Barbara, CA: ABC-CLIO, 2014), 79–80.
16 John K. Fairbank and Merle Goldman, *China: A New History*, enlarged ed. (Cambridge, MA: Harvard University Press, 1998), 139.
17 James L. Hevia, *Cherishing Men from Afar: Qing Guest Ritual and the MacCartney Embassy of 1793* (Durham, NC: Duke University Press, 1995).
18 Takeshi Hamashita, "Tribute and Treaties: Maritime Asia and Treaty Port Networks in the Era of Negotiation, 1800–1900," in *The Resurgence of East Asia: 500, 150 and 50 Year Perspectives*, eds. Giovanni Arrighi, Takeshi Hamashita, and Mark Selden (London: Routledge, 2003), 17–50.
19 For more information on the early contact with the West, see: James A. Millward, *The Silk Road: A Very Short Introduction* (Oxford, UK: Oxford University Press, 2013); David M.

Robinson, *Empire's Twilight: Northeast Asia under the Mongols* (Cambridge, MA: Harvard University Press, 2009); Laurence Bergreen, *Marco Polo: From Venice to Xanadu* (New York: Vintage, 2008).

20 The Dutch in fact had established themselves on Taiwan in 1621 and called the island "Formosa" ("beautiful one"). The Dutch maintained their settlement until 1658 when Ming General Zheng Chenggong (Cheng Ch'eng-kung) landed his troops and drove the Dutch from the island. See Xiaobing Li and Michael Molina, "Taiwan," in *Oil: A Cultural and Geographic Encyclopedia of Black Gold*, eds. Xiaobing Li and Michael Molina (Santa Barbara, CA: ABC-CLIO, 2014), 2: 671.

21 Ray Huang, *1587, A Year of No Significance: The Ming Dynasty in Decline* (New Haven, CT: Yale University Press, 1981), 187–188, 204–206.

22 Fairbank and Goldman, *China*, 137, 138.

23 Frederic Wakeman, Jr., *The Fall of Imperial China* (New York: The Free Press, 1975), 96.

24 Michael J. Seth, *A Concise History of Korea: From the Neolithic Period through the Nineteenth Century* (Lanham, MD: Rowman & Littlefield, 2006), 211.

25 Geoff Simons, *Korea: The Search for Sovereignty* (New York: St. Martin's Press, 1995), 109.

26 Seth, *A Concise History of Korea*, 218.

27 John K. Fairbank, Edwin O. Reischauer, and Albert M. Craig, *East Asia: Transition and Transformation*, revised ed. (Boston, MA: Houghton Mifflin, 1989), 320.

28 Liu, "From Five 'Imperial Domains' to a 'Chinese Nation'," 31.

29 R. Keith Schoppa, *Revolution and Its Past: Identities and Change in Modern Chinese History*, 3rd ed. (New York: Prentice Hall, 2011), 54.

30 For *Tongmenghui*, see: Hsu, *The Rise of Modern China*, 462–465.

31 Fairbank, Reischauer, and Craig, *East Asia: Transition and Transformation*, 746.

32 June Grasso, Jay Corrin, and Michael Kort, *Modernization and Revolution in China: From the Opium Wars to World Power*, 3rd ed. (Armonk, New York: M.E. Sharpe, 2004), 75–77.

33 James L. McClain, *Japan: A Modern History* (New York: W. W. Norton, 2002), 41–43.

34 Michael S. Neiberg, *Warfare in World History* (London: Routledge, 2001), 25.

35 Andressen, *A Short History of Japan*, 75.

36 Fairbank, John K., Edwin O. Reischauer, and Albert M. Craig, *East Asia: Transition and Transformation*, rev, ed. (Boston, MA: Houghton Mifflin, 1989), 490–491.

37 Mikiso Hane and Louis G. Perez, *Modern Japan: A Historical Survey*, 4th ed. (Boulder, CO: Westview, 2009), 75.

38 Hane and Perez, *ibid.*, 85–86.

39 Andressen, *A Short History of Japan*, 87.

40 Hane and Perez, *Modern Japan*, 143.

41 W. G. Beasley, *The Rise of Modern Japan*, 2nd ed. (New York: St. Martin's, 1995), 61.

42 Hane and Perez, *Modern Japan*, 258.

43 Anne Walthall, *Japan: A Cultural, Social, and Political History* (Boston, MA: Houghton Mifflin, 2006), 183.

44 Hane and Perez, *Modern Japan*, 283.

2 The Asian-Pacific War (1937–1945)

By 1937 armed clashes between the Japanese and Chinese troops at Lugouqiao, or the Marco Polo Bridge outside Beijing, had escalated into all-out war between China and Japan. Japan's imperialist attempt to turn North China into a second Manchukuo led to the full-scale military confrontation between these two East Asian countries. Unlike the first Sino-Japanese War in 1894–1895, the second Sino-Japanese War, or the Anti-Japanese War in Chinese, was a long struggle of attrition that ended only by Japan's unconditional surrender to the Allies in 1945. Japan's territorial ambition on the Asian mainland was thwarted not by an Asian power, but by the Western power. On September 1, 1939, when the German army invaded Poland, World War II started in Europe. This war was fought between the Axis powers, including Germany, Italy, and Japan on one side and an Anglo-French coalition on the other. However, it eventually widened to include most of the nations in the world.

After Japan attacked Pearl Harbor, Hawaii, on December 7, 1941, the Allied powers expanded to include the United States, China, and Korea. Between the war against Germany in Europe and the war against Japan in East Asia, World War II in the Asian-Pacific region is known as the Pacific War, the War in the Pacific Theater, or simply the War against Japan. Through the war, nationalism strengthened its hold on the East Asian people. It is interesting to note that Tokyo called it the "Greater East Asia War" at a cabinet meeting on December 10, 1941, after it attacked US military bases at Pearl Harbor. The militarist-controlled government promoted its propaganda of "Asia for the Asians," freeing Asian peoples from European colonization and replacing the West to build a new Asian empire. Believing that Europe and America sought to slow down or even stop Japanese survival and success in building a strong military and modern country, Japanese militants decided to fight back by challenging the existing international order. The militarists' domination in the government doomed any diplomatic effort and peace negotiation.

Before the Pearl Harbor attack, Japan had already conquered Manchuria, Eastern and Central China, French Indochina, and British Hong Kong. After Pearl Harbor, Japan continued its attacks on Southeast Asia, and occupied American Philippines; British Malaya, Singapore, and Burma; and independent Thailand. In June 1942, Japanese armed forces conquered the Dutch East Indies, and began to invade Australia and New Zealand. By that summer, Japan possessed a vast oceanic and continental empire stretching 4,000 miles from the Western Aleutian Islands south almost to Australia, and 6,000 miles from Burma in the west to the Gilberts in the east. Many people at home showed a strong support and appreciation of the superior military power of the Japanese invading forces.

As Milton W. Meyer has argued:

> Until Japan's defeat, no power in world history had achieved in Asia precisely the same extended imperial stature and the same widespread imperial boundaries. But Japan's temporary wartime supremacy was gained only at a great human cost to all parties concerned, built as it was on force and servitude. In 1941, Japan's position in Asia and the Pacific was paramount; in 1945, it became minimal.[1]

From 1937 to 1945, more than 600 million East Asian people took part in the Asian-Pacific War, about one-third of the world total (1.7 billion) involved in WWII. A total of twenty-nine million individuals were mobilized for military service on both sides, including twelve million Japanese, eleven million Chinese, and four million Korean soldiers. More than six million were killed during the war; about five million of those soldiers were from China and Japan. Japan suffered an ultimate defeat and had to relinquish its long, hard-fought ambition to become a nation of the Asian mainland.

Japan's attacks on China and Pearl Harbor (1937–1941)

In 1937, while Japan reorganized the nation's economy, it also called into question the validity of the European-centered economic order in Asia. The Konoe cabinets (1937–1939, 1940) tried to establish a new Japan-centered economic order in East Asia. This in turn sped up Japan's expansions on the Asian continent and Pacific islands. In 1937, the Japanese forces launched a total war in China from Manchuria which they had occupied since 1931. The Lugouqiao, or Marco Polo Bridge, Incident began the second phase of the Japanese invasion of China and marked the start of the total conflict between the countries. On July 7, 1937, Japanese army troops demanded entry into the town of Wanping, about ten miles west of Beijing in Hebei province. The town was held by forces loyal to the Nationalist (Guomindang, GMD; or Kuomintang, KMT) government. When the Chinese troops denied entry to the Japanese, the Japanese threatened the use of force at Lugouqiao, where the opposing sides met. On July 17, 1937, Jiang Jieshi, President of the ROC, informed the Chinese people that "the hope for peace has been shattered" and that the Chinese people had to fight the Japanese "to the bitter end" in order to expel the "invader."[2] After the Marco Polo Bridge Incident, China mobilized the entire population and launched a total resistant war against Japan's invasion.

Japan's invading army, however, scored victories over most major Chinese cities during the first year of the war. In August 1937, Japanese occupied Beijing and Tianjin. In November, Japan concentrated 220,000 troops and began an offensive campaign against Nanjing, China's capital. Jiang and the GMD high command deployed nearly 700,000 troops to defend the Nanjing-Shanghai region. On November 7, the Japanese Tenth Army successfully landed at Hangzhou Bay. In December, they seized Nanjing. The Chinese defense forces suffered heavy casualties, with 50,000 deaths including seventeen army generals. In *The Rape of Nanking: The Forgotten Holocaust of WWII*, Iris Chang stated that after the Japanese troops entered the capital city, they killed 90,000 POWs and 260,000 civilians.[3]

Jiang's army continued its ineffective defense into 1938 despite a few victories in the Battle of Taierzhuang (Shandong, March–April, 1938) and the Battle of Wanjialing (Jiangxi, October 1938). By March 1938, almost all of North China fell into the enemy's hands. In October, Guangzhou and Wuhan also fell. The GMD government was forced to move its capital to Chongqing in Sichuan province. Jiang's troops suffered heavy casualties. From July 1937 to November 1938, Jiang lost one million GMD troops while eliminating 250,730 Japanese soldiers. The GMD Army withdrew to China's Southwest and Northwest to conserve some of their troops when Jiang removed the seat of his government from Nanjing to Chongqing.[4] By 1939, when WWII started in Europe, the GMD Army had lost the coastal and other port cities that once had been their bases of power.[5] In the meantime, Japanese forces slowed down their southward advance, stopping short at China's southwestern region. The Chinese war of resistance entered a protracted phase of six years.

Japan's imperial expansion, fueled by the invasion of China, did not achieve the objectives of the Japanese leaders in Tokyo. They had expected economic returns – in the form of fuels and raw materials – to at least cover the cost of the war. What made it even worse was that "the American government answered each Japanese move," beginning with a trade embargo on Japan by banning the sale of airplanes in July 1938, then extending to oil and petroleum products in December 1939, and lastly to scrap iron, munitions, and other implements of war in July 1940.[6] The US government refused to recognize Japan's military occupations of Indochinese countries and demanded an immediate withdrawal of all Japanese troops from China. After the spring of 1941, trade negotiations failed between Tokyo and Washington. That July the US government froze Japanese financial assets and signed agreements with the Dutch and British to also end their oil exports to Japan.

At an imperial conference in early July, Japanese naval officers proposed a navy-led southward drive into southeast Asia, where crude oil, coal, and other natural resources were accessible for Japan's needs to continue the war. In the summer of 1941, Japanese military leaders had to reassign divisions from China to carry out the invasions of Hong Kong, the Philippines, Malaya, and Burma (present-day Myanmar). These steps, an effort to cut off the Chinese from US aid flowing from India, brought US retaliation against Japan in the form of an economic embargo on certain critical war materials, especially oil. In turn, this triggered Japan's decision to go to war against the United States. Meyer states that "the U.S. and Japanese positions had become irreconcilable," and that it was "against the backdrop of irreconcilable positions" that Japan made "the decision to go to war" against the United States.[7] Japan's 1941 attack on Pearl Harbor and its war with Britain and the Netherlands broadened the conflict into a general Pacific war and severely strained its capability to conduct offensive operations in China.

In 1941 the United States had significant military strength in the Pacific, which would be an obstacle for Japan's ocean-going expansion into the Western Pacific. In September Admiral Yamamoto Isoroku planned a surprise attack on Pearl Harbor to cripple the US Pacific Fleet there. In October, Army General Tojo Hideki became prime minister, and decided to put the war plan into action. On November 1, Yamamoto issued the orders for an attack on Pearl Harbor. On November 26, the Pearl Harbor Striking Force, including six aircraft carriers, two battleships, three cruisers, and nine destroyers, left Etorofu in the Kuriles. In the meantime, an American decoding project named *Magic* had been successful in breaking the Japanese diplomatic code, and it provided information leading to the conclusion that Japan would launch military operations in Southeast Asia, but it was uncertain about target and timing.

On December 7, 1941, the Japanese Strike Force launched a surprise attack on the US military bases at Pearl Harbor in Hawaii. Nearly 200 Japanese aircraft attacked the

US Pacific Fleet and sank four of the fleet's battleships, and damaged four more. Another 200 aircraft smashed the US Army and Navy airfields and destroyed about 350 aircraft. The raid lasted less than two hours, killing more than 2,400 Americans, and almost crippling US defenses in the Pacific. For Japan, however, the attack was only temporarily successful since its pilots failed to destroy oil storage facilities at Pearl Harbor and the three aircraft carriers of the US Pacific Fleet were not at Pearl Harbor that day. After the US Congress endorsed President Franklin D. Roosevelt's (FDR) call for a declaration of war on December 8, the US Navy was able to build a huge naval power in the Pacific over the next year. On December 11, both Hitler and Mussolini declared war against the United States, bringing the US into all-out war with the Axis powers in both East Asia and Europe.

Japan's attack on Pearl Harbor refueled public enthusiasm in China. A frustrated Jiang Jieshi and exhausted Chinese forces in the fourth year of their fruitless resistance became suddenly encouraged and extremely motivated by seeing that the United States was then fighting on their side against Imperial Japan in the Pacific. The Chinese government thereafter enjoyed unprecedented activism in allied diplomacy through the war for international support in general and US aid in particular. The new vigor of nationalism revealed a profound change taking place in China. As Liu states, external factors seem the only reasons behind this change, partly because of "China's own tenacious resistance against Japan and partly from Washington's promotion."[8] While Jiang and his government attempted to improve the ROC's international status in Cairo and Moscow where he attended the Allied summits as one of the international leaders, his efforts actually strengthened the Nationalist leadership at home, which Jiang had never before enjoyed. Important internal reasons also drove this crucial turn for the GMD government. Chinese warlords, urban merchants, and intellectuals saw clearly the need for a fully centralized government to protect their local interests, and Jiang was willing to establish a united front that included all political parties and social groups.

Conquest and home front (1942–1945)

On the same day Pearl Harbor was attacked, Japan also invaded the Philippines, Thailand, Malaya (present-day Malaysia), British Hong Kong, American Wake Island, and Guam. On December 8, Thailand surrendered to Japanese invading forces, and the Thai government began cooperating with Japan on December 21. The US defense collapsed on both Guam and Wake Island on December 25. At the same time, British and Canadian forces lost Hong Kong to Japanese landing forces. In January 1942, after losing Kuala Lumpur and Rabaul, British forces were driven out of Malaya. Then, Japanese forces invaded Borneo, Burma (present-day Myanmar), Dutch Indonesia, New Guinea, and the Solomon Islands. Chief among the major military disasters of the Allied forces in Southeast Asia were the defenses of Singapore and the Philippines. During the Battle of Singapore, the Allied forces lost the city to the Japanese invading forces in February 1942, and about 130,000 British, Australian, and Dutch troops became prisoners of war. American defense of the Philippines continued until May 1942, when more than 80,000 US soldiers were ordered to surrender to the Japanese. General Douglas MacArthur, Supreme Allied Commander of the Southwest Pacific, left Manila for Australia before the fall of the Philippines.

In early 1942, Japan planned an invasion of Australia. Japanese forces took over the Australian Territory of New Guinea in January/February and established naval and air bases there. In March, MacArthur formulated a defense plan for Australia and moved his headquarters to Melbourne. On April 1, 1942, the Pacific War Council was established in Washington with US President Roosevelt and representatives from Britain, China, Australia, and other countries. The council and the Doolittle Air Raid on Japan in April were politically symbolic, but offered a huge international morale boost among the Asian countries under either Japanese attacks or occupation. The war situation in the Pacific Theater did not change in favor of the Allied forces until June 1942.

From 1942 to 1944, Japanese government tried to establish colonial governments in its occupied countries. Tokyo promoted its propaganda of "Asia for the Asians," according to its spokesman's own Monroe Doctrine for the Asian continent. As pointed out by John K. Fairbank, Edwin O. Reischauer, and Albert M. Craig, the "liberated" countries found Japan's "New Order" to be harsher than the former colonial rule. Still, changes occurred during the Japanese occupations that made the re-establishment of the colonies after the war impossible. In the long run, this may have been the most significant consequence of the Pacific War.[9] In November 1942, Tokyo established the Ministry of Great East Asia to handle the national puppet governments to develop a colonial empire under its political and military control. The Japanese colonial pattern which had developed in Korea and Manchuria could be applied in these countries.

After the total war broke out between Japan and China, Tokyo founded the Mongolian autonomous government on October 27, 1937 in the north of the ROC, today's Republic of Mongolia. On March 28, 1938, Japanese established a puppet Chinese government in Nanjing after Jiang Jieshi moved the seat of the ROC government from Nanjing to Chongqing in November 1937. Since then, Chongqing became Jiang's wartime capital to resist Japanese invasion of China until 1945. In March 1945, the Japanese military arrested the French authorities and formed the Empire of Vietnam under the leadership of the Bao Dai Emperor (r. 1932–1945). Nevertheless, the East Asian people did not consider the Japanese occupiers as "liberators" and the establishment of the puppet governments as "independence." The local responses to the Japanese conquests took the form of nationalist and communist resistance.

To meet the needs of its war in East Asia, Japanese government also created a "Great East Asia Co-Prosperity Sphere" as a self-sustaining economic community in the territories overrun by Japan. Since 1937, Japan's military expansions had been a war of attrition, in which Japan was over-stretched and drained by the war with China. The "East Asia Sphere" should have provided fuel, raw materials, labor, and markets for Japan's empire through the military occupation and economic exploitation. Bruce A. Elleman points out that "Tokyo authorized continued southward expansion in July 1941, and soon occupied Indochina. From this position, Japanese troops made further advances into Southeast Asia, a rich source of rubber, tin, oil, quinine, lumber, foodstuffs, and other raw materials."[10] Because of the war situation and strong resistance, Tokyo was unable to manage this economic community, which provided a little economic return to Japan's war effort. After 1943, the Japanese economy could not match the American industrial-military capacity for rapid expansion. In 1944, the Allied powers had successfully isolated Japan from its empire by cutting off its maritime transportation through naval, air, and submarine powers.

At home, the Tojo cabinet (1941–1944) mobilized the entire country for Japan's war effort by controlling of the country's economy. For instance, in the spring of 1941, the Iron and Steel Control Association was founded to coordinate wartime iron and steel productivities. Later that year, Tojo established several similar associations to control

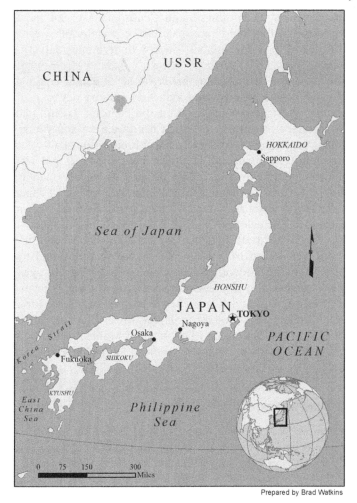

Prepared by Brad Watkins

Map 2.1 Japan

Japan's coal, cement, machinery, motor vehicles, foreign trade, and ship building industries. Individual companies still belonged in the private sector, according to James L. McClain, "but each control association became responsible for meeting production targets set by the supervising ministry."[11] The Japanese government began to direct the industrial war efforts through these control associations led by chairmen from one of the giant member companies such as Mitsubishi and Mitsui.

Japan spent more than $60 billion on its war-related production activities. Aircraft manufacturing increased from 1,080 fighters in 1941 to 2,935 in 1942, 7,147 in 1943, and 13,811 in 1944. Similarly, bombers production increased from 1,461 in 1941 to 2,433 in 1942, 4,189 in 1943, and 5,100 in 1944. Japan also increased naval capacity, building five aircraft carriers in 1941, six in 1942, three in 1943, and four in 1944 as well as nine destroyers in 1941, nine in 1942, fifteen in 1943, and thirty-one in 1944.[12] Nonetheless, it was a war of attrition, and Japanese war-fighting capability was worn down by a steady growth of American industrial-military power. The successes of the

US amphibious forces in the Southwest and Central Pacific and the US submarine victories cut the flow of food and raw materials, especially oil, from the Japanese-conquered territories to the home islands, thereby undermining Japan's war economy. The US submarines sank 1,300 Japanese vessels.[13] Already drained by the war with China for more than five years, soon the Japanese economy could not match the American capacity for rapid expansion of industrial-military power.

Moreover, a labor shortage became a serious problem for Japan's manufacturing in the early 1940s. Military recruitments drafted nearly ten million young men between sixteen and forty, according to the National Mobilization Law of 1938 and the National Service Draft Ordinance of 1939. As labor shortages got worse during the war, Prime Minister and Army Chief Tojo decided to replace men with women in seventeen industrial sectors. According to McClain, 42 percent of Japan's work force was female in February 1942, and about 60 percent of all employees in the communications industries were female by October 1944. McClain continues that from 1944 the government "began to draft students from middle school, eventually more than three million boys were called to work in war-related factories, and by August 1945 nearly one-fifth of all industrial workers were under twenty years of age."[14] During the war, Japanese government also impressed prisoners of war and foreign laborers from China, Taiwan, Hong Kong, and Korea. Between 1941 and 1945, for example, more than one million Koreans were brought to Japan. Meanwhile, as many as 250,000 to 400,000 Korean, Chinese, Filipino, and Dutch young women were forcibly sent to the brothels of the Imperial Army as "comfort women" for Japanese soldiers and colonial administrators.[15]

Anti-Japanese wars in East Asia

China's Anti-Japanese War (or Sino-Japanese War), sometimes known as the Second Sino-Japanese War, began against the backdrop of repeated efforts of GMD leader Jiang Jieshi to crush the forces of the Chinese Communist Party (CCP) led by Mao Zedong. From October 1934 to October 1935, Jiang pursued Communist forces through China's hinterlands to Yan'an in what became known as the Long March. When Mao's forces reached the relative safety of Yan'an in Northeastern Shaanxi province, Jiang ordered local warlords, nominally loyal to him, to continue the campaign against the Communists instead of concentrating on resisting Japanese expansion. The Xi'an Incident in December 1936, a coup staged by two GMD generals, forced Jiang to accept a United Front against Japan and helped focus Chinese Nationalist fervor against the Japanese.

The GMD government came to an agreement with the CCP on joint resistance. After the total war broke between China and Japan in July 1937, in September, the GMD made public a declaration for GMD-CCP co-operation and recognized the legal status of the CCP. Thus, an anti-Japanese united front formally came into existence.[16] This front is often called the Second United Front (1937–1945) to distinguish it from the First United Front of GMD-CCP cooperation (1924–1927). Moscow firmly supported the CCP-GMD coalition through the war. Although the Soviet leader, Josef Stalin, continued to send his financial aid to the CCP, he began to support Jiang's GMD Army as well.[17]

When Jiang lost some of his best troops in the war against the Japanese invasion, Mao's successful guerrillas recruited a large number of peasants into his forces. The units of the CCP's Eighth Route Army marched to the enemy-occupied territories, where they carried out guerrilla operations and established military and political bases.[18] The Eighth Route Army in North China increased from 46,000 men in 1937 to 220,000 men in 1939, and to 500,000 men in 1940. In the south, the CCP's New Fourth Army moved north and south of the Yangzi (Yangtze) River and established bases in southern Jiangsu and also north of the river. In each of the bases, the CCP established a government, reduced the peasants' rents and interests, returned land to poor peasants, and armed the masses. In February 1940, the Central Military Commission (CMC) ordered both armies to recruit 300,000 more soldiers within that year.[19]

From 1939 to 1945, China was divided into three distinctive regions. The first region were the Japanese-occupied territories (*Lunxianqu* in Chinese), including strategic areas in Manchuria, Northeastern China, Southeastern China, Hainan Island, and major coastal cities including Shanghai, Nanjing, Wuhan, Hong Kong, and Guangzhou – the most industrialized urban areas. In the occupied region which had about 36–40 percent of national population, some local warlords and their armies collaborated with the Japanese. In 1940, the Japanese established an alternative Chinese national government in Nanjing with Wang Jingwei, one of Jiang's political rivalries in the GMD, as the president. Many Chinese in the occupied region accepted Wang's government "because they had no choice, or because they saw the possibility of profiting from cooperation with Japan."[20]

The second region was the Nationalist-controlled region (*Guotongqu*), also known as "Free China," including Chongqing, the wartime ROC capital, and a few rear base cities such as Chengdu, Kunming, Guilin, and Central and Southwestern China. Under Jiang and his GMD government, the GMD-controlled region had about 48–50 percent of the total population and 60 percent of China's rice production. US aid to the Nationalists increased after December 1941, but China was a distant part of the China-Burma-India Theater. In April 1942, Japanese forces in Burma took Lashio and cut the Burma Road, the Nationalist-controlled region's only land route to the outside world. Thereafter, American aid had to be flown over "the Hump" of the Himalayas to reach Chongqing. Jiang's US military adviser, Lieutenant General Joseph Stilwell (1883–1946), tried to train and organize new Chinese divisions equipped by the United States, but he became increasingly frustrated with Jiang's refusal to commit them to fight the Japanese in Burma or in Southeastern China. There was also disagreement among US generals about aid to China. Major General Claire Lee Chennault (1893–1958) wanted to build on the success of the Flying Tigers and their high kill ratio against Japanese pilots to commit most aid to the new US Fourteenth Air Force in China.

The third region in wartime China was the Communist-controlled region, or the "liberated regions" (*Jiefangqu*) according to the historians in China. This region loosely incorporated scattered rural areas in remote northern and northwestern regions under the influence of the CCP with Yan'an as the political center through the war. In 1941–1942, the Japanese command concentrated 64 percent of its troops in China to launch "mopping-up operations" against the CCP bases behind its line, governed by a policy known as "Three Alls": kill all, burn all, and loot all. Slowly and gradually, they wanted to stop the guerrillas in their rear area of operations by eliminating their human and economic resources. To overcome the shortage of food and supply, the Chinese officers and soldiers devoted themselves to increasing production. Many of them participated in the opening up of wilderness for crop cultivation, the raising of hogs, and the making of cloth. After much hard work, many army units and offices succeeded in attaining total or partial self-sufficiency. The most difficult problems with logistical concerns for the bases were resolved by 1943, after which these areas continued to expand.[21] On July 22, 1944, the first team of the "American Observation Group" arrived in Yan'an. By the spring of 1945, the nation had nineteen "liberated areas" with a total population of ninety-five million.[22] By the fall of 1945, the CCP's regular army had grown to 1.27 million men, supported by militias numbering another 2.68 million.[23] The Eighth Route Army increased from three divisions in August 1937 to more than forty divisions in August 1945; the New Fourth Army increased from four divisions in 1937 to seven divisions in 1945.[24]

Allied support, operation, and atomic bombs (1942–1945)

Even though the Allied counterattack in East Asia was slowed by the Allied decision to defeat Germany first, the tide turned in the Pacific during the summer of 1942. In May, the American fleet defeated a Japanese armada in the Coral Sea north of Australia. Then, in the Battle of Midway on June 3–6, American planes sank four Japanese aircraft carriers, and Japan lost its Strike Force. Now with limited offensive capabilities, the Japanese were left to defend the many islands and territories they had occupied. The US island-hopping campaign began in August 1942, when US Marines landed on Guadalcanal in the southern Pacific. Thereafter, savage battles raged for control of the strategic islands in the Pacific. In 1943, American and British forces, along with Indian and Chinese allies, launched an offensive against Japanese outposts in Southern Asia. In mid-1943, Allied forces launched offensives in New Guinea and the Solomon Islands that eventually controlled the South Pacific. While the island-hopping campaign kept pressure on Japanese forces, the Allies landed in the Philippines in the fall of 1944. After the American fleet crushed the Japanese armada in one of the greatest naval battles in world history, the Allied forces liberated Manila, capital city of the Philippines, in February 1945. In the meantime, American forces also captured Iwo Jima, a crucial island group in the Pacific.

At the same time, Japanese forces in China launched a two-pronged offensive that highlighted continued Chinese military weakness. Operation ICHI-GŌ, which Japan conducted from April to December 1944, aimed to cross the Burma-India border through South China to seize Allied airfields at the western side of the Hump air-transport route, capture key north-south railroads in China, and seize Fourteenth Air Force airfields used to stage attacks on Japanese forces. The attack on Assam (an Indian state that borders Burma) failed, as Allied forces in Burma under Lieutenant General Sir William Slim (1891–1970) broke the siege of Imphal and then went on the offensive. But the Japanese attack in China succeeded. The Japanese first won control of the key north-south railroad between the Yellow River and Yangzi River; they then seized the airfields used by the Fourteenth Air Force, and later in 1944 they secured Guilin province as well as Nanning and Liuzhou in Guangxi province. The ICHI-GŌ operation was the high point of Japanese military operations in China. Thereafter, Tokyo began transferring its best divisions from China and Manchuria to meet the US drive across the Pacific into the Philippines and later the Bonin Islands and the Ryukyus. Remaining Japanese forces in China were badly overextended, and Japanese commanders sought to consolidate, especially by summer 1945, to face a possible Soviet attack.

In the wake of the Allied Forces' offensive campaign against the fascists and militarism across the globe, East Asian countries developed a new vigor of nationalism which revealed a profound change taking place in the former colonies and occupied territories. This new nationalism was no longer a traditional, Eastern cultural or ethnic nationalism, but a modern, Western-style state nationalism that emphasized national independence, self-government, state interests, and territorial sovereignty.

In early 1945, the Allies began large-scale bombing of Japan. In one raid in March, Allied planes dropped bombs across Tokyo, unleashing a firestorm in which more than 100,000 people died. In April, MacArthur, commander in chief of Allied Forces in the Pacific, ordered the invasion of Okinawa. To defend the Japanese island, thousands of suicide pilots, known as *kamikaze*, crashed their bomb-laden planes into American ships. During the landing, Allied forces suffered 49,100 casualties, while thirty-four warships were sank. MacArthur estimated a total of 350,000 American casualties for the landing campaign on Japan's major islands, which became one of the important factors for the Truman administration's decision to drop the atomic bombs on Japan to end the war.

President Roosevelt established a government-sponsored atomic research project in May 1943, known as the "Manhattan Project." After Roosevelt's death in April 1945, Harry S. Truman became the president and carried on the nuclear bomb development in Hanford, Washington; Oak Ridge, Tennessee; and Los Alamos, New Mexico, continuing to race for an atomic bomb before Germany. On July 16, the first successful atomic bomb was exploded at Alamogordo in the New Mexican desert. President Truman saw no reason not to use the atomic bomb against Japan to save American lives and to end the war. After the Japanese failed to respond to the Allied ultimatum – Japan must surrender unconditionally – Truman issued the order to drop the bomb. On August 6, the first bomb was dropped on the city of Hiroshima, incinerating about 100,000 people and destroying nearly 96 percent of buildings. Three days later, after the Japanese government still refused to surrender, the second atomic bomb was dropped at Nagasaki, killing about 90,000 people.

Even after these catastrophes, the Japanese military remained unmoved. At an imperial conference on August 14, the cabinet split 3:3, and Emperor Hirohito gave his support to the group favoring surrender. When the emperor's surrender speech was broadcast, it surprised a civilian populace prepared for a final "battle of Japan." On August 15, 1945, Hirohito made a public speech on radio asking all Japanese to lay down their arms and wait for repatriation. On September 2, the instrument of surrender was signed by MacArthur and the Japanese government on the US battleship *Missouri*, in Tokyo Bay. Japan was defeated, ending a war started in 1937. Over the eight years, 3.1 million Japanese had lost their lives, including 2.3 million military deaths and 800,000 civilians in the war. China had sustained military casualties alone of more than five million, with more than three million dead. The number of civilian dead is estimated to be between nine to twelve million.

Japan's surrender ended its occupations and colonial governments in China, Korea, Taiwan, and Hong Kong. Although the war was over in East Asia, peace was not there. The national unification, independence, self-government, and democracy, which had been fought for by Asians and supported by the Allied powers, did not consequently happen after the war ended in August 1945. Instead, the European powers returned, expecting to re-establish their pre-war colonial order in East and Southeast Asia. In 1946, the First Indochina War broke out between the French army and the Communist force in North Vietnam. At the same time, the pre-WWII civil war resumed in China between the GMD and CCP less than one year after they had won the victory of the Anti-Japanese War, which they had been fighting together for eight years. In 1948, the Korean Communist Party founded the Communist state in the North, while the Republic of Korea (ROK) was established in the South after a general election. The political, economic, and military struggles in East Asia continued into the post-WWII era.

Notes

1 Milton W. Meyer, *Japan: A Concise History*, 4th ed. (Lanham, MD: Rowman & Littlefield, 2013), 216.
2 Compilation Committee of the ROC History, *A Pictorial History of the Republic of China* (Taipei, Taiwan: Modern China Press, 1981), 1: 444.
3 Iris Chang, *The Rape of Nanking: The Forgotten Holocaust of World War II* (New York: Basic Books, 1997), 4.
4 Compilation Committee of the ROC History, *A Pictorial History of the Republic of China*, 1: 505.
5 Edward L. Dreyer, *China at War, 1901–1949* (New York: Longman, 1995), 7.
6 James L. McClain, *Japan: A Modern History*, 473.
7 Meyer, *Japan*, 210.
8 Xiaoyuan Liu, *A Partnership for Disorder: China, the United States, and their Policies for the Postwar Disposition of the Japanese Empire, 1941–1945* (Cambridge, UK: Cambridge University Press, 1996), 3.
9 Fairbank, Reischauer, and Craig, *East Asia: Transition and Transformation*, 808.
10 Bruce A. Elleman, *Modern Chinese Warfare, 1795–1989* (London: Routledge, 2001), 208.
11 McClain, *Japan*, 486.
12 Jerome B. Cohen, *Japan's Economy in War and Reconstruction* (Minneapolis: University of Minnesota Press, 1949), 211, 237, 262.
13 Fairbank, Reischauer, and Craig, *East Asia: Transition and Transformation*, 814.
14 McClain, *Japan*, 489.
15 Peipei Qiu, *Chinese Comfort Women: Testimonies from Imperial Japan's Sex Slaves* (New York: Oxford University Press, 2013), 6.
16 Elleman, *Modern Chinese Warfare*, 205–206.
17 Qian Haihao, *Jundui zuzhi bianzhixue jiaocheng* [Graduate Curriculum: Military Organization and Formation] (Beijing: Junshi kexue [Military Science Press], 2001), 39.
18 There are rich examples of CCP military operations behind the enemy lines in literature focused on the Resistant War against Japan. For example, in Feng Chih, *Behind Enemy Lines* (Beijing: Foreign Languages Press, 1979), chapters 2–5.
19 Li Baozhong, *Zhongwei junshi zhidu bijiao* [Comparative Study of Chinese Military System] (Beijing: Shangwu yinshuguan [Shangwu Press], 2003), 229.
20 Harold M. Tanner, *China: A History from the Great Qing Empire through the People's Republic of China* (Indianapolis, IN: Hackett, 2010), 2: 169.
21 Peter Zarrow, *China in War and Revolution, 1895–1949* (New York: Routledge, 2005), 324–325.
22 War History Division, National Defense University (NDU), *Zhongguo renmin jiefangjun zhanshi jianbian* [A Brief War-Fighting History of the PLA] (Beijing: Jiefangjun [PLA Press], 2001), 484.
23 NDU, *ibid*.
24 Qian, *Jundui zuzhi bianzhixue jiaocheng* [Graduate Curriculum: Military Organization and Formation], 39.

3 Cold War Japan: Occupation and reform (1945–1951)

During the Pacific War, the struggle against colonialism in East Asia gained popular support by resisting Japanese colonization. After Pearl Harbor, the nationalist movements in China, Korea, and Vietnam became internationalized through the war, and the anti-Japanese parties and armies, including the Communist forces, received the Allies' support and aid. As a result of the wartime alliance, the political parties in East Asia accepted the international leadership of the Allied powers such as the United States and Soviet Union, which promised peace, independence, and democracy after defeating and decolonizing the Japanese empire.

In the meantime, however, the Allied leaders considered post-war Japan, China, and Korea as international issues and practiced their conventional power politics. US President Roosevelt approached the issues of post-war East Asia from an inclusive and world-systemic standpoint, intending to maintain the momentum of US leadership in Asia. Thus, at the Cairo Conference in 1943 and the Yalta Conference in early 1945, Roosevelt discussed and finalized his policy planning toward East Asia, which was "primarily oriented toward dealing with other powers in Asia, but not with Asian people."[1] Most East Asian leaders found it difficult to establish a partnership for a post-war order with the Roosevelt administration. Roosevelt's policy toward East Asia was that there should be a transition (or occupation) period before the establishment of a united and sovereign government in these countries. For example, his initial Korean trusteeship plan called for a ten-to-forty-year tutelage, thoroughly ignoring the Korean people's eagerness to reclaim their free and independent standing at the earliest date. Nor was he aware of the fact that Koreans wanted to reject another foreign ruler regardless of who it might be. In fact, the president was not willing to listen to the very people whose future would be most directly affected by his policy. Although they fought on the same side during the war, their different backgrounds and strategic considerations drove them in different directions in their pursuit of political schemes for the future of East Asia.

While America's post-war policy failed to gain support from its East Asian allies, the post-war role of the Soviet Union in East Asia also remained unclear. It was expected that Russia would view the region with more sensitivity and understanding because its interests and involvement in East Asia had been much more direct and historical than America's. However, Ilya V. Gaiduk points out that in 1945 "Moscow was trying to consolidate its sphere of influence and attain a favorable position from which to deal with the West. Therefore ... Asia was not even the second front of Soviet confrontation with the West."[2] Soviet leader Josef Stalin's refusal to grant Roosevelt's repeated request to deploy the Red Army against Japan to open a second front in East Asia was interpreted not as a fundamental disagreement with Washington, but rather Moscow's wartime policy of Europe first. To gain Russian military engagement against Japan, Roosevelt was willing to yield Manchuria, North China, and northern Korea to Russia. In retrospect, it was an improvident deal even though it was made under the assumption that Japan's military in Manchuria would not offer a swift capitulation.

The sudden surrender of Japan in August 1945 provided an opportunity for both US power politics and Soviet influence in East Asia. The anti-Japanese governments and forces continued to request international support to complete their national movements, which had been escalated in the Pacific War. But President Truman, who entered the White House after Roosevelt died in the spring of 1945, inherited "broad outlines" of US East Asian policy adapted by FDR.[3] Lacking foreign policy experience and a personal familiarity with any Asian leaders, the new president heavily relied on advice from officials in Roosevelt's cabinet and State Department. Many historians agreed that Truman let others, such as Secretary of State Dean G. Acheson, NSC Policy Planning Staff Director George Kennan, and more importantly, Special Ambassador John Forster Dulles, take charge of the East Asian problems in 1945–1949. It wasn't until June 1950 – when North Korea invaded South Korea – that Truman shifted his East Asian policy-making from "hands-off" to "hands-on" and engaged East Asian countries in the Cold War.

The origin of the Cold War (1945–1947)

Soviet and American interests clashed in Eastern Europe after WWII ended in 1945. Stalin used the Russian Red Army, which had occupied East Europe during the war, to install communist governments in many countries such as Poland, Bulgaria, Romania, Albania, and later Czechoslovakia and Hungary, by refusing to recognize their general elections. Soviet determination to create a security buffer zone in Eastern Europe directly conflicted with Washington's desire for a democratically elected and economically free continent. Truman's displeasure with the Soviet Union's policy towards Eastern Europe caused the administration, experiencing increasing pressure from Congress and the American people, to adopt a more adversarial role at the beginning of 1946. The deterioration of US-Soviet relations in East Europe occurred because the two nations had diametrically opposed strategic visions for the post-war world. Consequently, America and Russia's relentless pursuit of their irreconcilable policies in Europe drastically reduced their willingness to cooperate on a wide range of issues in Asia.

The Cold War began as an escalated propaganda war between Moscow and Washington. In February, Stalin warned the Russians that the Soviet Union must safeguard its interest against aggressive capitalist nations, which had historically begun wars over access to raw materials and foreign markets.[4] Stalin's speech immediately provoked a wide range of reactions in the United States. *Time Magazine* condemned the Soviet dictator's suspicions of his allies and labeled it "the most warlike pronouncement uttered by a top-rank statesman since V-J Day."[5] Conflicting national interest and ideological differences gradually undermined the wartime alliance and established the basis for the Cold War.

On February 22, 1946, George F. Kennan (1904–2005), the *Chargé d'affaires* at the US Embassy in Moscow, sent Washington the "Long Telegram" to explain aggressive Soviet foreign policy and provide the framework for America's evolving containment policy against the USSR (Union of Soviet Socialist Republics). Despite his dire warning, Kennan emphasized that the Soviet Union, unlike Nazi Germany, respected the "logic of force" and did not want to risk a war with the Western Powers.[6] Kennan's telegram made an immediate impact with officials in the US foreign policy establishment. In March, Truman accompanied former British Prime Minister Winston Churchill (from 1940–1945 and again from 1951–1955) to Fulton, Missouri, where Churchill made his famous "iron curtain" speech to denounce Soviet intention to divide Europe by a communist expansion. Churchill's powerful anti-Soviet speech elicited a strong response from America's media, public, and political establishment. Not surprisingly, the Kremlin condemned the British statesman's speech and tried to exploit the controversy surrounding it. Stalin described Churchill's speech as "a call to war against the USSR."[7]

After Kennan's cable was widely circulated in the State Department, the Truman administration attempted to use America's economic power as diplomatic leverage against the Soviet Union. On March 12, 1947, Truman addressed a special joint session of Congress to request $400 million in aid for Greece and Turkey. The president argued that communist subversion threatened to undermine Athens and Ankara's sovereignty, thus hindering democratic development in these nations. Thus, he claimed, US national security required Washington to adopt a more proactive strategy in the post-war world.[8]

Thereafter, Truman's new policy, or the "Truman Doctrine," became the comprehensive US foreign policy to contain the Soviet Union's worldwide aggressions. As the result, the National Security Act of 1947 created a Department of Defense (DOD), including a separate air force, and formalized the existence of the Joint Chiefs of Staff (JCS). It also gave the president a National Security Council (NSC), a National Security Agency (NSA), and the Central Intelligence Agency (CIA). Its precepts also provided the rationale for America's military intervention in Korea, Vietnam, and the Taiwan Straits. Confronted by the deepening Cold War, the State Department reorganized, creating a Policy Planning Staff and growing fivefold.

While most Cold War scholarship incorporates the Truman Doctrine Speech within larger studies concerning the origins of America's and Russia's post-war conflict, some historians such as Gaddis reject the event as the turning point in the Cold War.[9] Others even downplay the role of ideology, and instead point out the bureaucratic factors in the Truman administration. For instance, Bruce R. Kuniholm applies Gaddis' post-revisionist ideas in his work and questions the Truman speech's "imagery and rhetoric which encouraged a misleadingly simplistic view or model of the world."[10] He concludes that this erroneous conception helped create the mindset that made the Korean and Vietnam Wars possible. Along with the Truman Doctrine, moreover, the President tied himself to containing communism but mainly focused on Europe, as demonstrated by the 1948 Marshall Plan and formation of NATO (North Atlantic Treaty Organization) in 1949. James I. Matray points out that there were two themes that co-existed in Truman's containment policy: realism in Europe and idealism in East Asia.[11] And unlike most US-Soviet conflicts in Europe, the Cold War lacks an easily discernible starting point in East Asia. Its origins, however, arguably began during the American Occupation of Japan in 1945–1952 when latent national rivalries amongst the Allies threatened to undermine their certain victory over Tokyo.[12]

SCAP policy and the 1947 Constitution

After Japan surrendered on August 15, 1945, the Allied forces landed at Tokyo Bay on August 30. General Douglas MacArthur accepted the official surrender signed by Japanese Foreign Minister Shigemitsu on board *USS Missouri* in Tokyo Bay on

September 2. When Truman approved the "US Initial Post-Surrender Policy for Japan" on September 6, the American Occupation of Japan (1945–1952) began. By the end of the year, there were about 350,000 US troops participating in the Occupation.

At that moment, the devastation of war was evident across the country: more than 45 percent of national assets had been lost by 1945; about 119 cities, including Hiroshima and Nagasaki, were in ruin; more than 2.4 million residential houses were destroyed; and millions of war prisoners and refugees returned from the former colonies in 1946. Japan's production in 1947 was below 30 percent of the pre-war level. Because of the lack of coal, most of the steel and iron mills remained closed, and more than an half of the locomotives were not in operation. While the people were starving, the country experienced drastic inflation because the first two post-war cabinets, Prince Higashikuni (1945) and Kijuro Shidehara (1945–1947), failed to deal with the financial difficulties. The retail prices in 1946 were 4.6 times higher than those in 1945, and then continued to increase to 13.8 times by 1947, and 36.5 times by 1948. Added to inflation, Japanese citizens faced the shortage of daily essentials, a high unemployment rate, and foreign occupation.

Many Japanese expected a cruel and harsh occupation, but found a democratic one. More and more Japanese became cooperative or "even enthusiastic" with the new authorities of the Occupation administration under MacArthur, Supreme Commander for the Allied Powers (SCAP).[13] Truman's policies toward Japan marginalized Japan within the context of East Asian international politics. Germany, in contrast, quickly became and remained crucially contested territory between the two great power blocs in Europe.[14] In Japan, Truman's foreign policy left a legacy of political stability and economic prosperity, conditions which helped make Japan a quiet corner of an otherwise noisy and threatening East Asia. Japan never featured prominently in the rivalry between the superpowers in East Asia.

The American Occupation succeeded because it built on earlier trends, yet also broke with the pre-war system in revolutionary ways. As Iriye points out in his study of Japanese-US wartime relations, even though Japan and the United States were involved in a struggle for power in the war, their views on a peaceful international structure in post-war East Asia were basically in agreement because their leaders had a shared past and believed in the same principles.[15]

According to the agreement, the Occupation of Japan after its surrender was international. It was to be administered by a four-power Allied Council for Japan in Tokyo under MacArthur. In fact, the Occupation was carried out almost entirely by MacArthur, his staff, and the American troops under his command. Meyer states that "the occupation was run by predominantly military personnel."[16] It was a natural result of defeating Japan. Thus, Truman's appointment of MacArthur as SCAP led to American unilateralism. The United States provided the leadership, the bulk of the troops, and funds for its occupation.

The Soviet Union declared war on Japan on August 8, a week before Japan's surrender. The next day, Soviet Red Army entered Manchuria. On August 12, the Soviet Army marched into North Korea. When Japan surrendered on August 15, the Red Army did not stop their advance until it occupied all the territory promised to the Soviet Union at the Yalta Conference. Historically, the Russian primary interest in East Asia had been its security concerns. Stalin was interested in installing a buffer zone along the Russian borders with Korea, Manchuria, China, and Mongolia. Having occupied all the regions, Stalin announced the end of hostilities on August 23. US Admiral William

Leahy, Roosevelt's military chief of staff, caustically observed at the end of the Yalta Conference that the language of the final agreement "was so elastic that the Russians can stretch it all the way from Yalta to Washington without technically breaking it."[17]

From 1945 to 1947, the US policy was aimed at eliminating militarism and imperialism, and empowering Japanese people. With the emphasis on the political reforms, the American Occupation began with the liquidation of the apparatus of Japanese militarism. The empire was dismembered and all Japanese abroad, both soldiers and civilians, were returned to Japan. The military services were demobilized; paramilitary organizations were dissolved. MacArthur issued orders to destroy the home islands' defenses immediately after his arrival.

The Truman administration also sent economic aid to Japan from the very beginning of the Occupation, setting the United States on course to providing half a billion dollars between 1945 and 1947. In retrospect, US foreign aid enabled Japan to engage with the United States in the Cold War against the Soviet Union and its allies and also helped bring about Japanese political and economic reforms that laid a foundation for an extended period of stability and prosperity. The Truman administration's foreign aid policies resulted in the demilitarization and democratization of Japan. Before the end of 1945, land reform began, and universal adult suffrage was enacted. In early 1946, elections were held. Then, labor protection laws were passed and freedom of workers' assemblies and strikes was also granted.[18]

Within two years, MacArthur had implemented all of the changes outlined at the Potsdam Conference. Among other tasks, armaments industries were dismantled, the Home Ministry was abolished, and the police were decentralized. Next, the Occupation removed the imperial leadership. In 1946, Hirohito was forced to publicly renounce his divinity.

The Military Tribunal for the Far East was held in Tokyo between 1946 and 1948. Twenty-five of the top leaders were brought to trial for having begun the war. Seven of them, including Tojo, were hanged in December 1948. Of approximately 6,000 people charged with war crime, 920 were executed. The SCAP also purged about 200,000 former politicians and military officers. War-time political prisoners were released from jail. Shinto was disestablished. The *zaibatsu* were targeted during the Occupation. The first wave of reforms dissolved eighty-three *zaibatsu* holding companies. In December 1947, the SCAP issued a new act to further deconcentrate about 1,200 companies. It also forced the Japanese government to shift macroeconomic policy to an export-driven economic recovery as the priority.

The most significant reform was the 1947 Constitution, drafted by SCAP staff, with which sovereignty was given to the people and a democratic system of government was adopted. Under the new Constitution, the emperor was the symbol of the state, but he had no powers related to government. He performed only those acts that were stipulated in the Constitution. His succession, according to the Imperial House Laws, came through the eldest male heir. Although there was debate over the Emperor Hirohito's responsibility for Japan's war in 1931–1945, the United States and SCAP decided to retain the emperor, a decision which was very popular in Japan. Meyer considers it a wise decision, "allowing MacArthur to effect SCAP measures through the emperor to ensure peaceful continuity in the country and loyalty of the people, which made reforms all the easier."[19]

The present system is built on the separation of powers of the three branches of government – legislative, executive, and judicial – which act to check and balance one another. According to the 1947 Constitution, all men and women over the age of twenty had political rights. In the first post-WWII election held in 1949, forty-two million Japanese voted, out of a total population of seventy-eight million. Along with the reforms, the Occupation helped the women's movement and labor unions. Workers were given the rights to organize, bargain, and strike.

One of the most well-known changes is specified in Article IX in the new constitution, in which "the Japanese people forever renounce war as a sovereign right of nation," and will never maintain "land, sea, and air forces" or "other war potential."[20] After the Korean War broke out in June 1950, the National Police Reserve was organized for national security. It was renamed the National Safety Force in 1952, and the Japan Self-Defense Forces (JSDF) in 1954.

In contrast to its experience in Germany, the Truman administration allowed a certain degree of self-governance for the Japanese during the early American Occupation. "The Japanese government, although it was subordinated to MacArthur, was left in a position to implement U.S. operations." Meyer believes that "This necessary approach also was based on the prohibitively high costs of direct U.S. government that would necessitate huge staffs."[21]

Policy change: Reform and rebuilding (1948–1950)

After 1947, the US government applied the Truman Doctrine, also known as the containment policy, against worldwide communist expansion, to Japan. Confronted by the increasing influence of the Soviet Union on the Asian mainland, Truman's strategic dilemma in the Asia-Pacific region was the limited resources for global containment. His primary concern was to determine what the United States could possibly do to prevent the Asian Communist movements, including the on-going wars in China and Vietnam, from further challenging US security interests in the long run. Regarding Europe, not Asia, as its strategic focus, the Truman administration did not want its effort, attention, and resources diverted in East Asian countries like China and Vietnam.

Given these assessments, Truman's advisors had reached a consensus that Communist-controlled China alone would not enhance the Soviet ability to undertake military aggression unless the Communists controlled Japan as well. Japan would be of vital strategic importance for US containment in the Asia-Pacific region. Therefore, the idea of a "defensive perimeter" in the Western Pacific became the predominantly accepted solution. Kennan argued in February 1948 that an American security system in the region should be based on "what parts of the Pacific and Far Eastern world are absolutely vital to our security." In his view, Japan and the Philippines would be "the cornerstones of such a Pacific security system." The objective of such a defense system, Kennan stressed, was "to prevent the assembly and launching of any amphibious forces from any mainland ports in the east-central or northeast Asia [with our] Okinawa-based air power plus our advanced naval power."[22]

Thereafter, US policy toward Japan shifted from focusing on political reform to re-building a new economy. The goal was to make Japan a Cold War leader against communist expansions in the Asia-Pacific region. Kennan and his newly created Policy Planning Staff modified the US policy and made it clear in the NSC Document No. 13/2 of 1948 that "Japan was to be strengthened economically and socially ... SCAP was to shift responsibilities to the Japanese."[23] Howard B. Schonberger describes it as the "reverse course" for the entire post-war US-Japan relationship. He points out Japan's geopolitical importance in the Cold War:

> The economic recovery of Japan, however, was a central feature of Kennan's global geopolitical containment strategy which ultimately contemplated the creation of such tension within the Soviet empire as to lead to a 'mellowing' of Soviet power or its complete collapse.[24]

 The strategic status of Japan in East Asia was promoted as a stronghold of the Free World in the Cold War. The Truman administration and his successors tried almost everything to assure Japan's safety and loyalty to the "Western Camp" under America's leadership. Hane and Perez point out that "U.S. policy toward Japan shifted from focusing on demilitarization to rebuilding it as a link in the anti-Communist chain along the Eastern Pacific rim."[25]

In 1947–1948, SCAP worked with the cabinet to embody many constitutional provisions into laws to endorse democracy and civil liberties. Among the important laws included were: gender equality in the working-place; human rights in general, especially the "right to life, liberty, and the pursuit of happiness"; the guarantee of freedom of assembly; the guarantee of workers' rights to organize and bargain collectively, and of minimum labor standards; the establishment of an independent judicial system; and the establishment of free and equal public education. Key was the political right to vote given to all adults over twenty. For the first time in the country's history, women gained universal suffrage. Andrew Gordon points out that:

> In response to these reforms, a virtual fever of 'democratization' swept Japan in the late 1940s and 1950s. Democracy and equality were understood in extremely expansive terms by their advocates; the terms meant far more than voting and land reform. They implied to many – and this was both promise and threat – a remaking of the human soul.[26]

In December 1948, the State Department and US Army HQs issued a joint statement of the "Nine Principles for Economic Stabilization" to end the financial disorder and retail inflations. In February 1949, Joseph Dodge, board chairman of the Detroit Bank, visited Japan as the presidential envoy and financial advisor of SCAP. During his visit, Dodge proposed what became known as the "Dodge Financial Reform," instructing the Japanese government to reinforce tax collection, reduce governmental subsidies, and freeze salaries. Although the "Dodge Line" was very controversial, James L. McClain credits it with "extinguishing the flames of Japan's post-war inflation, sweeping away economic deadwood, and clearing the fields for subsequent growth."[27]

After October 1949, when the Chinese Communist Party (CCP) won the Chinese Civil War and established the People's Republic of China (PRC) on mainland China, the US government increased its support to Japan and other allies in Asia hoping to prevent further communist expansion in East Asia. It also began to build up its military bases in Okinawa as its East Asian bastion after the founding of the PRC. In June 1950, North Korea invaded South Korea. The Truman administration shifted its Cold War efforts from Europe to East Asia. From 1949 to 1951, the US government provided Japan with a total of $2.3 billion in financial loans and economic aid.

After the Korean War broke out in 1950, SCAP created the National Police Reserve (NPR) with 75,000 men to prepare for any possible foreign (or communist) landing on Japan. Two years later, the National Safety Agency (NSA) was established as the national commanding headquarters to supervise the NPR force. In 1954, the NSA was renamed the Japanese Self-Defense Agency, and the NPR became the Japan Self-Defense Force (JSDF, *Jieitai*). At the beginning of the twenty-first century, the JSDF had nearly 250,000 troops. Its army, the Japan Ground Force, included five infantry armies, totaling 150,000 troops. Its navy, the Japan Maritime Self-Defense Force, commanded five maritime districts with 44,000 sailors and soldiers. And its air force, the JSDF Air Force, had three air defense forces, totaling 45,000 men. The service branch chiefs worked at the Joint Staff Office under the minister of defense, who as a civilian cabinet member controlled the Japanese military.

Yoshida cabinets and economic recovery (1948–1951)

The 1947 Constitution placed the executive branch of the government in the center of power with the prime minister and his cabinet. One of the significant segments of the first post-war decade was the era of Prime Minister Yoshida Shigeru (from 1946–1947 and 1948–1954) as the implementer of Occupation reforms. Meyer emphasizes that "in contrast to their record in Germany, the US administrators in Japan utilized the Japanese as much as possible inasmuch as there was a dearth of Japanese-speaking Americans."[28] During his two terms, Yoshida cooperated with SCAP and convinced MacArthur and his staff that Japan had a new, potent political leader capable of abiding by Occupation reforms and a peace treaty. Soon Yoshida became a Japanese hero next to MacArthur when he served as the foreign minister after WWII and prime minister in 1947 and 1948–1954.

The first post-war decade emerged as Japan's period of economic recovery. First of all, after SCAP dissolved hundreds of *zaibatsu* headquarters and their holding companies, Prime Minister Yoshida employed the existing pyramidal structure of the centralized administration with SCAP support. The political centralization and economic nationalization had been established by the Konoe Fumimaro cabinet in 1937–1940 for national mobilization with the support of militarists for war. Although the imperial system under the new constitution was sharply reduced, the Yoshida cabinet was able to utilize a centralized government for national economic recovery during 1947–1954. For example, the government used the Economic Stabilization Board (ESB), established in August 1946, and the Reconstruction Finance Bank (RFB) to plan the nation's economic recovery, decide on production and purchases, allocate financial resources for certain industries, control imports and exports, and regulate minimum wages. MacArthur and his SCAP supported the Yoshida administration in organizing the nation's recovery, involving the government in business, and micro-managing the nation's economy.

The Board and Trust had adopted "focused production methods," by which the government concentrated its limited resources to ensure the recovery of certain key industries first. For instance, the shortage of fuel, especially coal, was the biggest problem for Japan's economic recovery in 1946–1948. The board focused its efforts on promoting coal production and transportation, while the trust provided industrial loans of 47.5 billion yen for the coal companies as financial support in 1947–1948, about 36 percent of the total national loans. In 1947, the annual coal production reached 29.3 million tons, about a 30 percent increase from that in 1946. By 1948, the coal production had reached 90 percent of the pre-war level, while steel and iron industry about 49.2 percent. At that moment, Japan's economy began its recovery.[29]

By 1949, with US financial and economic aid, the Japanese government had a surplus in its annual budget for the first time after the war, and the drastic inflation was finally under control. In 1950, Japan issued its new Foreign Investment Laws to attract capital from Western countries like the United States. A year later, Japan joined the World Bank and International Monetary Fund, fully participating in the global financial community.

Then, Yoshida successfully prevented Japan from being drawn into the Cold War through the 1950s, especially during the Korean War (1950–1953). Yoshida, the first post-war prime minister, developed an overall foreign policy for a new Japan, sometimes called the "Yoshida Doctrine," giving primacy to economic growth and not getting entangled in the Cold War.[30] He believed that being drawn into the American-Soviet Cold War and consequently wasting resources on military spending was a great danger to post-war Japan. If that danger could be avoided, Japan might survive.

To expel North Korea's invasion of South Korea, the United Nations (UN) Security Council organized the UN Forces (UNF) and appointed MacArthur as the commander in chief of UNF in the summer of 1950. The danger Japan faced at that moment was a possible involvement in the Korean War which would lead to a huge amount of military spending. Yoshida refused the demand made by John Foster Dulles in June 1950, later the Secretary of State, to rearm Japan to participate in the Korean War. Yoshida refused the US government's request by citing Article IX of the constitution.[31]

With the radical transformation of American fortunes in the Korean War, MacArthur soon turned Japan into an economic base for the UNF intervention in Korea. Yoshida emphasized economic recovery in a political context, which provided Japan a well-balanced position during the Korean War. But, meanwhile, Yoshida had maintained a close relationship with the United States to receive American military orders of $4 billion during the war, more than half of the nation's total exports. Yoshida called the war "a gift from the gods."[32] The revenues from manufacturing war supplies increased from $149 million in 1950 to $809 million in 1953. War supply industries also promoted other major industries such as steel, machinery, ship building, textiles, and construction. The war also stimulated the service industry such as vehicle repairs, ship rebuilding, food processing, and medical assistance. By 1951, the nation's industrial production had reached pre-war levels.

When Truman dismissed MacArthur as SCAP in April 1951, General Matthew Ridgway (1895–1993) had a smooth transition to take over the position in Tokyo since the SCAP had carried out the reforms through the Yoshida cabinet. The first decade after the Pacific War set the pattern for Japan's post-war future. The American Occupation from 1945 to 1952 successfully broke with Japan's pre-war system and made revolutionary changes in terms of government, economy, society, and military. Occupied Japan, unlike Korea and China, never became a worrisome partisan issue in Washington.

Without being militarily involved in the Korean War – which lasted until 1953 – on September 8, 1951, Japan signed a peace treaty with the United States and forty-seven other nations in San Francisco. In retrospect, Tokyo's way of handling the improved international relations helped to continuously marginalize the "Japan question" in East Asian international politics. Compared with the "German question," which had occupied a central position in defining the agenda of big power politics in Europe throughout most of the twentieth century, including a large part of the Cold War period, the

"Japan question" did not have such a long history and overwhelming influence. However, clearly the origins of, as well as the actual historical path leading to, the Second World War in Asia (or Pacific War), were closely related to the complex "Japan question." Thus the great powers paid adequate attention to this particular question during the early post-war period. Yet, throughout the Cold War period, settling the "Japan question" never occupied a central position in the making of Washington's and Moscow's grand strategy toward East Asia.[33] Indeed, even the "question itself had not been clearly defined. After the Vietnam War, "détente" and Sino-US rapprochement further pushed the "Japan question" to the periphery of the agenda of big-power politics in East Asia. All of these factors contributed to the re-emergence of the question as a sensitive political issue in the post-Cold War era in the 2000s.

Aftermath: Political and social changes

According to the Peace Treaty, on April 28, 1952, Japan regained its independence, and the Occupation ended. On the same day, the US government also provided what Japan wanted most: a long-term guarantee of its security, later referred to as the "nuclear umbrella." The US protection of Japan thereafter held the cost of Japanese defense at minimum, about one percent of GDP through the 1990s. Some critics later accused Japan of enjoying a "free ride" through the Cold War. Last but not least, Japan enjoyed minimum spending on defense throughout the Cold War because of the American "nuclear umbrella" and mutual defense treaty. The low annual military budget was another contributor to Japan's economic advance, even though the country had established a small armed force, the Self-Defense Forces, in 1954. The cost of this force was very low, about one percent of Japan's GDP in through the 1960s.[34]

The Japanese government and conservative parties liked the new security agreement as an improvement over the Peace Treaty since it was a pact concluded between equals. The liberals and radical parties, such as the Socialists, labor leaders, and intellectuals, criticized the mutual defense treaty since its contending provisions that had clearly linked Japan to the United States in the Cold War, and that could draw Japan into a military alliance against the communist nations, particularly North Korea and China. These groups began to organize political rallies and political campaigns to protest the treaty and the administration in the 1950s. They also raised their voice against US military presence in Japan and Okinawa as well as US nuclear testing.[35]

In 1955, several conservative political parties formed the Liberal Democratic Party (LDP, *Jiyu Minshuto*) to control national politics as the majority party with Yoshida as its first chairman against the left-wing groups. The LDP was the party in power in the 1970s–1990s. It emphasized free enterprise, the expansion of foreign trade, government aid to small business, and close relations with the United States and Europe. Nevertheless, McClain points out that:

> Organizationally the LDP functioned as a party of factions. Throughout its political heyday a half of dozen or so major alliances jockeyed with one another for influence. Each faction constituted a separate entity that raised its own campaign funds, promoted the careers of its members, negotiated with other factions for control of high party and cabinet posts, and rotated the office of prime minister among themselves.[36]

Thereafter, the LDP dominated the Diet until 1993. As a conservative party, LDP usually gained two-thirds of the popular votes in the elections from the 1950s to 1980s. In contrast, the Japan Socialist Party emphasized the nationalization of major industries and expanded social welfare. The party also favored a policy of neutrality in foreign affairs. Other parties were founded in the 1960s–1970s by groups that broke away from those two, following middle-of-the-road policies.

Politically, the country continued to witness one-party domination by the LDP. According to the representation in the Diet, the majority political parties in the 1990s were the LDP, the Japan Socialist Party (JSP), the Clean Government Party (*Komeito*), the Democratic Socialist Party (DSP), and the Communist Party of Japan. According to the 1947 Constitution, the Diet is the supreme organ of the government power and sole law-making body of the country. As a bicameral body, it consists of the House of Representatives (lower house) with 480 members, and the House of Councilors (upper house) with 242 members. Elected by universal suffrage, the representatives serve for four-year terms, while the upper house members for six-year terms. Elections for one-half of the membership are held every three years in Japan. The lower house is the more powerful of the two since it retains control over legislation, dealing with treaties, and control over the national budget. It can also veto the decisions made by the upper house. In the 1950s, one-party control, historically referred to as the "1955 System," provided a new political stability in Japan. Hane and Perez conclude that "The LDP's dominance of the political world did not translate into a monopoly of power. Intraparty factionalism kept the LDP from becoming a steamrolling power machine. The presence of major factions made compromises and mutual accommodations necessary."[37]

In the first half of the 1950s, continuing economic growth transformed Japan into an independent economy. Nevertheless, the government continued its successful post-war policy of central control by introducing a state monopoly of key industries like steel, iron, coal, electricity, and ship building. Following the Yoshida Doctrine, the Japanese government ensured its pro-business policies by being more deeply involved in economic planning, financial support, and trade promotion than any other non-socialist state. The government made central plans for these industries, provided low interest loans to them, reduced tax rates, controlled imports and exports, improved their infrastructure, and updated equipment. Since the state monopoly protected them by reducing the competition and guaranteeing their profits, these industries were able to attract more than 40 percent of private investment and continued to enjoy a rapid growth after the Korean War in the 1950s. In the meantime, the government established the Bank of Japan which backed commercial banks in providing capital investment. The Japanese Diet passed resolutions to protect growing industries at home and limit foreign competitions in these fields. The government only welcomed foreign investment that brought in new technologies, like those made by the United States. It was cheaper and faster to license new technology than to develop it at home.

During the early 1950s, the industrial priority was the development of heavy industry, especially iron and steel and including products like ship-building and heavy machinery. By 1954, Japan's manufacturing had returned to pre-war levels, while agriculture had surpassed pre-war levels. By 1955, Japan had recovered from the devastation of war, and provided enough rice for the entire population. In 1955, Japan's annual GNP totaled $24 billion, and its per capita GNP was $268, above the pre-war level. By 1955, Japan's manufacturing capacity had reached pre-war levels. By 1956, the Japanese economy was ahead of other Asian countries. Its economic growth continued through the following decade with an average annual economic growth rate of 9 percent, compared with the United States' 4 percent, Great Britain's 2.5 percent, France's 4.2 percent, and West Germany's 5.7 percent during the same period of time. In the late 1960s, Japan had obtained an economic level comparable to that of Europe.[38]

Moreover, Washington was willing to share American science and technology with Japan. President Dwight Eisenhower (1890–1969; in office from 1953–1961) and his administration believed that a strong Japan was important and necessary for the United States to curb the communist expansion and influence in the Asian-Pacific region after the Korean War. The United States did not only make the new technologies available for Japanese industry, but also made its domestic market available for Japanese manufactured items such as toys, shoes, clothing, and apparel in the 1960s. The availability of the American market was vital to Japanese products, not only because of mass consumption in America, but also because it introduced the American public to the high quality and low cost of Japanese manufactured items. Soon Japan became the manufacturing factory of Asia. Exports increased to $2 billion in 1955.[39]

In the meantime, education had transformed the post-war society by narrowing the gap between the masses and social elite. By the 1960s, the social and educational gap between the elite and masses had disappeared. Moreover, almost 90 percent of the Japanese people – high school and university graduate – defined themselves as middle class. As a result, Japan became urbanized after the war, when more than 50 percent of Japanese lived in the cities. The rapid expansion of manufacturing opened up a large labor market in the 1950s. In less than one decade, millions of Japanese people had moved from rural areas into the cities seeking work. As the result of urbanization, the physical setting in rural Japan had begun to change by the late 1950s. Factories were built in rural areas to take advantage of lower costs. With its economic recovery and growth, the country had generated a substantial portion of capital for the urbanization. In 1956, the Japanese government published its Economic White Book to review the economic recovery in the preceding ten years and announced that "By now, Japan is no longer in the post-war era. The recovery is over, and we are facing a new era, which is different from the past decade."[40]

Notes

1 Liu, *A Partnership for Disorder*, 301.
2 Ilya V. Gaiduk, "The Second Front of the Soviet Cold War: Asia in the System of Moscow's Foreign Policy Priorities, 1945–1956," in *The Cold War in East Asia, 1945–1991*, ed. Tsuyoshi Hasegawa (Stanford, CA: Stanford University Press, 2011), 65, 68.
3 Robert G. Sutter, *U.S.-Chinese Relations: Perilous Past, Pragmatic Present* (New York: Rowman & Littlefield Publishers, 2010), 48–49.
4 Stalin's speech to announce the start of a new Five-Year Plan is quoted in Richard Sakwa, *The Rise and Fall of the Soviet Union, 1917–1991* (London: Routledge, 1999), 289–293.
5 *Time Magazine*, February 18, 1946, 29–30.
6 George F. Kennan to Secretary of State James F. Byrnes, "Long Telegram," February 22, 1946, in the US Department of State, *Foreign Relations of the United States, Eastern Europe, the Soviet Union* (Washington, DC: Government Printing Office, 1985), 5: 707–708. Hereafter cited as *FRUS*.
7 Jeremy Black, *The Cold War: A Military History* (London, UK: Bloomsbury Academic, 2015), 42.
8 Felix Belair, Jr., "New Policy Set Up: President Blunt in Plea to Combat 'Coercion as World Peril," *New York Times*, March 13, 1947, 1.
9 In this regard, Gaddis concurred with some revisionist assessments concerning some of the misconceptions embraced by the Truman administration. Furthermore, the authors agreed

that both the US and Soviet Union shared responsibility for starting the Cold War. Gaddis, *The United States and the Origins of the Cold War, 1941–1947* (New York: Columbia University Press, 1972), 356, 360; Gaddis, "Was the Truman Doctrine a Real Turning Point?" *Foreign Affairs* 52, no. 2 (January 1974): 387.

10 Bruce R. Kuniholm, *The Origins of the Cold War in the Near East: Great Power Conflict and Diplomacy in Iran, Turkey, and Greece* (Princeton, NJ: Princeton University Press, 1980), xv, 415, 418.

11 James I. Matray, "Opening Remarks" at the International Symposium, "The Legacy of Harry S. Truman in East Asia: Japan, China, and the Two Koreas," Key West, FL, May 14–15, 2010.

12 Stephen E. Ambrose and Douglas G. Brinkley, *Rise to Globalism: American Foreign Policy since 1938* (New York: Penguin, 1997), 52–53.

13 Fairbank, Reischauer, and Craig, *East Asia: Transition and Transformation*, 817.

14 Chen and Li, "China and the End of the Global Cold War," 123.

15 Akira Iriye, *Power and Culture: The Japanese-American War, 1941–1945* (Cambridge, MA: Harvard University Press, 1981), vii, 265.

16 Meyer, *Japan*, 222.

17 Admiral William Leahy's words are quoted in LaFeber, *America, Russia, and the Cold War*, 16.

18 For more details of the American Occupation and reforms in 1945–1947, see: W. G. Beasley, *The Rise of Modern Japan: Political, Economic and Social Change since 1850*, revised ed. (New York: St. Martin's Press, 2000), 213–226; John W. Dower, *Embracing Defeat: Japan in the Wake of World War II* (New York: Norton, 1999).

19 Meyer, *Japan*, 237.

20 Article 9 in the Constitution is quoted from Dale M. Hellegers, *We, the Japanese People: World War II and the Origins of the Japanese Constitution* (Stanford, CA: Stanford University Press, 2002), 2: 576.

21 Meyer, *Japan*, 222.

22 George F. Kennan, "Memorandum to the Secretary of State, February 24, 1948," *FRUS, 1948*, 1: 525.

23 For the complete text of NSC Document 13/2, see *FRUS, 1948*, 6: 857–862.

24 Howard B. Schonberger, *Aftermath of War: Americans and the Remaking of Japan, 1945–1952* (Kent, OH: Kent State University Press, 1989), 169, 282.

25 Hane and Perez, *Modern Japan*, 396.

26 Andrew Gordon, "Society and Politics from Transwar through Postwar Japan," in *Historical Perspectives on Contemporary East Asia*, eds. Merle Goldman and Andrew Gordon (Cambridge, MA: Harvard University Press, 2000), 279.

27 McClain, *Japan*, 573.

28 Meyer, *Japan*, 222.

29 Schonberger, *Aftermath of War*, 231–234.

30 Glen D. Hook, Julie Gilson, Christopher W. Hughes, and Hugo Dobson, *Japan's International Relations: Politics, Economics, and Security*, 2nd ed. (London, UK: Routledge, 2005), 73–74.

31 For more details on Article IX, see Schonberger, *Aftermath of War*, 58.

32 Andressen, *A Short History of Japan*, 125.

33 Chen and Li, "China and the End of the Global Cold War," 123.

34 Hook, Gilson, Hughes, and Dobson, *Japan's International Relations*, 146–147.

35 James L. Huffman, *Modern Japan: A History in Documents* (New York: Oxford University Press, 2011), 163.

36 McClain, *Japan*, 565.

37 Hane and Perez, *Modern Japan*, 391.

38 Mikiso Hane, *Eastern Phoenix: Japan Since 1945* (Boulder, CO: Westview, 1996), 100.

39 Beasley, *The Rise of Modern Japan*, 245–246.

40 Sachiko Hirakawa, "Japan: Living in and with Asia," in *Regional Community Building in East Asia*, eds. Lee Lai To and Zarina Othman (London: Routledge, 2017), chapter 12.

4   The Nationalists vs. the Communists in China

Japan's surrender in August 1945 did not automatically bring peace and independence to East Asians, who soon found themselves returned to civil war or struggling for independence against colonialism. While America undertook some policy planning for a post-war East Asia after the Allies' victory over Japan, Washington was unable to specify and finalize the plans with the government of the Republic of China (ROC). Compared with US foreign policy planning, China had a focused and much narrower agenda, which proved pragmatic in their tenacious pursuit to gain national independence. China did not have the American sense of superiority, but rather a fear of the return to inferiority as a second-class nation like before the war. Both Nationalist and Communist Parties approached post-war issues from an exclusive, China-centered, absolute nationalist calculation for an "independent and strong China."[1] They did not expect US or Soviet hegemony, nor restoration of pre-war European colonial powers in China.

Although Washington and Chongqing, the wartime ROC capital under Jiang Jieshi of the Chinese Nationalist Party (Guomindang, GMD), cooperated diplomatically in 1945 on designing a new international order for post-war East Asia by decolonizing the Japanese empire, the policy never materialized because of the developing Chinese Civil War of 1946–1949 between the GMD and the CCP. Therefore, the United States failed to forge an effective, long-term partnership that might have prevented the Soviet Union from expanding to the Pacific region and thus avoided Cold War turmoil in East Asia for many decades to come. General Jiang Weiguo (Chiang Wei-kuo, 1916–1997), former secretary general of the ROC's Council of National Security and President Jiang Jieshi's son, said that Jiang was convinced that the Roosevelt administration did not have a strategic plan for post-war China, nor did it consider China as a new power that would replace Japan in the position of dominance in East Asia after the war.[2] Even though the United States and the ROC fought as allies during the war, the leaders of the two countries found it extremely difficult to establish a partnership for a post-war order due to conflicting backgrounds and beliefs and incompatible visions for the future of East Asia. Moreover, the Truman administration's aid to Jiang has largely been ignored, or treated only briefly by historians, because the GMD, as well as Truman, "lost China" to the CCP by the end of the Chinese Civil War. This joint effort is all too commonly dismissed as solely a sterile phase of the wartime alliance or as a precursor of the upcoming CCP takeover, both of which have been given more detailed attention.

In retrospect, President Truman's foreign aid programs to East Asia played a pivotal role in US policy toward the post-WWII world. Truman's aid to Japan, China, and Taiwan enabled those countries to engage in a global Cold War against Soviet and communist aggressions while providing a foundation and opportunity for their political and economic reforms and domestic development. In the early 1950s, Truman's policy led to the demilitarization and democratization of Japan, as well as the neutralization and stability of the Taiwan Straits. East Asia's early Cold War experiences contributed significantly to shaping the specific course of the Cold War but more importantly, helped create conditions for the Cold War to remain "cold" between the two superpowers: the United States and the Soviet Union.[3]

The Chinese Civil War (1946–1949)

During the period of the second CCP-GMD coalition, the Communist-controlled areas grew significantly. In 1944, the "liberated areas" (or *Jiefangqu*) under CCP control launched partial counter-offensives and won important victories against Japan. By the spring of 1945, the nation had nineteen "liberated areas" with a total population of ninety-five million. When Japan surrendered in August 1945, Jiang and the ROC faced a very serious challenge from Mao Zedong's army, totaling 1.27 million men, which was supported by militias numbering an additional 2.68 million men.[4]

Jiang found himself far away from the country's economic and population centers and facing an unprecedented challenge from Mao and the CCP. At that time, the GMD had a total of 4.3 million troops, including two million regulars.[5] They were better equipped than the CCP forces since they had received most of the weapons and equipment surrendered by Japanese troops in China and also continued to receive US military aid after the Pacific War. The GMD forces controlled three-quarters of the country with three-quarters of the population, more than three hundred million people. They occupied all of the large cities and controlled most of the railroads, highways, seaports, and transportation hubs.[6]

The US government wanted to maintain the wartime coalition between the ROC and Mao's Communists. In the fall of 1945, President Truman sent Patrick Hurley, the US ambassador to Yan'an in China, the CCP capital, to pick up Mao and escort him to Chongqing for negotiations with Jiang.[7] The Chongqing Talks lasted forty-three days. In October 1945, Jiang and Mao signed an agreement which provided for a joint coalition government under Jiang's leadership.[8] However, since both sides had different political agendas, the negotiations failed, and the two parties resumed their military conflicts in North China. As the "Double Tenth Agreement" went public, hundreds of thousands of the CCP troops moved from Central to Northeast China.

The GMD-CCP post-war struggle focused on the Northeast, the location of China's heavy industry, coal, oil, and chemical sources, established by the Japanese from 1931–1945. Japan's surrender, along with the Russian Red Army's withdrawal, created a power vacuum in that strategic region and invited GMD-CCP competition over its cities, industrial and commercial centers, and key points of transportation. In 1946, Jiang reinforced the Northeast with a large number of his best troops. For the first time in its history, the CCP Central Committee transferred 110,000 troops with 20,000 party cadres with the goal of transforming its military from a regional to national level. The Northeast thereafter became its strategic base, which secured communications and transportation between the Soviet Union and the CCP. Fighting between the ROC and the Communists erupted in Northeastern China in late 1945. Hurley, feeling Jiang had gone against his agreement with the Communists, resigned on November 26. Nevertheless, the United States continued its wartime economic and military aid to China, which in fact went exclusively to the Jiang government. When military conflict erupted in Northeastern China, contrary to the early assurances by Jiang of a political resolution, the Nationalist forces needed the US military aid more than ever.[10]

Following Hurley's resignation, Truman appointed General George Marshall, Secretary of State and former head of the JCS, as his envoy to China in December 1945. Marshall tried to use US aid, which the ROC desperately needed, as a negotiating tool to force Jiang to accept terms which would also be acceptable to Mao. Marshall believed that even the threat of a reduction of US aid to China would bring Jiang around. In fact, neither Jiang or Mao would compromise and they refused to cooperate with one another. The Chinese Civil War began on June 26, 1946 when Jiang launched an all-out offensive against CCP-held areas, culminating in a major attack in Central China and other attacks throughout the country.[11] Seeing the momentum of civil war growing, Marshall announced in January 1947 that his mission had failed.[12]

In the summer of 1946, the Chinese Communist and Nationalist armed forces began a full-scale war against each other for control of the country. Chinese military historians divide the Civil War into three phases. The first phase of the war began on June 26, when Jiang launched an all-out offensive campaign against Mao's "liberated regions" with a major attack in Central China and other offensive campaigns from south to north.[13] From September to November, the GMD troops moved northward along the four major railroad lines, and tried to advance into the CCP liberated regions. Jiang believed that if he could squeeze the CCP forces out of their bases within three to six months, he could win the war.

The Communist forces made full preparations for fighting a new war against the GMD. The CCP forces totaled 1.68 million troops by the beginning of the war, even though the Red Army was, in fact, an army equipped with "millet plus rifles." They controlled the countryside with a population of about a hundred million, while the GMD held the cities with larger population. Mao adopted a new strategy in late 1946, "giving them tit for tat and fighting for every inch of land,"[14] and "offense in the north; defense in the south."[15] The goal was to maintain and concentrate a superior force in order to destroy the GMD's effective strength.

In 1946, the CCP successfully reserved most of its troops and stayed in its "liberated areas" during Jiang's all-out offensive campaign. Soon after, the CCP offensive campaign began in the north and then swept into the south. The CCP managed to maintain their control of one-quarter of the country. Westad points out that the key to the CCP's success in mobilizing the Chinese masses was their ability to manipulate local politics. Moreover, the party cadres made their own decisions and practiced their skills without "undue interference."[16]

US aid to Jiang (1947–1948)

As the ROC offensive stalled and the CCP began counterattacking, Jiang asked Washington for more aid. In 1947, Truman began to implement his containment policy, the so-called "Truman Doctrine," to stop Russian-sponsored Communist expansion around the globe. Even though debate over various types of assistance to China appeared repeatedly in the official communications throughout the Chinese Civil War, the Truman administration continued to support Jiang's government. On October 27, 1947, the United States and the ROC signed an agreement stipulating that the United States would give $270 million in economic aid by congressional appropriation "for purposes of post-UN Relief and Rehabilitation Administration."[17] Secretary Marshall initiated the aid package in a November 1947 speech delivered to a joint session of the House and Senate Committees on Foreign Affairs and Relations, implementing Truman's containment policy against communist expansions in the global Cold War. Marshall announced the intention of the State Department to present to Congress an aid program for China: "The United States and all other world powers recognize the National government as the sole legal government of China ... we should extend to the Government and its people certain economic aid and assistance."[18]

American policymakers realized from the beginning that the CCP would not like the United States providing aid to Jiang's regime. Furthermore, Chinese Communist leaders believed that the United States had intervened in the Chinese Civil War by providing Jiang with military equipment and financial aid. In February 1948, a CCP spokesman criticized the aid proposal which Truman sent to Congress, which included the China Aid Act, as "US imperialism's plot to extend the Chinese civil war and a part of US imperialism's aggressive plan to enslave the people in both Asia and the world and to destroy world peace."[19] Although Chinese Communist leaders watched angrily as the Truman administration increased its aid to the ROC, they were able to use the American involvement in China to mobilize the Chinese masses and to undermine the ROC war effort. As shown by recently available Chinese documents –including documents from Chinese Party archives,[20] PRC archives,[21] and the papers of key leaders[22] – Mao used propaganda to change the perceived character of the Civil War from one between two Chinese sides to one between the Chinese Communists and "US imperialists and their puppets." He calculated a total of $5.9 billion (in 1945–1949) which had been given by the Truman administration "to help Chiang Kai-shek slaughter several million Chinese."[23]

The CCP's massive propaganda campaigns helped the Communists form a united front in opposition to "US imperialism" and the Jiang regime – the two firmly linked together by propaganda. Corruption within the ROC, spiraling inflation, and the factional struggles within the GMD also assisted in making Communist propaganda popular and successful. Exploiting widespread complaints about Jiang's government and also the strong desire for peace after WWII, the CCP organized a second front against Jiang in major cities through student-led anti-government, and anti-war movements to politically isolate the ROC. In 1947, for instance, students from more than sixty cities demonstrated for the patriotic and democratic movement, opposing hunger, civil war, and persecution. Regarding these demonstrations, John Carter Vincent reported to Washington that:

> the Chinese university students would inevitably be swayed in their attitudes and approaches by any widespread campaign, whether of Communist or other origin, directed against American military aid to China and would in turn become strongly anti-American. The anti-American feeling in China might possibly take an even more serious turn than at present.[24]

In twenty-nine cities, including Shanghai and Tianjin, 3.2 million workers staged strikes and demonstrations in early 1947. As Westad concludes, the CCP's skillful propaganda juxtaposed a "new China" against the deeply flawed old China headed by Jiang. Mao mobilized the Chinese masses, especially the peasants, by exploiting Jiang's weaknesses and mistakes, and by expanding his revolution across the country.[25]

The second phase of the Chinese Civil War started in March 1947 and ended by August 1948. Since his all-out offensive campaign was failing, Jiang changed his war strategy from broad assaults to attacks on key targets. Jiang concentrated his forces on two points: the CCP-controlled areas in Shandong and Shaanxi, where the CCP Central Committee and its high command had been since 1935. Jiang failed again.

When the GMD offensive slowed down, a CCP strategic offensive began. Between June and September 1947, the CCP launched some offensive operations and the main battlefields had by this time moved to the GMD-controlled areas. For example, Deng Xiaoping led 120,000 troops across the Yellow River, breaking through Jiang's line, which brought the GMD offensive to an end in Central China.[26] Some Western historians attribute Mao's victory over Jiang's offensives during the early years of the Civil War to the CCP popularity, political propaganda, and land reforms to gain peasants' support.[27] In October 1947, the PLA (People's Liberation Army) issued a manifesto calling upon the people to "overthrow Jiang Jieshi and liberate all China." It put forward this political program:

> United workers, peasants, soldiers, intellectuals and businessmen, all oppressed classes, all people's organizations, democratic parties, minority nationalities, overseas Chinese and other patriots; form a national united front; overthrow the dictatorial Jiang Jieshi government; and establish a democratic coalition government.[28]

In December, through its economic policy, the CCP again promised the peasants that the party would confiscate land from the landlords and redistribute it among the peasants. Not surprisingly, the new policy received wide support from the peasants.

The military failure forced Jiang to ask for more US aid. On November 11, 1947, the Secretary of State requested a congressional appropriation of $300 million for the ROC government in 1948. John Leighton Stuart (1876–1962), US ambassador to China, supported Marshall's plan in a cable on November 24 stating that "American aid could be based on the desire to help the populace in Government territory to have the twin benefits of the freedom essential to democracy and economic welfare which is the only protection against Communist penetration."[29] The Jiang government, however, was ready to demand more aid from the United States in December, requiring "$500 million for the first year, the same amount for the second year, $300 million for the third year, and $200 million for the fourth year, totaling 1.5 billion US dollars."[30] Chen states that:

> The escalation of the CCP-GMD confrontation presented a deepening dilemma to the Americans ... Both for checking the expansion of Soviet influences in East Asia and for maintaining stable order in China, it was necessary for the United States to provide aid to the GMD government (although many Americans disliked Jiang and his regime) and to help promote China's political democratization.[31]

The Truman administration submitted its finalized aid package for China to Congress on February 18, 1948. It totaled $570 million for economic aid through June 1949. After extensive discussion in committee, Congress passed the aid program legislation, called the China Aid Act of 1948 – Title IV of the Foreign Assistance Act of 1948, which funded the Marshall Plan – on April 2. It provided for $338 million of economic and construction assistance, and a $125 million grant "for aid of military character."[32] As a result, the 1948 China Aid Act was extended to February 25, 1950, and the United States continued to be bound to the GMD by a program of economic assistance as well as shipments of arms.

Mao's fight for victory (1948–1949)

The third phase of the war lasted from August 1948 to October 1949. In the fall of 1948, the CCP armed forces reorganized as the People's Liberation Army (PLA) and began launching offensives from rural areas against GMD defenses in urban areas. This phase included three of the most important PLA campaigns in the war: the Liao-Shen Campaign (in Northeastern China), Ping-Jin Campaign (in the Beijing-Tianjin region), and Huai-Hai Campaign (in Eastern China).

The Liao-Shen (Liaoning province and Shenyang) Campaign was the first of three large campaigns which, according to Christopher Lew, "effectively destroyed the Nationalist army in mainland China during the Chinese civil war."[33] The PLA under Lin Biao initiated the offensive campaign on September 12, 1948. The main effort was against Jinzhou, which was defended by eight Nationalist divisions. Jiang ordered the siege lifted by dispatching a force from Shenyang. GMD field generals balked at this, having anticipated a Communist ambush. However, Jiang persisted and the GMD troops departed Shenyang on October 1. The PLA launched an all-out assault on Jinzhou on October 14. After nearly twenty-four hours of fighting, they captured the city and inflicted 90,000 casualties – most of them prisoners of war who would soon be integrated into the Communist ranks – while they suffered 24,000 of their own.

At this point, the GMD defenses began to unravel with alarming speed. On October 19, the Changchun garrison surrendered. Despite this, Jiang insisted that the GMD armies continue on their course and recapture Jinzhou. He believed they could still destroy the PLA in the field while the Communists were disorganized and weakened after the fight for Jinzhou. With PLA units piling on, the weight of numbers proved decisive and the Communists prevailed on October 28. Flush with victory, the PLA swept over Shenyang, capturing what remained of its garrison on November 1. The Communists continued their pursuit to Yingkou, capturing the town just as the last Nationalist troop ship departed. By all accounts, the Liao-Shen Campaign was a crushing strategic and tactical defeat for the GMD. Official PLA records cite 472,000 GMD casualties, which included 109,000 defections and 306,200 prisoners of war.

The Huai-Hai Campaign was the largest military operation in the Chinese Civil War. It took place between the Huai River in the west and Huang Hai (Yellow Sea) in the east, spanning from November 1948 to January 1949. Jiang decided to hold the key city of Xuzhou, near the Grand Canal and a key railway junction. He mobilized 920,000 GMD troops from seven armies and three military zones. The troops of the PLA, totaling 600,000 men with 600,000 militia fighters and over one million peasant laborers, were under the command of Deng Xiaoping, Liu Bocheng (Liu Po-ch'eng, 1892–1986), Chen Yi (Ch'en Yi, 1901–1972), and Su Yu (1907–1984). On November 6, 1948, 300,000 Communist troops of the East China Field Army attacked the GMD Seventh Army near Haizhou District, Lianyungang, and the long-awaited Huai-Hai Campaign began. Lew points out that "the GMD battle plan did not work."[34] On November 23, the Seventh Army was eliminated at Nianzhuang. On November 30, Jiang ordered the Nationalist armies to retreat to the south.

An all-out attack was launched by the Communist armies on January 6, 1949. The GMD defense collapsed. General Du Yuming was captured, and General Qiu Qingquan was killed in action while trying to break out of the Communist siege with his Second Army. Only General Li Mi was able to escape through the line. The Huai-Hai Campaign was a catastrophe for Jiang and the ROC government. By the spring of 1949, nearly all of Jiang's best troops were wiped out by the PLA. As the result of the campaign, the country north of the Yangzi (Yangtze) River was taken over by the CCP. Thereafter, the PLA troops were poised to threaten Nanjing, the capital of the ROC. After the failure of the campaign, ROC Vice President Li Zongren forced Jiang to resign from his presidency on January 31, 1949.

The Beijing-Tianjin Campaign (Ping-Jin Campaign) was the last of the three large campaigns which effectively destroyed the GMD Army in mainland China during the Chinese Civil War. The battle took place primarily in Hebei (Hopeh) and the municipalities of Beijing (Peking, or Beiping) and Tianjin (Tientsin) from late October 1948 to January 31, 1949. Shortly after Lin Biao's army destroyed the Nationalist army in Manchuria (Liao-Shen Campaign), the Communists turned their attention towards Fu Zuoyi's (Fu Tso-yi, 1895–1974) General Headquarters for Bandit Suppression in North China. This army consisted of almost half a million men. Fu's army manned a four-hundred-mile defense line that started at the port in Tanggu, ran through Tianjin and Beijing, and ended at Zhangjiakou. Nonetheless, by November 23, Lin's army seized Shanhaiguan and severed the Beijing-Tianjin railroad. As Lin's army continued its infiltration, Nie Rongzhen (Nieh Jung-chen, 1899–1992) deployed the Second Army, commanded by Yang Dezhi, and Yang Chengwu's (Yang Ch'eng-wu, 1914–2004) Third Army to attack Zhangjiakou. Fu dispatched his best force, the Thirty-Fifth Corps, to relieve the city but this element was trapped by the Third Army at Xinbao'an. Fu's rescue attempts failed at the cost of 13,000 men.

Despite the danger, Fu insisted on staying put, believing Lin's main force was still a month away. In this, he severely miscalculated, as the majority of Lin's army had already assumed their assigned positions by December 12. Having surrounded and isolated the major strong points of the GMD defenses, the Communists began a series of secret talks to convince Fu to surrender. These were facilitated by Fu's own daughter, Fu Dong, who was a member of the Communist underground. When these negotiations reached an impasse on December 19, Lin unleashed the Second and Third Armies, which proceeded to destroy the Thirty-Fifth Corps and capture Zhangjiakou. This action severed Fu's escape route west and cost him another 60,000 men. After Fu left the bargaining table for a second time, the Ping-Jin Committee decided to attack Tianjin and cut the Nationalists off from the sea. The Communists captured the city on January 15, inflicting 130,000 casualties in a day long battle. On January 22, Fu left Beijing and his army, still a quarter of a million men strong, were integrated into the Communist ranks. This act brought the campaign to a close.

The three campaigns lasted altogether 142 days, during which 1,54 million GMD troops were killed, wounded, captured, or had revolted against Jiang's regime.[35] In terms of scale, or the number of enemies destroyed, the three campaigns were unprecedented in Chinese military history. As a result of these offensive campaigns, all of the areas north of the Yangzi River were liberated. Nearly all of Jiang's best troops were wiped out. In early 1949, the PLA had fifty-eight infantry armies, numbering four million men.[36]

The Chinese Civil War situation turned against the GMD government and forced the Truman administration to re-evaluate its policy toward China. In September 1948, George Kennan, then the director of the Office of Policy Planning of the State Department, submitted a report, the "PPS/39 Document," suggesting a wait-and-see policy or a gradual disengagement from the Chinese Civil War after it ended. Under domestic and international pressure, on January 1, 1949, Jiang asked for cease-fire talks. In connection with this declaration, Mao, on January 14, refused Jiang's request and made public his viewpoint on the current situation.[37] Jiang retired from his presidency on January 21, and vice president Li Zongren came to the forefront. The peace talks between the GMD and CCP began on April 1 and ended on April 20 when both sides failed to reach an agreement.[38]

On February 4, 1949, Kennan's policy suggestion was accepted by the State Department and later by the NSC, and became known as NSC No. 34 and 34/1 documents.[39] But the Truman administration faced strong criticism, both from a Republican Congress and the "China Lobby." The State Department was persuaded to continue its limited assistance to the GMD government to satisfy demands by some Republican senators for increased assistance. On March 25, an executive proposal was sent to the House to allow the Chinese Nationalists to spend the remaining appropriations after the original expiration date of April 2. Truman would be authorized to use these remaining funds, of approximately $54 million, for economic assistance to the GMD government. On April 12, the House passed the amendment of the 1948 China Aid Act and then referred it to the Senate. During debate, the Senate did not have strong opposition.[40]

The PLA then ordered one million troops to cross the Yangzi on April 21. Two days later, Nanjing, the capital of the ROC, fell. Jiang evacuated the seat of his government with one million troops and government officials and fled to Taiwan. The PLA pressed on in its drive into the Northwest, Southwest, and Central China. By September, the PLA occupied most of the country except for Tibet, Taiwan, and various offshore islands. The GMD lost seven million troops and its control of mainland China to the Communists in the Civil War. The PLA suffered a total of 260,000 killed, and further 1.04 million wounded.[41]

Who lost China?

By the fall of 1949, Mao's forces had occupied most of China. The ROC had lost several million troops and was restricted to a few small areas on the mainland. On August 5, 1949, the State Department issued its "White Paper on China," officially known as *United States Relations with China*, a move to defend US–China policy. Dean Acheson, then Secretary of State, explained US–China policy from 1946–1949, arguing that the situation of China's Civil War was out of America's control. The 1,054-page document calculated a total of $3 billion as US aid provided by the Truman administration for the Jiang government during the Chinese Civil War. Acheson emphasized that the major reason for the GMD military failure was its armed forces, which "did not have to be defeated; they disintegrated."[42] After its publication, the *China White Paper* was sharply criticized by all sides, especially the Chinese Communist leaders, who seemingly had found evidence to back up their accusation that the United States had supported Jiang's war efforts and had sent money and weapons for Jiang to kill millions of Chinese people. They believed that the *China White Paper* went into particular detail of how, in the five years from the last part of the War of Resistance against Japan until 1949, the United States pursued a policy of support for Jiang and of anti-communism, opposed the Chinese people by every possible means, and finally met with defeat. "Thus, in its objective effect, the *China White Paper* became a confession by U.S. imperialism of its crimes of aggression against China."[43]

On August 12, Xinhua News Agency, mouthpiece of the CCP, published an editorial, "A Reluctant Self-confession," to attack the US Department's *China White Paper*. Then, Mao himself wrote another five editorials and articles from August 14 to September 16 to criticize the *China White Paper*. Mao states: "The White Paper is a counter-revolutionary document which openly demonstrates U.S. imperialist intervention in China."[44] Mao used it as "teaching material by negative example," saying that Chinese people should "thank" Acheson, because, first of all, "he has explicitly confessed to the fact that the United States supplied the money and guns and Chiang Kai-shek the men to fight for the United States and slaughter the Chinese people;" secondly, "Acheson himself confessed that the great, sanguinary war of the last few years, which cost the lives of millions of Chinese, was planned and organized by U.S. imperialism."[45]

On October 1, 1949, Mao declared the birth of the People's Republic of China (PRC). After Chinese Nationalist forces were ousted from mainland China, on December 8, 1949, Jiang moved the seat of his government to Taiwan. News of the Communist victory in China swept over the United States like wildfire. The politicians, the media, and members of the public criticized the Truman administration for having not given enough support to Jiang's government and for thus having "lost China."

Some historians in the West argue that the CCP's victory over the GMD was politically predestined, given the conflicts between two parties, the failure of American involvements, the critiques from intellectuals of GMD leaderships, student movements against the GMD, and the popularity of CCP land reforms. Some, however, have questioned whether the Chinese Civil War is best examined through the use of these categories of analysis. Joseph Esherick, for example, observes that early works on the Civil War and land reforms featured overly simplistic and idealized descriptions of CCP actions. Esherick advises not to think the Chinese revolution explainable by "anti-pole" structures such as "China and the West, state and society, urban-rural or class contradictions."[46] Suzanne Pepper stresses that, although the CCP land reform succeeded in gaining support to match the GMD, people's attitudes toward the two were not totally either advantageous or disadvantageous for either party during the war. Nevertheless, the CCP was one of the minority parties and was not accused of being responsible for the war, which the GMD, already powerful, could not escape.[47] It is conceivable that the draconian rule of the Japanese caused the Chinese people to turn against the Chinese state. In fact, it appears more likely that it was the failure of state-building during the GMD's control in the mainland that cost the Chinese state its "legitimacy" – if indeed the "loss of legitimacy" is the best way to interpret the GMD defeat. The GMD had a chance to promote major changes short of revolution. The failure to do so accounts for the rise of communism in mainland China. Edward Dreyer explains the outcome of the Civil War in conventional military-historical terms: "The Nationalists sent their best formations into a series of traps in Manchuria and North China, lost them, and afterwards never had a chance. Mao's revolution was a consequence, rather than a cause, of the Communist victory on the mainland."[48]

Nevertheless, Truman's foreign aid programs for East Asia played a pivotal role in US foreign policy in the post-war world. US foreign aid enabled Japan, China (pre-1950), and Taiwan (post-1949) to engage with the United States in the Cold War against the Soviet Union and its allies and also helped bring about in Japan and Taiwan political and economic reforms that laid a foundation for an extended period of stability and prosperity. Truman's aid policies resulted in the demilitarization and democratization of Japan and, by neutralizing the Taiwan Straits, stopped the Chinese Civil War before the last great battle – the battle for Taiwan – could be fought. In retrospect, Truman's foreign aid policies in East Asia not only significantly contributed to shaping the character of the Cold War, but helped create conditions which would keep the Cold War from ever turning into a new world war.[49]

Notes

1 Lanxin Xiang, *Recasting the Imperial Far East: Britain and America in China, 1945–1950* (Armonk, NY: M. E. Sharpe, 1995), 30–31.

2 General Jiang Weiguo (Chiang Wei-kuo, GMD Army, ret.), son of Jiang Jieshi, and adoptive brother of Jiang Jingguo (Jiang Ching-kuo), president of the ROC from 1978–1988, interview by the author at Rongzong [Glory's General] Hospital in Taipei, Taiwan, on May 25–27, 1994.

3 For recent publications on these events, including the Korean War (1950–1953), First Indo-china War (1946–1954), two Taiwan Strait Crises (1954–1955 and 1958), and the Vietnam War (1964–1975), see: Chen Jian, *China's Road to the Korean War: The Making of the Sino-American Confrontation* (New York: Columbia University Press, 1994); Shuguang Zhang, *Mao's Military Romanticism: China and the Korean War, 1950–1953* (Lawrence: University Press of Kansas, 1995); Xiaobing Li, Allan R. Millett, and Bin Yu, trans. and eds., *Mao's Generals Remember Korea* (Lawrence: University Press of Kansas, 2000); Mark A. Ryan, David M. Finkelstein, and Michael A. McDevitt, eds., *Chinese Warfighting: The PLA Experience since 1949* (New York: M. E. Sharpe, 2003); Xiaobing Li, *Voices from the Vietnam War: Stories from American, Asian, and Russian Veterans* (Lexington: University Press of Kentucky, 2010).

4 Xiaobing Li, *A History of the Modern Chinese Army* (Lexington: University of Kentucky Press, 2007), 70.

5 Compilation Committee of ROC History, *A Pictorial History of the Republic of China*, 2: 255–256.

6 Zarrow, *China in War and Revolution*, 330–331.

7 In 1944, to avoid a collapse of the CCP-GMD coalition, US Ambassador Hurley visited Yan'an, Mao's wartime capital, and proposed a joint postwar government in China. See Patrick Hurley, "Aide Memoirs," September 25, 1944; and his letter to President Roosevelt accompanying the memoirs, September 25, 1944, *Ambassador Patrick Hurley Papers*, University of Oklahoma Library, Norman, Oklahoma.

8 Compilation Committee of ROC History, *A Pictorial History of the Republic of China*, 2: 259.

9 Dean Acheson and John C. Vincent, "China Memo, Top-Secret," September 6, 1945, US State Department Records of the Office of Chinese Affairs, 1945–1955. National Archives, Washington, DC. Digitized by Gale, *Archives Unbound Collection*, available at: http://go.galegroup.com.vortex3

10 Dean Acheson and John C. Vincent, "China Memo, Top-Secret."

11 Xiang, *Recasting the Imperial Far East*, 142.

12 Li, *A History of the Modern Chinese Army*, 71–77.

13 For more detailed information on the Chinese Civil War, see: Li, *ibid*.

14 Mao Zedong, "The Situation and Our Policy after the Victory in the War of Resistance against Japan," in *Selected Works of Mao Tse-tung* (Beijing: Foreign Languages Press, 1977), 4: 14.

15 Mao, "Greet the New High Tide of the Chinese Revolution," *ibid.*, 4: 119–24.

16 Odd Arne Westad, *Decisive Encounters: The Chinese Civil War, 1946–1950* (Stanford, CA: Stanford University Press, 2003), 107.

17 The Chinese Ambassador Wellington Koo in Washington to the US Secretary of State, "Agreement between the U.S. and China regarding Relief Assistance to China, signed October 27, 1947," in *FRUS, 1947, The Far East: China* (Washington, DC: Government Printing Office, 1972), 7: 1293.

18 Secretary Marshall's recommendation to Congress on November 10, 1947, in US State Department, *United States Relations with China: With Special Reference to the Period 1944–1949* (Washington, DC: Government Printing Office, 1949), 371–372. Hereafter as *China White Paper*.

19 The statement of the CCP Central Committee from *Zhonggong zhongyang wenjian xuanji, 1921–1949* [Selected Documents of the CCP Central Committee, 1921–1949], 17: 60–61.

20 The CCP party documents include CCP Central Archives comps., *Zhonggong zhongyang wenjian xuanji, 1921–1949* [Selected Documents of the CCP Central Committee, 1921–1949],

vols. 1–18; CCP Central Archives, Central Archival and Manuscript Research Division, and CCP Organization Department comps., *Zhongguo gongchandang zuzhishi ziliao, 1921–1997* [Documents of the CCP Organization's History, 1921–1997], vols. 1–14; Southern Bureau of the CCP Central Committee, *Nanfangjiu dangshi ziliao* [Party History Records of the CCP Southern Bureau]; and Nanjing Bureau of the CCP Central Committee, *Zhonggong zhongyang Nanjingjiu: zhonggong lishi ziliao* [The Nanjing Bureau of the CCP Central Committee: CCP Historical Documents].

21 Among the government documents are the Archives of the PRC Ministry of Foreign Affairs, formerly in the Archives Section of the General Office of the Foreign Ministry, which include 330,000 volumes of documents, mainly in paper form, with some microfilm, photographs, audio and video tapes, and compact discs, recording China's foreign policy and diplomatic activities since the founding of the PRC in 1949. The Archives declassified about 10,000 volumes of the documents in 2004 and 60,000 in 2006.

22 Chinese leaders' papers and manuscripts include: *Mao Zedong waijiao wenxuan* [Selected Diplomatic Papers of Mao Zedong]; *Mao Zedong wenji* [Collected Works of Mao Zedong], vols. 1–8; *Mao Zedong junshi wenji* [Collected Military Works of Mao Zedong], vols. 1–6; *Mao Zedong junshi wenxuan: neibuben* [Selected Military Papers of Mao Zedong: Internal Edition], vols. 1–2; *Jianguo yilai Mao Zedong wengao, 1949–1976* [Mao Zedong's Manuscripts since the Founding of the State, 1949–1976], vols. 1–13; *Zhou Enlai junshi wenxuan* [Selected Military Works of Zhou Enlai], vols. 1–4; *Zhou Enlai waijiao wenxuan* [Selected Diplomatic Papers of Zhou Enlai]; Liu, *Jianguo yilai Liu Shaoqi wengao, 1949–1952* [Liu Shaoqi's Manuscripts since the Founding of the State, 1949–1952], vols. 1–4; Deng, *Selected Works of Deng Xiaoping*, vols. 1–3.

23 Mao, "'Friendship' or Aggression?" An article as commentaries was written by Mao for the Xinhua News Agency on August 30, 1949, *Selected Works of Mao Zedong*, 4: 448.

24 John C. Vincent, "Memorandum by the Director of the Office of Far Eastern Affairs (Vincent) to the Secretary of State," February 5, 1947, in *FRUS, 1947*, 7: 787.

25 Westad, *Decisive Encounters*, 279.

26 National Defense University (NDU), *Zhongguo renmin jiefangjun zhanshi jianbian* [A Brief History of the PLA Revolutionary War] (Beijing: Jiefangjun [PLA Press], 2001), 566.

27 Military History Research Division, China Academy of Military Science (CAMS), ed. *Zhongguo renmin jiefangjun quanguo jiefang zhanzhengshi* [History of the PLA in the Chinese Civil War] (Beijing: Junshi kexue [Military Science Press], 1997), 3: 1–3.

28 "Manifesto of the Chinese People's Liberation Army," in *Selected Works of Mao*, 4: 150. This political manifesto was drafted by Mao at Shenchuanpao, northern Shaanxi, for the General Headquarters of the PLA. It was issued on October 10, 1947, and known as the "October 10 Manifesto."

29 Leighton Stuart, US Ambassador in China, to the Secretary of State, November 24, 1947, *FRUS, 1947*, 7: 372.

30 The ROC Government's Letter to US Ambassador Leighton Stuart in China, December 22, 1947, "Some Fundamental Considerations on American Aid to China," *China White Paper*, 377.

31 Chen, *Mao's China and the Cold War*, 32.

32 US State Department, "Confidential History of the China Aid Program" Office of Chinese Affairs, 1945–1955. National Archives, Washington, DC. Digitized by Gale, *Archives Unbound Collection*, 8.

33 Christopher Lew, "Liao-Shen Campaign," in *China at War*, ed. Li, 229–232.

34 Lew, "Huai-Hai Campaign," *ibid.*, 171–175.

35 Westad, *Decisive Encounters*, 205–211.

36 Qian Haihao, *Jundui zuzhi bianzhixue jiaocheng* [Graduate Curriculum: Military Organization and Formation], 40.

37 After Jiang proposed a cease-fire, Mao issued several speeches and articles to explain why he and the CCP could not have any peace talk with Jiang: Mao, "On the War Criminal's Suing for Peace," "Statement on the Present Situation by Mao Tse-tung, Chairman of the Central Committee of the CCP," and "Comment by the Spokesman for the CCP on the Resolution of the Nanking Executive Yuan," in *Selected Works of Mao*, 4: 309–324.

38 Mao, "Order to the Army for the Country-wide Advance," *ibid.*, 387–397.

39 NSC No. 34 and 34/1 in *FRUS, 1949*, 9: 474–475.

40 Senate Foreign Relations committee, *Hearings in Executive Session: Economic Assistance to China and Korea, 1949–1950* (Historical Series, 1974), 193–194; House committee on Foreign Affairs, *Report on Amending the China Aid Act of 1948*, House of Representatives, no. 329, 81st Congress, 1st Session, 1949, 5; and *Report on Extension of European Recovery Program*, House of Representatives, no. 323, 81st Congress, 1st Session, 1949, 2: 5. See also: Congressional Records, 81st Congress, 1st Session, 1949, 95, 3: 3820–3822, 3829, 3738.

41 Military History Research Division, China Academy of Military Science (CAMS), *Zhongguo renmin jiefangjun quanguo jiefang zhanzhengshi* [History of the PLA in the Chinese Civil War] (Beijing: Junshi kexue [Military Science Press], 1997), 5: 146–211; Military History Research Division, CAMS, *Zhongguo renmin jiefangjun de qishinian, 1929–1997* [Seventy Years of the PLA, 1929–1997] (Beijing: Junshi kexue [Military Science Press], 1997), 357.

42 Richard M. Fried, *Nightmare in Red* (New York: Oxford University Press, 1990), 89.

43 Mao, "Cast Away Illusions, Prepare for Struggle," *Selected Works of Mao*, 4: 431.

44 Mao, "Why It Is Necessary to Discuss the White Paper," an article as commentaries written by Mao for the Xinhua News Agency on August 28, 1949, *ibid.*, 4: 442.

45 Mao, "The Bankruptcy of the Idealist Conception of History," *ibid.*, 4: 451.

46 Joseph W. Esherick, "Revolution in a Feudal Fortress," *Modern China* 24, no. 4 (October 1998), 370.

47 Suzanne Pepper, *Civil War in China: The Political Struggle, 1945–1949* (Berkeley: University of California Press, 1978), 75.

48 Dreyer, *China at War*, 7.

49 For recent publications on these events, including the Korean War (1950–1953), First Indochina War (1946–1954), two Taiwan Strait Crises (1954–1955 and 1958), and the Vietnam War (1964–1975), see: Chen Jian, *China's Road to the Korean War: The Making of the Sino-American Confrontation* (New York: Columbia University Press, 1994); Shuguang Zhang, *Mao's Military Romanticism: China and the Korean War, 1950-1953* (Lawrence: University Press of Kansas, 1995); Xiaobing Li, Allan Millett, and Bin Yu, trans. and eds., *Mao's Generals Remember Korea* (Lawrence, KS: University Press of Kansas, 2000); Mark A. Ryan, David M. Finkelstein, and Michael A. McDevitt, eds., *Chinese Warfighting: The PLA Experience since 1949* (New York: M. E. Sharpe, 2003); Xiaobing Li, *Voices from the Vietnam War: Stories from American, Asian, and Russian Veterans* (Lexington: University Press of Kentucky, 2010)

5 The People's Republic of China and Taiwan (1949–1957)

The first generation of the Chinese Communist Party (CCP) leaders became founders of the People's Republic of China after twenty-eight years (1921–1949) of military and political struggles on the road to increased power.[1] The CCP had acquired sufficient experience and self-confidence to create a new Communist state; its alliance with the Soviet Union reinforced the new government's capability of following the Russian model. In 1949, Mao Zedong, chairman of the CCP until his death, transformed the party from a rebellious force against the Nationalist government to a ruling apparatus of the PRC. Mao converted China into a single-party Communist state, nationalized industry and business under state ownership, and carried out socialist reforms in all areas of Chinese society. His theoretical contributions to the communist ideology, along with his military strategies, are commonly recognized as Mao Zedong Thought.[2] Having moved to center stage and gaining national power, Mao and his comrades were characterized as communist ideologists and radical revolutionaries against an "old" world order, the post-WWII international system.

After the Korean War ended in 1953, China quickly adjusted its position in international affairs and willingly moved onto center stage of ideological and military confrontations between the two contending camps, headed by the Soviet Union and the United States, respectively. The active role that China played in East Asia turned this Cold War battlefield into an odd "buffer" between Moscow and Washington because, with China and East Asia standing in the middle, it was less likely that the Soviet Union and the United States would become involved in direct military confrontation.[3] Some Western historians agree that the alliance between Beijing and Moscow was the cornerstone of the communist international alliance system in the 1950s.[4] Mao continued his revolution by calling to "learn from the Soviet Union" and by launching a series of political campaigns through the 1950s. While Chinese society became more radicalized in order to maintain its identity within the communist camp, its foreign policy became more active in supporting the worldwide communist movement to keep up with its new power status. The alliance between Beijing and Moscow had become the cornerstone of the global communist alliance system in the Cold War.

By the late 1950s, the CCP had grown beyond the Leninist party system which depended on secrecy and institutional control and had developed a self-improvement mechanism and functionality which adapted to a new environment and allowed for changes within the party. According to Patrick F. Shan, the party's association with Chinese grass-roots society "in a total native social setting" guaranteed its flexibility and adaptation to an ever-changing China during the continuing revolution.[5] David Shambaugh concludes: "The CCP exhibited many classic symptoms of an atrophying and decaying Leninist party – but at the same time, it is also showing itself capable of significant adaptation and reform in a number of key areas."[6] The relatively neglected lessons learned by the CCP have helped to re-define the party's characteristics and have changed it in numerous ways. Its leaders acted according to their own consistent logic in its political agenda with their political experience within the context of Chinese society and global Cold War environments.

Mao's request for Soviet aid

Before the founding of the People's Republic, Mao had declared the "lean-to-one-side" policy, according to which the new republic would favor the Soviet Union and join the socialist and communist camps in the post-WWII world.[7] After Mao proclaimed the PRC on October 1, 1949, his new government was still confronting more than one million GMD fighters in Taiwan and Southwest China. Mao's first priority was to consolidate the new state by eliminating all remnants of Jiang's Nationalist forces on Taiwan and other offshore islands.[8] Since the PLA lacked enough air and naval power, Mao required Soviet aid to cross the Taiwan Strait.

Mao paid a state visit to the Soviet Union on December 16, 1949, hoping to get what the new China desperately needed through an alliance treaty between the PRC and the USSR. Josef Stalin, however, was never easy to deal with, not even with his next-door communist comrade. Mao, frustrated after two fruitless meetings in December, became even more upset when he had not yet had a chance to meet Stalin during three weeks in January 1950.[9] Nevertheless, during his long stay in Moscow, a total of sixty-five days, Mao had a better understanding of Stalin's objective. Among other things, the Soviet leader hoped to convince Mao that the Soviet Union had its own difficulties; there would be no "free ride" for China and that China should share responsibility for the worldwide communist movement. Stalin also made it clear that China should support international communist movements in Asian countries. During their second meeting on December 24, it is recorded that "Stalin did not mention the treaty at all," and instead discussed with Mao "the activities of the Communist Parties in Asian countries such as Vietnam, Japan, and India."[10] Stalin, preoccupied with European affairs, needed China to help with ongoing Asian Communist revolutions such as the anti-French war in Indochina.[11]

Mao understood Stalin's demand that China share "the international responsibility" of global communist movements by supporting the Asian revolutionary wars like Ho Chi Minh's First Indochina War. From a geopolitical point of view, it seemed to make sense to Chinese leaders that China could secure its southwestern border, earn Soviet aid and technology, and modernize its armed forces, by helping the Democratic Republic of Vietnam (DRV) fight the French forces. Having noticed Stalin's priority and intent, Mao accepted Stalin's perception of a "worldwide communist revolution," and was ready to share "the international responsibility." In Moscow, Mao agreed to support Ho's war against the French because Mao also considered internationalism as one of the fundamental principles of the CCP.[12]

On February 14, 1950, the Sino-Soviet Treaty of Friendship, Alliance, and Mutual Assistance was signed in Moscow. The Soviet Union committed its nuclear protection and military aid to the new People's Republic. On February 16, Stalin hosted a banquet to celebrate the signing of the Sino-Soviet treaty.[13] Mao then signed a huge naval order with Stalin in Moscow. The Soviet Union agreed to arm a new Chinese naval force with warships and equipment worth $150 million, half the total loan package that Stalin granted through the treaty.[14] After his return to Beijing, Mao began in March 1950 to send hundreds of Chinese officers as advisors and huge military aid to Vietnam to support Ho's war against the French forces. After the Korean War broke out that summer, Mao sent three million Chinese troops to Korea against the UN/US forces in 1950–1953.

To strengthen the PRC militarily as the frontrunner of the Cold War in East Asia, the Soviet Union re-armed the Chinese forces. During the Korean War, Stalin helped Mao establish the Chinese air force with brand new Russian-made jet fighters. The PLA Air Force (PLAAF) had less than 100 fighters in 1950, increasing to 3,000 fighters and bombers by 1953, and totaling 5,000 by 1955.[15] In five years, this made China's air force the third largest in the world, after the United States and the Soviet Union. The Soviets also helped China build its navy by providing technology and advisory assistance during the Korean War. By the end of 1955, the Chinese navy totaled 188,000 men with 519 Russian-made warships and 341 support vessels. It had nineteen artillery regiments with 343 heavy coastal artillery pieces (mostly 130mm Russian-made coastal cannons), and eight anti-aircraft artillery regiments with 336 AAA guns.[16] The navy also commanded six air force divisions and two independent air force regiments that included 515 bombers, fighters, reconnaissance, and cargo planes.[17] The Soviet Union also re-armed sixty infantry divisions for the PLA between 1951 and 1954, and thereafter Chinese weaponry was standardized.[18] While the PLA continued the Chinese military tradition, it assimilated new Soviet technology and operational tactics. The Chinese armed forces modernized and the Chinese ways of war evolved through Chinese interaction with, and observation of, Russian advisors in the 1950s. Soviet support in military, economy, government, and international affairs was critical for the new regime's political consolidation and economic reconstruction. If the Soviet model had shaped the revolutionary and communist nature of the new China, Russian aid and military technology helped the Chinese military with its transformation in the early 1950s from a peasant army into a modern professional force.[19]

Russian model: The Party-state

Mao soon established a party-state after the Soviet totalitarian model. The Party's membership increased from 2.7 million in 1947, to 6.1 million in 1953 and 10.7 million in 1956 when the CCP Eighth National Congress was held in Beijing. At that Congress, Mao was again elected chairman of the Central Committee with Liu Shaoqi, Zhou Enlai, Zhu De, and Chen Yun (Ch'en Yun, 1905–1995) as vice chairmen and Deng Xiaoping as secretary general.[20] The Central Committee of the CCP, composed of approximately 300 members, did not have legislative power; however, it had constitutional power since the most important and high-ranking officials of the Chinese government were all members of the Central Committee. The Politburo, lodged within the Central Committee, consisted of twenty-five people who controlled the CCP. Theoretically, members of the Central Committee elected the Politburo. Politburo members held offices in China's national government and regional offices concurrently so as to strengthen the CCP's power in government and provincial affairs.[21] The Standing Committee within the Politburo was composed of seven to nine persons, who held the maximum power in the overall Chinese governing hierarchy. This group met weekly to discuss national policies. Since all power was concentrated in the hands of these seven to nine people, or ultimately in the hands of the supreme leader, the National Congress became essentially a rubber stamp that only approved decisions that had been made by the Standing Committee of the Politburo or by the paramount leader.

The CCP also dominated local governments by controlling their legislative, executive, and judicial branches. The party employed similar methods to have political control of the provincial, district, metropolitan, and county governments by appointing CCP members to the local posts and approving or disapproving the nominations. Most of the provincial governors, lieutenant governors, city mayors, district executives, county heads, and local congressional leaders were CCP members. Under the local party committees were grass-roots party committees in township, districts, and neighborhoods; in business enterprises, commercial companies, manufacturing factories, and retail stores; in all universities, public school districts, and research institutes; and in all military army, divisional, regimental, and battalion commands. Each grass-roots party committee had a secretary, deputy secretaries, and committee members, who were elected at the grass-roots level and approved by the next higher level. These committees supervised the general party branches and party branches in the villages, departments, offices, and PLA companies. Each party branch elected a secretary, a deputy secretary, and a committee, and led the party teams which, as the most basic unit in the CCP organization, had three to ten party members. One of the important tasks for the party teams was to recruit new party members.

To gain political support from the country, the CCP organized the Chinese People's Political Consultative Conference (CPPCC) in September 1949 under leadership of the CCP. It served as a national coalition, including the national democratic parties, non-communist associations, religious groups, industrial and commercial chambers, various political organizations such as the Revolutionary Committee of the Guomindang, Democratic League, Democratic National Construction Association, Association for Promoting Democracy, and Chinese Peasants' and Workers' Democratic Party. Due to the overwhelming majority of the CCP representatives, the First CPPCC supported the CCP to found the PRC in October 1949. Thereafter, the CPPCC exercised the functions and powers of the legislative branch, as the national congress was not convened until 1954. Its delegates passed the Common Program at the First Plenary Session in Beijing. The Common Program served as China's provisional constitution from 1949 to 1954 and established the Central People's Government under the leadership of the CCP, with Mao as the first PRC president from 1949 to 1954. Zhou Enlai elected second, third, and fourth in 1954, 1959, and 1965; and Deng Xiaoping the fifth in 1978.[22]

On September 20, 1954, the First National People's Congress (NPC) passed the first formal constitution by secret ballot and promulgated the Chinese Constitution. This document included a preamble and was divided into 106 articles in four chapters, much like the Soviet Union's Constitution of 1936, which can be regarded as a civil law system. Parts of the Soviet legal code were directly translated into Chinese, and Russian legal experts assisted in rewriting the code to better fit the conditions in China. The 1954 Constitution stipulated the president as chief executive, the NPC as the main legislative body (a unicameral parliament), the State Council as the executive body, and the Courts and procurates as the judicial branch. According to the Constitution, the NPC exercised most of its power on a day-to-day basis through the Standing Committee in Beijing. Due to its overwhelming majority in the Congress, the CCP had total control over the composition of this committee.[23] Until the late 1980s, the NPC and its Standing Committee played only a symbolic role as a powerless rubber-stamping legislature. They followed the Party Center's instructions and made sure to pass all the Party's decisions at the congressional meetings. All local governments at the provincial, district, county, city, and town levels served as agents of the central government in Beijing.

As a result of party control, the legal system is also highly centralized in China. The Constitution authorizes the NPC Standing Committee to select, appoint, and dismiss Supreme Court justices and procurators at the national level. The Supreme Court is the highest judicial organ of the state. In 1954, the NPC created the Ministries of Justice and Public Security. In 1955, the Ministry of Public Security granted local party committees authority to manage the public security and police force at its level. After 1958, local party committees became the main source of law enforcement in their areas. The standing committees of the local congresses could appoint and dismiss local judicial personnel. Moreover, all the local judges, court clerks, police, detectives, and public attorneys were hired as civil service staff of the national government, and many were CCP members. The CCP government consistently circumvented the legal system in Mao's continued political campaigns to eliminate any opposition. The reputation of legal institutions, including the courts and due process, fell drastically, and lawyers began to stop practicing in the late 1950s. The Ministry of Justice was closed in 1959, not to re-open until twenty years later, in 1979.

The NPC elected Mao as the PRC's president on September 27, 1954. According to the 1954 Constitution, the NPC was the highest state body and the only legislative house in China. Until the 1990s, its representatives were determined by the CCP, which maintained effective control over the composition of the body at various levels. Each village could elect its own representative, with no restriction on the number of candidates, as the lowest level in the electoral system.[24] Only this representative could enter the next level as a candidate to become the town or city congressional representative. After approval of the Party committee of each town or city, each elected official could then enter the county level election. At this level, the Party exercised additional control over the process by limiting the number of candidates in proportion to the number of seats available. At the election of the county's people's congress (about 2,861 counties and county-level administrations in 2004), a maximum of 130 candidates were allowed per 100 seats. Following the approval of the county's Party committee, each elected representative could serve a five-year term and enter as a candidate at the district election. The next higher up was the provincial election, at which level the ratio was 120 candidates per 100 seats. Delegates who were re-elected by the provincial people's congresses could then enter the election for the NPC where, at this highest level, the ratio decreased again to only 110 candidates per 100 seats. This tiered electoral structure made it impossible for a candidate to become a member of a higher legislative body without Party approval. In 2013, about 3,000 delegates attended the Twelfth NPC.[25] Again, the CCP leadership demonstrated its ability to adapt to a new political and social environment by inventing a new system, a party-state.

Political movements and control

The Party's experience of working with the masses during the Chinese Civil War had convinced CCP leaders that they could consolidate power and solve the country's problems by thorough mobilization, such as they had done during the "people's war." During the 1950s, Mao launched one political movement after another to engage the masses in a class struggle and to eliminate those labeled as established or potential counterrevolutionaries through initiatives such as land reform, the Three Antis movement, the Five Antis movement, and the anti-Rightist movement; all of which turned into violent reactions against millions of people. During the early years, the CCP believed that it needed charismatic authority and absolute power to achieve its idealistic goals. The Communists' successful military struggle against the GMD had convinced the leaders that violent means were necessary, not only for establishing national power, but also for continuing their Communist revolution after the founding of the PRC. The ideology, experience, and nature of this transformation left little room for civil liberties of Chinese citizens.

The movement to suppress counterrevolutionaries in the early 1950s became a brutal struggle against former officials and supporters of the GMD government. During the campaign, Chinese leaders called for the execution of all enemy elements. The new regime realized the necessity of stamping out all resistance in its efforts to consolidate political control. The campaign then became swift and decisive, as thousands of suspected enemies of the revolution were rounded up, tried – sometimes on extremely limited evidence – and arbitrarily sentenced. According to Mao, around 1.27 million were incarcerated and 800,000 were executed. The Common Program stipulated in Article 75 that "By law, the trials in the People's Court shall be conducted through the People's Assessors System."[26] Many of the accused, however, did not have a lawyer, a hearing, or even a trial before they were sentenced or executed. Through a massive peasant movement, landlords and rich peasants, as a social class, were eliminated by a campaign that shocked much of the rural population, most of whom were unaware of the wrath of the revolutionary state.

While this suppression of counterrevolutionaries disturbed rural areas, two additional movements, the Three Antis and Five Antis, expressed the will of the new regime to impose order in industry and commerce by all-out assaults on the bourgeoisie in the cities. China's intervention during the Korean War in 1950–1953 dragged the country into a significant conflict with the UN/US forces on the Korean peninsula.[27] To meet the drastic war needs, the CCP had to strengthen its economic and financial control more than ever. The government launched the Three Antis and Five Antis movements from 1951–1954 to target the private manufacturing, commerce, trade, financial, and real estate sectors in urban areas. The Party Center mobilized and encouraged manufacturing workers, company employees, and bank clerks to report their employers' wrongdoing and the companies' illegal activities. Most private entrepreneurs were found guilty in one way or another, and almost all of their businesses, properties, and even their homes were confiscated by the government. It was an action made possible by the forceful deprivation of private property and individual rights. The criteria for punishable crimes and their accompanying sentences became noticeably harsher against business owners, and more than 200,000 of these individuals and their families died during the two campaigns, resulting in the virtual elimination of the bourgeoisie as a class.[28] These movements made China a Soviet-style state, in which the government owned 98 percent of all industry, commerce, finance, and trade. The Chinese leaders had constructed a communist institution that put severe limits on individual freedoms, such as movement, employment, and economic activities.[29]

Between 1954 and 1956 tension mounted between the specialists and the cadres, who were more concerned about communist ideology than about the legal system. Also, the intellectuals questioned the wisdom of emulating the 1936 Soviet Constitution, since Stalin never intended to grant the Russian people freedom, liberties, or fair trials. In

1956, Mao called for the "Blooming of the Hundred Flowers" movement to encourage the public, especially the intellectuals, to express their grievances on the mistakes, corruption, and mismanagement both in the government and in the Party. When the criticism spread like wildfire across the country a year later, the chairman attempted to stop the complaints by launching another political movement, the "Anti-Rightist" campaign.[30]

The Anti-Rightist movement targeted non-party members and those not interested in Communist politics. In schools and in the mass media, party committees and branches mobilized the masses to identify "rightists" among faculty members, researchers, and educated employees who might have said something derogatory about the government and the Party during the "Blooming of the Hundred Flowers" campaign. By the end of the year, over 550,000 intellectuals had been labeled as "rightists," meaning enemies of the people. Many of these individuals were purged and denied the right to work, teach, or live with their families. A large number were exiled to labor camps or to remote villages for re-education. Numerous others were jailed or executed. The accused received no respect for their human dignity, let alone their rights and liberties. Jonathan D. Spence states that a whole generation of artists, scientists, journalists, educators, and even college and high school students were penalized.[31]

During the "Blooming of the Hundred Flowers" movement, several legal experts, lawyers, and judges identified legal problems in the system such as the Party's power abuses by overruling court decisions, by excessive use of police force, and other violations of civil rights in the earlier political movements. Subsequently, in the 1957 Anti-Rightist movement, all of them were accused of using the law to oppose the Party, including four judges on the Supreme Court. Thereafter, the PRC government consistently circumvented the constitution and the legal system in Mao's continued mass campaigns to eliminate any opposition. The reputation of legal institutions, including courts and procuratorates, fell drastically, and attorneys stopped practicing law. The number of law schools was reduced from eighty-three to only twelve. The Ministry of Justice was closed in 1959, not to re-open until twenty years later, in 1979. Political security was a major concern for Chinese intellectuals and legal professionals from the late 1950s through the 1960s. Many young and middle-aged legal experts left the judicial system, which was considered a sensitive and dangerous field. The fear factor in Mao's harsh, endless political campaigns against intellectuals was effective.[32] There is no political challenge, major opposition, or election campaign at the national level. The military, or the PLA, belonged to the party rather than the state, since the CCP controlled resources and personal management for the military budget and for professional careers. The party used the government, including the military, to serve its political agenda as a totalitarian authority from 1949 to 1990 and as an authoritarian regime after the 1990s.

US Taiwan policy change

David Finkelstein points out that, even though President Truman did not recognize new Communist China after it was founded in October 1949, he neither gave full support to Jiang Jieshi on Taiwan after Jiang removed the seat of the ROC government to the island later that year with two million Nationalists from the mainland. Truman and his Secretary of State Dean Acheson vigorously warded off pressures from domestic critics of their policy. They never used the US Navy to protect Taiwan from an attack from the mainland. At a NSC meeting in December 1949, Truman rejected the JCS recommendation of helping the GMD government to defend Taiwan and dispatching a military mission to the island.[33] On December 23, 1949, the State Department sent a secret memorandum on Taiwan to its diplomatic and consular officials in the Far East, informing them of the US hands-off policy toward Taiwan. The memo pointed out that the fall of Taiwan to the Chinese Communists was widely expected. The island had no special military significance. It was politically, geographically, and strategically a part of China, and "Formosa is exclusively the responsibility of the Chinese government."[34]

Confronted by the increasing influence of the Soviet Union, Truman's strategic dilemma in China in early 1950 was the limited resources for a global containment. His primary concern was to determine what the United States could possibly do to prevent the Chinese Communists from further challenging US security interests in the long run. Given these assessments, Truman's advisors had reached a consensus by early 1950 that China alone, under Communist control, would not enhance the Soviet capability of undertaking military aggression on the basis of Asia's strategic potential unless the Communists controlled Japan as well.

Therefore, according to Zhang, a complete fall of China to the CCP should not necessarily result in an immediate threat to US security interests in the Asian-Pacific area, at least in the foreseeable future.[35] Thus, the idea of a "defensive perimeter" in the Western Pacific became the predominantly accepted solution. In Acheson's address before the National Press Club on January 12, 1950, he outlined this "defensive perimeter" as it had been described in NSC Document No. 48/1 two weeks earlier. The American defense perimeter in the Western Pacific ran along the Aleutians through Japan and the Ryukyus to the Philippines. The Taiwan area was left out of this defense line.[36] Apparently, strategic and security considerations were the decisive factors structuring Truman's policy toward Taiwan in early 1950. A general line to guide this hands-off policy "is to conduct a strategic offensive in the 'West' and a strategic defensive in the 'East'."[37] Zhang argues that regarding Europe, not Asia, as its strategic focus, the Truman administration did not want its effort, attention, and resources diverted in China.[38] The outbreak of the Korean War in the summer of 1950 not only changed America's strategic concerns in Asia, but also changed US policy toward Taiwan.[39]

On June 27, 1950, two days after the Korean War broke out, having reached a consensus with Capitol Hill and the Pentagon, Truman announced that the US Seventh Fleet would be deployed to the Taiwan Strait to prevent a Chinese Communist attack on GMD-held Taiwan. Truman's order became the turning point in the US Taiwan policy and had a strong impact on the future of Taiwan. Under the Presidential Directive, the United States for the first time committed its armed forces to the defense and security of the ROC government. The Truman administration shifted its strategy on Taiwan from the hands-off policy to a military commitment. However, Finkelstein argues that Truman's order to the Seventh Fleet was not just to keep the Communists from invading Taiwan, but also to keep the GMD from attacking the mainland, thus widening the war beyond Korea. Finkelstein makes it clear that "Taiwan was neutralized for purely military-strategic reasons. Washington could not allow the island to be occupied by enemy forces while US ground troops were committed to a land war in Korea."[40] The Truman administration operated under the auspices of the 1950 NSC Document No. 68, which laid out four "possible courses of action."[41] The island's status quo has inherited much since that summer. It secured the ROC on Taiwan from a major military showdown with the PRC on the mainland in the 1950s, it preserved the political unity and social stability of Taiwan through the 1960s, and it provided an opportunity for the island's economic take-off in the early 1970s.

In retrospect, Truman's new policy of 1950 was disengaging the Chinese from their hot civil war while engaging them in the global Cold War. The Truman legacy was keeping the military struggle "cold" in the Taiwan Strait and creating the foundation and opportunity of political and international competition in which both Chinese parties could find alternatives or even a peaceful solution over their civil struggle. Truman did not intend to postpone the Chinese Civil War or provide Beijing with a different reason to attack Taipei. Nancy Bernkopf Tucker points out that "Truman had no plans to create two Chinas or to secure independence for Taiwan."[42] The newly declassified Chinese documents show that the Chinese Communist leaders in Beijing took Truman's policy change seriously, and that they had to stop their landing operation against Taiwan. China had been preparing its landing campaign against Taiwan since the founding of the People's Republic. The Seventh Fleet's presence in the Taiwan Strait totally changed the balance of military power in the Chinese Civil War. The Communist leaders faced a serious challenge – America's direct involvement in the Chinese civil struggle, which would transform the conflict into an international confrontation. With Washington's direct involvement in the Taiwan Strait, the PLA now confronted the most advanced military force in the world – the US armed forces.

On February 9, 1951, Washington and Taiwan reached an agreement of "mutual defense and assistance." On February 16, 1951, the Defense Department received a financial package of $67.1 million as military aid to Taiwan and Thailand, $50 million of which was for Taiwan.[43] In May, the Truman administration provided $21 million in military aid to Taiwan's naval and air force improvement.[44] On May 1, the US "Military Advisory Assistant Group" (MAAG) was established in Taiwan. To ensure the island's safety, the American advisors became actively involved in improving the combat effectiveness of GMD forces, including re-organizing Jiang's troops into thirty-one infantry divisions. In August, General William Chase (1895–1986), leading advisor of the American group in Taiwan, reported to Washington that he and his advisory group had planned to aid and train a total of 600,000 Chinese Nationalist troops.[45] By the end of September 1951, the total of American military advisors numbered 280.[46]

US aid and the 1954 Taiwan Strait Crisis

US aid to Taiwan from 1951 to 1953 was a successful case to show how the Truman administration had created situations of strength to maintain a balance without renewing the Chinese Civil War. When the Jiang government moved to Taiwan, its economy was characterized by high inflation, low productivity, and an influx of population from the mainland. In 1949, the inflation rate reached 181 percent.[47] Only a few industries remained from the heavy bombing of Allied Forces during the Pacific War. On May 17, 1951, the NSC passed the No. 48/5 Document and decided to provide more economic and military aid to Taiwan in order to further strengthen Taiwan's economy and to guarantee Taiwan's defense.[48] By the end of the year, US aid to Taiwan reached $98 million, but only about 13 percent of the total was military aid while 87 percent consisted of economic and technology aid. In 1952, US aid to Taiwan totaled $81.5 million, including only $13.3 million in military aid. In 1953, the United States annual aid increased to $105 million, with more than 74 percent of the total allocated to economic and technology aid to Taiwan. Besides the governmental aid, the United States also provided financial and material aid to Taiwan through the industrial CFP (counterpart fund), JCRR, and other assistant projects during the early 1950s.[49]

With the help of US economic and technology assistance, Jiang instituted new policies aimed at promoting economic development and industrialization. The first, and one of the most important ones, was land reform. John F. Copper points out that the land reform "was a resounding success; so much so that Taiwan's land reform program still provides a model for other countries to study and emulate."[50] Land reform and Taiwan's overall successful economic development plans, both of which were overseen by US aid advisors, also made Taiwan a showcase of US foreign aid and improved the Nationalist government's image in the international community. After successful land reform, the start of its industrialization process, and some years of peace and stability, Taiwan introduced a new monetary system and initiated interest rates, foreign exchange, and trade control, with a major priority of the government program aimed at developing electricity, fertilizer, and textile industries.

In the years 1947 to 1953, the Truman administration's aid to the ROC had the effect of disengaging both the ROC and the new PRC from their civil war and thrust them into the Cold War struggle. Although the PRC gave up its plans for an amphibious invasion of Taiwan in 1950, its presence in East Asia turned this new Cold War battlefield into an odd buffer between the United States and the Soviet Union. The PRC stood in the middle, between the two superpowers, thus helping to ensure there would be no military confrontation.[51] The Cold War in East Asia remained cold, at least in part because of the PRC.[52]

Chinese military involvements in Korea from 1950 to 1953 had certainly promoted CCP to international status, projecting a powerful image of China as the vanguard of the communist countries against Western powers such as the United States. After the Korean Armistice was signed in July 1953, China shifted its attention and efforts against "American imperialists" from Korea to Taiwan. When the Korean War was over, Beijing had hoped to see US withdrawal from the Taiwan Strait, but the Korean Armistice did not end the Taiwan problem, nor did it lead to the Seventh Fleet's withdrawal. Instead, America's increasing involvement dashed Beijing's hopes for a possible end to the Chinese Civil War. Chinese leaders suspected that the United States was carrying out a policy of "unleashing Jiang." Since the establishment of the PRC, the question of how to deal with the United States was not only a foreign policy issue for Beijing; rather, it had become an issue concerning the very essence of the Chinese revolution.[53]

In 1954, Beijing perceived unmistakable indications that Taipei-Washington collaboration was accelerating. If China did not send a quick and effective message to the United States, Beijing believed, American cooperation would legitimize Taiwan within international politics, hindering Beijing's goal to gain full acceptance as a significant member of the international community. The Central Military Commission (CMC) of the CCP decided in July that the PLA would launch attacks in September on the Dachen Islands off the Zhejiang coast and the Jinmen (Kinmen or Quemoy) Island off the Fujian coast in the Taiwan Strait.[54]

On September 3, the PLA artillery in the Fujian front began a heavy bombardment of Jinmen and Mazu to reduce the re-enforcement and supply shipments from Taiwan to these islands.[55] The Taiwan Strait Crisis of 1954–1955, or the First Taiwan Strait Crisis, began between China and Taiwan. On November 1, the PLAAF and PLAN began their air and naval assault on the Dachens. For four days, PLA bombers and fighters raided the Dachens, flying more than 100 sorties and dropping over 1,000 bombs. By late November, the PLA had completed construction of a torpedo-boat base and coastal artillery positions opposite Yijiangshan. They now dominated both air and sea around the Dachens, and a landing at Yijiangshan seemed imminent.[56] Nonetheless, General Jiang Weiguo recalled that his father, Jiang Jieshi, visited the Dachens, and strengthened the garrison's morale by clearing some rumors that Taiwan's high command would evacuate the GMD troops from these islands. Then, the Dachens' garrison received reinforcement and more supplies.[57]

The PLA high command called a halt to await the outcome of negotiations on a US-Taiwan mutual defense treaty that might or might not include the offshore islands. President Dwight Eisenhower continued Truman's policy to disengage the Chinese in the Taiwan Strait. The Washington-Taiwan Mutual Defense Treaty was signed by the Eisenhower administration during the First Taiwan Strait Crisis on December 2, 1954.[58] This made any further amphibious operations from the PLA very difficult, if not impossible, without risking war with the United States.

On December 16, the PLA generals selected Yijiangshan, a half square mile islet seven miles north of the major Dachen Islands, as the first target of the landing campaign. On January 18, 1955, the PLA launched the Yijiangshan landings. The GMD garrison at Yijiangshan numbered only about one thousand troops armed with some sixty artillery pieces and 100 machine guns. The PLA's 10,000 men attacking forces had overwhelmingly numerical superiority.

The Eisenhower administration, for its part, persuaded Jiang Jieshi to withdraw his troops from the Dachens with American assistance. Between February 8 and February 12, the Seventh Fleet helped the GMD evacuate some 25,000 military and 18,000 civilian personnel from the Dachen Islands.[59] At the same meeting that decided the Dachens' evacuation on January 20, 1955, Eisenhower and Secretary Dulles agreed that abandoning all the offshore islands would be a "great blow to Nationalist morale and that the United States must therefore assist in defending Quemoy and Matsu as long as the PRC continued to threaten Taiwan."[60] To implement this policy, Eisenhower requested authorization from Congress for the United States to participate in the defense of Jinmen, Mazu, and other islands in the Taiwan Strait. On January 29, Congress passed the "Formosa Resolution," which authorized Eisenhower to employ US armed forces to protect Taiwan from a possible PLA invasion.

To stop further Chinese Communist invasion of Jinmen and Taiwan, the United States began to utter fearsome nuclear threats. On March 6, Eisenhower and Dulles reaffirmed their commitment to the defense of the offshore islands and concluded that this would require drastic measures, including "the use of atomic missiles," by which they evidently meant tactical nuclear weapons.[61] The United States appeared willing to risk a war, even a nuclear war, over the Taiwan Strait against Chinese Communist aggression just one year after the Korean Armistice. Beijing backed down on April 26 when the Chinese premier offered a negotiation with the United States at the Bandung Conference. Zhou Enlai said that the PRC wanted no war with America, that "the Chinese people are friendly to the American people," and that his government was willing "to negotiate with the United States for the reduction of the tensions in the Taiwan Strait."[62] The 1954–1955 Taiwan Strait crisis was over. On August 1, 1955, the Chinese-American Ambassadorial Talks began at Geneva.

In the meantime, US aid poured in to help the Taiwan economy's recovery. From the 1950s, much of the US aid was used in infrastructure and the agricultural sector.

American advisors stationed in Taiwan, and Taiwanese sent abroad for education, were all directed at rebuilding the economy. The growth rate of the GDP reached 12 percent in 1952. In 1953, the Taiwanese government implemented its First Four-Year Economic Plan. Its emphasis on import-substitution policy aimed at making Taiwan self-sufficient by producing inexpensive consumer goods, processing imported raw materials, and restricting other imports. By 1959, 90 percent of exports were agriculture or food-related. Increased production and higher income resulted in low inflation and capital accumulation, as importing food was unnecessary. Realizing Taiwan's small domestic market, its government adopted a second policy of "export promotion" in the late 1950s and continued throughout the 1960s. From 1961 to 1964 Taiwanese exports averaged a growth rate of 31 percent per year. Its economic growth rate rose steadily and in 1964 reached double-digit figures, 12.6 percent, for the first time since 1951.[63] Soon Taiwan secured an international reputation as an exporter to the world.

In 1964, US aid to Taiwan stopped; almost simultaneously, Taiwan's economy took off. Starting from the Fourth Four-Year Economic Plan in 1965, Taiwan began its first economic plan without US economic aid. In 1966, the share of heavy industry in total industrial output reached 52 percent, exceeding that of light industry for the first time. By 1968, the output of manufacturing industry hit 24 percent, for the first time exceeding the share of agriculture (about 22 percent).[64] Over two decades, Taiwan enjoyed the world's fastest growing economy. A decade and a half of successful Nationalist rule after 1949 had made Taiwan more prosperous than it had ever been.

Economic development fostered governmental and social reforms, including political openness and educational reforms. Taiwan began to create a more honest and efficient government. Jiang and his GMD Party made moves to rid the government and ruling party of corruption and incompetence. Jiang even organized elections and made efforts to democratize Taiwan's political system at the local level. The Taiwanese felt that democracy at the local level would eventually work its way to the top. The government allowed local elections of village, township, city, and district leaders and assemblies as well as provincial assembly elections to be routinely held. The Nationalist government also permitted discussion and debate of Western liberalism and allowed regime critics to hold public meetings and critically evaluate the regime as long as the authorities judged such behavior did not threaten party-state rule. The Taiwan government even passed a law in 1969 permitting a small quota of national representatives to be elected every three years. Linda Chao and Ramon H. Myers point out that the balancing act between maintaining authority and power and nurturing a democracy paved the way to later democratic movement.[65] The Taiwanese people gradually learned to play by the rules of democracy.

Notes

1 Cheng Li, *China's Leaders: The New Generation* (Lanham, MD: Rowman & Littlefield, 2001), 9.
2 For studies of Mao, see: Alexander V. Pantsov and Steven I. Levine, *Mao: The Real Story* (New York: Simon & Schuster, 2012); Jung Chang and Jon Halliday, *Mao: The Unknown Story* (New York: Knopf, 2005); Ross Terrill, *Mao: A Biography* (Stanford, CA: Stanford University Press, 1999); Philip Short, *Mao: A Life* (New York: Henry Holt, 1999); Jonathan D. Spence, *Mao Zedong* (New York: Viking, 1999); Li Zhisui, *The Private Life of Chairman Mao: The Memoirs of Mao's Personal Physician* (New York: Random House, 1994).
3 Chen and Li, "China and the End of the Global Cold War," 121–122.

4 For the importance of the Sino-Soviet alliance, see: Lüthi, *The Sino-Soviet Split*; Westad, *Brothers in Arms*; Michael M. Sheng, *Battling Western Imperialism: Mao, Stalin, and the United States* (Princeton, NJ: Princeton University Press, 1997); Zubok and Pleshakov, *Inside the Kremlin's Cold War*; Gordon H. Chang, *Friends and Enemies: The United States, China, and the Soviet Union* (Stanford, CA: Stanford University Press, 1990).

5 Patrick Fuliang Shan, "Local Revolution, Grassroots Mobilization and Wartime Power Shift to the Rise of Communism," in *Evolution of Power: China's Struggle, Survival, and Success*, eds. Xiaobing Li and Xiansheng Tian (Lanham, MD: Lexington Books, 2014), chapter 1.

6 David Shambaugh, *China's Communist Party: Atrophy and Adaptation* (Berkeley: University of California Press, 2008), 5.

7 Xiaobing Li and Xiansheng Tian, "Introduction: Evolution of the CCP: Progress, Problems, and Prospects," in *Evolution of Power: China's Struggle, Survival, and Success*, eds. Li and Tian (Lanham, MD: Lexington Books, 2014), xxii.

8 Mao Zedong's Telegram to Lin Biao on October 31, 1949, "My Suggestions on Your Troops Disposition and Battle Array," in *Jianguo yilai Mao Zedong wengao* [Mao Zedong's Manuscripts since the Founding of the State] (Beijing: Zhongyang wenxian [CCP Central Archival and Manuscript Press], 1989), 1: 107. Hereafter cited as *Mao's Manuscripts since 1949*. Lin was the commander of the PLA Fourth Field Army, totaling 1.2 million troops, in South China in late 1949.

9 For Mao's "anger" over the "ill-treatments" and his "half prisoner," see: Lüthi, *The Sino-Soviet Split*, 31–33; Chang and Halliday, *Mao*, 351–353; Short, *Mao*, 424.

10 Pei Jianzhang, *Zhonghua renmin gongheguo waijiaoshi, 1949–1956* [Diplomatic History of the People's Republic of China, 1949–1956] (Beijing: Shijie zhishi [World Knowledge Publishing], 1994), 18.

11 Luo Guibo, "An Exceptional Model of Proletarian Internationalism: Remember Mao Zedong and the Assistance of Vietnam and Resistance against France," in *Zhongguo junshi guwentuan yuanyue kangfa shilu: dangshiren de huiyi* [The Records of the Chinese Military Advisory Group (CMAG) in Assisting Vietnam and Resisting France: Personal Accounts of the Veterans], ed. Compilation Team (Beijing: Zhonggong dangshi [CCP Party History Press], 2002), 3–4.

12 Mao's concluding speech at the CCP Seventh National Congress on May 31, 1945, in CCP Central Archives comps., *Zhonggong zhongyang wenjian xuanji, 1921–1949* [Selected Documents of the CCP Central Committee, 1921–1949] (Beijing: Zhonggong zhongyang dangxiao [CCP Central Party Academy Press], 1989–1992), 15: 98–106.

13 Zhang Guanghua, "The Secret Records of China's Important Decisions to Assist Vietnam and Resist France," in *Zhongguo junshi guwentuan yuanyue kangfa shilu: dangshiren de huiyi* [The Records of the CMAG in Assisting Vietnam and Resisting France: Veterans' Accounts], ed. CMAG Compilation Team (Beijing: Zhonggong dangshi [CCP Party History Press], 2002), 25.

14 Xiaobing Li, "Truman and Taiwan: A U.S. Policy Change from Face to Faith," in *Northeast Asia and the Legacy of Harry S. Truman: Japan, China, and the Two Koreas*, ed. James I. Matray (Kirksville, MO: Truman State University Press, 2012), 122–123.

15 Li, *A History of the Modern Chinese Army*, 123, 125.

16 Military History Research Division, China Academy of Military Science (CAMS), *Zhongguo renmin jiefangjun de qishinian, 1927–1997* [Seventy Years of the PLA, 1927–1997] (Beijing: Junshi kexue [Military Science Press], 1997), 455, 461.

17 Zhang Aiping, *Zhongguo renmin jiefangjun* [The Chinese People's Liberation Army] (Beijing: Dangdai zhongguo [Contemporary China Press], 1994), 1: 540.

18 The Soviet Union delivered weapons to China for sixteen infantry divisions in 1951 and for forty-four divisions in 1952–1954. See: Marshal Xu Xiangqian, "The Purchase of Arms from Moscow," in *Mao's Generals Remember Korea*, trans. and eds. Xiaobing Li, Allan R. Millett, and Bin Yu (Lawrence: University Press of Kansas, 2000), 140–142.

19 Li, *A History of the Modern Chinese Army*, 127.

20 Fairbank and Goldman, *China*, 350.

21 Xiaobing Li, "Chinese Communist Party," in *China at War*, ed. Xiaobing Li (Santa Barbara, CA: ABC-CLIO, 2012), 58–63.

22 Li, *Modern China*, 99–101.

23 Xiaobing Li, "The Dragon's Tale: China's Efforts toward the Rule of Law," in *Modern Chinese Legal Reform: New Perspectives*, eds. Xiaobing Li and Qiang Fang (Lexington: University Press of Kentucky, 2013), 87.
24 Xiaobing Li, *Civil Liberties in China* (Santa Barbara, CA: ABC-CLIO, 2010), 8–9.
25 According to governmental records, 2,987 NPC delegates were elected in China by February 27, 2013, and thirteen special delegated were from Taiwan, totaling 3,000 delegates.
26 In fact, the People's Assessors System did not formalize in the new republic until September 1951 when the "provisional Regulations for the Structure of People's Court Organization" were stipulated.
27 Li, Millett, and Yu, trans. and eds., *Mao's Generals Remember Korea*, 3–5.
28 Yi Sun and Xiaobing Li, "Mao Zedong and the CCP: Adaptation, Centralization, and Succession," in *Evolution of Power: China's Struggle, Survival, and Success*, eds. Xiaobing Li and Xiansheng Tian (Lanham, MD: Lexington Books, 2014), 39.
29 Li, *Civil Liberties in China*, 5–7.
30 Xiaobing Li and Qiang Fang, "Introduction: Legal Reforms in Twentieth-century China," in *Modern Chinese Legal Reform: New Perspective*, eds. Xiaobing Li and Qiang Fang (Lexington: University Press of Kentucky, 2013), 10.
31 Jonathan D. Spence, *The Search for Modern China*, 3rd ed. (New York: Norton, 2013), 512.
32 Jieli Li, "In Transformation toward Socio-Legality with Chinese Characteristics," in *Modern Chinese Legal Reform: New Perspective*, eds. Xiaobing Li and Qiang Fang (Lexington: University Press of Kentucky, 2013): 115–116.
33 "Foreign Relations: Two Decisions," *Time Magazine*, January 2, 1950, 11–12.
34 US Department of State, "Military Situation in the Far East: Policy Memorandum of Formosa, December 23, 1949," *Hearings before the Committees on Armed Services and on Foreign Relations*, Senate, 82nd Congress, First Session (Washington, DC: Government Printing Office, 1951), part iii, 1667–1669.
35 Zhang Guanghua. "The Secret Records of China's Important Decisions to Assist Vietnam and Resist France," in *Zhongguo junshi guwentuan yuanyue kangfa shilu: dangshiren de huiyi* [The Records of the Chinese Military Advisory Group (CMAG) in Assisting Vietnam and Resisting France: Personal Accounts of the Veterans], ed. Compilation Team (Beijing: Zhonggong dangshi [CCP Party History Press], 2002), 18.
36 US Department of State, *State Department Bulletin* xxii, no. 551 (January 23, 1950), 116.
37 Doak Barnett, *China and the Major Powers in East Asia* (Washington, DC: Brookings Institution, 1977), 223–224.
38 Shuguang Zhang, "Revolution, Security, and Deterrence: The Origins of Sino-American Relations, 1948–1950," in *Chinese Historians* 3, no. 1 (January 1990), 22.
39 David Finkelstein, *Washington's Taiwan Dilemma, 1949–1950: From Abandonment to Salvation* (Fairfax, VA: George Mason University Press, 1993), 208.
40 Finkelstein, *ibid.*, 332–333.
41 NSC Document, No. 68, 1950, in US Department of State, *FRUS, 1950, National Security Affairs: Foreign Economic Policy* (Washington, DC: Government Printing Office, 1977), 1: 237, 252–253, 262–263, 264, 282, 290.
42 Nancy Bernkopf Tucker, *Strait Talk: United States-Taiwan Relations and the Crisis with China* (Cambridge, MA: Harvard University Press, 2009), 13.
43 Truman to the Secretary of State, February 16, 1951; Truman to the Secretary of Defense, February 16, 1951; and "Memorandum for the President, February 16, 1951," in Mutual Defense File, *Papers of Harry S. Truman*, Box 26, Truman Library.
44 Truman to the Secretary of State, May 4, 1951; Truman to the Secretary of Defense, May 4, 1951; and "Memorandum for the President: Request for Allocation of Mutual Defense Assistance [MDA] Funds to Provide Additional Military Assistance to Formosa, May 3, 1951," in Mutual Defense File, Folder 4, Confidential File, *ibid.*
45 US Department of State, *FRUS, 1951*, 6: 37–38.
46 Karl Lott Rankin, *China Assignment* (Seattle, WA: University of Washington, 1964), 174.
47 Zuohong Pan, "Democracy and Economic Growth: A Taiwan Case Study," in *Taiwan in the Twenty-First Century*, eds. Xiaobing Li and Zuohong Pan (New York: University of America Press, 2003), 144.
48 US Department of State, *FRUS, 1951*, 6: 37–38.

49 For more details about the financial and economic aid, see Air Pouch 181, October 14, 1954, 794a, 5-MSP/1054, RG, *National Archives.*

50 John F. Copper, *Taiwan: Nation-State or Province?* 4th ed. (Boulder, CO: Westview, 2003), 47.

51 For more detailed discussions, see: Chen, *Mao's China and the Cold War,* 2–5.

52 Chen and Li, "China and the End of the Global Cold War," 120.

53 For example, Mao, "Address to the Preparatory Meeting of the New Political Consultative Conference," *Mao Zedong xuanji* [Selected Works of Mao Zedong] (Beijing: Renmin [People's Press], 1991), 4: 1447, 1465–1466.

54 Xiaobing Li, "PLA Attacks and Amphibious Operations during the Taiwan Straits Crises of 1954–1955 and 1958," in *Chinese Warfighting: the PLA Experience since 1949*, eds. Mark A. Ryan, David M. Finkelstein, and Michael A. McDevitt (New York: M. E. Sharpe, 2003), 148.

55 GMD and CIA officers on the scene were surprised by the timing of the artillery shelling. See CIA, "Report on the Chinese Offshore Islands Situation, September 9, 1954," CIA Official File, 50318-Formosa (1), box 9, International Series, Dwight D. *Eisenhower Papers.* Dwight D. Eisenhower Library, Abilene, Kansas.

56 Han Huaizhi, *Dangdai Zhongguo jundui de junshi gongzuo* [Contemporary Chinese Military Affairs] (Beijing: Zhongguo shehui kexue [China's Social Science Press], 1989), 1: 216–217.

57 Jiang Weiguo (Chiang Wei-kuo), son of Jiang Jieshi, and adoptive brother of Jiang Jingguo (Jiang Ching-kuo), President of the ROC from 1978–1988, interview by the author at Rongzong [Glory's General] Hospital in Taipei, Taiwan, on May 25–27, 1994.

58 Thomas J. Christensen, *Useful Adversaries: Grand Strategy, Domestic Mobilization, and Sino-American Conflict, 1947–1958* (Princeton, NJ: Princeton University Press, 1996), 60, 194.

59 In February 1955, the Seventh Fleet deployed aircraft carriers, cruisers, and up to forty destroyers, to cover the evacuation of the Dachens. *New York Times,* January 25 and February 7, 1955.

60 "Memorandum of Discussion at the 232nd NSC Meeting, January 20, 1955," *FRUS, 1955–1957,* 2: 70–71.

61 Gordon H. Chang, "To the Nuclear Brink: Eisenhower, Dulles, and the Quemoy-Matsu Crisis," *International Security* 12, no. 4, (Spring 1988): 106.

62 Xinhua News Agency, *China's Foreign Relations: A Chronology of Events, 1949–1988* (Beijing: Foreign Languages Press, 1989), 525.

63 Pan, "Democracy and Economic Growth: A Taiwan Case Study," 146.

64 Copper, *Taiwan: Nation-State or Province?,* 48.

65 Linda Chao and Ramon H. Myers, *The First Chinese Democracy: Political Life in the Republic of China on Taiwan* (Baltimore, DE: The Johns Hopkins University Press, 1998), introduction.

Part II
The East vs. the West

6 The Korean War (1950–1953)

[handwritten annotation: not ↑ v. ↓ Koren war was US v. Soviet (China)]

The Korean War was a watershed conflict within the Cold War. It was the first shooting war and also the first limited war of the nuclear age. The Korean War was a formal benchmark for the opening of the military conflict between the United States and the Soviet Union. It represented a serious international challenge to both the world communist movement and Western democracy. From the early stage of the conflict, the war ceased to be a civil war between the North and South Koreas to unify the divided country, and instead became a "proxy" war representing the two sides of the Communist East-Capitalist West rivalry. The fact that President Truman justified US involvement by claiming the necessity to prevent a third world war sufficiently illustrated the US disposition toward the war. The US government was determined to make a point by displaying its will and military might to its communist adversary.

General Douglas MacArthur and United Nations Command (UNC) not only failed to prepare for the sudden intervention of the Chinese Communist forces in the war, but also refused to believe that Beijing would not or could not operate independently of Moscow against the US forces. In October 1950, China sent its army, in Mao Zedong's words, to "resist America, aid Korea, defend the homeland, and safeguard the country (*Kangmei yuanchao, baojia weiguo*)."[1] Over the next three years, over 3.1 million Chinese troops fought US-led UN Forces (UNF), in reality making the Korean War a conflict between China and the United States, which provided 90 percent of the UNF. Mao's decision to send Chinese troops into the Korean War had been widely debated. The Chinese intervention was by no means a simple miscalculation but rather a manifestation of complex regional politics that preordained the unique outcome of the conflict. Facing vastly superior fire-power, China suffered 1,027,146 casualties.

China's intervention secured its northeastern borders, strengthened Sino-Soviet relations, and saved the North Korean regime. China acted as a major military power for the first time since the Opium War against Britain in 1840. However, some historians in China, and many more in America, challenge this "wise-decision" argument and condemn Mao for gross misjudgments and an "idiosyncratic audacity" that cost the lives of hundreds of thousands of Chinese soldiers.[2] Modern Chinese history, however, has demonstrated that neither foreign invasion, nor support of an international power, could create a strong, centralized national government. Instead, power status depended more on China's political stability and its military strength than on its foreign relations. In this sense, by entering the Korean War, it is possible that Mao perceived his chance to continue the communist movement at home and to project New China's power image abroad. His strategic priorities included establishing the legitimacy the CCP needed as the ruling party; national security through winning the last battle of the

Chinese Civil War against the GMD on Taiwan; an economic recovery; and military modernization. His decision may also have been based on the PLA's superiority in manpower, giving Mao and his generals overconfidence in their capacity to drive the UNF out of the Korean Peninsula.

Two Koreas (1945–1950)

Controlled by Japan in 1910–1945, Korea was divided in half after WWII. Wartime agreements called for the United States to temporarily occupy Southern Korea up to the 38th Parallel, while the Soviet Union did the same north of that line under the US-Soviet Joint Commission as the international trusteeship. On September 9, 1945, US General John R. Hodge (1893–1963) set up his military occupation command in Seoul. American soldiers were warmly received by the Koreans as their saviors. In spite of good intentions, harmony was absent between the occupiers and the occupied from the outset of the new era. The Korean people, underestimating the formidable task they had to overcome, were only too eager in hoping that America would provide quick and constructive guidelines for a new era of nation building. Moreover, Koreans were scarcely informed about the developing international power politics from which the new nation could not depart from regardless of its preference. Hodge's occupation command was interested in helping the new nation, but only under the framework of US post-war strategic interests.

Russian forces entered Northern Korea on August 10, 1945, only five days before the Japanese surrender. Scoring a rapid advance against retreating Japanese forces, the Russians managed to occupy most of Northern Korea's major cities by August 24. Unlike the American forces that were not able to reach Korea until the early part of September, Russian forces fought against Japanese forces on Korean soil, even though Japanese resistance was generally light. Nevertheless, the Russians entered Korea not only as victors of the Pacific War, but also as comrades-in-war to the Koreans and were received favorably by the Korean public. Russians squandered no time in implementing their extensive programs to establish a Communist society in northern Korea.

The Russian occupation in the North remained largely behind the scenes from the beginning. Although their domination in the North should have been nearly absolute, Russia managed the occupation chores largely through its Korean allies, the Korean Communist Party. Russia's sensitive scheme was effective in re-establishing the badly-mangled social order while protecting the public image of the Russian occupation command. The Russians successfully projected themselves as liberators of Korea in the North, a notable success in comparison to America's policies that left the South still struggling under extreme political uncertainty. The Russians were confident of their capacity to earn the respect of the Korean people and eager to engage in a political game against their counterparts in the South. Russia's most pronounced success in the early period of its occupation of Northern Korea was extensive land reforms, which were greatly aided by the peculiar socioeconomic structure of the northern half.

The Cold War brought the permanent division of Korea into two states. Bruce Cumings states that:

> The political and ideological divisions that we associate with the Cold War were the reasons for Korea's division; they came early to Korea, before the onset of the global Cold War, and today they outlast the end of the Cold War everywhere else.[3]

Efforts to establish a unified Korea failed, and in September 1947 the United States referred the issue to the UN, which called for a unified Korean government and the withdrawal of occupation forces. In January 1948, Soviet authorities refused to permit a UN commission to oversee elections in Northern Korea, but elections for an assembly proceeded in Southern Korea that spring. By August 1948, the ROK had officially formed with its capital at Seoul and was headed by seventy-year-old Syngman Rhee, a staunch conservative.[4] Washington then terminated its military government and agreed to train South Korea's armed forces. In September 1948, the Communists formed the Democratic People's Republic of Korea (DPRK) with its capital at Pyongyang and led by veteran communist Kim Il-sung. Kim had fought the Japanese occupation and ended WWII as a major in the Soviet Army. The United States withdrew all its troops from South Korea by June 1949.

Syngman Rhee was well known among Koreans associated with independence movements, although he had not been in Korea for more than twenty years prior to his return home in September 1945. He thus had not had an opportunity to build a political power base or a large number of followers within Korea until his return. As a result, for the public, he was more of a legendary figure associated with the faraway nation of America. His superb educational achievement, a doctoral degree from Princeton University, and long exposure to Washington politics made him a strong contender for the political leadership of the new nation under American tutelage. The ruling class of the South that was dominated by Rhee and the conservative Korean Democratic Party (KDP) were never too eager to take genuine steps needed to unite the South with their Communist brothers in the North. They would have been receptive to do so only under their own terms. Being fiercely political and typically divisive, they were capable of settling for a short-term advantage even at the expense of long-term national interests. Moreover, a speedy Sovietization of North Korea might have convinced the rightist leaders in the South that a compromise was impractical.

Unlike Rhee in the South, Kim Il-sung was largely unknown except for his legendary name. He was believed to be a young, anti-Japanese guerrilla leader who at times commanded several hundred guerrilla fighters. Considering the extremely limited number of Koreans fighting the Japanese during the 1930s–1940s, his force still might have been one of the most active Korean resistance movements. Kim joined the Chinese Communist Party in the 1930s and served some years as an officer in the Soviet Red Army in WWII. He was introduced to the North Korean public on October 14, 1945. Political consolidation developed much faster in the North than in the South. The credit for the success in the North, however, did not solely belong to the Russian occupation command, but also to the Korean Communists. Kim was pursuing a separate government in the North as early as 1946 when the Provisional People's Committee for North Korea was established with him as its chairman. Having set up a governmental structure, the Communists drafted a constitution in November 1947. The election for the Supreme People's Assembly was held on August 25, 1948, and the new constitution was ratified by the assembly on September 8. Kim was named premier of the DPRK on September 10. Thus, two Koreas emerged from the occupied zones, sponsored by respective powers, although the support given to Kim and Rhee was by no means identical.

Beginning in 1948, sporadic fighting began along the 38th Parallel. Kim planned to use his military superiority to invade and quickly conquer South Korea. Twice he consulted Soviet leader Josef Stalin, promising him victory in a matter of weeks, assuring him that there would be a Communist revolution in South Korea, and insisting that Washington would not intervene.[5] North Korea was actively preparing for the invasion as early as the spring of 1949, and Russian military advisors assisted in its planning. Stalin pledged military assistance but not direct Soviet military involvement. He also insisted that Kim meet with PRC leader Mao Zedong and secure his assent to the plans. In late 1949, Mao released the PLA 164th and 166th Divisions of Korean volunteers who had fought against the Japanese and in the Chinese Civil War, providing North Korea with 30,000–40,000 seasoned troops.[6]

Northern invasion and the UNF Inchon landing (1950)

On June 25, 1950, North Korea, or the DPRK, launched a surprise attack on South Korea, which signaled the beginning of the Korean War as a civil war. The invading divisions, the North Korean People's Army (NKPA), equipped with Russian-made tanks and heavy artilleries quickly threw the South into chaotic confusion. The northern Communist troops captured Seoul in four days, forcing the Rhee government to flee the capital city. The UN Security Council called for an immediate cease-fire and the withdrawal of North Korean forces, a resolution that went unchallenged because of a Soviet UN boycott. Nonetheless, the military situation deteriorated daily as the invasion columns encountered only token resistance. It was evident that the South possessed neither manpower nor equipment to stop the invaders.

On June 27, the Security Council asked UN member states to furnish assistance to South Korea. Truman also extended US air and naval operations to include North Korea and authorized US Army troops to protect the port of Pusan. Upon MacArthur's recommendation, Truman committed US Far Eastern ground forces to Korea on June 30.[7] At the request of the UN Security Council, the UN set up a military command in Korea on July 7. Washington insisted on a US commander, and on July 10 Truman appointed MacArthur to head the UNC. Seventeen nations contributed military assistance, and at peak strength UNC forces numbered about 400,000 South Korean troops, 250,000 US troops, and 35,000 troops from other nations. Two British and Canadian units formed the First Commonwealth Division. Turkey provided a brigade, and there were troops from Australia, Thailand, the Philippines, Colombia, Ethiopia, France, Greece, Belgium, Luxembourg, the Netherlands, and New Zealand. Other nations provided medical units.[8]

By mid-July UNC troops had been pushed back into the so-called Pusan Perimeter, an area of thirty to fifty miles around the vital port of Pusan on the southeastern coast of Korea. The NKPA failed to employ its early manpower advantage to mount simultaneous attacks along the entire perimeter. By the middle of August, after mostly uninterrupted retreat and futile resistance, the UNF and their ROK Army were able to muster enough strength to stall the advancing columns; they finally secured a precious redoubt from which they could regroup and wage counterattacks. On August 31, Kim launched his last offensive campaign against the UNC stronghold at Pusan. At that point, the NKPA had suffered 58,000 casualties and lost 120 of the 150 Russian-made tanks and one-third of its artillery pieces in the previous two months.[9] After his failure, Kim could not launch another major attack. On September 10, the UNF and ROK forces launched their first major counter-offensive. Even as the battle for the Pusan Perimeter raged, MacArthur was planning an amphibious assault behind enemy lines. The Inchon landing was a risky venture, and few besides MacArthur favored it.

On September 15, MacArthur successfully landed American troops behind the North Korean forces at Inchon, rapidly changing the military situation in Korea. The NKPA's offensive quickly collapsed. Among the 70,000 American troops, Major General Edward Almond's X Corps of the First Marine Division and the Seventh Infantry Division commenced the invasion. Supported by naval gunfire and air attacks, the Marines secured Inchon with relatively few casualties. UNC forces re-entered Seoul on September 24.[10] At the same time, the US Eighth Army, having survived the precarious seizure, broke out of the Pusan Perimeter and drove north, linking up with X Corps on September 26. Only one-quarter to one-third of the NKPA escaped north of the 38th Parallel. On September 28, the UNF re-took Seoul. The same day, Kim issued a new order to all the North Korean troops to slow down the enemy offensive, save the main part of the NKPA, and organize a strategic withdrawal to the North.

Soon the advancing UNF faced a momentous decision on whether or not to expand operations north of the 38th Parallel. Yet taking measures of precaution, the United States chose an all-out assault on the North Korean forces. On October 1, South Korean troops crossed the 38th Parallel into North Korea. On October 7, the UN General Assembly passed a resolution calling for a unified, independent, and democratic Korea, and two days later MacArthur ordered US forces across the 38th Parallel. In a meeting with Truman at Wake Island on October 15, MacArthur had assured the president that the war was about won but that if the Chinese were to intervene, their forces would be slaughtered. UNC airpower, he believed, would nullify any Chinese threat.[11] Pyongyang fell on October 19 as stunned NKPA forces fled north. The Eighth Army crossed the Chongchon River at Sinanju, and by November 1 elements of the 24th Division were only eighteen miles from the Yalu. Several days earlier a South Korean unit had reached the Yalu, the only UNC unit to get there.

After asking the Soviet Union for help, Kim proposed to Soviet leader Josef Stalin that China should send troops to Korea. After careful consideration, on October 5, Mao, chairman of the CCP, and the Politburo of the CCP Central Committee decided to send Chinese troops to Korea.

China's intervention (1950–1953)

From the moment the "new China" came into being, Beijing's leaders regarded the United States as China's primary enemy while, at the same time, consistently declaring that a fundamental aim of the Chinese revolution was to destroy the "old" world order dominated by US imperialists.[12] Through endless propaganda campaigns and constant indoctrination efforts, Beijing portrayed the United States as the bastion of all reactionary forces in the world.[13] For almost two decades, the United States had been thoroughly demonized in Chinese popular image. As a result, in Mao's efforts to legitimize his "continuous revolution," the theme of "struggling against US imperialism" had occupied a central position. Chen explains the Mao revolution's international aim as to supposedly serve as a "constant source of domestic mobilization, helping to legitimatize the revolution at home and to maintain its momentum."[14]

As early as July 1950, the situation in Korea was beginning to worry Mao.[15] Between July 7 and 22, Beijing mobilized forces in Northeast China, or Manchuria, leading to an important strategic shift from defense towards intervention by early August. Alarmed over possible US bases adjacent to Manchuria, Mao had issued warnings about potential Chinese military intervention. He believed that the United States would be unable to counter the Chinese numerical advantage and viewed American troops as soft and unused to night fighting. MacArthur's Inchon landing and the collapse of the NKPA led to accelerated military preparations and serious policy debates among the top leaders in early October. Eventually, all these culminated on October 4 in a final decision to commit Chinese troops to Korea.

According to Mao's Cold War theory, a clash between China and the United States would inevitably occur sooner or later. The Chinese military should thus have its own initiative, advantage, and alternative prior to this inevitable conflict. In the 1950s, the United States intruded into, and threatened, China's security in three areas: Korea, Vietnam, and the Taiwan Strait. Concerned with the geopolitics, regional economy, and transportation capacity of these three areas of conflict, the Chinese believed America's intervention in Korea was the most critical threat to the new regime. Mao described American involvements in those three areas as similar to three knives around China's body: America in Korea was like a knife over her head; America in Taiwan was one around her waist; and Vietnam was one on her feet.[16] Thus, Korea was considered the most immediate threat. Therefore, Korea was chosen as the first place for China to fight against the United States.[17]

On the same day, Mao informed Stalin that China would enter the war. Stalin agreed to move Soviet MiG-15 fighters already in China to the Korean border. In this position they could cover the Chinese military buildup and prevent US air attacks on Manchuria. Soviet pilots began flying missions against UNC forces on November 1 and bore the brunt of the Communists' air war. Stalin also ordered other Soviet air units to deploy to China, train Chinese pilots, and then turn over aircraft to them.[18]

On October 8, Mao created the Chinese People's Volunteers Force (CPVF). By using the name "volunteers," the Chinese leaders expected to convince the world that the CPVF was not organized by the Chinese government. By officially entering Korea, China risked full-blown war with the United States and sixteen additional countries that had joined the UNF and theoretically could invade China. In fact, the "volunteer" soldiers were Chinese regular troops, commanded by Chinese officers. Mao's and the Party Center's role represented unprecedented activism in the Korean War; China was no longer playing a minute, passive spectator, or an adjunct, in world-power politics. This innovative vigor of internationalism revealed a profound change taking place in New China.

The first echelon of Chinese forces – three infantry armies and three artillery divisions, a total of approximately 260,000 troops – entered North Korea on October 19, 1950. China kept its military intervention secret, and not until November would the PRC publicly acknowledge that Chinese forces had entered Korea to assist North Koreans in repelling the American invasion. By late November, China had made a sizable commitment to Korea – thirty-three divisions, totaling more than 450,000 men.[19] On November 8 the first jet battle in history occurred when an American F-80 shot down a MiG-15 over Sinanju.

Beginning in October 1950, the CPVF launched the first of its "Five Offensive Campaigns" against UN/US forces in Korea. This rapid and unexpected development surprised American generals. The CPVF's sheer numbers enabled the Chinese to overcome their inferiority in equipment and technology. In the First Phase Campaign, from October 25 to November 7, the CPVF stopped the UNF's northward advance and stabilized the situation for North Korea for the first time since the Inchon landing.

The initial Chinese intervention had consisted of eighteen volunteer divisions. In early November they moved an additional twelve divisions into Korea, totaling some

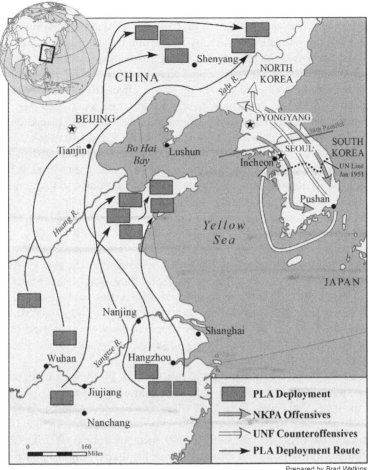

Prepared by Brad Watkins

Map 6.1 The Korean War

300,000 men. MacArthur responded by ordering the air force to destroy the bridges over the Yalu. Washington revoked the order, but MacArthur complained that this threatened his command. Washington gave in. On November 8, 79 B-29s and 300 fighter-bombers struck bridges and towns on either side of the Yalu. The bombing had little effect. At the time most of the Chinese were in North Korea, and the Yalu was soon frozen.

In the Second Offensive Campaign, from November 25 to December 24, the Chinese recaptured Pyongyang and pushed the battle line back to the 38th Parallel. During their Third and Fourth Offensive Campaigns between January and March of 1951, the CPVF crossed the 38th Parallel into South Korea, took Seoul, the capital city of South Korea, and pushed UNF south to the 37th Parallel. By mid-April, the Chinese had 950,000 troops in Korea, including forty-seven infantry divisions, eight artillery divisions, and four anti-aircraft artillery divisions.[20] MacArthur seemed oblivious to any problems, seeing the advance as an occupation rather than an offensive. It went well on the first day. On the night of November 25, the Chinese attacked the Eighth Army in force.[21] The Americans held, but on November 26 the South Korean II Corps disintegrated, exposing UNF's right flank. The Chinese poured eighteen divisions into the gap, endangering the whole Eighth Army. In a brilliant delaying action at Kunu-ri, the US Second Division bought time for the other divisions to re-cross the Chongchon. MacArthur now ordered a retirement just below the 38th Parallel to protect Seoul.

The Korean War had entered a new phase: in effect, the UNC was now fighting China. MacArthur refused to accept a limited war and publicized his views to his supporters in the United States, making reference to "inhibitions" placed on his conduct of the war. UNC morale plummeted, especially with General Walker's death in a jeep accident on December 22. Not until Lieutenant General Matthew Ridgway arrived to replace Walker did the situation improve. In the United States, Truman found himself under heavy pressure from Republicans to pursue the war vigorously. But the administration reduced its goal in Korea to restoring the status quo *ante bellum*.

UNC forces again had to retreat when the Chinese launched a New Year's offensive, retaking Seoul on January 4.[22] But the Chinese outran their supply lines, and Ridgway took the offensive. His methodical, limited advance was designed to inflict maximum punishment rather than to secure territory. Nonetheless, by the end of March, UNC forces recaptured Seoul, and by the end of April they were again north of the 38th Parallel. On April 11, 1951, Truman relieved MacArthur of command, appointing Ridgway in his stead. Although widely unpopular at the time, MacArthur's removal was fully supported by the JCS, as MacArthur had publicly expressed his disdain of limited war. He returned home to a hero's welcome, but much to his dismay, political support for him promptly faded.

On April 22 the Chinese counterattacked in Korea. Of all these campaigns the Chinese Fifth Phase Offensive, or the Spring Offensive Campaign, proved the most decisive. Lasting from April 22 through June 2, 1951, it was the largest and longest Communist military operation of the war, as well as the largest battle since WWII. The CPVF-NKPA Joint Command deployed more than 700,000 men, including 600,000 CPVF troops, against 340,000 UNF troops. As Marshal Peng Dehuai (P'eng Te-huai), chief of the CPVF-NKPA Joint Command, anticipated, "this is the battle [that] will determine the fate of the Korean War."[23] The CPVF Spring Offensive failed. The UNF put up a strong defense, drove the Communists back north of the 38th Parallel, and inflicted 105,000 casualties. After the Chinese failure in this one-million-men battle, the war settled into a stalemate and a more conventional pattern of trench warfare along the 38th Parallel. The Chinese pushed the UNC south of the 38th Parallel, but the offensive was halted by May 19.[24] UNC forces then counterpunched, and by the end of May the front stabilized just above the 38th Parallel.

Ridgway, commander in chief of the UNF Command after MacArthur's dismissal, launched several offensives designed to destroy CPVF-NKPA personnel and supplies while also building confidence and fighting skills in the UNF during the early spring of 1951. Lieutenant General James A. Van Fleet (1892–1992), commander of the US Eighth Army, consolidated the supply line and emphasized training of the ROK divisions.[25]

After the Chinese forces lost their Spring Offensive Campaign, the Communists never again came so close to Seoul, nor mounted another major southward incursion of such magnitude. Their defeat forced Mao to reconsider both his political and military aims. Realizing the huge gap between Chinese capabilities and the ambitious aim of driving the UNF from the peninsula, the Chinese leadership became willing to accept a settlement without total victory. The Chinese Spring Offensive Campaign was the turning point that not only shaped the rest of the war, but also led to truce negotiations in July 1951.

From trench warfare to the cease-fire (1951–1953)

The war was now stalemated, and a diplomatic settlement seemed expedient. On June 23, 1951 Soviet UN representative Yakov Malik proposed a cease-fire. With the Chinese expressing interest, Truman authorized Ridgway to negotiate. Meetings began on July 10 at Kaesong, although hostilities would continue until an armistice was signed.[26]

UNC operations from this point were essentially designed to minimize friendly casualties. Each side had built deep defensive lines that would be costly to break through. In August armistice talks broke down, and later that month the Battle of Bloody Ridge began, developing into the Battle of Heartbreak Ridge that lasted until mid-October. In late October negotiations resumed, this time at Panmunjom, although the fighting continued. Half of the war's casualties occurred during the period of armistice negotiations.[27] By 1952, Chinese forces in Korea had grown to a record high of 1.45 million men, including fifty-nine infantry divisions and fifteen artillery divisions.

In November 1952 General Dwight Eisenhower was elected president of the United States on a mandate to end the war. With US casualties running 2,500 a month, the war had become a political liability. Eisenhower instructed the JCS to draw up plans to end the war militarily including the possible use of nuclear weapons, which was made known to the Communist side. More important in ending the conflict, however, was Stalin's death on March 5, 1953. As the armistice negotiations entered their final phase in May, the Chinese stepped up military action, initiating attacks in June and July to remove bulges in the line. UNC forces gave up some ground but inflicted heavy casualties.

Their military operations and tactics reflect the Chinese view of war. The security concerns, strategic decisions, and consistency through war-fighting experience illustrate Chinese methods for conducting a war. Some of their methods were holistic, effective, flexible, and as successful as others in the West. Scholars in Europe and America have studied the 2,500-year Chinese warfare and military thoughts, including Sunzi's (Sun-Tzu) classic *The Art of War* and Mao's views on guerrilla warfare.[28] Mao's military theories, drawing heavily on ancient classics like Sunzi's book, remain a vital component of the Chinese military history and expertise. Mao's generals recognized the traditional form or style of Chinese warfare.[29] In comparison to the West, Chinese experience offers a mixed picture. Countless parallels can be drawn between the CPVF and UNF in the Korean War.[30]

The chief stumbling block to peace was the repatriation of POWs. The North Koreans had forced into their army many South Korean soldiers and civilians, and thousands of them had subsequently been captured by the UNC. If all NKPA prisoners were repatriated, many South Koreans would be sent to North Korea. Also, many Chinese POWs sought refuge on Taiwan (Formosa) instead of returning to the PRC.[31] Truman was determined that no prisoner be repatriated against his will. This stance prolonged the war, but some US officials saw a moral and propaganda victory in the Chinese and North Korean defections. The Communist side rejected the UNC position out of hand.

Following intense UNC air strikes on North Korean hydroelectric facilities and the capital of Pyongyang, the Communists accepted a face-saving formula whereby a neutral commission would deal with prisoner repatriation. On July 27, an armistice was signed at Panmunjom, and the guns finally fell silent.

Of 132,000 North Korean and Chinese military POWs, fewer than 90,000 chose to return home. Twenty-two Americans held by the Communists also elected not to return home. Of 10,218 Americans captured by the Communists, only 3,746 returned. The remainder were murdered or died in captivity. American losses were 142,091, of whom 33,686 were killed in action. South Korea sustained 300,000 casualties, of whom 70,000 were killed in action. Other UNC casualties came to 17,260, of whom 3,194 were killed in action. North Korean casualties are estimated at 523,400 and Chinese losses at more than a million.[32] Perhaps three million Korean civilians also died during the war.

China gained greatly from the war in that it came to be regarded as the preponderant military power in Asia. This is ironic, because the Chinese Army in Korea was in many respects a primitive and inefficient force. Nonetheless, throughout the following decades exaggeration of Chinese military strength was woven into the fabric of American foreign policy, influencing subsequent US policy in Vietnam.

The Korean War effectively militarized the containment policy. Before the war, Marshall Plan aid had been almost entirely non-military. US aid now shifted heavily toward military rearmament. The war also marked a sustained militarization of American foreign policy, with the Vietnam War a logical consequence. Additionally, the Korean War solidified the role of the United States as the world's policeman and strengthened the country's relationship with its West European allies and NATO. The war facilitated the rearmament of West Germany. It also impacted Japan and was a major factor fueling that nation's economy.

Post-war Koreas (1954–1968)

The war devastated Korea and hardened the divisions between North and South. No formal peace has ever been concluded in Korea. Technically, the two Koreas remain at war, and the 38th Parallel remains one of the Cold War's lone outposts. It was also a sobering experience for the United States. After the war, the US military establishment remained strong. For America, the Korean War institutionalized the Cold War national security state. It also accelerated the racial integration of the armed forces, which in turn encouraged a much wider US civil rights movement.

The armistice was expected to signal the return of the region's pre-war external equilibrium, a standoff between two superpowers. Yet the war introduced an element that quickly proved to be a significant barrier in the North's return to its pre-war external relations: the Soviet Union's overwhelming influence. The rise of the political leverage of Communist China in North Korea, a direct result of its effective military intervention in the Korean War, was to complicate North Korea's external relations and to some notable extent the post-war relations of the two communist giants in the region. It was an interesting turn of events that the conflict facilitated by the rivalry between two occidental powers had enabled China to emerge as a threat to the Soviet Union's influence in North Korea. As post-war North Korea was obliged to accommodate the rising prestige of Communist China, its closest comrade-in-arms during the war, the Soviet Union, lost some of its preeminent influence in North Korea. In that sense, North Korea's problematic relations with its two powerful communist neighbors were preordained when Chinese troops crossed the Yalu River in late 1950.

The Soviet Union continued to be North Korea's primary source of economic and military support during the post-war period. It was still the only power capable of providing political support for the Pyongyang regime on the international stage.

Although Kim ruthlessly removed his major domestic political rivals, his control of the Communist Party was anything but complete. His vindictive purge of pro-Soviet and pro-China factions in the party and governmental hierarchies continued for some time. In spite of his crafty and brutal drive for absolute control of North Korea, his leadership was often challenged by determined adversaries who still had strong ties with the Chinese or the Russians. The flow of foreign aid to North Korea was by no means adequate for its herculean tasks. Worse yet, it started to dwindle quickly. In addition, the North's wavering stand in the Sino-Soviet rivalry in the late 1950s had a direct impact on the amount of foreign aid the nation was receiving. The generosity of fellow communist brothers was contingent on Pyongyang's political submission to the Soviet Union. Even under such pressing circumstances, however, Kim and his colleagues displayed their extreme uneasiness for taking sides with either of the two contending communist superpowers.

Instead, Kim Il-sung elected to pursue the policy of *Juche*, an ideology of independence and self-reliance that includes the doctrine of *Jaju* (political independence), *Jarip* (economic self-sustenance), and *Jawi* (military self-defense).[33] In essence, Kim had declared ideological independence from his chief and dominating benefactors in 1958 and, simultaneously, had made it clear to the masses of North Korea that their economic recovery had to be completed through their own hard work and sacrifice. Dae-Sook Suh argues that the *Juche* idea is nothing more than xenophobic nationalism that has little ideological relevance to communism.[34] Regardless of its uncertain acceptability to the world socialist and communist movement, the declaration of the *Juche* ideology was a momentous development for the Korean nation. It was fresh and highly symbolic for this nation that had historically been dominated by its stronger neighbors and was able to maintain its precarious survival only by adopting Sadaeism (open appeasement). Notwithstanding its outmoded nature in this increasingly interdependent world, the North Korean regime has maintained the idea of *Juche* as the national doctrine to date. (Pyongyang government refers to the doctrine as Kimilsungism, an effort to promote it as an idea invented by its leader.)

After the Korean War, the democratization in the South developed slowly against the military junta which dominated the politics in the 1950s and 1960s. President Rhee's efforts centered on securing Washington's economic as well political support, seen as critical to resuscitating the Republic of Korea's lethargic economy. Once the aid packages were arranged, however, he demanded that the United States allowed him discretionary power over the funds. His extensive dependency on the United States, which resulted both from choice and sheer necessity to compete against North Korea, did not mean that his rule was based on an American system. In reality, his brand of democracy in 1954–1960 was far from the one advocated by the United States. In spite of his familiarity and frequent contacts with that nation, he had been a poor student of the plural democratic system with which America was often identified. Still, the president was absolutely confident of his loyalty and ability to lead the troubled nation. Naturally, his authoritarian rule was of constant concern to the US; it was opposed by his vocal domestic rivals in the national assembly, whom Rhee did not hesitate to suppress by force.

On April 19, 1960, the presidential election in South Korea was swept by student demonstrations against Rhee's dictatorship. On April 26, Rhee announced his resignation, which ended his twelve-year rule and the domination of his Liberal Party. South Koreans placed expectations on the new ruling Democratic Party. However, the party had neither the experience nor the preparation to lead the nation. As political instability worsened, some of the nation's conservatives openly advocated military intervention.

In 1961, the South Korea military launched a coup, using national salvation as its sole justification. The generals portrayed themselves as saviors of the nation rather than as usurpers of power. Eager to salvage the country from chaotic social disorder and political drift, they immediately undertook a number of corrective measures in military fashion. Thus began the first period of South Korea's extensive military rule. In response to the Western criticism of its abolishment of a duly elected government, the military junta promised that a civilian government would be installed in mid-1963. Two years later the South Korean military complied with its own promise by transferring power to a civilian government as scheduled. However, the transfer of military rule to a civilian administration did not mean the military's withdrawal from politics. Instead, the military elite chose to remain the nation's ruling political force in the new civilian government. In the ensuing general election, the military leader General Park Chung-hee, was elected as the new president.

The Park administration's first and most urgent priority went to normalizing its relations with Japan. The junta realized that normalized relations with Japan were a matter of critical importance for South Korea in economic, diplomatic, and security dimensions. This was vital to America's strategic interests in the Far East. Washington had poured over $3 billion into South Korea's struggling economy in 1945–1964. In spite of this massive aid, however, the economy was still suffering from shortages, excessive unemployment, hyper-inflation, negligible growth performance, and increasing import dependency. By 1964, its GDP per capita income was about $104 and comparable with levels in the poorer countries of Africa and Asia. Washington actively pursued an avenue for placing South Korea under the joint efforts by the United States and Japan. On August 14, 1965, the National Assembly adopted the South Korea-Japan normalization bill. The Park government thus established a solid ground for its close cooperation with Japan in the economic sphere. The government began to emphasize industrial development in the late 1960s, with increasing importance placed on petroleum refining and the production of chemicals and fertilizers. By the 1970s, South Korea had achieved rapid economic growth with per capita income rising to seventeen times the level of North Korea. The government promoted the import of raw materials and energy sources, and focused on the exports of its manufacturing goods. Its exports, comprising half of its GDP, increased at the remarkable annual rate of 27.2 percent during the 1970s.

Notes

1 Mao's quote is from the following sources: Xu Yan, *Mao Zedong yu kangmei yuanchao zhanzheng* [Mao Zedong and the War to Resist the US and Aid Korea], 2nd edition (Beijing: Jiefangjun [PLA Press], 2006), 3; Shen Zhihua, "China Sends Troops to Korea: Beijing's Policy-making Process," in *China and the United States: A New Cold War History,* eds. Xiaobing Li and Hongshan Li (Lanham, MD: University Press of America, 1998), 13.
2 Andrew B. Kennedy, "Military Audacity: Mao Zedong, Liu Shaoqi, and China's Adventure in Korea," in *History and Neorealism*, eds. Ernest May, Richard Rosecrance, and Zara Steiner (Cambridge, UK: Cambridge University Press, 2010).
3 Bruce Cumings, *Korea's Place in the Sun: A Modern History* (New York: Norton, 1997), 186.
4 Cumings, *ibid.*, 211–212.

5 Xu, *Mao Zedong yu kangmei yuanchao zhanzheng* [Mao Zedong and the War to Resist the US and Aid Korea], 53–54.

6 Col. Lee Jong Kan, interview by the author in Harbin, Heilongjiang, in July 2002. Also see Lee, "A North Korean Officer's Story," in *Voices of the Korean War: Personal Stories of American, Korean, and Chinese Soldiers,* eds. Richard Peters and Xiaobing Li (Lexington: University Press of Kentucky, 2004), 76–84. Lee served as a battalion political commissar in the 33rd Regiment, Twenty-sixth Division of the North Korean People's Army in 1950.

7 Harry S. Truman, *Memoirs, Years of Trial and Hope*, vol. 2 (Garden City, NY: Doubleday, 1956), 335–340.

8 Max Hastings, *The Korean War* (New York: Simon and Schuster, 1987), 15–22, 58; Bevin Alexander, *Korea: The First War We Lost*, revised ed. (New York: Hippocrene Books, 1998), 32–45.

9 Lee, interview; Lee, "A North Korean Officer's Story," 81.

10 Roy E. Appleman, *South to the Naktong, North to the Yalu (June–November 1950), US Army in the Korean War* (Washington, DC: Office of the Chief of Military History and US Government Printing Office, 1961), 587, 600–604.

11 Allan R. Millett, *The War for Korea, 1950–1951: They Came from the North* (Lawrence: University Press of Kansas, 2010), 282–283.

12 For a more detailed discussion, see: Chen, *China's Road to the Korean War*, 63–69; Niu Jun, "The Origins of the Sino-Soviet Alliance," in *Brothers in Arms: The Rise and Fall of the Sino-Soviet Alliance, 1945–1963*, ed. Odd Arne Westad (Stanford, CA: Stanford University Press, 1998), 47–89.

13 Mao, "Report to the Second Plenary Session of the CCP Seventh Central Committee," *Mao Zedong xuanji* [Selected Works of Mao Zedong], 4: 1425–1426, 1428.

14 Chen, *China's Road to the Korean War*, 8.

15 Xu, *Mao Zedong yu kangmei yuanchao zhanzheng* [Mao Zedong and the War to Resist the US and Aid Korea], 64–65.

16 Mao's conversations with Wang Jifan and Zhou Shizhao on October 27, 1950, from the recollections of Wang Yuqing, grandson of Wang Jifan, in *Guandong zhuojia* [Authors from Northeast China] no. 9 (2003), 88–93; *Zhiqingzhe shuo* [The Inside Stories] 2 (2005): 3–4.

17 For more details about Mao's decision to intervene in the Korean War, see Li, *China's Battle for Korea*, chapter 1.

18 Li, Millett, and Yu, trans. and eds., *Mao's Generals Remember Korea*, 4–5.

19 Mao's telegram to Zhou Enlai who was in Moscow, October 14, 1950, agreed to send 260,000 Chinese troops to Korea at once. And Mao's telegram to Stalin on November 13, 1950 informed the Soviet leaders of reinforcement of eight more Chinese divisions to Korea. In *Jianguo yilai Mao Zedong junshi wengao* [Mao Zedong's Military Manuscripts since the Founding of the PRC] (Beijing: Junshi kexue [Military Science Press] and Zhongyang wenxian [CCP Central Archival and Manuscript Press], 2010), 1: 258–259, 349. Hereafter as *Mao's Military Manuscripts since 1949*.

20 Xu Yan, "Chinese Forces and Their Casualties in the Korean War," trans. Xiaobing Li, *Chinese Historians* 6, no. 2 (Fall 1993): 50.

21 From November 25 to December 24, 1950, the Chinese launched the Second Offensive Campaign. The CPVF had a total of 240,000 men on the Western front against 130,000 UN troops, and another 150,000 men on the Eastern front against 90,000 UN troops – a ratio of nearly 2:1. On the evening of November 25, two days after Thanksgiving, the CPVF launched the Second Offensive Campaign against MacArthur's "home-by-Christmas" offensive. Four Chinese armies conducted an all-out attack on the US Eighth Army's I and IX Corps on the west. On the Eastern front, the three CPVF armies attacked the US X Corps, including the First Marine and Second Infantry Divisions. General Walton Walker, commander of the US Eighth Army, was killed in a traffic accident. The CPVF suffered 80,000 Chinese casualties.

22 From December 31, 1950 to January 8, 1951, the CPVF launched its Third Offensive Campaign against a strong UNF defense along the 38th Parallel. In a matter of eight days, the CPVF crossed the 38th Parallel, moved into South Korea, recaptured Seoul, and pushed the UNF down to the 37th Parallel. The UNF was forced to retreat eighty miles south. According to Chinese reports, the CPVF and NKPA lost 8,500 men during the Third Offensive Campaign, including 5,800 CPVF and 2,700 KPA casualties.

23 Peng Dehuai, *Peng Dehuai junshi wenxuan* [Selected Military Papers of Peng Dehuai] (Beijing: Zhongyang wenxian [CCP Central Archival and Manuscript Press], 1988), 379. Hereafter as *Peng's Military Papers*.

24 Li, *China's Battle for Korea*, 176–177.

25 William T. Bowers, ed., *Striking Back: Combat in Korea, March–April 1951* (Lexington: University Press of Kentucky, 2010), 409.

26 For more details, see: Xiaobing Li, "Chapter 29: Military Stalemate," in *Ashgate Research Companion to the Korean War*, eds. James I. Matray and Donald W. Boose, Jr. (Surrey, UK: Ashgate Publishing, 2014), 383–394.

27 Yafeng Xia, *Negotiating with the Enemy: U.S.-China Talks during the Cold War, 1949–1972* (Bloomington: Indiana University Press, 2006), 43–75.

28 Among the recent publications, see: Ralph D. Sawyer, ed., *The Seven Military Classics of Ancient China* (New York: Basic Books, 2007); Jeremy Black, *Rethinking Military History* (New York: Routledge, 2004); and John Keegan, *A History of Warfare* (New York: Knopf, 1993).

29 Mao highly praised *The Art of Warfare* and considered it a scientific truth by citing Sunzi in his military writing, "know the enemy and know yourself, and you can fight a hundred battles with no danger of defeat." See Mao, "Problems of Strategy in China's Revolutionary War," in *Selected Works of Mao Tse-tung* (Beijing: Foreign Languages Press, 1977), 1: 190.

30 Da Ying, *Zhiyuanjun zhanfu jishi; xuji* [Voices from the CPVF POWs (continued)] (Beijing: Zhongguo qingnian [China's Youth Press], 1993), 20, 84–88; Zhang Zeshi, ed., *Meijun jizhongying qinliji* [Personal Stories of the CPVF POWs in UN/U.S. Camps] (Beijing: Zhongguo wenshi [China History and Literature Publishing], 1996), 1–3. Zhang served as an army staff sergeant in the 180th Division, Sixtieth Army, Third Army Group of the CPVF during the Korean War. He was captured by the UNF during the Chinese Spring Offensive Campaign in May 1951.

31 Li, "Chapter 29: Military Stalemate," 383.

32 According to Chinese military records, Chinese casualties in the Korean War break down as follows: 183,108 dead, 383,218 wounded, 455,199 hospitalized, 21,400 prisoners of war, and 4,221 missing in action, totaling 1,047,146 casualties. See Li, *China's Battle for Korea*, 239.

33 Dae Sook-Suh, *Kim Il Sung: The North Korean Leader* (New York: Columbia University Press, 1988), 300–302.

34 Suh, *ibid.*, 303–313.

7   China and the First Indochina War

As a communist state bordering North Vietnam, China actively supported the revolutionary movement of Ho Chi Minh (1890–1969) after the founding of the PRC in 1949.[1] The Chinese government was involved in the First Indochina War (1946–1954) against the French and also joined North Vietnam against South Vietnam in the Vietnamese civil war (1955–1963). China's military involvement in the First Indochina War became a historical precursor for Chinese intervention in the Vietnam War (1964–1973) against America. Chinese intent in Indochina can best be understood in historical terms by four elements: an overall foreign policy of the PRC in a global cold war context, formed to a large extent by the United States and the Soviet Union; national security concerns; domestic political stability; and military means and economic resources available at that moment. Chinese leaders' security considerations and policy decisions to assist Vietnam and resist France in the First Indochina War reflected a new strategic culture that advocated concepts of an active defense to protect the newly established communist state from an immediate threat from a perceived foreign invasion.

Upon Soviet leader Stalin's request, Mao decided to involve China in the French-Indochina War in late December 1949 when he visited the Soviet Union. Mao understood Stalin's demand that China share "the international responsibility" of the global communist movement by supporting the Asian revolutionary wars in general and Ho's First Indochina War in particular. From a geopolitical point of view, it seemed to make sense to Chinese leaders that China could secure its southwestern border, earn Soviet aid and technology, and modernize its armed forces, by helping the Democratic Republic of Vietnam (DRV) fight the French forces. Having noticed Stalin's priority and intent, Mao accepted Stalin's perception of a "worldwide communist revolution," and was ready to share "the international responsibility." In Moscow, Mao agreed to support Ho's war against the French because Mao also considered internationalism as one of the fundamental principles of the CCP.[2]

On February 6, 1950, Ho, hoping for Soviet aid, arrived in Moscow. Mao followed Stalin's advice and met Ho in Moscow. Ho explained to Mao why the Viet Minh needed international help in their war against the French. Mao made it clear to Ho at their meetings that China would support North Vietnam in order to win the war against the French. Mao also "stressed the importance of reciprocating friendship."[3] Thereafter, China began to engage in the global Cold War by supporting Ho's war against the French in Indochina.[4]

Ho and the CCP: Comrade-in-Arms

Ho Chi Minh was no stranger to the Chinese leaders. They had established a long-time mutual friendship through their revolutionary careers as members of the Comintern

(Communist International Congress) in Moscow, alumni of the Russian Oriental University, and comrades-in-arms during WWII. After the Soviet Union was founded in October 1917, Vladimir I. Lenin (1870–1924), the Soviet creator, expected a worldwide communist revolution. To globally spread the communist movement, the Russian Communist Party (Bolshevik) founded the Comintern in Moscow in 1919 as a political association of communist parties of the world. In September 1920, the Comintern held an "International Conference of Asian Nations" at Baku (in present day's Azerbaijan).[5] Thereafter, the Comintern created the University of the Toilers of the East (or the Oriental University) to train communist leaders from Asian countries. Following the Bolsheviks' guideline and Comintern's instructions, the Oriental University provided military training, consulting, and advising, as well as technology assistance to Asian Communist-armed rebellions against their non-communist governments. Many Chinese Communist leaders received their training through the Comintern in the 1920s. In 1921–1922, Liu Shaoqi, the future president of China, studied at the Oriental University in Moscow.[6] His learning experience in Moscow later contributed to his successful organization of Chinese trade unions, worker strikes, and underground party committees.[7]

Ho, then Nguyen Tat Thanh, came to Moscow the summer of 1923 and began his studies at the Oriental University. Fluent in Chinese and having had some Chinese friends in France in 1922–1923, Nguyen soon developed close relations with the Chinese Communists and changed his name to Ho Chi Minh. His first book published during his studies was titled *China and the Chinese Youth*.[8] When Lenin died on January 21, 1924, Ho, together with his Chinese classmates, attended the funeral.[9] The communist fraternity, among the Asian Communist leaders that had developed in the Soviet Union, continued and flourished when they returned to lead their own revolutions.[10]

Ho spent many years in China building up his revolutionary career and the Vietnamese Communist Party. He had been sent to China by the Comintern after completion of his training in 1924.[11] His assignment was to assist Soviet representative Mikhail Borodin, the Comintern envoy to the Chinese Nationalist (GMD) Revolutionary Committee in Guangzhou. Ho worked for Borodin as his Chinese interpreter during the day, while jogging around the mansion and practicing with pistols and rifles after work. The southern Chinese city of Guangzhou hosted a large number of Vietnamese refugees and political exiles. Ho organized the Association of Vietnamese Revolutionary Youth, or *Thanh Nien*, a group "which eventually became the forerunner of the Indochinese Communist Party" (ICP).[12] In 1925, Ho opened a political training school for young Vietnamese revolutionaries. He invited Liu Shaoqi, then national leader of China's labor movement, to lecture in his classes. After his return to China, Liu soon became one of the most promising party organizers from 1922–1926, and an elected member of the Party's Central Committee. As vice chairman of the China National Trade Union, Liu trained union leaders and mobilized urban workers for the communist movement in Guangzhou, where a friendship grew between Liu and Ho.[13] Qiang Zhai argues that personality was "an important factor in shaping Beijing's attitude toward revolution in Vietnam." The CCP and PLA leaders did not ignore "the close personal ties and revolutionary solidarity that they and Ho Chi Minh had forged in the years of common struggle in the past."[14]

It was in China that Ho Chi Minh founded the Vietnamese Communist Party on February 3, 1930, and then renamed it the Indochinese Communist Party (ICP) in October to include Communists in Cambodia and Laos. In the early 1930s, Ho had been eclipsed by ICP figures who were willing to support more immediate revolutionary efforts. While they organized the Nghe-Tinh uprisings, he remained north of

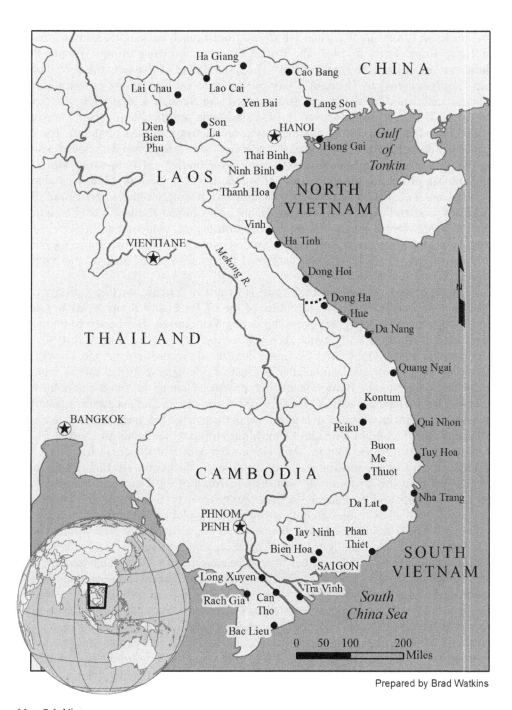

CHINA

Ha Giang

Cao Bang

Lai Chau

Lao Cai

Yen Bai

Lang Son

Dien
Bien
Phu

Son
La

HANOI

Hong Gai

Gulf
of
Tonkin

Thai Binh

Ninh Binh

LAOS

Thanh Hoa

NORTH
VIETNAM

Vinh

Ha Tinh

VIENTIANE

Dong Hoi

Mekong R.

Dong Ha

Hue

Da Nang

THAILAND

Quang Ngai

Kontum

Qui Nhon

Peiku

Buon
Me
Thuot

Tuy Hoa

BANGKOK

CAMBODIA

Da Lat

Nha Trang

PHNOM
PENH

Tay Ninh

Phan
Thiet

Bien Hoa

SAIGON

SOUTH
VIETNAM

Long Xuyen

Tra Vinh

South
China Sea

Rach Gia

Can
Tho

Bac Lieu

0   50   100   200
                      Miles

Prepared by Brad Watkins

Map 7.1 Vietnam

the border in China. In 1931, under pressure from French authorities, he was arrested in Hong Kong. Early in 1933, the British Governor of Hong Kong, William Peel, decided to quietly release Ho Chi Minh. The future father of the Vietnamese revolution was quietly escorted to Shantou, a city on the coast of Guangdong province on the Chinese mainland.[15] From there, Ho made his way through several Chinese cities to the Soviet Union, where he arrived in 1934, and remained there until 1938.[16] For most of this period, he remained an obscure castoff on the fringe of the Comintern. The ICP leadership declared that his "nationalist tendencies" were out of step with Soviet policies at the time, which emphasized class struggle over finding common cause with non-communists in fighting imperialism.[17] However, by 1937 Ho Chi Minh was able to benefit from a change in Soviet policy. With the increasingly bellicose policies of Nazi Germany and the rapid expansion of Japan into Chinese territory, the Comintern's policy shifted toward making alliances with anti-fascist, non-communist forces. This shift coincided with the advent of the Second United Front between the CCP and GMD in China (1937–1945), and it favored the production of such frontist policies among Vietnamese Nationalists.

After the Sino-Japanese War broke out, Ho came to Yan'an, wartime capital of the CCP in 1938, serving in the branch office of the CCP's Eighth Route Army in Guilin and southwestern Guangxi, a province bordering Vietnam. In 1939 he served under the command of Marshal Ye Jianying (Yeh Chien-ying, 1897–1986).[18] In May 1940, Ho recruited Pham Van Dong, later the prime minister of North Vietnam, and Vo Nguyen Giap, later a general and commander in chief of Vietnamese armed forces, into the Indochinese Communist Party at Kunming, provincial capital of Yunnan in Southwest China, a border province with Vietnam.[19] In October, Ho and his supporters established a base at Guilin in China and began to call themselves the League for Vietnamese Independence (Viet Nam Doc Lap Dong Minh Hoi), or Viet Minh for short.[20]

After his return to Vietnam in 1940, Ho worked with ICP leaders in Indochina and founded a new Communist-dominated united front in Vietnam at the Eighth Plenum of the ICP, to fight the Japanese. Ho was the Chairman of the Plenum, thus completing his rehabilitation; and the Plenum declared that henceforth, their focus would not be on an "anti-feudal" class revolution but instead on a "revolution of national liberation."[21]

Gadkar-Wilcox points out that in the next two years, the Ho-led Viet Minh government struggled unsuccessfully to gain recognition from the military authorities in the GMD and to compete with another frontist organization.[22] That group was the Vietnamese Revolutionary League, which was led by prominent non-communists and therefore favored by GMD leaders.[23] Ho Chi Minh was so unsuccessful in gaining notice for the group that he was arrested by GMD authorities on suspicion of being a spy in August 1942.[24] The Viet Minh successfully consolidated its military base in the northern border areas. Giap, Ho's lieutenant, organized the party's troops, Armed Propaganda Team, on December 22, 1944, which became the birthday of the Vietnamese Communist armed forces. With Allied support, Giap's guerrilla army along the Vietnamese-Chinese border grew to 5,000 men.[25] Since his army was under the Vietnamese Communist leadership, the force is also popularly known as the Viet Minh.

The DRV, GMD, and the French-Indochina War (1946–1954)

The sudden surrender of Japan in August 1945 created a power vacuum in Indochina. The Viet Minh were in an excellent strategic position to take advantage of the passivity of Japanese troops and the lack of action from the government in Hue. Ho and Viet Minh launched the "August Revolution" to take over the country by sending their cadres and troops to the major cities. Among others was General Giap, commander in chief of the Viet Minh army, who entered Hanoi with 1,000 troops on August 18. As various Nationalist groups acted to assert authority over various regions, the Viet Minh benefited from a better organizational structure, the support of Northern peasants, and better information.

In the wake of the August Revolution of 1945, the Viet Minh sought to accomplish two goals. Domestically, first of all, their aim was to consolidate their hold on the major cities of Vietnam and to be in a position to retain that hold in the face of the two military forces of the Allies – the British army in the southern part of Vietnam and the Chinese Nationalist (GMD) army in the North – who were tasked with securing the surrender of Vietnamese troops. At the Potsdam conference in July 1945, the Allies had agreed on dividing Vietnam at the 16th parallel, just above Da Nang and below Hue, and to have British forces take a Japanese surrender below this line and GMD forces take the surrender above this line.

Internationally, the Viet Minh's goal was to gain diplomatic recognition that would ensure their continued ability to govern even in the face of British and GMD occupations. Of particular importance was to secure diplomatic recognition from the United States, which the good relationship fostered between the Viet Minh and the OSS in the spring and summer of 1945 made seem possible. Gadkar-Wilcox points out that in reality, the Viet Minh were unsuccessful at these two goals, though they did benefit from GMD delays in handing power in Northern Vietnam back to the French. This led Ho to adopt a conciliatory posture toward the French in 1946, and led to nearly a year of diplomatic negotiations.[26] However, these negotiations ultimately failed, leading to a French takeover of Hanoi in December 1946. The Viet Minh were forced to flee into the "resistance zone" in the countryside, and the First Indochina War began.

By September 2, 1945, the August Revolution had resulted in *de facto* Viet Minh control of the major cities of Vietnam. Emperor Bao Dai, whom the Viet Minh had forced to abdicate the throne with the famous statement that he would rather be "a citizen of a free country than a king of a slave state."[27] Ho proclaimed the independence of Vietnam and founded the Democratic Republic of Vietnam (DRV) in the North, with himself as president and Hanoi as its capital.[28] After the armed conflict began between the Communist North and French forces in 1946, Vietnam became part of the Cold War in Asia.

In the South, the British forces were under the command of General Douglas Gracey (1894–1964). Within two weeks of Gracey's landing in Saigon on September 13, 1945, he had evicted the Viet Minh from the former Governor-General's palace, turned major ammunition depots and other key infrastructure points over to a small French unit, declared Martial law and enforced it with the help of the Japanese troops he was charged with disarming, and armed former French prisoners of war.[29] By early October 1945, Saigon was back in French hands.

The situation in the North was more complicated. When GMD General Lu Han (1895–1974) arrived with 100,000 Chinese troops in Hanoi on September 14, 1945, he promptly kicked out the French representative Jean Sainteny (1907–1978), met with Ho Chi Minh, and made clear that the Viet Minh government was to remain in place so long as they could maintain law and order.[30] At the same time, it became clear by October that the Chinese troops intended to remain in Indochina for some time to come. The Chinese position had two motivations. First, they recognized that the Viet Minh government in Hanoi was entrenched and popular enough that removing them would cause a backlash.[31] Second, allowing the Viet Minh to remain in place provided the Chinese diplomatic leverage against the French that they could use to bolster the GMD position in China.[32] Peter Worthing argues that the Chinese "made a substantial contribution to the Vietnamese Revolution" because they provided "time and opportunity for the Viet Minh to consolidate and triumph over domestic rivals ..."[33] According to Worthing, Ho's newly established DRV survived with the Chinese Nationalist protection in 1945–1946.

The decision of Lu Han to leave the Viet Minh in place prompted several months of diplomatic negotiation and positioning on both the parts of the Viet Minh and the French. The Viet Minh sought diplomatic recognition, particularly from the United States, and to avoid antagonizing their Chinese Nationalist occupiers. To do so, they officially dissolved the Indochinese Communist Party, at least on paper, in November 1945. Bowing to GMD pressure, they guaranteed non-communist representation in the national assembly by reserving seats for two non-communist parties. Famously, they appealed for support from the American government and from American industry. Ho wrote several letters to President Truman and to Secretary of State James Byrnes calling for the diplomatic recognition of Vietnam, and through 1946 the Viet Minh made contacts with American oil and insurance companies. The motorcycle manufacturer Harley-Davidson even sent an agent to Hanoi to explore commercial contacts.[34] Ultimately, however, the advent of the Cold War and the US desire to maintain good relations with France prevented any decisive action in favor of the Viet Minh.

By early 1946, the Viet Minh were forced into a position of negotiating with the French. In February of that year, the GMD concluded an agreement with the French in which the French gave up territorial claims in China in exchange for GMD recognition of French sovereignty in Indochina.[35] However, Lu's troops, not wishing to be caught in the middle of a French-Viet Minh war, pressured Ho Chi Minh and Jean Sainteny to come to an agreement and would not allow French troops to reach Hanoi without it. On March 6, 1946, they agreed that Vietnam would be a "free state" within a loose confederacy of the French Union. In return, 15,000 French troops would be allowed into the northern part of Vietnam, and other more difficult problems, such as the status of Cochinchina, would be worked out through a future referendum and further negotiations.[36]

For the rest of 1946, French and Viet Minh authorities attempted without success to iron out details of a comprehensive agreement. With these attempts at peace falling flat, both sides prepared for the eventuality of war. On November 20, 1946, French forces reoccupied Haiphong harbor, and on December 17, they reoccupied Hanoi, forcing the Viet Minh into the countryside and beginning the First Indochina War. In November, North Vietnam passed its first constitution and established its Defense Ministry with Giap as its first defense minister and commander-in-chief of the North Vietnamese armed forces.

In 1947 and 1948, the First Indochina War quickly ground to a stalemate. Viet Minh forces were not strong enough to remove French troops from major cities or from key transportation routes; French forces were unable to locate and successfully annihilate Viet Minh leadership in the resistance zone. Militarily, this series of inconclusive battles would remain the norm until 1949, when the Viet Minh could take advantage of additional support from the North owing to the CCP's victory over the GMD in the

Chinese Civil War. In the meantime, the Viet Minh became a more openly hard-line communist organization, ejecting non-communists, from whom it could no longer gain significant political advantage, from its ranks, restricting future Communist party membership to people from proper class backgrounds, and formulating a more radical land policy in occupied areas.[37] By 1951, this process was complete; the ICP created separate Communist parties for Laos and Cambodia and renamed itself the Vietnamese Labor Party in support of a class struggle line and in line with the aspirations of the CCP.

In the meanwhile, the French sought to gain international legitimacy and support for their position in the First Indochina War by creating a plausible but pliable non-communist government. They turned to the former Emperor Bao Dai, who had lived in Hong Kong after abdicating the throne during the August Revolution of 1945. At that point, the former emperor slowly became receptive to French plans for him to become involved in a non-communist government that had been favored by High Commissioner d'Argenlieu. In March 1949, an accord was signed at the Élysée Palace in Paris announcing the organization of a new State of Vietnam. The Élysée Accords allowed Bao Dai to create a State of Vietnam with himself as Head of State. However, the French retained control of foreign affairs, retained extraterritorial rights for French citizens, and specified that for as long as a state of war existed, the Vietnamese army would take orders from a French commander.[38]

In reality, Bao Dai probably lacked sufficient popular support to rally non-communists to his side, and his efforts at securing major French concessions fell flat. As Gadkar-Wilcox argues, the State of Vietnam was not inconsequential. Instead, seeing a quasi-legitimate Vietnamese polity come to fruition made it more palatable for the United States to act in Indochina. Still reeling from having "lost China" to the Communists, the United States recognized the State of Vietnam in 1950 and began to direct material support to French operations in Indochina shortly thereafter.[39]

Chinese aid and Dien Bien Phu

In the meantime, as the situation for the Viet Minh continued to improve, French forces adopted new tactics.[40] In response, the French sent General Jean de Lattre de Tassigny (1889–1952), a hero from WWII, to take over not only as Chief of the Expeditionary Corps but also as High Commissioner for Indochina, making him effectively in charge of both the French military and political apparatuses in Indochina. The hope was that de Lattre could eliminate petty disputes and implement an aggressive policy against the Viet Minh.[41] In 1950 and 1951, de Lattre implemented a much more aggressive campaign against the Viet Minh, trying to reduce the effectiveness of their forces by limiting their access to supplies and food through a "scorched earth" campaign that burned crops near areas of concentrated Viet Minh attacks. This policy produced some tactical successes but was a strategic failure, as it deprived not only the Viet Minh but also local villagers of necessary food, supplies, and transportation, and thus only increased the ire of locals against the French.

After Beijing established diplomatic relations with Hanoi in January 1950, the focus of the CCP's policy toward Vietnam shifted from party relations to a state relationship. The Chinese leaders' main concerns changed from their political cooperation and moral support to the current national interests and border security.[42] The newly founded republic was to establish political order, national unity, domestic tranquility, and to reorganize in order to defend against foreign invasion. From this point forward, the

PRC adopted a geopolitical strategy stressing defensive military measures to consolidate a new regime and to protect its territorial gains. Since the end of 1949, Chinese leaders had shifted their strategic thinking from taking over the country to focusing on national defense and homeland security. The concept of national defense against a possible Western invasion developed in early 1950, becoming the cornerstone of China's strategic thinking and its military modernization through the 1970s. In 1950, according to Mao's perception of the Cold War, Western imperialist powers threatened China's national security in three areas: Korea, Vietnam, and the Taiwan Strait.[43]

Mao believed China should secure its southwestern border by eliminating any Western power's presence in Vietnam. Mao again promised Ho that the PRC would be primarily responsible for providing support for the Viet Minh.[44] Duiker points out that "The possibility of an outright military triumph appeared increasingly probable after Mao Zedong's Communist Party came to power in China in 1949, a stunning shift in the regional balance of power that provided the Vietminh with a powerful new ally."[45]

On August 11, General Wei Guoqing led the Chinese Military Advisory Group (CMAG), numbering approximately 250 officers, and accompanied by Hoang Van Hoan, then Vietnamese Ambassador to Beijing, into Vietnam from Guangxi province. They arrived at Quang Uyen, Northern Cao Bang province, on August 12. After China sent its forces to the Korean War in late 1950, Mao paid more attention to the French Indochina War to make sure Beijing would not fight against the Western powers on two fronts. To secure the border, in 1951 Mao instructed the CMAG to exploit the victory of the Border Campaign in the Northeast by expanding base areas into the Northwest, along the border. From April to September 1950, China shipped 14,000 automatic rifles, 1,700 machine guns, 450 artillery pieces, and food supplies for forty days, in order to secure the success of the Border Offensive Campaign in September–October. The PLA also received and treated 1,143 wounded Viet Minh soldiers in China during the campaign.[46]

In 1950, the North Vietnamese armed forces were reorganized and renamed as the People's Army of Vietnam (PAVN; commonly known as the North Vietnamese Army, or NVA) with 50,000 troops. By the end of the French Indochinese War in 1954, the NVA totaled 120,000 regulars. The Chinese also trained the Vietnamese in China, opening an officer academy, communication, technology, and mechanic schools in Guangxi and Yunnan, two Chinese-Vietnam border provinces.[47] The Viet Minh high command sent entire units to China for training and re-arming. For example, in 1951 the 308th Division and the 174th and 209th Regiments traveled to China for training, and while there received new arms, weapons, and equipment from the PLA. In 1952, 799 Vietnamese medic personnel and 176 surgical doctors also received training in China. By 1954 the Chinese had provided, within China, military and technology training for 15,000 Vietnamese officers and soldiers.[48]

By the end of 1954, China had armed five Vietnamese infantry divisions, one artillery division, one anti-aircraft artillery (AAA) division, and one security regiment.[49] According to Chinese government statistics, from 1950 to 1956 China had shipped 155,000 small arms, fifty-eight million rounds of ammunition, 4,630 artillery pieces, 1.08 million artillery shells, 840,000 hand grenades, 1,200 vehicles, 1.4 million uniforms, 14,000 tons of food, and 26,000 tons of fuel to Vietnam.[50] From August 1950 to March 1954, the Chinese government shipped additional goods, war materials, medicine, and fuel worth $43.2 billion, to Vietnam.[51] In 1954, Chinese imports increased, and included trucks, gasoline, generators, and four million meters of cotton materials.[52] By the end of 1954, China had armed five Vietnamese infantry divisions, one artillery division, one anti-aircraft artillery division, and one security regiment.[53]

By May 1953, the French had again gone in a different direction, appointing Henri Navarre (1898–1983) as Chief of the Expeditionary Corps. French troops then implemented what has come to be known as the Navarre Plan. This plan called for French forces, assisted by Bao Dai's Vietnamese National Army, to use their advantage in technology and force of arms to hold key territory and strategic points along roads between them. The intent of this plan was to force the Viet Minh into a position of negotiation by fighting them into an impasse. Whatever gains the Viet Minh might make in the countryside, Navarre's defenses would prevent the Communists from having any reasonable chance at taking cities or holding major roads.[54]

In late 1953, the French sent more than 10,000 troops into the Dien Bien Phu area in the Northwest, threatening Viet Minh bases and connections with Laos. Navarre's plan proved to be a failure at the conclusive and most famous battle of the First Indochina War: the Battle of Dien Bien Phu in 1954. Dien Bien Phu is a town along a main route between Hanoi and Vientiane, the capital of Laos. As such, it was a critical military and transportation route, and was heavily fortified by French troops who were supplied by aircraft. Unfortunately for the French, Dien Bien Phu is also ringed by mountains. In November 1953, the Viet Minh high command and the CMAG planned a response to the French occupation of Dien Bien Phu. The Central Committee of the Vietnamese Workers' Party (VWP, *Dang Lao Dong Viet Nam*) approved the plan on December 6.

From December 1953 to early March 1954, the Viet Minh concentrated the 304th, 308th, 312th, 316th Infantry Divisions, and the 351st Artillery Division – a total of more than 40,000 troops – and encircled 15,000 French troops at Dien Bien Phu. In the meantime, the PLA sent to Dien Bien Phu one Vietnamese rocket battalion and one 75mm recoilless gun battalion, which had been equipped and trained in China. To support the Dien Bien Phu Campaign, among other supplies, China also shipped into Vietnam 2.4 million rounds of ammo, 60,000 artillery shells, 3,000 machine guns, 100 heavy artillery pieces, 200 trucks, 10,000 barrels of gasoline, and 1.7 million kg of grain. The CMAG also helped the Viet Minh prepare for field medical care and for campaign hospital readiness. Most of the 9,124 wounded NVA soldiers received proper care during the offensive campaign.[55]

On March 13, 1954, the Viet Minh launched attacks to isolate French strong points at Dien Bien Phu. By late April French troops held only three points. On May 6, the Viet Minh launched its final attack. The newly-arrived, Chinese-manufactured six-rocket launchers, heavy artillery pieces, and anti-aircraft guns played an important role in the final assaults. The very next day, the French surrendered. After eight years of fighting, Ho and the Viet Minh had finally defeated 120,000 French troops in what was later called the First Indochinese War.[56]

By the end of the French Indochinese War in 1954, the NVA totaled 120,000 regulars. In May 1955, the NVA established its Navy, followed by its Air Force in September 1956. Under the order of Giap, Viet Minh forces pushed anti-aircraft guns up the peaks and simply shot down French resupply aircrafts, effectively laying siege on French positions at Dien Bien Phu. After months of this siege, the French will to fight the war waned, and the French made the decision to conclude the war in talks at Geneva that were already underway. The resulting Geneva Accords were quite comprehensive, but their most salient effect was the partition of Vietnam at the 17th parallel, north of the city of Hue, with the Communist-led Democratic Republic of

Vietnam in the North and the non-communist forces of the State of Vietnam under Bao Dai in the South.

The 1954 Geneva Convention

During the battle of Dien Bien Phu, an international conference on Indochina began at Geneva in April 1954. Delegations from France, North Vietnam, China, the Soviet Union, the United States, and four other countries attended peace talk meetings.[57] The Soviet Union was represented by Minister of Foreign Affairs Vyacheslav Mikhailovich Molotov (1890–1986), and the United Kingdom was represented by Secretary of State for Foreign Affairs Anthony Eden (1897–1977). The United States, which was represented by Secretary of State John Foster Dulles (1888–1959), largely stayed on the sidelines of these discussions.[58] China was represented by Premier Zhou Enlai.

The main interest of the major powers at the conference was to keep a civil war in Vietnam from arising and escalating into a major Cold War battlefront – in other words, to avoid precisely the events that actually occurred during the 1960s. In France, Prime Minister Joseph Laniel (1889–1975) and the French political right were hoping to find a way "to bring an end to the war on terms that could be profitable to French interests in Indochina and could still be made to look honorable."[59] However, the debacle at Dien Bien Phu collapsed the Laniel government. On June 18, 1954, leftist Pierre Mendès France (1907–1982) replaced him as prime minister. He insisted the Geneva Conference produce an agreement to end the war within thirty days.[60] It is an important but infrequently noted fact that a resolution of the Indochina question was but one aim of the Geneva Conference. The other was to resolve the remaining outstanding issues in the wake of the Korean War, which had ended in an armistice in 1953 but has not formally been ended by treaty even to the present day.

All sides were wary of repeating the experience of Korea in Vietnam. The Soviet Union was only a little more than a year removed from the death of Josef Stalin, and First Secretary Nikita Khrushchev's position in power was still far from secure. China had lost more than 180,000 soldiers in the Korean War, less than a year before the Geneva negotiations. China's First Five-Year Plan (1953–1957) required soldiers to perform key land reform and industrial tasks that made a protracted conflict in Vietnam unpalatable to China.[61]

Given the geopolitical situation at the time, the most prudent course for the major powers was to partition Vietnam. However, the Vietnamese representatives at the conference were universally opposed to partition of the country. Agreement required some convenient way to placate Vietnamese parties – especially the Viet Minh – on the partition issue.

Since Ho did not attend the Geneva Conference, Zhou met him in Liuzhou, Guangxi province. At their meeting in China, the premier pressured Ho to accept a peace settlement in Indochina. Vietnamese leaders like Le Duan rallied against Mao's idea and Zhou's pressure, blaming China for a "lost South Vietnam" in 1954. Le Duan reviewed the Sino-Vietnamese relations many years later and stated that:

> When we had signed the Geneva Accords, it was precisely Zhou Enlai who divided our country into two [parts]. After our country had been divided into northern and southern zones in this way, he once again pressured us into not doing anything in regard to southern Vietnam. They forbade us from rising up [against the US-backed RVN].[62]

Later, Mao admitted his mistake by asking the Vietnamese to replace their military struggle with a political struggle. Mao told Pham Van Dong, who represented the DRV at the Geneva Conference in 1954 and visited Beijing in November 1968:

> I did say that we had made a mistake when we went to the Geneva Conference in 1954. At that time, President Ho Chi Minh wasn't totally satisfied. It was difficult for President Ho to give up the South, and now, when I think twice, I see that he was right.[63]

In July of 1954, the Indochina Settlement was signed at Geneva by the Viet Minh, French, Chinese, and Soviets. The United States did not sign the Geneva agreements. According to the 1954 Geneva Accord on the restoration of peace in the Indochinese region, as a temporary arrangement the Viet Minh army would withdraw from Southern Vietnam to the areas north of the 17th parallel, paving the way for a French departure and a mandatory national election in 1956.[64] The election was to be held in July 1956 to produce a national government for the entire country. The Viet Minh's withdrawal began in August. On October 10, 1954, after eight years of fighting in the jungle, the Viet Minh eventually returned to Hanoi, capital of the DRV. The CMAG HQs also moved into Hanoi along with a total of 237 Chinese advisors.[65]

When the Geneva Conference secured the Vietnamese Communists' power in North Vietnam, Ho strengthened his efforts in social and political reform movements. In 1959, the DRV government passed its new constitution, stating that the DRV was a people's state, an alliance between workers and peasants led by the VWP, and resulting from Ho's re-organization of ICP. According to the constitution a national congress would take place every five years, although in practice they were convened on an *ad hoc* basis to approve decisions already passed by the Central Committee and Politburo of the VWP. The Politburo (*Bo Chinh Tri*), the top decision-making body, enabled senior party and military leaders to handle day-to-day issues between plenary sessions of the Central Committee. The ten members met approximately once a week.[66]

After the Republic of Vietnam (RVN) was founded in Saigon in 1955, the Communist leadership in Hanoi rejected the government in South Vietnam, calling for a national reunification by its Communist forces. In the South, RVN President Ngo Dinh Diem (1901–1963) cooperated with the US government by suppressing a large number of suspected communists. In 1957–1958, angry Southern rebels launched anti-government rebellions in rural areas. To grasp a leadership opportunity for the Southern mass movement, the Viet Minh organized the National Liberation Front (NLF) in December 1960 as an umbrella organization to mobilize the masses against the Diem government. Diem labeled the NLF the "Viet Cong," meaning Vietnamese Communists. At that time the Southerners joined the Northern Communist revolution against the RVN government and US involvement in South Vietnam. In February 1961, the People's Liberation Armed Force (PLAF) was formed, under a united military command with Tran Luong as the head. He was soon replaced by several Northern generals of the NVA, veterans of the war against France.[67]

After the Geneva Conference, China continued to provide weaponry, equipment, and military training to North Vietnam. By the end of 1960, Chinese foreign aid had totaled $6.7 billion. One-third of China's total foreign aid of $1.9 billion went to Vietnam, another $133.9 million to Cambodia, and $670,000 to Laos. Each year's foreign aid from 1950 to 1960 consisted of 1.2 percent of total governmental annual expenses.[68] In

Beijing in the summer of 1962, Mao agreed with Ho that China would provide grain and weapons to Viet Cong in South Vietnam through the "Ho Chi Minh Trails," a mountainous transport route between North and South Vietnam through Laos and Cambodia.[69] After Ho left Beijing, the Central Committee decided to provide free weaponry and equipment to re-arm 230 Vietnamese infantry battalions, over 180,000 men. In March 1963, Luo Ruiqing, chief of the PLA General Staff, led the Chinese military delegation to Hanoi to discuss more details on how to assist the NLF in South Vietnam, and how the PLA could better cooperate with the Vietnamese.[70]

Between 1955 and 1963, Chinese military aid to North Vietnam totaled $320 million, while its economic aid totaled $1.1 billion from 1955–1958 alone. Russian economic aid was 531 million rubles in Russian currency (about $177 million). China's massive supply and support to North Vietnam in the early 1960s helped Ho intensify guerrilla warfare in South Vietnam.[71] Ho supported the Southern Communist guerrilla warfare against the southern government and the Army of the Republic of Vietnam (ARVN) by providing logistical support, experienced officers, and a small number of NVA troops. Between 1959 and 1960, North Vietnam sent 4,500 NVA officers and troops to the South to advise the NLF's guerrilla force against Diem's RVN government. By 1961, Northern advisors had increased to 6,200 men.[72] Later, Hanoi increased its infiltration by sending NVA regulars, nearly 100,000 a year, through the the the Ho Chi Minh Trail.[73] In the summer of 1962, China began aiding the NLF by providing weapons, ammunition, and supplies to the Vietnamese Communist forces in the South through the Ho Chi Minh Trail.

Notes

1 Gadkar-Wilcox, writing sections in "East Asia and the West," by Li, Sun, and Gadkar-Wilcox (unpublished manuscript), chapter 8.
2 Mao's concluding speech at the CCP Seventh National Congress on May 31, 1945, in CCP Central Archives comps., *Zhonggong zhongyang wenjian xuanji, 1921–1949* [Selected Documents of the CCP Central Committee, 1921–1949] (Beijing: Zhonggong zhongyang dangxiao [CCP Central Party Academy Press], 1989–1992), 15: 98–106.
3 Qiang Zhai, *China and the Vietnam Wars, 1950–1975* (Chapel Hill: University of North Carolina Press, 2000), 5.
4 Yang Kuisong, "Mao Zedong and the Indochina Wars," in *Zhongguo yu yindu zhina zhanzheng* [China and the Indochina Wars], ed. Li Danhui (Hong Kong: Tiandi Tushu [Heaven and Earth Books], 2000), 58.
5 Huang Zheng, *Hu zhimin yu zhong guo* [Ho Chi Minh and China] (Beijing: Jiefangjun [PLA Press], 1987), 9.
6 Huang Zheng, *Liu Shaoqi yisheng* [Life of Liu Shaoqi] (Beijing: Zhongyang wenxian [CCP Central Archival and Manuscript Press], 2003), 20–21.
7 Jin Chongji, "Shanyu duli sikao de zhanlujia he lilunjia" [A Great Strategist and Theorist with His Own Thoughts], keynote speech at the opening ceremony of the conference on Liu Shaoqi Studies, Chuzhou, Anhui Province, October 29, 1996, in *Liu Shaoqi yanjiu pingshu* [On the Studies of Liu Shaoqi], ed. Chen Shaotao (Beijing: Zhongyang wenxian [CCP Central Archival and Manuscript Press], 1997), 3–6. Jin is deputy director of the Archival and Manuscript Research Division of the CCP Central Committee.
8 Ho Chi Minh's book, *China and the Chinese Youth*, was first published in French in France in 1925. Then, he translated it into Russian and published it in the Soviet Union in 1926.
9 Wang Yizhi, "Huiyi Zhang Tailei" [Recollections of Zhang Tailei], *Jindaishi yanjiu* [Journal of the Modern History Studies] 2 (1983), 23–27.
10 See Huang Zheng, *Hu zhimin yu zhong guo* [Ho Chi Minh and China], 9; Robert Strayer, *The Communist Experiment; Revolution, Socialism, and Global Conflict in the Twentieth Century* (Boston, MA: McGraw Hill, 2007), 118.

11　For more details about Ho's training in the Soviet Union, see David Halberstam, *Ho* (New York: Alfred Knopf, 1987), 41–44.

12　Halberstam, *ibid.,* 45–46.

13　Huang Zheng, *Liu Shaoqi yisheng* [Life of Liu Shaoqi], 20–21.

14　Zhai, *China and the Vietnam Wars*, 5.

15　Sophie Quinn-Judge, *Ho Chi Minh: The Missing Years, 1919–1945* (Berkeley: University of California Press, 2002), 194–195; William J. Duiker, *Ho Chi Minh: A Life* (New York: Theia, 2000), 205–209.

16　Pierre Brocheux, *Ho Chi Minh: A Biography* (New York: Cambridge University Press, 2007), 56–58.

17　Brocheux, *ibid.*, 64.

18　Mai Ly Quang, ed., *Chuyen ke: cua nhung nguoi giup viec Bac Ho* [Personal Recollections: Years Working and Living with Uncle Ho] (Hanoi: The Goi [World Publishing], 2004), 11, 111–112.

19　Roger Hilsman, "Foreword" to *People's War, People's Army: The Viet Cong Insurrection Manual for Underdeveloped Countries*, Vo Nguyen Giap (New York: Praeger, 1968), ix–xi.

20　Quinn-Judge, *Ho Chi Minh*, 246.

21　Huynh Kim Khanh, *Vietnamese Communism, 1925–1945* (Ithaca, NY: Cornell University Press, 1982), 256–261; Mark Philip Bradley, *Imagining Vietnam and America: The Making of Postcolonial Vietnam, 1919–1950*(Chapel Hill: University of North Carolina Press, 2000), 110.

22　Gadkar-Wilcox, writing sections in "East Asia and the West," by Li, Sun, and Gadkar-Wilcox (unpublished manuscript), chapter 8.

23　Bradley, *Imagining Vietnam and America.,* 112–114; Keith W. Taylor, *A History of the Vietnamese* (New York: Cambridge University Press, 2013), 531.

24　Brocheux, *Ho Chi Minh*, 79.

25　George C. Herring, *America's Longest War: the United States and Vietnam, 1950–1975*, 3rd ed. (New York: McGraw-Hill, 1996), 6.

26　Gadkar-Wilcox, writing sections in "East Asia and the West," by Li, Sun, and Gadkar-Wilcox (unpublished manuscript), chapter 8.

27　Bui Diem with David Chanoff, *In the Jaws of History* (Bloomington: Indiana University Press, 1987), 42.

28　General Vo Nguyen Giap (NVA, ret.), *People's War, People's Army: The Viet Cong Insurrection Manual for Underdeveloped Countries* (New York: Praeger, 1968), 8–10.

29　David Marr, *Vietnam: State, War, and Revolution, 1945–1946* (Berkeley: University of California Press, 2013), 186–187.

30　Marr, *ibid.*, 266.

31　Taylor, *History of the Vietnamese*, 537.

32　Archimedes L. A. Patti, *Why Viet Nam? Prelude to America's Albatross* (Berkeley: University of California Press, 1980), 213.

33　Peter Worthing, *Occupation and Revolution: China and the Vietnamese August Revolution of 1945* (Berkeley: University of California Press, 2001), 173.

34　Bradley, *Imagining Vietnam and America,* 126–132.

35　Stein Tønneson, *Vietnam 1946: How the War Began* (Berkeley, CA: University of California Press, 2010), 41.

36　Mark Atwood Lawrence, *The Vietnam War: A Concise International History* (New York: Oxford University Press, 2008), 32; Tønneson, *Vietnam 1946*, 40.

37　Tuong Vu, "'It's Time for the Indochinese Revolution to Show Its True Colors': The Radical Turn of Vietnamese Politics in 1948," in *Journal of Southeast Asian Studies 40*, no. 3 (October 2009), 519–542.

38　Nguyen Phut Tan, *A Modern History of Viet Nam* (Saigon: Khai Tri, 1964), 567–574.

39　Gadkar-Wilcox, writing sections in "East Asia and the West," by Li, Sun, and Gadkar-Wilcox (unpublished manuscript), chapter 8.

40　In 1951, the Viet Minh front officially ceased to exist as it came to be entirely subsumed into the Lien Viet Front, another umbrella organization of the Vietnamese Communists. Also in 1951, the Vietnamese Communists came to be organized under the title Vietnamese Workers' Party, which was designed to reflect their renewed commitment to class struggle. For the purposes of simplicity and reflecting the conventions of English-language sources at the time, until 1954 this book will refer to the forces of the People's Army of Vietnam as the Viet Minh.

41 Fredrik Logevall, *Embers of War: The Fall of an Empire and the Making of America's Vietnam* (New York: Random House, 2014), 260–264.
42 China had a long border with Vietnam about 850 miles inland and 600 miles offshore in the Tonkin Gulf. The Chinese-Vietnamese borders are still controversial between the two governments. The information in this work is based upon the Chinese official documents and literature. See: Guo Ming, *Zhongyue guanxi yanbian sishinian* [Uncertain Relations between China and Vietnam, 1949–1989] (Nanning: Guangxi renmin [Guangxi People's Press], 1992), 135–136, 139–140.
43 Mao's conversations with Wang Jifan and Zhou Shizhao on October 27, 1950, from the recollections of Wang Yuqing, grandson of Wang Jifan, in *Junshi lishi* [Military History], vol. 88, 93; *Guandong zhuojia* [Authors from Northeast China] no. 9 (2003); and *Zhiqingzhe shuo* (The Inside Stories) 2 (2005), 3–4.
44 Wang Xiangen, *Yuanyue kangmei shilu* [True Stories of Aiding Vietnam and Resisting America] (Beijing: Guoji wenhua [International Culture Publishing], 1990), 42.
45 William J. Duiker, "Foreword: The History of the People's Army," in *Victory in Vietnam: The Official History of the People's Army of Vietnam, 1954–1975*, Military History Institute of Vietnam, trans. Merle L. Pribbenow (Lawrence: University Press of Kansas, 2002), xi.
46 Li, *A History of the Modern Chinese Army*, 212.
47 CCP Central Committee's telegram to Luo Guibo and ICP Central Committee on Establishing Military Academies in Vietnam on April 21, 1950, drafted by Liu, *Jianguo yilai Liu Shaoqi wengao, 1949–1957* [Liu Shaoqi's Manuscripts since the Founding of the State, 1949–1957] (Beijing: Zhongyang wenxian [CCP Central Archival and Manuscript Press], 2013), 2: 73–75. Hereafter cited as *Liu's Manuscripts since 1949*,
48 Guo Zhigang, "A Foreign Military Assistance after the Founding of the New Republic," in *Junqi piaopiao; xinzhongguo 50 nian junshi dashi shushi* [PLA Flag Fluttering: Facts of China's Major Military Events in the Past Fifty Years of the PRC], ed. by Military History Research Division, China Academy of Military Science (CAMS) (Beijing: Jiefangjun [PLA Press], 1999), 1: 161.
49 Han, *Dangdai Zhongguo jundui de junshi gongzuo* [Military Affairs of Contemporary China's Armed Forces], 1: 520; Military History Research Division, CAMS, *Zhongguo renmin jiefangjun de qishinian, 1927–1997* [Seventy Years of the PLA, 1927–1997], 403.
50 Han, *Dangdai Zhongguo jundui de junshi gongzuo* [Military Affairs of Contemporary China's Armed Forces], 1: 576; Guo Zhigang, "A Foreign Military Assistance after the Founding of the New Republic," 1: 161.
51 Ministry of Foreign Trade, "1953 Zhongguo yu yuenan maoyi xieding" [Agreement of China's Trade with Vietnam in 1953], File# 106-00078-02 (1) 3 (10 pages), Archives Department, PRC Ministry of Foreign Affairs, Beijing. Hereafter cited as *PRC Foreign Ministry Archives.*
52 Ministry of Foreign Trade, *ibid.*
53 Han, *Dangdai Zhongguo jundui de junshi gongzuo* [Military Affairs of Contemporary China's Armed Forces], 1: 520; CAMS, *Zhongguo renmin jiefangjun de qishinian, 1927–1997* [Seventy Years of the PLA, 1927–1997], 403.
54 CAMS, *Zhongguo renmin jiefangjun de qishinian* [Seventy Years of the PLA], 355–356.
55 CMAG History Compilation Team, *Zhongguo junshi guwentuan yuanyue kangfa douzheng shishi* [Historical Facts of the CMAG in the Struggle to Assist Vietnam and Resist France], 114.
56 Herring, *America's Longest War*, 32–34.
57 For more details on the Chinese diplomacy at the Geneva Conference in May-July 1954, see Zhou's telegrams to Mao, Liu, and other leaders on June 10, 18, and July 20, 1954, File# 206-Y0050 (2) and 206-Y0051 (3), *PRC Foreign Ministry Archives.*
58 Taylor, *History of the Vietnamese*, 560.
59 Taylor, *ibid.*, 489.
60 Edward Miller, *Misalliance: Ngo Dinh Diem, the United States, and the Fate of South Vietnam* (Cambridge, MA: Harvard University Press, 2013), 89.
61 Li, *China's Battle for Korea*, 239; Meg E. Rithmire, *Land Bargains and Chinese Capitalism: The Politics of Property Rights under Reform* (New York: Cambridge University Press, 2015), 37.

62 Le Duan, "Document: Comrade B on the Plot of the Reactionary Chinese Clique against Vietnam," in *Behind the Bamboo Curtain: China, Vietnam, and the World beyond Asia*, ed. Priscilla Roberts (Stanford, CA: Stanford University Press, 2006), 468.
63 Mao's conversation with Pham Van Dong, Beijing, November 17, 1968, "Selected Conversations of Asian Communist Leaders on Indochina," in *Behind the Bamboo Curtain*, ed. Roberts, 504.
64 "Final Declaration of the Geneva Conference on Indochina, 1954," in *Major Problems in the History of the Vietnam War: Documents and Essays,* ed. Robert J. McMahon (Lexington, MA: Heath, 1995), 124–126.
65 CMAG History Compilation Team, *Zhongguo junshi guwentuan yuanyue kangfa douzheng shishi* [Historical Facts of the CMAG in the Struggle to Assist Vietnam and Resist France], 141.
66 William J. Duiker, *Sacred War: Nationalism and Revolution in a Divided Vietnam*(Boston, MA: McGraw-Hill, 1995), 106–108, 120.
67 George Donelson Moss, *Vietnam: An American Ordeal.* 6th edition. (Upper Saddle River, NJ: Prentice Hall, 2010), 106.
68 The Bureau of Foreign Economy and Liaison, "Report on the Current Foreign Aid and Proposal for the Future Tasks," September 1, 1961.
69 Mao decided that China must support the "excellent armed struggles" in South Vietnam and Laos unconditionally during a Central Work Conference of the CCP Central Committee at Beidaihe in August 1962. See: Yang Kuisong, "Mao Zedong and the Indochina Wars," 72–73.
70 Han Nianlong, *Dangdai zhongguo waijiao* [Foreign Affairs of Contemporary China] (Beijing: Zhongguo shehui kexue [China's Social Science Press], 1990), 159.
71 Zhai, *China and the Vietnam Wars*, 115–116.
72 Marilyn B. Young, *The Vietnam Wars, 1945–1990* (New York: HarperCollins, 1991), 71.
73 William J. Duiker, *Vietnam: Revolution in Transition*, 2nd ed. (Boulder, CO: Westview, 1995), 69.

8　New Japan (1952–1996)

The Japanese people, proud of their heritage and conscious of their economic power, desired to take the place in world affairs to which they felt they were entitled. A new awareness and a readjustment were taking place in both foreign relations and international trade. In both cases it was ultimately not for the politicians or the bureaucrats but for the people as a whole to determine the outcome. The consistent US drive to restore Japan as a preeminent power in the region was a source of constant irritation for China, the Koreas, and Vietnam. Having fallen into an assumption that it would be in its best interest to install Japan as the leader in the Western Pacific, the American government had openly returned to its pre-WWII policy (in the 1920s) of supporting and encouraging Japan to re-emerge as the regional leader. This peculiar attitude might have reflected a historical pattern that the United States had never been comfortable with exercising a dominant political influence in the region. Washington's pro-Japan stand hardly pleased any government and its people in East Asia; either it had to compete with America's favorite, or had to fight against it.

Nevertheless, Washington's pro-Japan policy continued its support and aid to post-war reforms in the country. Washington was willing to share American science and technology with Japan. President Eisenhower and his administration believed that a strong Japan was important and necessary after the Korean War, for the United States, in order to curb communist expansion and influence in the Asian-Pacific region. Tokyo received the new "détente" policy, as laid out by President Richard Nixon, with a great deal of apprehension and some positive reaction. The doctrine meant the withdrawal of the United States from Southeast Asia in 1972–1973.[1] In 1972, the United States reinstated administrative control of Okinawa and the Ryukyus Islands to Japan. In September, only months after Nixon's visit to Beijing, Japan and China established a formal diplomatic relationship. (The diplomatic relationship between Beijing and Washington was not established until January 1, 1979.) Japan and China went further and signed a treaty of friendship and mutual co-operation in 1978. When China's "Reform and Opening" process began to unfold in the late 1970s and early 1980s, Japan was the first among all major industrial/capitalist countries to provide China with substantial technological and financial support.[2]

Among the major reasons behind Japan's economic growth in 1956–1979 were Tokyo's policies: domestic working force, international trade opportunities, and Washington's financial and technology aid. The United States not only made the new technologies available for Japan's industry, but also made its domestic market available for Japanese manufactured items. As Japan's largest trading partner, the United States had bought more than 22 percent of Japanese exports in 1975. Since then, the Japan-US trade has become imbalanced in favor of Japan, with tens of billions of dollars going to Japan every year through the first decade of the twenty-first century.

Japan-US relations: Aid and trade (1956–1965)

Soon after the peace treaty, Japan began a transitional era to complete the American reforms imposed after the Occupation and through the 1950s. Following the Yoshida Doctrine, the Japanese government increased its pro-business policy by becoming more deeply involved in economic planning, financial support, and trade promotion than any other non-Socialist state. For example, the government established the Bank of Japan, which backed commercial banks in providing capital investment. The Japanese Diet passed resolutions to protect growing industries at home and to limit foreign competitions in these fields. The government only welcomed foreign investment that brought in new technology, such as that made by the United States. It is cheaper and faster to license new technology than to develop it yourself.

After the early post-WWII period ended, the decade of 1956–1965 had transformed Japan into a new nation in terms of economy. By 1954, Japan's manufacturing had resumed to the pre-war level, and by 1956 the Japanese economy was ahead of other Asian countries. From 1956 to 1973, Japan's annual GDP had an average higher than 10 percent of the growth rate, which had never before been seen in any other industrial country. In 1956, private investment in the infrastructure and equipment had increased 54.6 percent from the previous year. Thereafter, this increase continued, with more than 70 percent in the steel and iron, machinery, electricity, and chemical industries. These traditional industries also provided a solid foundation for newly-established industries, such as automobile, electronic instruments, petro-chemistry, and plastic manufacturing. Because of the availability of the capital, these new industries were able to import new technology, equipment, and even entire manufacturing facilities from Western countries such as the United States, Germany, and France. Japan imported 1,148 foreign technologies between 1950 and 1955, and 2,273 advanced technologies in 1956–1965.

For Japan, as for most other East Asian countries in the Cold War from the fifties to the seventies, foreign policy developed within the nuclear balance between the United States and the Soviet Union. Edwin Reischauer and Albert Craig point out that "Throughout this era and beyond, the central principle of Japan's foreign policy was to maintain close ties to the United States."[3] Washington had made efforts to persuade Japan and South Korea to come to a settlement in the 1950s in order to complete the normalization of the Japan-Korean relations. As discussed in Chapter 5, this was vital to America's strategic interests in East Asia. Moreover, as South Korea remained far from reaching a self-sustaining economy, Washington was eager to share the cost with an increasingly prosperous Japan. In a sense, the United States was anxious to relinquish its role as South Korea's sole financial supporter. Thus, Washington actively pursued an avenue for placing South Korea under the joint custody of the United States and Japan.[4] On the other hand, Japan was hardly in a position to overlook Washington's wish, as its rapidly expanding industrial economy needed continuing access to the vast consumer market, as well as the capital and technology pool in America.

The Sato administration desired to resolve the unpleasant past by opening a new chapter of neighborly cooperation. First of all, the Japanese were anxious to secure the

Korean market for their industrial products. They were also observant of the opportunity to exploit South Korea's abundant but highly educated labor force. Aggressive business leaders of both countries exerted pressure on their respective governments for an early conclusion of normalization talks in 1964. The ensuing developments proved that the judgment of these business communities was generally correct and justifiable. By 1965, the treaty was concluded between the two countries, and Japan normalized its diplomatic relationship with South Korea. Japanese business re-entered the Korean market after twenty years since it was forced to withdraw from the peninsula at the end of the Pacific War.[5]

The United States not only made the new technologies available for Japan's industry in the 1950s, but also made its domestic market available for Japanese-manufactured items such as toys, shoes, clothing and apparel. Between 1956 and 1964, Japan's exports had an average annual growth rate of 13.5 percent, higher than any Western country. The United States became Japan's most important single trading partner. With the availability of the huge US market, Japan's exports reached its pre-war level in 1959. Tokyo continued its governmental control of exports and imports through the 1950s in favor of importing new technology and advanced machinery, while protecting domestic industry by limiting similar foreign imports. Eventually, in 1960, the Japanese government issued the Free Trade and Exchange Outlines, lifting some of the governmental controls over imports and opening part of the domestic market for foreign goods. By the end of the year, free imports consisted of 41 percent of total imports, and increased to 93 percent by 1964. Japan joined the GATT (General Agreement on Tariffs and Trade) in 1963, and IMF (International Monetary Fund) in 1964.[6]

After the completion of the transitional era, in 1960 Japan entered a new period of development and growth with many new economic programs of its own. In 1960, its annual GDP almost doubled to $43 billion with per capita GDP of $461. In 1965, Japan's GDP doubled and increased to $88 billion with per capita GDP of $898. By 1970, its annual GDP increased to $203 billion, more than doubled, and its per capita GDP reached $1,939. In another five years, by 1975, Japanese GDP doubled again and increased to $484 billion with per capita GDP of $4,320. In the same year, Japan had obtained a productive level comparable to that of Europe.

Japan's energy system had shifted from coal production to oil importation and consumption in the same period. In the early 1950s, oil production experienced tremendous development in the Middle East, while the United States and other oil-importing countries were able to control the oil price for their low-cost importation. Since the cost of importing oil from the Middle East was lower than producing coal in Japan, the country began to import crude oil and change its energy consumption structure. In 1956, coal consumption consisted of more than 50 percent of the nation's energy total, while oil consumed only 21.9 percent. But by 1964, oil consumption increased to 55.7 percent of the nation's total, while coal decreased to 29.2 percent.[7] Oil importation helped keep the cost of production low, and also supported the petro-chemical industry, ship building industry, steel and iron, and harbor construction. Soon, however, Japan expanded its exports and moved far beyond cheap manufacturing by including plastic products, polymers, and automobiles..

The availability of the American market was vital to Japanese products, not only because of the mass consumption in America, but also by its introduction of good quality and low cost Japanese manufactured items. Japan soon became the manufacturing factory of Asia. Its exports increased from $2 billion in 1955 to $8.45 billion in 1965, and to $55.75 billion in 1975. At that time, Asia took up to 28.4 percent of Japan's exports while Europe had 14.4 percent.

Last but not least, Japan had minimum spending on its defense through the Cold War because of the American "nuclear umbrella" as well as the mutual defense treaty. The low annual military budget was another contributor to Japan's economic advance, even though the country had established a small armed force, the Japanese Self-Defense Forces (JSDF, including army, naval, and air forces), in 1954. The cost of this force was very low, about one percent of Japan's GDP through the 1960s to 1980s. In 1974, for example, Japan spent only $1.9 billion on defense, while the United States spent $63.3 billion, the Soviet Union $61.9 billion, and West Germany $7.8 billion.[8] By the 1970s, the JSDF numbered a quarter of a million troops and one thousand jet war-planes. The Japanese Self-Defense Forces had not been deployed outside Japan until the First Persian Gulf War in 1991.

The International Olympic Committee (IOC) awarded the 1964 Summer Olympic Games to Tokyo. It was a dramatic juncture for the nation, which had survived almost total destruction at the end of the war in 1945, and occupation by foreign forces in 1945–1952. It was the first such international recognition for the Rising-Sun nation. The IOC decision galvanized Japan. Tokyo spent billions of dollars constructing ultra-modern Olympic facilities. Being eager to fully exploit such a rare opportunity, Japan poured in numerous resources to make the Olympics a showcase. The 1964 Tokyo Olympics helped elevate the worldwide prestige of industrial Japan. The island nation staged the games with unparalleled grandeur and professionalism. Unlike their forebears who hopelessly procrastinated in opening the nation to the West, contemporary Japan was eager to show its progress and success to the world community. Without doubt, the event served to enhance the prestige and international recognition of Japan. McClain concludes that "Most Japanese treasured the Olympic experience as a time of national bonding, a shining moment when the nation came together to affirm its political, economic, and spiritual recovery from the horrors of war and defeat."[9]

Economic taking-off and international relations (1966–1973)

Among the major areas of economic growth, during the 1960s –1970s, was that the automobile industry took the lead in the country's manufacturing. From 1966, Japan enjoyed a continuing growth over the next five years. By 1970, private investment in equipment improvement increased more than 23 percent.

First, to be able to compete in the international market, key industries such as steel and iron, the petro-chemical industry, and electronic companies, began developing into giant corporations with mass production through merging and reorganizing. The super-sized steel mills were completed with an annual productive capacity of over ten million tons of steel each after 1965. The huge steel complexes significantly increased the nation's steel products from 41 million tons in 1965 to 120 million tons in 1973. During the same period, other industries had also been super-sized with huge shipyards building 500,000-ton capacity ships, giant petro-chemical facilities producing 300,000 tons of ethylene annually in each factory, and super-power generations producing 500,000 kW of electricity annually in each plant. Japan's heavy and chemical industries increased from 42.7 percent of the nation's industries in 1955, to 51.1 percent in 1965, and up to 68.9 percent of the total industry in 1970. By then, Japan had become number one or two in steel production, electric power, automobile manufacturing, ship building, and plastic products, in the advanced countries.

Also, Japan had gained its own technology development in the late 1960s, while it continued to import new technologies from advanced countries such as the United States. Japan imported approximately 15,000 new technologies from foreign countries between 1965 and 1973. In the meantime, however, Japan had crafted a strategy that focused on greatly expanding its utilization of research and development. If we can say that Japan was merely a copier and reproducer of existing Western technologies in the early 1950s, and became an adapter and modifier in the late 1950s and early 1960s, then Japan engaged in technological innovations at a global level in the late 1960s and early 1970s. From 1966 to 1973, research and development funds had increased three times. By the early 1970s, there were twenty-one scientific researchers among every 10,000 Japanese citizens, the second highest research personnel rate in the world only after the United States. Japan began demonstrating its capacity for designing and producing relatively advanced new technologies and manufacturing systems. This was especially the case in high quality home appliances, such as color televisions, watches, cameras, tape-recorders, and electron microscopes with high magnifications. Japan appeared to have strong potential indigenous technological capabilities, to compete with the advanced countries, including the United States. By the early 1970s, Japan's productive quality had become one of the best in the world. The perfection of manufacturing also improved labor productive efficiency with an increase of 12.4 percent between 1966 and 1973.

After 1965, Japan had maintained a surplus in its international trade with most trading partners in the world, including the United States. Its exportation totaled $8.32 billion in 1965 with a surplus of $1.9 billion that year. By 1972, its exportation had increased to $28.03 billion (more than triple that in 1965), with a surplus of $8.97 billion (more than four times that in 1965). Among the major exports, industrial items increased rapidly from 62.4 percent of total exports in 1965 to 73 percent in 1970, and up to 84 percent of total exports in 1977. The steady incoming trade surplus had brought in much hard currency to Japan and increased the nation's gold reserves.[10]

The international status of Japanese yen had improved, and its strong financial status had made Japan a wealthy country with a huge capital surplus and many overseas investment opportunities. In 1961, Japan's overseas investment totaled $381 million. Its total foreign investment increased to $1,066.8 million in 1965, with a majority of the investments in textile, mining, and chemical industry in Third World countries such as Asia, Africa, and Latin America. After the 1970s, however, Japanese direct investments entered the United States and other industrialized countries in Europe.

Japan obtained a balance development in 1966–1973 between agriculture and industry; between big corporations and small- and medium-sized factories; and between manufacturing and service industries. With a rapid growth of industry, Japanese farmers lost two-thirds of their labor force in the 1960s. Farming labor decreased from 41 percent of the entire labor force in 1955, down to 24.6 percent in 1965, and continued to decease to only 13.8 percent of the national total by 1975. Nevertheless, the Japanese government continued to improve agriculture and to support local farmers. In 1961, the Basic Agricultural Laws were promulgated with increasing farmers' loans and governmental subsidies. By 1973, agriculture had achieved new developments through its modernization with machineries, new irrigation systems, and fertilization.

In the 1950s, small and medium-sized companies had considered the huge enterprises as enemies or threats to their business. The government modified industrial structure during merging and super-sizing in the late 1960s in a manner that meant the small- and medium-sized companies operated around the large enterprises to provide parts, service, and supportive roles. Through reorganization, these small- and medium-sized companies became mutually beneficial with the large enterprises. They enjoyed an average annual increase of their production of more than 17 percent between 1966 and 1973. During the same period, Japan's service industries, including public utilities, transportation and communication, finance and banking, commerce and retails, medical and legal services, also had tremendous development. The total service labor force increased from 35.1 percent in 1955, to 43.4 percent in 1965, and up to 52.1 percent of the national total labor force in 1975.

The annual average of Japanese GDP growth rate remained at 10.5 percent between 1966 and 1973. Its GDP exceeded the British and French in 1967, and it moved ahead of Germany in 1968, becoming the third largest economy in the world only after the United States and the Soviet Union. Its economy in 1973 was as much as 2.4 times what it was in 1964.

Nevertheless, Japan made major changes in its foreign policy-making in the late 1960s and early in 1970, after the "Nixon shock" in 1969 and the first "oil shock" in 1973. After winning the election of 1968, President Nixon carried out his new policy toward the Vietnam War, including the "Vietnamization," to build up the South Vietnamese armed forces so that American forces could withdraw without the Communists overrunning the South. This is what he had promised to the American voters in his presidential campaign. In his Guam Doctrine, or the Nixon Doctrine, the president asked all American allies, including Japan, to take on a greater role to increase their responsibility for regional defense against the communist aggression. Historians likely agree that Japan exploited the opportunity offered by the US alliance system to pursue improved relations with communist states such as China. Glenn D. Hook, Julie Gilson, Christopher W. Hughes, and Hugo Dobson point out: "What is more, Japanese policy-makers became less consistent in following U.S. foreign policy goals as the strength of U.S. global hegemony began to wane and multi-polarity in the international system started to wax in the early 1970s."[11]

According to Hane and Perez, "The major focus of United States-Japan relations from the 1970s on was trade between the two nations. The United States has remained Japan's biggest trading partner since the end of the war."[12] In 1970, 30.7 percent of Japan's exports and 29.4 percent of its imports were to and from the United States, and the figure remained in the 20 to 30 percent range to the 1990s. From the 1970s to 1980s, Japan experienced rapid economic growth through its export-oriented manufacturing. Its "economic miracle" transformed the country into a world-class economic power. The export-oriented manufacturing provided many job opportunities for Japanese people in the 1960s to 1970s and had a strong impact on demographic changes.

New challenges and new foreign policy (the 1970s)

The closeness of the Japanese government's ties to the United States caused problems. Japan's foreign relations were intimately bound up with its economic ups and downs. The major change in its foreign policy-making took place in the early 1970s. Japan was admitted as a full member to the Asian Development Bank and then to the International Development Bank. The United States sponsored Japan's re-entry into the UN and World Bank. In April 1973, in a major speech in New York, Henry Kissinger, then Secretary of the State in the Nixon administration, proposed "a new Atlantic Charter," which created for the Atlantic nations a new relationship which Japan could share in. The United States became Japan's largest single market, and the source for most of its technology.

Tokyo received the new "détente" policy, as laid out by President Richard Nixon, with a great deal of apprehension and some positive reaction. The doctrine meant the withdrawal of the United States from Southeast Asia in 1972–1973.In 1972, the United States returned administrative control of Okinawa and the Ryukyus Islands to Japan. In the same year, Nixon visited Beijing to carry out the Nixon Doctrine as the first US president that had ever visited the Communist state since its founding in 1949. The Nixon Doctrine was born against the backdrop of political uncertainty in East Asia. By then the United States was not expected to achieve a clean victory in Vietnam; the nation with the most modern weaponry and tactics but which was politically divided and unsure of its mission in the region, failed to subjugate the ill-equipped but determined Vietnamese guerrilla force. Confronted by the prospect of a long military stalemate and worsening anti-war sentiments at home, the Nixon administration was anxious to end the war by withdrawing its forces. The new initiative reflected Washington's strong interest in improving its relations with Beijing. Kenneth Henshall points out that:

> The Nixon Shocks were not as damaging as the Oil Shock, but they were disturbing to the Japanese. They clearly signaled a cooling in American attitudes and good-will towards Japan. Nevertheless, Japan rode them all out, and by the end of the 1970s many Japanese were starting to wonder if they needed American good will anyway.[13]

Although there was a fear among Japanese that the United States might use Japan as a bargaining chip for a Sino-American rapprochement, the Japanese government moved forward to improve its relations with Communist China. Having followed US policy toward the PRC, Japan hadn't had any relationship with mainland China since 1949, and a formal diplomatic relationship with Taiwan. In 1952, Prime Minister Yoshida signed a peace treaty with the Taiwanese government, since the latter was not among the forty-six signatories of the peace treaty at San Francisco in 1951. In the 1960s, some improvement of the economic and cultural relations between Tokyo and Beijing occurred when trade began between the two countries. Japan voted with the United States in the UN for replacing Taiwan with China in 1970 and 1971.

Although Tokyo was "completely caught off guard" in the summer of 1971 when Washington suddenly announced Nixon's plan to visit Beijing in February 1972, Japanese leaders quickly followed suit.[14] In that September, only months after Nixon's visit to Beijing, Japan and China established a formal diplomatic relationship. (The diplomatic relationship between Beijing and Washington was not establish until January 1, 1979.) The trade between China and Japan increased from $1.1 billion in 1972 to $3.8 billion in 1975. The trading amount between the two countries in 1975 was 25 percent of China's total foreign trade. Reischauer and Albert point out that "China was attracted by Japanese technology but had little to offer in return and it was reluctant to be simply a supplier of oil and other raw materials."[15] Then the two countries went further and signed a peace treaty of friendship and mutual cooperation in 1978. When China's "Reform and Opening" process began to unfold in the late 1970s and early 1980s, Japan was the first among all major industrial/capitalist countries to provide China with substantial technological and financial support.

As a result, the 1980s became "a decade of impressive economic growth for Asian countries on the whole." Iriye states that: "By the end of the decade, South Korea, Taiwan, Hong Kong, and Singapore – the so-called 'newly industrializing economies' or 'little dragons' – were fast moving in the same direction, and the countries of Southeast Asia, also did not lag far behind."[16] Iriye, however, credits the spectacular Asian "economic miracle" to the United States, which provided a military presence necessary for the security and stability of East Asia and the Pacific, where there had been two large-scale wars, Korea and Vietnam.

Through 1952–1978, despite the growth of the JSDF, there was little coordination between the Japanese and the American military. After the end of the Vietnam War, as Reischauer and Craig point out, "Japan feared a general American withdrawal from Asia, so it began more actively to coordinate the efforts of the two forces with respect to logistics, strategic planning, and military intelligence."[17]

Then, during his long tenure as prime minister, Nakasone Yasuhiro thought to strengthen Japan's SDF further in 1982 when he took over the cabinet. At that moment, he was concerned by overflights of Russian backfire bombers and by the basing of over one-third of the nuclear and conventional forces of the USSR in the East Asian region opposite Japan. The United States was certainly anxious to have Japan undertake responsibility for the naval defense of the sea-lanes for 1,000 miles off the Japanese coast. Nakasone's efforts were successful; the defense budget rose from $11 billion in 1983 to $13 billion in 1984, and then $15 billion the following year. However, Nakasone had to move with great caution. The Japanese people had no wish to return to any kind of military posture. For years, it had been an unwritten rule that the defense budget should not exceed 1 percent of the country's GDP. That barrier was broken in 1986. By the next year, the barrier was abandoned and the defense budget settled under a five-year plan, bearing no relation to the GDP.

Another question was that of sending Japanese troops to serve abroad. The problem first arose during the Persian Gulf War. In October 1987, two Japanese-operated oil tankers were attacked by Iranian gunboats in the Persian Gulf. The Persian Gulf countries were the source of 55 percent of Japan's oil, and the US government criticized the Japanese for not offering more help to the international effort to control the region. The Japanese thereupon offered technical aid and more funds to finance the US forces stationed in Japan.

Japan's economic growth had not always been steady because of its energy dependency on foreign oil and natural gas. The energy crises in the 1970s slowed Japan's economic development. The post-war economy had been geared to cheap oil. The formation of OPEC (Organization of the Petroleum Exporting Countries) and oil price shocks of 1972 and 1979 hit Japan hard.

After the Yom Kippur War between Arabic countries and Israel broke out in the Middle East during October 1973, the OPEC imposed an oil embargo on the United States and European countries, in order to dissuade the United States from selling armaments to Israel and to align oil dependent countries with OPEC (or Arabic countries) rather than with Israel. Japan totally depended on imported oil – 99.5 percent of its oil had to be imported, and 88 percent of the oil import came from the Middle East in 1973. OPEC then began raising the oil price drastically. The price increased from $2 a barrel to $11 in 1973.

In 1973–1975, government officials and industrial leaders in Japan formulated plans to deal with the oil crisis by cutting back the use of oil and readjusting industrial production. As a result, there was a shift of manufacturing "from heavy industries to the production of high-tech goods such as precision machineries and electronic products."[18] In the meantime, after the 1973 Oil Crisis, American consumers began looking for smaller, high-mileage, gas-saving cars. Japan was ready to supply in place of large American cars. Japan only produced 165,000 cars in 1960, but its manufacturing of passenger cars totaled 3,178,000 in 1970, and increased to 6,176,000 in 1975. Japanese cars soon began flooding the US auto market.

After 1972, as the gap between Japan and other advanced nations closed, the 11 percent growth rate of the previous two decades declined to 4 percent or slightly less. This was still at the high end of growth rates among advanced nations. Some of the favorable factors that had helped Japan earlier continued: high-quality labor, the propensity to save, low defense costs, open world markets, and so on. But other advantages were lost, such as free and cheap Western technology, cheap oil, and cheap labor. Another earlier advantage had been the combination of cheap labor and high productivity. By the late seventies, this advantage had passed to South Korea, Taiwan, Hong Kong, and Singapore. Labor was no longer cheap, and slower growth meant a rising proportion of more expensive older workers. Government costs also rose.

Social and political changes (1970s–1980s)

The seventies, and especially the late seventies, saw the emergence of an era in Japan with a new and different character. McClain points out that "The unprecedented economic boom changed life dramatically for Japan's citizens."[19] First, Japan had experienced unprecedented social transition with the establishment and growth of its middle class. After twenty years of economic growth, increasingly more Japanese had improved their standard of living and moved up to the social middle. In the 1960s, upward social mobility diminished the boundaries between different social statures that had been clearly and rigidly marked before the war. The loosening government control over people's mobility further allowed farmers to take up occupations originally only available to urban residents. All of this helped to diversify the homogeneous group of farmers into different social groups and quickly boosted a considerable number of them into a higher income stratum. The developing middle class included engineers, managers, specialists, professional technicians, legal service staff, business administrators, and private business owners. Since the 1970s, the rapid change of Japan's traditional social strata has been largely perceived as beneficial to the healthy growth of its society. It increased opportunities for the general public, and helped to bring the social mechanisms of choice and award to the general populace; a norm that did not exist in the 1930s–1940s.

Second, education transformed the post-war society by narrowing the gap between the masses and the social elite. The number of all school-age children in high schools increased from 43 percent in 1950 to 93 percent in 1975, totaling 4.3 million in that year. Then, the high school enrollments inched up to 5.4 million in 1987. By the late eighties, though not compulsory, 96 percent of middle school graduates went on to high school. Post-secondary enrollments also increased: in 1987, 1.9 million students were enrolled at four-year universities, 438,000 at two-year colleges, and 50,000 at higher technical schools. In 1950, about 84,000 students enrolled in colleges, only 8 percent of the college-age population. By 1975, about 1.7 million students enrolled in colleges, more than 44 percent of the college-age total. By that time, the social and educational gap between the elite and masses had disappeared. Moreover, almost 90 percent of the Japanese people – high school and university graduate – defined themselves as middle class.

Third, Japan became urbanized after the war, with more than 50 percent of the population living in the cities. With its economic growth in the 1960s, Japan had generated a substantial portion of capital for the urbanization. Among the major cities were Tokyo, Yokohama, Osaka, Nagoya, Sapporo, Kobe, Kyoto, and Fukuoka. In 1972, one of every nine Japanese lived in Tokyo, and one out of every four lived in the Tokyo-Osaka industrial belt. The number of farm families had decreased from 6 million in 1960 to 5.67 million in 1965, and down to 4.95 million in 1975. In the 1970s, farming in Japan became an enterprise for profit, not subsistence. As a result, the average annual farm family income had increased from $1,143 in 1960 to $11,086 in 1975. And balanced trade gave way to huge export surpluses, which made Japan the world's premier financial power. Consumerism and the habits of affluence also appeared both in the urban and rural societies.

Fourth, in this urban society, as a social consequence, the status of women rose. Nearly all girls received primary education, while most girls went to high school and many to college. The legal rights of women increasingly became accepted. The government passed several major legislations to protect women's rights and to improve their social and economic status. For example, the Diet passed the Equal Employment Opportunities Law in 1986, the Tax Exemption Act for Low-Income Females in 1988, and Leave Laws in 1992. The cabinet also created the Gender Equality Council which oversaw and enforced the regulations and labor standards. In 1993, the first sexual harassment suit was tried in court. By the 1990s, Japanese women were working in 50 percent of teaching jobs, 32 percent of government employments, and 16 percent of medical, legal, and engineering occupations. About 14 percent of CEOs, high-ranking managers, and board directors were women, while 9 percent of elected Diet members were women. In regards to the institution of marriage, post-war changes reached into the eighties. In the early post-war period, most marriages were still arranged by go-betweens with the approval of the parents. This gave way in the sixties and seventies to "love marriages," in which the partners made their own arrangements, although sometimes asking an office superior or teacher to serve as an honorary go-between. During this time most young couples lived apart from their parents, and by the eighties almost four out of five marriages were of this new type. The old-fashioned "arranged marriage" became a fallback device for those who had failed earlier to find partners on their own by their late twenties.

Fifth, one significant social change in post-war Japan, and one that distinguished Japan from China and most other nations in Asia, was the decline in the growth rate of its population. After 1950, the overall rate of increase in Japan's population had been stabilized with a total of 72 million in 1945, 89 million in 1955, 98 million in 1965, 112 million in 1975, and 120 million in 1990. During the same period of time, China's population increased from 400 million in 1945 to 800 million in 1965, and to 1,200 million in 1990. One of the explanations for Japan's stabilization of population could be credited to evolution of social institutions along the course taken by other advanced nations. Medical facilities, had improved, more education meant later marriages and fewer children, and the educated were more willing to accept a two-child ideal. One trend of the eighties was the continued moderation of the rate of population growth. By the late eighties, there were 122 million Japanese. During this era, the Japanese life span had advanced to a European level. By the late eighties, the Japanese were living longer than any other people in the world: women had gained four years for an average longevity of eighty-one, and men's average lifespan had gone up three years to seventy-five.

One may expect some dislocations and social unrest with the rapid pace of social changes in Japan. Instead, the society had maintained a high degree of political stability and social integration in the 1960s–1980s. In the late 1980s, the government changed policy so that Japanese people received more benefits from the nation's wealth, including improving public health, social welfare, and retirement. On January 7, 1989, Emperor Hirohito died as the longest monarch in the country since 1926. His eldest son, Akihito (or Emperor Heisei) ascended the throne as Japan's 125th emperor on November 12, 1990.

The LDP enjoyed popular support from the constituencies that received benefits from LDP legislation and domestic policies. Into the 1980s, however, a burst of political conservatism reversed the twenty-year decline of the LDP's popular vote and ended the "age of parties." More Japanese began to criticize LDP political dominance, personal networking, and scandal and corruption. One clear political trend in the transition from the seventies to the eighties was a growing conservatism. Discussions of national character, long a favorite topic in magazines and journals, became decidedly upbeat. The benefit took the form of a reversal of the twenty-year decline in the popular votes for the LDP. In the late 1980s, the party was beset by exposures of corruption, including political bribery, sex scandals, and mismanagement. It was also undermined by the defection of a number of party elites who had been part of the political establishment in the past. In the election of 1993, the LDP failed to gain a majority for the first time in thirty-eight years. The New Party won a governing majority in the Diet, and its leader, Hosokawa Morihiro, assumed the position of prime minister in 1993, thus terminating the LDP's dominance since 1955. A second political development of the eighties was a debate within the conservative camp over how to position Japan to meet the challenges of the twenty-first century. This debate was sparked by a new awareness that Japan could no longer look to foreign models and that henceforth it would have to define its own future goals.

Among other problems in the 1980s were an aging population, out-of-date college entry examinations, and pollution. Because the age distribution in Japan was affected by WWII and the post-war baby boom, the new longevity also portended a serious future problem: at the turn of the century, Japan had a higher percentage of non-working elderly people than any other country. After the war, the gate to higher education remained narrow. In 1986, about 2.9 million students took the college entrance examinations, but only 436,000 were accepted. Twice as many students took the examinations as graduates from high school – more than half were putting themselves through "examination hell" for a second, third, or fourth time. By the 1980s, the greatest internal problem was pollution. Many air and water pollutants from the automobile and manufacturing industries included nitrous oxides, carbon monoxide, benzene, and mercury. These environmental issues had become increasingly problematic, especially in newly rapid industrializing areas. The government took some measures to strengthen environmental improvement in the 1990s, such as passing legislations, educating businesses and the public, and enforcing regulations. Although environmental protection had become a hot topic and had received more attention inside and outside the government, the GDP-based development policy made by the pro-business government only served the purpose of economic growth rather than environmental protection.

From high growth to economic recessions (1980s–1990s)

After the "oil shocks" of 1973 and 1979, the breath-taking high-speed growth was finished, but Japan still had an average annual growth rate of 5 percent in the mid-1970s, still higher than Western countries, including the United States. By 1980, Japan's annual GDP consisted of 13.3 percent of the world total among the industrial countries, and became the second largest economy in the world only after the United States. In 1985, Japan's GDP totaled $1,329 billion, comparing to $3,988 billion for the United States, $2,063 billion for the Soviet Union, $354 billion for China, and $190 billion for India. In 1988, Japan's GDP increased to $2,792 billion, and its per capita GDP was higher than the equivalent American figure.

However, in the first half of the 1990s, Japan suffered the most severe recession the country had known for forty years. It began when the Finance Ministry took steps to start deflating asset prices. The ministry was seeking to protect over-extended banks and other financial institutes from the effects of unwise lending. The result was a drop in the price of land and shares, sluggish consumption, and falling company profits. The years 1990 and 1991 saw price escalation, high unemployment, wide spread bankruptcies, and slumped economic growth rate. The annual rise in GDP for the year 1992 was the smallest since 1974 (the first "oil crisis"). Automobile sales fell in each of the three years 1991, 1992, and 1993. In 1993, the production of four-wheel vehicles fell by 12 percent, exports by over 18 percent, while Toyota announced a reduction in profits of nearly 35 percent in 1992. Kenneth Henshall states that "The government and the business world occasionally interpreted this and that event as a sign of imminent recovery, but this did not eventuate."[20]

Then, in the second half of the 1990s, a major economic crisis swept Asian countries and to some extent Japan bore the brunt of further economic decline. Before the crisis of 1997 and 1998, Asia had been known for the robustness of its economy, its high exports, its attractiveness to foreign investors, and its increasing wages. Rather than being the darling of capitalists, Asia faltered in 1997 and 1998. In 1996 and 1997, industrial productivity fell 50 percent in Thailand. These years suggest that the Asian Economic Crisis may have begun in Thailand. In 1997 Thailand had a $10 billion deficit, although by December of that year, possibly through austerity, it reduced its deficit to $40 million. In 1997 in Thailand, the sale of cars, steel, electronics, and other goods fell between 35 and 75 percent. By 1998, unemployment stood at 6 percent. In 1997 and 1998 South Korean businesses went bankrupt, pushing unemployment upward. In November 1998, South Korea announced 5 percent unemployment, a high number for that country. In 1998 South Korean GDP weakened by 6.7 percent. In 1998 Indonesia's GDP fell 13 percent in 1998 and its stock market fell as low as 84 percent. In 1998 unemployment increased the number of poor Indonesians from twenty-three million to forty million.

Overall GDP declined 7 percent in East Asia in 1998. Japan saw its GDP fall an additional 2 percent in that year. In the late 1990s, the country's trade surplus became smaller, as imports grew faster than exports. The fall was also the result of a series of diplomatic attempts to reduce the bilateral imbalance of trade between Japan and the United States under the Bush and Clinton administrations. In principle, some agreements to increase Japanese purchases in the automobiles and auto parts industries had been reached. Automobiles and auto parts were much the most significant item in dispute between the two countries, since they were accounting for about two-thirds of America's $60–80 billion annual trade deficit from the 1980s to the 2000s.

Among other negative impacts, Japanese consumers turned more and more to lower cost goods. These goods were becoming much more readily available in discount shops. Japanese prices, as a whole, were being driven down by Asian competition and crisis. This put the returns from established retail businesses under pressure.

Another consequence was that companies began cutting into the work force, including some of the giants, such as the electrical company Hitachi, the computer company Fujitsu, and the communications company NTT. Traditional life-time employment could no longer be guaranteed, nor could pensions. Some companies even found it difficult to keep the retirement age at sixty-five. Increasingly they turned to a compulsory retiring age of sixty for men and fifty-five for women.

In the meantime, the government also made new policies to reduce annual working hours to move Japan away from its reputation as a country of workaholics. But many observers believed that the change was best explained by economic crisis. A report at the end of the 1990s showed no significant reduction in the number of employees who worked over sixty hours a week.

Some of the large companies began to transfer their manufacturing capacity to Japanese-owned factories overseas, the so-called "hollowing-out" of Japanese industry. It was largely for the sake of market access: to circumvent the threats of protectionism directed from time to time against Japanese goods. It was accomplished most success-fully in China and the countries of Southeast Asia, which found themselves able, as a result, not only to take over certain Japanese export markets, but also to penetrate the Japanese market itself.

The government responses to recessions had usually been a series of economic rescue packages, designed to act as a stimulus to consumer spending. For example, in August 1992, the Miyazawa cabinet announced a spending program of 10,700 billion yen for public works, loans to small- and medium-sized business, and help to banks in dispos-ing of real estate. In February 1994, the Hosokawa cabinet decided to stimulate the economy by spending 15,300 billion yen, including an income-tax cut of 5,500 billion yen, in the coming year. After the mid-1990s, the government also began its "Restruc-turing and Deregulation" policy, which was to reduce government intervention in business such as to give less protection to Japanese firms in the domestic market and open it more fully to foreign goods. The new policy would break down some of the traditional relationships between business and government.

Among other reasons for the economic downturn, first of all, was the combination of a rapidly expanding economy, and a slowly growing population, produced a labor shortage in the late 1980s and 1990s. Moreover, for several decades Japan's economic success had rested on the manufacture of high-quality goods at low prices through mass production and heavy investment in technology. This achievement had been made possible by long working hours, low dividends, and restrictive arrangements between members of large businesses; a "company-centered" approach which had already had its day.

Secondly, the post-war generation also faced the lack of welfare, including healthcare, social welfare, and retirement. So much of Japan's economic surplus was put back into new investments that little remained for social programs. Welfare for the sick and old was minimal. Last but not least, the country had gone through a grave period from the late 1990s, when instability in the energy market and financial system came to the surface. In 2000, Japan's GDP stood at 511 trillion yen ($4.7 trillion), while that of the United States was $9 trillion. In the same year, its per capita GDP was $37,560, and the United States was $33,000. The 2011 Tohoku earthquake and tsunami hit Japan's economic recovery from the 2000 recession, and China replaced Japan as the second largest economy in the world in 2012.

Notes

1　Paul H. Clyde and Burton F. Beers, *The Far East: A History of Western Impacts and Eastern Responses, 1830–1975*, 6th ed. (Prentice-Hall,, 1975), 524–525.
2　Donald W. Klein, "Japan and Europe in Chinese Foreign Relations," in *China and the World: Chinese Foreign Policy Faces the New Millennium*, ed. Samuel S. Kim, 4th ed. (Boulder, CO: Westview Press, 1998), 138–139.
3　Edwin Reischauer and Albert Craig, *Japan: Tradition and Transformation*, revised ed. (Boston, MA: Houghton Mifflin, 1989), 314.
4　Walter B. Jung, *National Building: The Geopolitical History of Korea* (Lanham, MD: University Press of America, 1998), 300–301.
5　Jung, *ibid.*, 301–302.
6　McClain, *Japan*, 519, 580–581.
7　Xiaobing Li and Michael Molina, "Japan," in *Oil: A Cultural and Geographic Encyclopedia of Black Gold*, ed. Li and Molina (Santa Barbara, CA: ABC-CLIO, 2014), 2: 565–566.
8　Fairbank, Reischauer, and Craig, *East Asia*, 829.
9　McClain, *Japan*, 564.
10　Fairbank, Reischauer, and Craig, *East Asia*, 830.
11　Hook, Gilson, Hughes, and Dobson, *Japan's International Relations*, 33.
12　Hane and Perez, *Modern Japan*, 397, 422 n16.
13　Kenneth Henshall, *A History of Japan*, 2nd ed. (London, UK: Palgrave, 2004), 168.
14　Hane and Perez, *Modern Japan*, 401.
15　Reischauer and Craig, *Japan*, 319.
16　Iriye, *Power and Culture*, 380.
17　Reischauer and Craig, *Japan*, 315.
18　Hane and Perez, *Modern Japan*, 409.
19　McClain, *Japan*, 572.
20　Henshall, *A History of Japan*, 173.

9   The Communist Cold War and Vietnam (1958–1975)

After the Korean War ended in 1953, China quickly adjusted its position in international affairs and willingly moved onto the center stage of ideological and military confrontations between the two contending camps of the Cold War, headed by the Soviet Union and the United States respectively. The active role that China played in East Asia turned this Cold War battlefield into an odd "buffer" between Moscow and Washington because, with China and East Asia standing in the middle, it was less likely that the Soviet Union and the United States would become involved in direct military confrontation.[1] Some Western historians agree that the alliance between Beijing and Moscow was the cornerstone of the communist international alliance system in the 1950s.

Mao Zedong continued his revolution by calling to "learn from the Soviet Union" and by launching a series of political campaigns through the 1950s. As the leading party of the most populous "third world" country, the CCP's culture of "borrowing" or "copying" from other countries like the Soviet Union proved to be conducive to its evolution and re-creation. While Chinese society became more radicalized in order to maintain its identity within the Communist camp, its foreign policy became more active in supporting the worldwide communist movement to keep up with its new power status. David Shambaugh identifies the CCP's trait of adaptation as a key difference to the Soviet Union.[2]

Soviet and Chinese leaders, however, soon split on ideological and political issues, including their differing views on nuclear weapons in the late 1950s and early 1960s. This rift can be attributed to multiple, complicated domestic and international factors. The most important of the disputes was over whether Beijing should become a new center of the international communist movement, which contributed to the decline of the Sino-Soviet alliance. The great Sino-Soviet polemic debate in 1960–1962 undermined the ideological foundation of the communist revolution. Chen Jian states that, in retrospect, few events during the Cold War had played so important a role in shaping the orientation and essence of the Cold War as the Sino-Soviet split.[3] Moscow lost its total control of the international communist movement. The conflicts between the two communist parties extended to their strategic issues in the 1960s. The 1964 transition in the Soviet leadership from Khrushchev to Brezhnev did not improve Sino-Soviet relations. China's bellicose rhetoric in the early 1960s, and the Great Proletarian Cultural Revolution sweeping across China beginning in 1966, completely destroyed any hope that Beijing and Moscow might continue to regard each other as "comrades in arms."[4] As the Sino-Soviet relationship worsened, it gradually moved from hostility to outright confrontation during a border war in 1969–1972.

Soviet and Chinese military aid to North Vietnam between 1965 and 1973 did not improve Sino-Soviet relations, but rather created a new front and new competition as each attempted to gain leadership of the Southeast Asian Communist movements. The North Vietnamese knew that the Soviet Union and China were rivals in the communist camp, competing for the leadership in the Asian Communist movement, including Vietnam. Each claimed itself a key supporter of the Vietnamese Communists' struggle against the American invasion. So the Vietnamese brought both sets of communist troops into North Vietnam, increasing the competition between the Chinese and Soviet Communists in the Vietnam War of 1965–1975.

In retrospect, international communist support to North Vietnam, including troops, logistics, and technology, proved to be the decisive edge that enabled the North Vietnamese Army (NVA) to survive the American Rolling Thunder bombing campaign, and helped the National Liberation Front (NLF, Communists in South Vietnam, also known as the "Viet Cong") prevail in the war of attrition and eventually defeat South Vietnam.[5] Chinese and Russian support prolonged the war, making it impossible for the United States to win. As Chang and Halliday point out, "It was having China as a secure rear and supply depot that made it possible for the Vietnamese to fight twenty-five years and beat first the French and then the Americans."[6]

Mao's Great Leap Forward movement

Between 1949 and 1966, the Chinese unitary party-state maintained complete control of all social resources. The Chinese Communist Party Center controlled the government, including courts, law enforcement, and the legal system to serve its communist political agenda as a totalitarian authority. In order to solidify this new establishment, the CCP institutionalized discrimination against tens of millions of people on the basis of their wealth, or "class origin." People regarded as having a "bad class origin" were considered possible threats to the new China. They and their children, and even their grandchildren, were socially stigmatized, treated as political outcasts, and discriminated against in education, employment, and daily life, and often viewed as potential criminals who were watched with suspicion. Mao justified the necessity of class struggle and stated that the Chinese people could never have any rights or liberties until they took them away from their social enemies, or counterrevolutionaries. Thus, under the people's democratic dictatorship, class struggle continued year after year through ruthless suppression, antagonistic contradiction, and massive violations of civil and human rights through the 1950s–1970s.

During the 1950s, Mao launched one political movement after another to engage the masses in the class struggle and to eliminate those labeled as potential or already active counterrevolutionaries through initiatives such as land reform, the Three Antis movement, Five Antis movement, and anti-Rightist movement. All of these campaigns turned into violent reactions against millions of Chinese people. During the 1950s, the CCP believed they needed a charismatic authority and absolute power to achieve their idealistic goals. Their successful military struggle for power during the Chinese Civil War against the GMD had convinced the leadership that violent means were necessary not only for establishing national power, but also for continuing their Communist revolution after the founding of the PRC. The ideology, experience, and nature of this transformation left little room for the Chinese people's civil liberties.

In 1958, the Chinese state further expanded into all levels of society through Mao's Three Red Banners movement, including the General Line of Socialist Construction,

Great Leap Forward, and People's Communes. The campaign instituted a bold advance on a large scale. All the industrial production targets for the second five-year plan (1958–1963) were doubled, and agricultural production targets were raised by 20 to 50 percent. The Great Forward Leap was Mao's radical economic policy to industrialize the country through labor power and collectivization instead of technology.

In rural areas, most peasants were organized into communes that controlled their productivity and distribution. Private land ownership and independent farming were non-existent. Every peasant worked with others in a team and through collective production shared the annual yields. Each people's commune, including about 1,600–2,000 households, theoretically played the role of collective owner, managed the local land, and produced food. By 1975, 52,615 people's communes had been established, managing 677,000 production brigades, including 4.83 million production teams and 164.48 million households. In fact, the commune system met with serious difficulties and failed to provide the basic needs for the local peasants. A national peasant average income was about 200 yuan RMB ($60) a year in the 1960s. After 1976, the concept of Mao's People's Communes weakened considerably. Under the People's Commune System, peasants could not leave their units, and if they wanted to travel, permission from village cadres was required. Furthermore, the markets in rural areas were banned as cradles for the petty bourgeois economy. In the urban areas, residents were similarly denied freedom of movement without permission. Factory workers could not change or quit their jobs and were dependent upon their work units for everything from food, medical care, housing, and their children's education. The state controlled all the resources necessary for manufacturing, transportation, trade, banking, education, and social welfare. In 1958, tens of millions of people were mobilized in a nationwide movement of steel-making, an extremely costly operation in terms of labor, capital, and raw material. Traditional craftsmen were all forced to participate in collectivized firms. China had become a state based on the complete control of all resources by the party-run government.

The Great Leap Forward movement's consequences were more disastrous than those of earlier programs. Many people's communes plunged into agricultural disaster. The grain harvest was dismal, leading to the widespread famine of the three hard years (1960–1963), or "three-year natural disaster" (*sannian ziran zaihai*). In 1959–1962, China experienced a serious economic depression. It claimed more than ten to fifteen million lives due to serious shortages of food, fuel, and other necessities. The total grain production decreased from 200 million tons in 1958 to 144 million tons in 1960.

In 1960, starvation became a nationwide phenomenon. Some provinces lost 5 percent of their total population. In some areas, animals disappeared, birds were not to be seen in the sky, and even the grass and leaves were gone. People in the worst affected areas soon turned to cannibalism. At first, people dug up shallow graves and ate human bodies. Soon they ate diseased persons, then babies, small children, and young women. Cannibalism eventually became common in every area decimated by starvation.[7] Human flesh was also traded on the black market. Some estimated the death of twenty-three to forty-five million people by the end of the great famine. The government, however, blamed it on the bad weather and called it a "natural disaster."[8] The main culprit, moreover, became the Soviet Union. The ideological split between China and its main ally became public in 1961. The Chinese people were told that the Soviet Union betrayed them by withdrawing all aid and terminating all the contracts between the two countries. The Great Leap Forward movement emerged as one of the most controversial events in modern Chinese history. Mao never admitted that his policy led to massive failure and economic disaster, nor that the movement intended to eliminate the large rural population through poverty, even though he had stepped down as China's president in 1959.

In April 1959, Mao stepped down as head of state while retaining his other powerful positions as chairman of the CCP and of the CMC. After Mao's resignation, Liu Shaoqi became the PRC's second president. Liu had been vice chair of the Central People's Government, and he later assumed the title of the first vice chair of the NPC from 1954 to 1959. In April 1959 he succeeded Mao as president of the PRC. Liu's work concentrated on party administrative functions and ideological matters. Liu, a traditional Soviet-style Communist, supported state planning and expansion of heavy industry. He was publicly acknowledged as Mao's chosen successor in 1961.[9] Liu later, however, fell victim to the Cultural Revolution, the largest and longest mass movement in PRC's history. He was forced from the presidency in spite of the fact that legally he could not be removed from office; thus, the Constitution failed to protect the President of the Republic. Liu died in jail in 1969.

Sino-Soviet split (1958–1960)

The first ideological conflict between Beijing and Moscow came in 1956 when the new Soviet leader, Nikita Khrushchev, issued a "secret report" to the Communist Party of the Soviet Union Congress, denouncing Stalin as a dictator. In November 1957, Mao visited Moscow to attend the celebrations of the fortieth anniversary of the Russian Revolution. At a meeting of communist parties from around the world, Mao emphasized that they should not be frightened by the prospect of a nuclear war started by the imperialists, but instead should realize that such a war, although carrying a high price, would bring the imperialist system to its grave.[10] Chen points out that Mao's statement was "a deliberate challenge to Khrushchev's emphasis on the necessity and possibility of 'peaceful coexistence' with Western imperialist countries," and "it inevitably worried Moscow's leaders."[11] Yang Kuisong makes a further point that the Mao-Khrushchev split resulted from their differing world views and different visions for the future of communism after Khrushchev departed from Stalinist ideology.[12]

Thereafter, the great Sino-Soviet polemic debate further undermined the ideological foundation of the Sino-Soviet alliance. In a deeper sense, Beijing's confrontation with Moscow even changed the essence of the Cold War. As argued earlier, since its beginning in the late 1940s the Cold War had been characterized by a fundamental confrontation between two contending ideologies – liberal capitalism versus Communism. The dramatic Sino-Soviet split buried the shared perception among communists and their sympathizers all over the world that communism was a solution to the problems created by the worldwide process of capitalistic modernization.

Lastly, the Chinese also complained about Soviet control of advanced technology. In October 1957, for instance, Fleet Admiral Xiao Jinguang, chief of the PLAN, asked the Soviet high command in Moscow to help the Chinese navy build nuclear submarines with missile launching capacity. The chief of the Soviet Navy told Xiao that the Soviet Union would provide these submarines to the PLAN so that the Chinese did not need to develop and build their own nuclear submarines.[13] On 28 June 1958, China's premier Zhou wrote to Khrushchev that the Soviet designs and blueprints of the new warships and submarines should be available to the Chinese Navy. Domestically, some of the Chinese leaders began to question "learning from the Soviet

Union," and instead they asked for "learning from the Soviet lessons."[14] It meant that the Soviets were not always correct, and China should avoid their mistakes. Marshal Liu Bocheng, for instance, questioned the copying of the Soviet model and suggested that the PLA treasure the Chinese experience and not lose sight of the "people's war" doctrine.[15] In the late 1950s, Liu stressed Chinese experience, proposed Chinese ways to build a modern and regular army, and opposed entirely copying the Soviet model.

The conflicts between the two communist parties extended to strategic issues. Disappointed and frustrated, Khrushchev wanted to withdraw the Soviet military advisors from China. Among the 80,000 Soviet advisers sent to China each year in the 1950s, most were military advisors.[16] The Soviet Military Advisory Group (SMAG) General HQ in Beijing assigned its advisors to all PLA headquarters in the capital city, and sent many others down to the PLA regional, army, and divisional commands across the country. For instance, the PLA Navy had 711 Soviet advisors working at Navy HQs, bases, and academies. The Russian Navy had a strong influence on Chinese naval development through advisory assistance in the 1950s. Nevertheless, there were some disagreements between the Russian advisors and Chinese naval officers at all levels. In 1959, the PLA began to install listening devices on the Russian advisors' telephones, in their offices, and at their hotel rooms. The monitors recorded the advisors' phone conversations both with Chinese and with Russians in the Soviet Union. Many Russian advisors also complained that their mail and family letters had been opened and checked.[17] More and more naval advisors felt uncomfortable working with the Chinese naval officers.

The problems between China and the Soviet Union reached a new height when supporters of the Dalai Lama launched an armed rebellion in Tibet against the Chinese central government in March 1959. His independence movement received official support from the Indian government, suddenly raising tensions between India and China. Ignoring the information and suggestions from Beijing, Moscow issued an official statement on September 9, condemning Chinese and defending India's policy toward Tibet. Mao criticized Khrushchev as the "new revisionist," and as "having betrayed the international communist movement" with "socialist imperialist" aggressive policy.[18]

In 1960, the Soviet Union unilaterally ended 600 bilateral contracts and withdrew all Soviet experts from China. On June 20, 1960, the Central Committee of the Soviet Communist Party informed the CCP Central Committee that in order to achieve an agreement to partially ban nuclear tests, the Soviet Union must terminate the Sino-Soviet agreement on co-operation of nuclear development. On July 16, the Soviet government informed the Chinese government that they would withdraw all nuclear scientists and experts. By August 13, all 12,000 Soviet experts left China with their blueprints and designs. Among them were more than 200 working on nuclear research and development programs. The Soviets also stopped shipments of equipment and materials that the Chinese nuclear program desperately needed.[19] In 1961, the Soviets canceled all projects of scientific and technical co-operation, including the joint nuclear programs. Obviously, the Soviet Union did not want to see a strong, unfriendly neighbor. In 1962, Soviet agents instigated the migration of tens of thousands of Chinese citizens in Yili Prefecture to the Soviet Union.

In the spring of 1962, more than 67,000 Chinese fled Xinjiang to Soviet Kyrgyzstan. Beijing blamed the KGB, claiming that the Soviet security agency was behind the mass flight. In 1966 Mao launched the "Great Proletarian Cultural Revolution" sweeping across China against any "Chinese agents of the Soviet revisionists" and completely destroying any hope that Beijing and Moscow might continue to regard each other as "comrades in arms."

The Sino-Soviet split divided the PLA leaders between the so-called "rightist" or pragmatic group and the "leftist" or radical group according to their loyalty to Mao. Peng Dehuai's military career ended when Mao accused him of forming a "right opportunist clique" and conducting "unprincipled factional activity" in the party and army, charges that often reflected pro-Soviet political positions, and removed him from his post as minister of defense in the summer of 1959. Marshal Lin Biao, as the new defense minister, terminated most of the programs that Peng had embarked upon. A top-down purge went through the PLA. In less than half a year, 1,848 high and middle ranking commanders and officers were dismissed, criticized, or jailed, since they had questioned the Great Leap Forward and People's Communes, supported or expressed their sympathies to Peng.[20] That same year, Lin abolished a Soviet-style system of military ranks, established by Peng in 1955. Lin blamed this system for having changed the PLA tradition of equality among soldiers and commanders.[21]

The 1958 Taiwan Strait Crisis and 1962 Sino-Indian War

The Second Taiwan Strait Crisis erupted in August 1958 over the offshore islands of Jinmen (Quemoy) and Mazu (Matsu), when the PLA heavily bombarded the islands. In the following two months, several hundred thousand artillery shells exploded on Jinmen. At one point, a PLA invasion of the island seemed imminent. The Jinmen island group, lying less than two miles off Xiamen, with three sides surrounded by the mainland, was about 140 miles from Taiwan. At that time, the GMD had six infantry divisions and two tank battalions with 308 heavy artillery pieces stationed among the nine islands of the Jinmens. Some 88,000 troops and 50,000 residents totally depended upon supplies from Taiwan, requiring at least 400 tons of supplies per day – transportation and logistics thus were the critical vulnerabilities of the Jinmen garrison.[22] If the PLA could cut off or restrict the flow of supplies, it would undermine the garrison's effectiveness. The Chinese intended to crack down on the Jiang Jieshi Army's frequent harassment along the Fujian coast across from Jinmen and Mazu, and create a blockade of supplies, leading to a possible withdrawal of the GMD garrison from those islands, such as the Dachen evacuation in 1955.

On August 23, 1958, the PLA began an intensive artillery bombardment of the GMD-held Jinmen Islands. The first barrage was delivered by 459 artillery pieces from twenty-four artillery battalions that fired some 24,000 shells onto the Jinmens in just thirty-five minutes. In a total of eighty minutes, the PLA fired more than 30,000 shells onto the islands and killed some 600 GMD troops, including three vice commanders. The next day, the shelling continued, sinking one transport ship and damaging two others. The GMD also lost two fighters in the air engagements with the PLA fighters. One PLA plane was shot down by its own anti-aircraft artillery. By August 25, the PLA's heavy shelling had totally cut off the Jinmen Islands from Taiwan. After ten days of shelling, the Jinmen garrison only received a very small percentage of its regular supplies through a limited and ineffective airlift and some nightly shipping.

In response to the rapidly escalating PLA threat, the Eisenhower administration reinforced US naval forces in East Asia and directed US warships to help the GMD protect Jinmen supply lines. Khrushchev wrote twice to Mao in October 1958, offering Russian C-75 bombers with surface-to-air (SAM) missiles and Soviet advisors. In his replies, Mao only accepted Russian bombers and SAM missiles, but did not want to have any more Soviet advisors. Russian aid and new technology never came.[23]

On September 7, seven American warships (two cruisers and five destroyers) escorted two GMD supply ships sailing to Jinmen. The next day, Taiwan sent another American-Taiwanese fleet to Jinmen using the same escort pattern of the day before, with four GMD landing ships and five American ships (one cruiser and four destroyers). Around noon, the combined fleet reached Jinmen harbor. Mao gave the order to open fire at 12:43pm. Thirty-six artillery battalions and six coastal artillery companies fired 21,700 shells.[24] The American ships turned southward quickly and moved out of the PLA artillery range. They stayed six to twelve miles away from Jinmen without firing a shot, while the GMD ships suffered heavy losses.[25] Taiwan tried the escort tactic again on September 11, with four American ships escorting four GMD transport ships and seven GMD warships. At about 3:00pm, when the fleet was getting close to Jinmen, the PLA used forty artillery battalions and six coastal artillery companies to shell the combined fleet.

Meanwhile, US planes began escorting GMD shipments to Jinmen, and equipped GMD F-86 fighters with new air-to-air missiles, their first ever introduction to combat. These became a huge tactical obstacle for PLA pilots. The PLAAF only discovered that the GMD had air-to-air missiles on September 24 when PLA fighters were shot down by missiles in an engagement with GMD fighters.[26] The blockade of Jinmen was becoming more and more difficult to sustain. On October 5, GMD transport from Taiwan to Jinmen gradually resumed by using LVTs. By October 5, some 170 tons of supplies arrived per day, about 40 percent of the daily needs of the island garrison, a significant increase from the 5 percent they had received since late August.[27] Chinese leaders seemed willing to accept the fact that the PRC would not fight the United States over the offshore islands if the Americans made a commitment to their defense.

Such was the outcome of the test shelling of Jinmen. Despite forty days of shelling, new tactics, and reinforcements, the PLA's blockade of Jinmen was not fully effective and Taiwan showed no signs of withdrawing its garrison. The PLA high command now had to decide on its next step. Mao, however, had to find an excuse for his slowing down of the bombardment. Also on October 5, the CMC issued an instruction, drafted by Mao, that rationalized the slowdown in shelling by claiming that while the PLA could have seized Jinmen, it would have been merely a short-term victory. China would leave Jinmen linked to Taiwan to avoid giving the United States a pretext for instigating a "two Chinas plot." The nation's unification and the liberation of Taiwan were much more important in the long run than the recovery of a few offshore islands. The problem of the islands could eventually be solved along with the Taiwan problem. Mao called it the "noose strategy." It meant that Beijing would leave the islands such as Jinmen and Mazu in Jiang's hands as a burden on America. Beijing, however, could use the islands as the "noose" to serve its own goals in the international arena. China could now simply bombard Jinmen to put more pressure on America, or stop the bombardment to relax the tension.[28] Mark A. Ryan and Admiral Michael A. McDevitt view this "new policy" as another example of Mao's experienced tactics, "often rationalizing constrained options as successes."[29]

Thus, by October 5, 1958, the tension in the Taiwan Straits began to ease, though small-scale shelling of Jinmen continued in order to carry out Mao's "noose policy." From August 23 to October 6, 1958, the PLA shelled the Jinmen Islands and surrounding waters with 474,900 rounds. The PLA claimed to have sunk twenty-one

GMD gunships and transport ships, damaged another seventeen, shot down eighteen GMD airplanes, and inflicted more than 1,000 GMD casualties.[30] The PLA bombardment in the 1958 Taiwan Strait Crisis demonstrated a Chinese military paradox with some implications. A gap existed between Mao's political considerations and PLA operational goals on the ground in Fujian. While emphasizing loyalty and discouraging policy debates, the PLA generals had to find their own ways to fight and win their battles. Their operations may have had an unintended impact, in that they helped bring about the major international crisis of 1958. The relationship between Mao and Peng became more complicated when Mao had less counsel and fewer meetings with the latter toward the end of the crisis. Peng would be purged a year later at the Lushan Conference, which was, as Joffe describes, "the most serious leadership struggle since the establishment of the Communist regime."[31]

In 1959, the PLA and Tibetan army clashed in Tibet over political issues. In 1951, the central government had negotiated with Tibet and signed the "Agreement on Measures for the Peaceful Liberation of Tibet," on May 23. The PLA had entered Tibet to safeguard its borders with India and Nepal. The agreement affirmed Tibet's political autonomy, social system, and religious freedom. In 1959, however, the central government accused the Buddhist spiritual leader, the Dalai Lama, of organizing a separatist movement in Tibet. The PLA troops suppressed the rebellion. The fourteenth Dalai Lama escaped into India. Then, the central government imposed policies to abolish the traditional economic and political system in Tibet. In 1961, an election was held to uproot the Tibetan leaders. In September 1965, the First People's Congress of Tibet was convened, at which the Tibet Autonomous Region and the Regional Government was officially proclaimed. Thereafter, Tibet became one of the twenty-nine provinces and autonomous regions of the PRC.

The Chinese-Indian War arose over a border dispute along the Himalayan Mountains in Ladakh and Aksai Chin in the west and in the North-East Frontier Agency (NEFA) in the east.[32] Part of the difficulties in the east concerned the "McMahon Line," a border based upon a 1914 British-Tibetan agreement. Tibet had served as a buffer zone between the PRC and India since 1949, when Beijing recognized the autonomy of the Tibetan government. As a result, Chinese-Indian relations reached the lowest point since the founding of the PRC. Afterwards, the Indian government granted sanctuary to the Dalai Lama, who denounced China's "aggression" in Tibet and continued to be "active in exile."[33] Armed clashes escalated during the summer of 1959. On August 25, a small group of Indian troops crossed into the Longju area north of the McMahon Line and exchanged fire with a Chinese border patrol. On October 21, there was another small-scale incident along the border of the western sector at Kongka Pass. Both sides claimed that the other fired first. Primer Zhou suggested a "mutual withdrawal" in the NEFA to 12.4 miles behind the McMahon line.[34]

However, Prime Minister Jawaharlal Nehru and the Indian government did not respond and instead expanded its armed forces and reinforced the border areas to pressure the Chinese through this "forward policy." According to Cheng Feng and Larry M. Wortzel, India formulated its "forward policy" in 1960–1961, which placed "continuous pressure and forward movement on Chinese forces" along the disputed border.[35] Nehru also turned to the Soviet Union for more economic aid and military support.

In 1962, the CCP Central Committee and CMC instructed the PLA to mobilize the frontier troops and plan a "counteroffensive campaign." The PLA employed four

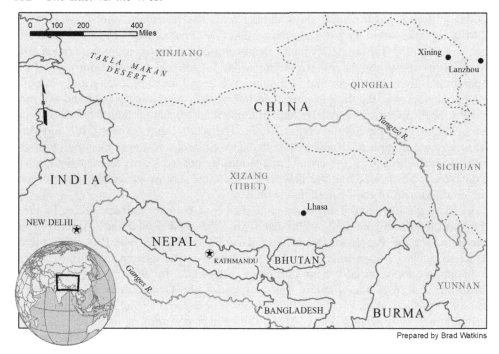

Prepared by Brad Watkins

Map 9.1 The Sino-Indian War

regiments in Tibet, about 13,000 men, and one regiment in Xinjiang, about 7,000 men. Large-scale attacks began on October 20 against the Indian garrisons in Ladakh and Aksai Chin and the NEFA. In the east, the PLA troops crossed the border and destroyed defense points of the Indian Army. On October 22, the PRC Defense Ministry announced that the PLA operation would not be limited by the "illegal McMahon Line."[36] By October 28, the PLA's Tibet regiments wiped out forty-three strong-points on the Indian side of the McMahon Line. In the west, Xinjiang's regiment crossed the border and took over thirty-seven Indian strong-points by traveling over 1,000 kilometers along the borders. The Indian troops, ill-prepared and poorly supplied, fell back under the PLA assaults. The Nehru administration, however, did not give up. While requesting military aid from the West, including the United States, Nehru reinforced the border areas with an additional 30,000 men in November. His defense effort still focused on the east. In early November, the Indian troops launched their own counteroffensive along the eastern borders.[37]

Facing the Indian attacks, the CMC deployed more troops to the borders. By mid-November, the PLA had eight infantry and three artillery regiments along the eastern borders; four regiments at the middle section of the eastern borders; and one regiment in the west. The troops in the east encircled the Indian troops and cut their supply lines by November 17. The next day, the eastern troops launched an all-out attack on the Indian troops. By November 21, the PLA eliminated the Indian presence along the eastern borders. In the west, the PLA also attacked the Indians. That day the PLA accomplished its goal. On November 22, the Chinese government announced a cease-fire along the Chinese-Indian borders. After December 1, Chinese forces began pulling out of Indian territories and returned to the old boundary, or "traditional border."

According to the Chinese reports, between October 20 to November 21, India lost 8,700 troops, including 4,800 killed and 3,900 captured. Total PLA casualties were 2,400 dead and wounded.[38]

The Vietnam War (1965–1975)

The direct engagement of the Chinese armed forces in North Vietnam enabled Hanoi to send more troops to South Vietnam. The level of infiltration from the North was significantly increased, and the main force units of the NVA began to stream South. Hanoi's main risk was that a further deterioration of security in the South would lead to increased US involvement, something neither Hanoi nor its allies in Beijing and Moscow desired. By the mid-1960s, the NVA units conducted guerrilla operations and a "people's war" to assist the NLF and Southern Communist troops, the People's Liberation Armed Forces (PLAF), to fight the Army of the Republic of Vietnam (ARVN) and the US armed forces in South Vietnam.

After the RVN was founded in Saigon in 1955, the Communist leadership in Hanoi rejected the Nationalist government in South Vietnam and called for a national reunification by its Communist forces. The civil war began between the North and South. William J. Duiker points out that:

> It was at this point that the United States first became directly involved in Vietnam. As French forces withdrew in accordance with the Geneva Agreement, the Eisenhower administration decided to sponsor the new anti-Communist regime in South Vietnam (Republic of Vietnam, RVN), with its capital in Saigon.

Ho Chi Minh and his government of the Democratic Republic of Vietnam (DRV) supported the Southern Communist guerrilla warfare against the Diem government and the ARVN by providing logistical support, experienced officers, and a small number of NVA troops.[39] "By the time John F. Kennedy entered the White House in January 1961, the situation in South Vietnam had become a major issue in the Cold War."[40]

Beginning in the early 1960s, North Vietnam sent its NVA regulars to the South to train and support the PLAF to fight the ARVN and the US forces in guerrilla operations. Later on, Hanoi further infiltrated by sending NVA regulars, nearly 100,000 a year, through the transportation network in Laos and Cambodia popularly known as "the Ho Chi Minh Trail."[41] As the Diem government was struggling to operate effectively, US support meant the American military would take a more prominent role in South Vietnam. By the end of 1961, US "advisors" numbered 3,205 men to provide advisory assistance to 170,000–270,000 men for the ARVN. During the next year, the figure jumped to 9,000. Kennedy's goal for Vietnam was not to put American troops on the ground, but to aid and support Diem in his endeavor to stop the Communists. At the time of President Kennedy's assassination in November 1963, the American forces totaled 16,700 men. Eventually Diem fell victim to a US-backed coup on November 1, 1963.

The common Western assumption is that the ARVN failed to defend its own country even with American direct intervention in the Vietnam War.[42] This assessment is unfair to the ARVN, which departed from traditional values and lost popular support only after the Americans transformed it into a modern army.[43] Its modernization or Americanization detached the ARVN from Vietnamese society. In other words, while providing advanced technology, military training, democratic ideas, and even

Christianity to the ARVN, the United States should have also promoted nationalistic pride to motivate the South Vietnamese soldiers to fight for their own country's independence and sovereignty. The advisors' ignorance and oversight of Vietnamese nationalism made the ARVN a hotbed of apathy. A man felt like he was fighting for his Catholic officers, President Diem, and American advisors, not for himself, his family, and the Vietnamese people.

President Lyndon B. Johnson continued Kennedy's policies and kept many of Kennedy's advisors. On August 2 and 4, 1964, North Vietnamese boats supposedly attacked American warships in the Gulf of Tonkin, giving Johnson a good opportunity to punish North Vietnam and to seek congressional support. The "Gulf of Tonkin Resolution" passed on August 7 with little debate and authorized President Johnson to escalate intervention in South Vietnam. At the same time, the United States shifted its war efforts increasingly toward North Vietnam. The Johnson administration finally decided to escalate the war in February 1965, sending in the first US combat troops and launching Rolling Thunder, a massive bombing campaign against North Vietnam. By March, the first US Marine combat soldiers arrived in Da Nang. Prior to that, though there were more than 20,000 US troops in Vietnam, their role was advisory in nature; they were not engaging in direct combat. These events would trigger an escalation of the US military role that would eventually lead to a buildup of around 500,000 US troops in Vietnam. The United States began assuming nearly total control over the actual fighting of the war.

Beginning in 1964, North Vietnam used the Ho Chi Minh Trail to infiltrate the South with an annual average of 100,000 troops, including some of the best NVA units. The NVA actually provided the main force of the Communist insurgency and its role had steadily increased in the South. In the fall of 1964, the NVA sent more infantry troops to the South. In the North, the NVA established five anti-aircraft artillery divisions and one radar division for air defense. In 1965, it formed two surface-to-air missile regiments.[44] The DRV government launched a massive mobilization to meet the manpower need for its new operations. The NVA divisions began to activate their reserves. Each NVA infantry division formed regionally. For example, most of the soldiers and officers of the 308th Division were from Hanoi, the capital city of North Vietnam. The 308th was also called the "Capital Division" as one of the first six divisions established in the First Indochina War. The 316th Division was an ethnic minority division in which many soldiers and officers were Tho, Miao, and Thai minorities from the northwestern mountainous region.

NVA grew to 350,000 troops by the end of 1964. In December, the 316th Division command called up all of its reserves for active duty. In the spring of 1965, Sgt. Thanh's company was sent to South Vietnam. From April to November, he fought in several battles around the Central Highlands and the surrounding mountainous areas. By 1966, the total number of NVA had doubled to 700,000, with two-thirds stationed in the North and the remainder in the South. In 1967, the NVA grew to 500,000 men. By the 1968 Tet Offensive, the NVA/PLAF in the South reached a total strength of 400,000 troops.

The Tet Offensive was a NVA/PLAF all-out attack at the major cities in January 1968. The plan was later modified to include the element of a "General Offensive and General Uprising," which meant that the purpose of the Tet Offensive was to spark a general uprising against the US and the regime in South Vietnam, as had been specified as a strategic goal by Resolution 9, passed in the aftermath of Diem's assassination as

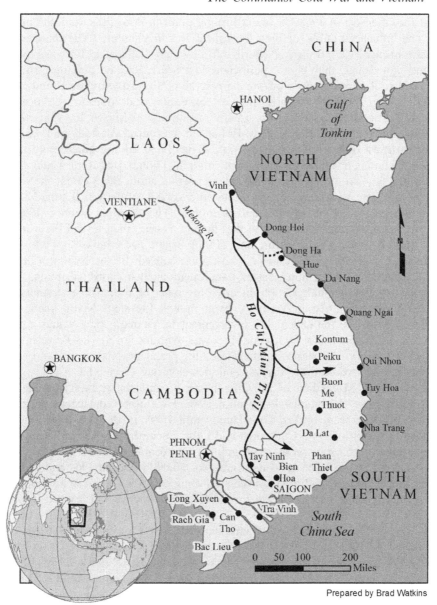

Map 9.2 The Vietnam War

a blueprint for the war.[45] By the end of the summer, a plan was devised to have the main force of the NVA troops occupy American troops in the countryside while the NLF and other NVA units attacked the city and town centers throughout the South. In a way, despite the tactical debacle of the Tet Offensive, the North did meet certain strategic goals. One of Le Duan's main purposes for the offensive was to weaken the Johnson administration's position in an election year and embolden the anti-war movement in the United States. From this point of view, the Tet Offensive was a strategic success.

The Tet Offensive of 1968 became a turning point in America's domestic politics at home and influenced public opinion toward the war in Vietnam. "The changes the Tet Offensive brought were decisive," Marilyn Young states. "Because Tet was reported as an American defeat, they claim, politicians lost heart, rejected making an increased effort, and took the first steps on the slippery slope toward withdrawal and admitted defeat."[46] After the Tet Offensive, military escalation and Johnson's political career derailed; the bombing scaled down. In the meantime, on March 16, 1968, three US platoons entered a village they called My Lai, on the central coast about 15 kilometers to the northwest of the city of Quang Ngai. They lined up and killed more than 300 villagers, including a significant number of children. Though this event would not come to be widely known until Seymour Hersh's reporting about the incident in November 1968, by that time it was only a coda to the other aspects of the war that had become a major issue in the 1968 presidential election.[47] The eventual winner, Republican Richard Nixon of California, pledged that he had a secret plan to end the war.

On May 10, 1968, Washington and Hanoi began peace talks in Paris, France. Eventually, on October 31, President Johnson announced the suspension of all US air raids, bombing, shelling, and coastal harassment against North Vietnam. Richard Nixon won the presidential election in early November by promising the voters that he would end America's war in Vietnam. Even though President Nixon knew that the voters wanted to see the end of US involvement in Vietnam, they would not accept another Communist victory. To end the war without losing it, President Nixon employed a few new war strategies after becoming president. Nixon's new war strategies included the Vietnamization of the war and incursion into Cambodia.

When Ho Chi Minh died in 1969, Le Duan became the secretary general of the North Vietnamese Communist Party until 1986. Ho's other concurrent position, the president of DRV, went to Ton Duc Thang until 1980. In the late 1960s, the PAVN expanded its operations into Cambodia and Laos. Then, the struggle in South Vietnam began to take on the signs of an open military confrontation between North Vietnam and the United States.[48] The NVA itself grew to 380,000 troops in 1964 and to 1 million men by 1972.[49] The NVA drafted all the adult males between eighteen and forty-five in the North. All the draftees received formal infantry training and learned how to use Russian and Chinese-made weapons.[50] In the late 1960s and early 1970s, the NVA/PLAF expanded its operations into Cambodia and Laos. From January 1961 to January 1973, the NVA/PLAF suffered 851,000 military deaths.[51]

The NVA then prepared a general offensive in the early 1970s in an attempt to convince Nixon and the American public that further escalation would lead to a US defeat. In late March 1972, the NVA launched the large-scale spring offensive against the South, which lost 25,000 men in defense against the Northern offensive.[52] To retaliate against the North, in April the Nixon administration responded to Hanoi's attack by resuming the extensive bombing, Operation Linebacker I, across North Vietnam, and mining harbors along the Vietnamese coast.[53]

In January 1973, nearly four years of negotiations between Kissinger and Le Duc Tho resulted in the Paris Peace Accords. This agreement specified that the United States would totally withdraw its military forces in sixty days, by the end of March 1973. In exchange, all United States' prisoners of war would be repatriated. Nguyen Van Thieu, the president of South Vietnam, was only coerced into going along with the agreement because President Nixon made it very clear that all US aid to Vietnam would be cut off if he did not agree, and that the United States would ensure that

North Vietnam would adhere to the terms of the agreement, including assurances that the United States would act if North Vietnam attacked across the 17th parallel and that substantial military aid would be forthcoming if Thieu agreed.[54] As the Americans disengaged from South Vietnam at a rapid pace, the South Vietnamese economy was thrown into turmoil.

The North had benefitted from a massive increase in supplies from the Soviet Union. For years, the rivals in the Sino-Soviet rift had competed for Hanoi's favor. Now, however, they could supply North Vietnam directly through Haiphong harbor and by railroad without fear of American bombing. As the end of March neared, South Vietnam's forces collapsed around the defense of Saigon, and Hue and Quang Tri were ceded to Communist forces.[55] Under pressure, Nguyen Van Thieu resigned as president on April 21, 1975. On April 30, Saigon fell to the Communist forces, and Vietnam was reunited under Communist rule.

Chinese and Russian aid to Hanoi

The US bombing against the North in 1964–1965 made North Vietnam desperate for help. In April 1965, Le Duan, first secretary general of the North Vietnamese Communist Party, and General Vo Nguyen Giap, defense minister, rushed to Beijing to ask China for increased aid and to send troops to Vietnam. On behalf of the Chinese leadership, Liu Shaoqi, president of the PRC and vice chairman of the CCP, replied to the Vietnamese visitors on April 8 that "it is the obligation of the Chinese people and party" to support the Vietnamese struggle against the United States. "Our principle is," Liu continued, "that we will do our best to provide you with whatever you need and whatever we have."[56] In April, China signed several agreements with the DRV government delegation concerning the dispatch of Chinese support troops to North Vietnam.

On May 16, Ho Chi Minh met Mao Zedong in Beijing. Ho requested that China send anti-aircraft artillery troops to Vietnam. In Van Tien Dung's meetings with Luo Ruiqing in early June, Dung specifically requested that China send two anti-aircraft artillery divisions to defend Hanoi and the areas north of Hanoi in the event of American air strikes. Luo agreed.[57] On July 24, the Vietnamese General Staff telegraphed the PLA General Staff, formally requesting that China send "the two anti-aircraft artillery divisions that have long completed their preparations for operations in Vietnam. The earlier the better. If possible, they may enter Vietnam on August 1." The next day, the Chinese General Staff cabled the Vietnamese General Staff, saying that China would send two anti-aircraft artillery divisions and one regiment to Vietnam immediately, and that these units would take the responsibility of defending the Bac Ninh-Lang Son section of the Hanoi-Youyiguan Railway and the Yen Bay-Lao Cai section of the Hanoi-Lao Cai Railway, two main railways linking China and North Vietnam.[58]

In July 1965, China began sending its troops to North Vietnam, including surface-to-air missiles (SAM), anti-aircraft artillery, railroad, engineering, minesweeping, and logistics units. Chinese forces operated anti-aircraft guns and SAM sites, built and repaired roads, bridges, railroads, and assembled factories. Chinese participation enabled Hanoi to send more NVA troops to the South to fight Americans. Between 1965 and 1968 China sent twenty-three divisions, including ninety-five regiments, totaling some 320,000 troops. The peak year was 1967 when 170,000 Chinese soldiers were present. Among the Chinese were 150,000 anti-aircraft artillery troops, who had engaged in 2,150 encounters.[59]

Beijing also provided a large-scale military aid to Hanoi through the Vietnam War. From 1964 to 1966, China shipped to Vietnam 270,000 rifles and machine guns, 540 artillery pieces, 900,000 artillery shells, 200 million rounds of ammunition, 700 tons of dynamite, along with other military supplies.[60] The Chinese doubled or even tripled their annual military aid through the second half of the 1960s. For example, China provided 80,500 automatic rifles in 1964, 141,531 in 1966, 219,899 in 1968, and 233,600 in 1973, almost three times more than the total aid of 1964. The heavy artilleries shipped totaled 1,205 pieces in 1964, 3,362 in 1966, 7,087 in 1968, and 9,912 in 1973. Artillery account increased by nine times between 1964 and 1973. The artillery shells provided were 335,000 shells in 1964, 1.06 million in 1966, 2.08 million in 1968, and 2.2 million in 1973. Tanks and vehicles totaled forty-one in 1964, ninety-six in 1966, 462 in 1968, and 8,978 in 1972. The deliveries of tanks and vehicles increased 200 times from 1964 to 1972.[61]

By 1974, China had sent Vietnam 2.14 million rifles and automatic guns, 1.2 billion bullets, 70,000 artillery pieces, 18.1 million artillery shells, 170 airplanes, 176 gunboats, 552 tanks, 320 armored vehicles, 16,000 trucks, 18,240 tons of dynamite, 11.2 million set of uniforms, as well as other war supplies. Between 1971 and 1972, China also shipped into Vietnam 180 Chinese-made Hongqi-2 anti-aircraft missiles and all the control equipment, radar, and communication facilities for a surface-to-air missile regiment.[62] From 1966 to 1973, China provided all the military aid totaling 42.6 billion yuan RMB (about $14 billion), including guns, ammunition, tanks, naval vessels, armored vehicles, trucks, airplanes, medicine, medical instruments, and other war materials. Thus, during the Vietnam War, China had provided North Vietnam with total aid of $20 billion.[63]

The DRV government and PAVN officially denied any foreign troops from the communist countries were involved in the Vietnam War during the 1960s. In fact, beside the Chinese troops, the North Vietnamese also invited anti-aircraft missile troops from the Soviet Union. The Soviet Union shifted its Vietnam policy from one of "staying away" until Nikita Khrushchev's fall from power in 1964, to "lending a hand" after Leonid Brezhnev's succession. In February 1965, Soviet Premier Aleksei Kosygin visited Hanoi and signed an agreement with the North Vietnamese to increase Russian military aid to 148,500 tons, including 55,000 tons of military aid, by year's end. It also requested a Soviet missile combat brigade, comprised of 4,000 Soviet troops, to arrive that spring.[64] After 1965, the Soviet Union continuously increased its aid to Vietnam, particularly intensifying its military assistance. Li Danhui describes Moscow's primary goal as to "infiltrate politically and win control over the strategically important Southeast Asian region, and Vietnam presented the best avenue whereby this objective might be achieved."[65] In 1967, Russia increased its military aid to Vietnam to over $550 million, exceeding that provided by the Chinese.[66] From 1965 to 1972, the Soviet Union provided a total of $3 billion aid to Vietnam, including $2 billion in military support.[67]

During the early years of the Cold War, the alliance between Beijing and Moscow was the cornerstone of the communist alliance system.[68] Yet beginning in the late 1950s, because of complicated domestic and international factors, the Sino-Soviet alliance began to crack apart. In addition, a polemical ideological debate between the PRC and the Soviet Union, following Stalin's death in 1953, helped to weaken the bonds between the two countries.[69] The mutual hostility reached a new peak in 1969 when two bloody clashes occurred on the Sino-Soviet border. Reportedly, Soviet leaders considered using a pre-emptive strike against the PRC.[70] Moscow's threats motivated the PRC to make a rapprochement with the United States.[71] All of this paved the way for President Nixon's historic visit to China in 1972.

Notes

1 Chen and Li, "China and the End of the Global Cold War," 121–122.
2 David Shambaugh, *China's Communist Party: Atrophy and Adaptation* (Berkeley: University of California Press, 2008).
3 Chen and Li, *ibid.*, 121.
4 For more detailed discussions, see: Niu Jun, "Mao Zedong's Crisis Conception and Origins of the Sino-Soviet Alliance's Collapse," in *Lengzhan yu zhongguo* [The Cold War and China], ed. Zhang Baijia and Niu Jun (Beijing: Shijie zhishi [World Knowledge Publishing], 2002), 273–296.
5 The term "Viet Cong" was used by President Diem to label the NLF (National Liberation Front), meaning "Vietnamese Communists," to discredit it. The South Vietnamese Communists and the NLF never used the term "Viet Cong" to describe themselves. The People's Liberation Army of Vietnam (PLAVN) was the armed force of the NLF. For their publications on NVA and PLAVN in English, see: Col. Dinh Thi Van, *I Engaged in Intelligence Work* (Hanoi: Gioi Publishers, 2006); Gen. Hoang Van Thai, *How South Viet Nam Was Liberated* (Hanoi: Gioi Publishers, 2005); Gen. Phung The Tai, *Remembering Uncle Ho: Memories in War Years* (Hanoi: Gioi Publishers, 2005).
6 Chang and Halliday, *Mao: The Unknown Story*, 357.
7 Frank Dikotter, *Mao's Great Famine: The History of China's Most Devastating Catastrophe, 1958–1962* (New York: Walker, 2010), 320–321.
8 For more details on the 1959–1962 "natural disaster," see: Spence, *The Search for Modern China*, 552–553.
9 For a review of Liu Shaoqi, see Lowell Dittmer, *Liu Shao-ch'i and the Chinese Cultural Revolution: The Politics of Mass Criticism* (Berkeley: University of California Press, 1974).
10 Mao, "Speech at the Moscow Conference of Communist and Workers' Parties, November 16, 1957," in *Mao's Manuscripts since 1949*, 5: 625–644.
11 Chen, *Mao's China and the Cold War*, 71.
12 Yang Kuisong. *Zouxiang polie: Mao Zedong yu Moscow de enen yuanyuan* [Road to the Split: Interests and Conflicts between Mao Zedong and Moscow] (Hong Kong: Sanlian shudian [Three Joint Publishers], 1999). 514–515.
13 Xiao Jinguang, *Xiao Jinguang huiyilu* [Memoirs of Xiao Jinguang] (Beijing: Jiefangjun [PLA Press], 1988), 2: 175–182.
14 Shen Zhihua, *Sulian zhuanjia zai zhongguo, 1948–1960* [Soviet Experts in China, 1948–1960] (Beijing: Zhongguo guoji guangbo [China International Broadcasting Publishing House], 2003), 253.
15 Xinghuo Liaoyuan Composition Department. *Zhongguo renmin jiefangjun jiangshuai minglu* [Marshals and Generals of the PLA]. Three volumes. (Beijing: Jiefangjun [PLA Press], 1992), 1: 6.
16 Shen Zhihua, *Mao Zedong, Sidalin he chaoxian zhanzheng* [Mao Zedong, Stalin, and the Korean War] (Guangzhou: Guangdong renmin [Guangdong People's Press], 2004), 371. Shen found the information in the archives of the Second Division, Defense Intelligence Agency, ROC Defense Ministry, in Taiwan. He believes that the numbers collected by the intelligence agents in the 1950s were incomplete.
17 Shen, *ibid.*, 358–359.
18 For example, Premier Zhou said on April 29, 1968 that the Soviet Union [like America] was apparently circulating and containing China. Li Danhui, "Conflicts between China and the Soviet Union in Their Efforts to Aid Vietnam and Resist America" in Zhang Baijia and Niu Jun, eds., *Lengzhan yu zhongguo* (The Cold War and China) (Beijing: Shijie zhishi, 2002), 373n1.
19 Nie Rongzhen, *Nie Rongzhen huiyilu* [Memoir of Nie Rongzhen]. Two volumes. (Beijing: Jiefangjun [PLA Press], 1984), 2: 806; Tang Xiuying, "A Sword Thrusting the Sky," in *Liangdan yixing: zhongguo hewuqi daodan weixing yu feichuan quanjishi* [A Complete Record of China's Nuclear Bombs, Missiles, Satellites, and Space Programs], ed. Political

Department of the PLA General Armaments Department (Beijing: Jiuzhou [Jiuzhou Press], 2001), 366.

20 China Academy of Military Science (CAMS), *Zhongguo gongchandang zhengzhi gongzuo 70 nian* [The Seventy Years of the CCP Political Tasks] (Beijing: Jiefangjun [PLA Press], 1992), 5: 238.

21 Xiaobing Li, "Chinese Military Ranking and Promotion," in *China Today: An Encyclopedia of Life in the People's Republic,* ed. Jing Luo (Westport, CT: Greenwood Press, 2005), 2: 402–405.

22 Chief General Hao Bocun (Hau Pei-tsun, GMD Army Ret.), interview by the author in Taipei, Taiwan, in May 1994. Hao served as the garrison commander on Jinmen from 1957 to 1960. Then, he became the Chief Staff of the GMD Army and the Defense Minister of the ROC in the 1970s and 1980s. He retired from the military and served as the ROC Premier in 1990–1993.

23 Li, *A History of the Modern Chinese Army,* 188–189.

24 Xu Yan, *Jinmen zhizhan* [The Battle of Jinmen] (Beijing: Zhongguo guangbo dianshi [China Broadcasting and Television Publishing], 1992), 250–251.

25 Shen Weiping, *8–23 Paoji Jinmen* [8-23 Bombardment of Jinmen] (Beijing: Huayi [China Literature Publishing], 1998), 2: 500.

26 Wang Dinglie *et al., Dongdai Zhongguo kongjun* [Contemporary Chinese Air Force] (Beijing: Zhongguo shehui kexue [China's Social Sciences Press], 1989), 345; History Compilation and Translation Bureau, ROC Defense Ministry, *8-23 Paozhan shengli 30 zhounian jinian wenji* [Recollection for the 30th Anniversary of the Victorious August 23 Artillery Battle] (Taipei, Taiwan: Guofangbu yinzhichang [Defense Ministry Printing Office], 1989), 33–34.

27 Xu, *Jinmen zhizhan* [The Battle of Jinmen], 256–257.

28 Mao, "Some Viewpoints about International Situation," speech at the Fifteenth Meeting of the Supreme State Council, September 8, 1958, in *Mao Zedong waijiao wenxuan* [Selected Diplomatic Papers of Mao Zedong] (Beijing: Zhongyang wenxian [CCP Central Archival Manuscript Press], 1994), 348–352.

29 Ryan, Finkelstein, and McDevitt, "Patterns of PLA Warfighting," in *Chinese Warfighting*, ed. Ryan, Finkelstein, and McDevitt, 15.

30 Shen, *8–23 Paoji Jinmen* [8–23 Bombardment of Jinmen], 2: 842; History Compilation and Translation Bureau, ROC Defense Ministry, *8–23 Paozhan shengli* [The Victorious 8–23 Artillery Battle], 30, 34.

31 Ellis Joffe, *The Chinese Army after Mao* (Cambridge, MA: Harvard University Press, 1987), 16.

32 Among the publications in English are: Kenneth Conboy and James Morrison, *The CIA's Secret War in Tibet* (Lawrence: University Press of Kansas, 2002); Allen S. Whiting, *The Chinese Calculus of Deterrence: India and Indochina* (Ann Arbor: University of Michigan Press, 1975); Neville Maxwell, *India's China War* (New York: Pantheon Books, 1970).

33 Elleman, *Modern Chinese Warfare,* 260.

34 Xinhua News Agency, *China's Foreign Relations,* 259.

35 Cheng Feng and Larry M. Wortzel, "PLA Operational Principles and Limited War: The Sino-Indian War of 1962," in *Chinese Warfighting,* ed. Ryan, Finkelstein, and McDevitt, 178.

36 Deng Lifang, "The First Anti-aggression War of the New Republic," in CAMS Military History Research Division. *Junqi piaopiao: xinzhongguo 50 nian junshi dashi shushi* [PLA Flag Fluttering: Facts of China's Major Military Events in the Past Fifty Years]. Two volumes. (Beijing: Jiefangjun [PLA Press], 1999), 2: 348.

37 Feng and Wortzel, "PLA Operational Principles and Limited War," 177.

38 Deng Lifang, "The First Anti-aggression War of the New Republic," 2: 356. The Indian statistics, different from the Chinese, record a total casualty of 7,000. See: "Sino-Indian War," in Richard Holmes ed., *Oxford Companion to Military History* (Oxford, UK: Oxford University Press, 2001), 840.

39 Zhai, *China and the Vietnam Wars,* 115–116.

40 Duiker, ""Foreword: The History of the People's Army," x.

41 Duiker, *Vietnam,* 69.

42 Interviews by the author in Ho Chi Minh City, Vietnam, in June 2006.

43 For further reading on the ARVN, see: Andrew Wiest, *Vietnam's Forgotten Army: Heroism and Betrayal in the ARVN* (New York: New York University Press, 2007); Robert K.

Brigham, *ARVN: Life and Death in the South Vietnamese Army* (Lawrence: University Press of Kansas, 2006).

44 The NVA missile troops developed fast in the 1960s with help from the Soviet Union. The NVA had twelve anti-aircraft missile regiments in the early 1970s. See: Douglas Pike, *Vietnam and the Soviet Union: Anatomy of an Alliance* (Boulder, CO: Westview Press, 1987).

45 Merle Pribbenow, "General Vo Nguyen Giap and the Mysterious Evolution of the Plan for the 1968 Tet Offensive," Journal of Vietnamese Studies 3, no. 2 (2008): 3.

46 Young, *The Vietnam Wars*, 222.

47 Heonik Kwon, *After the Massacre: Commemoration and Consolation in Ha My and My Lai* (Berkeley: University of California Press, 2006), 2–3; Kendrick Oliver, *The My Lai Massacre in American History and Memory* (Manchester, UK: Manchester University Press, 2006), 1–5.

48 Spencer C. Tucker, *Vietnam* (Lexington: University Press of Kentucky, 1999), 178–179; Duiker, *Sacred War: Nationalism and Revolution in a Divided Vietnam*, 230; Halberstam, *Ho*, 116–117.

49 For further reading on the NVA, see: Military History Institute of Vietnam, *Victory in Vietnam*; Michael Lanning and Dan Cragg, *Inside the VC and the NVA* (New York: Ballantine Books, 1992); Douglas Pike, *PAVN: People's Army of Vietnam* (Novato, CA: Presidio Press, 1986).

50 For more details on the NVA, also see: Sandra C. Taylor, *Vietnamese Women at War: Fighting for Ho Chi Minh and the Revolution* (Lawrence: University Press of Kansas, 1999) and Bao Ninh's historical novel from the NVA perspective, *The Sorrow of War* (New York: Penguin, 1996).

51 The military death total includes both NVA and Viet Cong. For more details, see: Moss, *Vietnam*, table C, 384.

52 For more details on the NVA 1972 spring offensive, or the Easter Offensive, see: *ibid.*, 314–320.

53 Stephen E. Ambrose, "Bombing Hanoi, Mining Haiphong, and the Moscow Summit," in *Light at the End of the Tunnel: A Vietnam War Anthology*, ed. Andrew Jon Rotter (Wilmington, DL: SR Books, 1999), 135–136.

54 Nguyen Phu Duc, *The Viet-Nam Peace Negotiations: Saigon's Side of the Story* (Christiansburg, VA: Dalley Book Service, 2005), 372–379; Diem, *In the Jaws of History*, 317; Van Nguyen Duong, *The Tragedy of the Vietnam War: A South Vietnamese Officer's Analysis* (Jefferson, NC: McFarland, 2008), 172.

55 *Ibid.*, 185–196; George J. Veith, *Black April: The Fall of South Vietnam, 1973–1975* (New York: Encounter Books, 2012), 288–292.

56 Liu Shaoqi's quote from Luo, "An Exceptional Model of Proletarian Internationalism: Mao Zedong and the War to Aid Vietnam and Resist France," in *Zhongguo junshi guwentuan yuanyue kangfa shilu* [The Records of the CMAG in Assisting Vietnam and Resisting France], ed. Compilation Team, 6.

57 Li Ke and Hao Shengzang, *Wenhua dageming zhong de renmin jiefangjun* [The PLA during the Cultural Revolution] (Beijing: Zhonggong dangshi ziliao [CCP Party Historical Archives Press], 1989), 423.

58 Han, *Dangdai Zhongguo jundui de junshi gongzuo* [Military Affairs of Contemporary China's Armed Forces] (Beijing: Zhongguo shehui kexue [China's Social Science Press], 1989), 1: 550.

59 The Chinese statistics show that Chinese anti-aircraft units had shot down 1,707 and damaged 1,608 US airplanes.

60 Wang Taiping, ed. *Zhonghua renmin gongheguo waijiao shi, 1957–1969* [A Diplomatic History of the People's Republic of China, 1957–1969] (Beijing: Shijie zhishi [World Knowledge Press, 1998]), 2: 35.

61 Chen, *Mao's China and the Cold War*, Table 1, 228.

62 Major General Chen Huiting, "Establishing a Vietnamese Surface-to-Air Missile Regiment," in *Yuanyue kangmei: zhongguo zhiyuan budui zai yuenan* [Aid Vietnam and Resist America: China's Supporting Forces in Vietnam], eds. Major General Qu Aiguo, Bao Mingrong, and Xiao Zuyue (Beijing: Junshi kexue [Military Science Press], 1995), 34. Chen was the head of the Chinese Missile Training Group in Vietnam from 1972 to 1973.

63 Wang Xiangen, *Zhongguo mimi da fabing: yuanyue kangmei shilu* [The Secret Dispatch of Chinese Forces: True Stories of Aiding Vietnam and Resisting the U.S.], Ji'nan: Ji'nan chubanshe [Ji'nan Publishing], 1992, 137.

64 For the details of the Soviet aid, see: Li Danhui, "The Sino-Soviet Dispute over Assistance for Vietnam's Anti-American War, 1965–1972," http://www.shenzhihua.net/ynzz/000123.htm 4–5. Her source is from Foreign Trade Bureau, "Minutes of Meeting between Chinese and Vietnamese Transportation Delegates," July 26, 1965, International Liaison Division Records, *PRC Ministry of Railway Administration Archives*, Beijing, China.

65 Li, "The Sino-Soviet Dispute over Assistance for Vietnam's Anti-American War," 1–2.

66 Ilya V. Gaiduk, *The Soviet Union and the Vietnam War* (Chicago: Ivan Dee, 1996), 59.

67 Guo, *Zhongyue guanxi yanbian sishinian* [Uncertain Relations between China and Vietnam], 103.

68 For studies on the rise and decline of the Sino-Soviet alliance, see: Lüthi, *The Sino-Soviet Split*; Westad, *Brothers in Arms*; Sheng, *Battling Western Imperialism*; Zubok and Pleshakov, *Inside the Kremlin's Cold War*; Chang, *Friends and Enemies*.

69 For a chronological development of the Sino-Soviet split, see: Chen, *Mao's China and the Cold War*, chapter 3; Yang Kuisong, *Zouxiang polie* [Road to the Split], chapters 13–14.

70 For example, Henry Kissinger recorded in his memoir that in August 1969, a Soviet diplomat in Washington inquired about "what the US reaction would be to a Soviet attack on Chinese nuclear facilities." Kissinger, *White House Years* (New York: Little, Brown, 1978), 183.

71 For a detailed discussion concerning Mao's foreign policy change in general and his policy toward the United States in particular, see Chen, *Mao's China and the Cold War*, 7–10, 241–242.

Part III
From bi-polar, triangle, to global

10 The Cultural Revolution and Sino-US Rapprochement

Shambaugh believes that the Cultural Revolution and Sino-US Rapprochement marked the beginning of "the stage – the transition from being a developing country to a newly industrialized one – that much of China has now entered."[1] The CCP may have learned from its negative lessons, adapted to a new international environment, re-built or reformed itself, and sustained its political legitimacy in the future. President Richard Nixon's visit to China in February 1972 further reshaped the Cold War world. First and foremost, it ended the total confrontation between the United States and China that had lasted for almost a quarter of a century, opening a new chapter in relations between the world's most powerful country and its most populous nation.[2] Within the context of this Sino-American rapprochement, Beijing's relations with Japan also improved. In September, only a few months after Nixon's visit, China and Japan established a formal diplomatic relation. In 1978, the two countries went further and signed a treaty of friendship and mutual cooperation. Consequently, a new crucial feature in the Cold War in East Asia as well as in the world emerged – international politics became dominated by a specific "triangular structure."[3] Taking the "Soviet threat" as an overriding concern, Beijing and Washington established a "quasi strategic partnership."[4]

The Chinese Cultural Revolution (1966–1976)

By the mid-1960s, questions about Mao's Great Leap Forward policy and dissenting opinion inside the Party were, to some extent, spreading. Liu Shaoqi's disapproval of Mao's policies had given rise to the latter's profound displeasure and distrust. To make the government more competent and dedicated to communist values, Liu himself presided over the enlarged Politburo meeting that formally started the Cultural Revolution. However, he quickly lost control of the movement while Mao and his political allies tried to use this opportunity to take over political power and destroy Mao's alleged enemies – Liu and Deng Xiaoping. Liu disappeared soon after the Cultural Revolution started. With Marshal Lin Biao by his side Mao responded to the opposition with a new effort to mobilize support from outside the party, including soldiers and students, and launched the Great Proletarian Cultural Revolution.

On May 16, 1966, the Politburo passed the "May 16th Circular," which had been drafted by Mao, pointing out the need to purge the "bourgeois representatives who wormed their way into the party, government, and army."[5] Fang Zhu considers the meeting a "turning point" in the Cultural Revolution; for after it, "the Maoists gained control over the party leadership."[6] On May 28, the Politburo organized the Central

Committee's "Cultural Revolution Leading Group" as the foremost organ to guide the national movement. In August, when Jiang Qing, Mao's wife, became its chairman, the "Cultural Revolution Leading Group" gradually replaced the Politburo in 1966–1967 as the Party's ultimate authority over the massive political campaign.[7]

In the summer of 1966, the Cultural Revolution became a nationwide political struggle with extensive purges. Mao used mass organizations such as the Red Guard (*Hongweibing*) youth to publicly attack, or "bomb" (*paoda*), CCP and PRC top officials, including President Liu Shaoqi and Party Secretary General Deng Xiaoping. The Red Guards, mostly college, high school, and middle school students, were empowered by Mao who called for "bombing the headquarters," by saying "rebellion is justified," and advocating "learning revolution by making revolution." From June to August 1966, all high schools and colleges dismissed classes and allowed students to participate in the new revolution. There were three months of "red terror," or "great chaos under the heavens" (*tianxia daluan*) as Mao called it. The Cultural Revolution was engineered from top to bottom. Lin Biao, Jiang Qing, and other leftists took advantage of the revolutionary enthusiasm and naiveté of the students, inflaming them with demagogic rhetoric. In a letter to Jiang Qing on July 8, Mao wrote: "Complete confusion leads to complete stability. The task today for the entire Communist Party, for the entire nation, is to fundamentally destroy the rightists."[8]

On August 12, 1966, at the Eleventh Plenary Session of the CCP Eighth National Congress, Lin became vice chairman of the CCP, second only to Mao. At this meeting Mao described the ongoing Cultural Revolution as a political struggle inside the party. "This is repression, terrorizing," Mao told the Standing Committee members of the Politburo, and "The terrorizing comes from the Central Committee." More specifically, he added, "There are ox demons and venomous spirits sitting here among us ... to rebel is justified!"[9] On August 18, at a mass meeting celebrating the Great Proletarian Cultural Revolution, Lin exhorted the youthful Red Guards to "smash all the old concepts, culture, customs, and habits of the exploiting classes."[10] Two days later, the Red Guards in Beijing took the lead in an unprecedented assault against the "Four Olds." Such furor quickly swept the country, as the Red Guards, having deserted schools, blanketed the land in a "revolutionary Red Terror." Instigated by Lin, and spurred into a frenzy by the "Cultural Revolution Leading Group," they went on a wild spree of home searches, property destruction, free-for-all fights, and even murders. By the end of the year, social stability had vanished while disturbances and conflicts increased. Industry, agriculture, and commerce were violently disrupted, causing widespread public fear and resentment. At the same time, the numerous Red Guard organizations became seriously factionalized, constantly arguing and debating heatedly amongst themselves, as a result of their differing interpretations of the "supreme instructions." China's vast land rumbled and seethed. It had indeed reached the "ideal" stage of Mao's "great chaos under the heavens" so earnestly sought by the revolutionary seer.[11] With Mao's support and encouragement, the Red Guards seemed ready to take over the country. Some even traveled to Vietnam, wanting to "fight against the American imperialists" there.

Lin used the Cultural Revolution and the Red Guards to reshape the PLA as radical political and military institutions. Before long, the new high command "subverted the programs of the professional military for ideological and political reasons."[12] The PLA's poor performance in the Vietnam War during 1966–1967 began to show its outdated war-fighting tactics, lack of combat training, and an outdated, ineffective weapon system.

On August 23, 1966, at the CMC Standing Committee meeting, Lin called for "three-month turmoil" in the PLA. On October 5, the CMC and Department of General Political Tasks (DGPT) of the PLA issued an urgent instruction that all military academies and institutes should dismiss their classes, allowing their cadets to become fully involved in the Cultural Revolution. Through the fall, with PLA logistical support, some eleven million Red Guards traveled to Beijing for a succession of mass rallies, then dispersed over the country.[13] In December 1966, Grand General Luo Ruiqing, chief of the PLA General Staff and head of China's Vietnam War command, was accused of "conducting anti-party activities" and "planning a plot to take over the power"; charges that were often raised against those who had differing opinions from Mao. In 1967, encouraged by Mao and Lin, the Red Guards began a direct attack on government officials at various levels and demanded that all government and Party officials accused of being counterrevolutionaries and capitalist roaders be removed from their positions. In October 1968 Liu was relieved of all his posts, and in 1969 his position as the successor of Mao was officially passed on to the Defense Minister, Marshal Lin Biao. On November 12, 1969, Liu died in prison in Kaifeng, Henan province, of medically neglected diabetes, thus ending an enduring yet tragic political career. Thereafter, two acting presidents served until 1975 when the new constitution abolished the position of China's presidency.

In Beijing, certain marshals and generals tried to stop the Maoist attempt to involve the PLA in the Great Cultural Revolution. Their efforts failed, and they were branded as the "February Countercurrent" against the Cultural Revolution. Mao asked them to leave their posts and engage in self-criticism. In March 1967, Lin mentioned several times the need to identify "a small handful in the army" and burn them to death. The Cultural Revolution Leading Group then moved into power, replacing the Politburo. Lin used the mass movement to purge military leaders who did not agree with his strategy and policies. He mobilized PLA soldiers and commanders in Beijing to look for "bourgeoisie agents in the PLA" and subsequently, with Mao's approval, dismissed and jailed many marshals and generals.[14] Among those marshals was He Long, Lin's long-time rival, who was labeled the "biggest bandit," and who died in prison. In early 1968, the Central Committee dismissed and jailed General Yang Chengwu, chief of the General Staff, and General Yu Lijin, chief of the Air Force. Lin then appointed his loyal followers to these positions. Most marshals and generals lost their positions, and were jailed or publicly criticized.

In Beijing, all PLA headquarters became paralyzed, as commanders and officers were expelled from their positions. In the course of cruel questioning sessions, many were tormented or beaten to death. From 1967 to 1969, more than 80,000 officers were accused and purged. Among them, 1,169 officers died of torture, starvation, or by execution. Many military institutes were shut down and research programs were cancelled. The number of military academies was reduced from 125 to forty-three, accompanied by the destruction of many defense works and the cessation of regular training. The PLA suffered the "most serious damage since the founding of the PRC."[15]

After early 1967, the situation worsened across the country as the Cultural Revolution entered the phase of a "total take-over" by authorities. The Red Guards, seizing government offices at all levels, jailed the officials and administrators of provincial and local affairs. To make matters worse, different factions within the Red Guards had contradictory political orientations and divergent plans, leading to violent conflicts that amounted to a civil war within the Red Guards in many places.

At local levels, regional and provincial commands were either paralyzed or divided into two or more factions because they had become involved in local factional activities. For example, in July 1967 the Wuhan Regional Command had an armed clash with the Hubei Provincial Command because of differing opinions over the local factional mass organizations. Known as the "July 20th Incident," the conflict pulled the entire province into essentially a civil war. During and after the incident, more than 180,000 were killed or wounded in the city streets of Wuhan, including officers, soldiers, and civilians.[16] Many officers brought the same attitude and problems back into the PLA, leading to the rise of two opposing factions in many units within the military.

To stop the national turmoil, Mao ordered the PLA to control the situation by "three supports and two militarizations" (support Leftist masses, manufacturing production, and agricultural production; and apply the martial law with military administration and training of civilians). Mao employed the PLA to restore social and political order and to prevent a possible civil war in the country. On January 23, the Central Committee, CMC, State Council, and Central Cultural Revolution Leading Team, issued a joint directive about the PLA's new task. Two months later, the CMC ordered all PLA units to be fully engaged in the "supports and militarizations" task to stop the armed conflicts and to stabilize social order across the country. Thereafter, tasking headquarters were established at regional and provincial commands, and the tasking offices were opened at army and divisional levels.

Moving to center stage and under Lin's command from 1967 to 1972, the Chinese military replaced civilian governments at provincial, district, county, and city levels through its military administration, or the "Military Administrative Committee." The PLA used its officers as administrators for schools, factories, companies, villages, and farms.[17] More than 2.8 million officers and soldiers participated in these tasks. By February 1967, the military administration took control of nearly 7,000 enterprises of mass media, defense industry, law enforcement, foreign affairs, transportation, finance, and other pivotal activities. Moreover, PLA administrative teams took over all universities, colleges, high schools, and elementary schools across the country. They also organized professors, teachers, administrators, and students for military training and daily drills. The PLA takeover promoted military-civilian integration and contributed to another increase in military services. By the mid-1970s, the PLA numbered more than six million troops.[18] From 1967 to 1971, the PLA was the dominant political force in the country, and Lin's power grew to an unprecedented level. At the CCP Ninth National Congress in April 1969, the Central Committee and the entire party recognized Lin as Mao's "close comrade in arms and successor."[19]

In 1970, the Cultural Revolution took a sudden and unexpected turn. A new political struggle between Chairman Mao and Marshal Lin erupted, one that would rip an enormous hole in a political arena already gasping for breath from the battering that it had endured. Lin and Mao differed in strategy, foreign policy, and domestic politics.[20] For instance, when Mao proposed that the PRC Constitution be amended to eliminate the post of Head of State, Lin made a counter-proposal that Mao should assume the presidency. Mao repeatedly turned down the offer and said, "I cannot do this job. The suggestion is inappropriate." On the surface this was only a question of whether or not to retain the post of Head of State. Actually, it concealed a host of contradictions.[21]

These contradictions burst forth at the Second Plenum of the Ninth CCP Central Committee at Lushan in August–September 1970. In his opening speech as the second party leader next to Mao, Lin again advocated creating the office of Head of State. His generals voiced their support, but the military leaders overplayed their hand in the party. Mao summoned an enlarged meeting of the Politburo at Lushan and sternly criticized Lin and the military, thus dooming Lin's fate. The plenum ended on September 6, when Mao's concluding speech struck the party leaders like a thunderclap. After the stormy meeting at Lushan, some of Lin's lieutenants were criticized, compelled to make self-criticisms or be removed from office. Angry and disappointed, Mao considered Lin's motivations and personal influence in the military to be dangerous. Mao had never expected that Lin would challenge his authority and openly stand up against him as an equal, and he decided to confront Lin – head on. In August and September 1971, Mao traveled around the country, talking to key people, both military and civilian, and stressing how serious the situation had become. In the Mao-Lin struggle, most of the military leaders chose Mao and denounced Lin.[22]

Lin and his family realized that Mao was directing the spearhead of his political struggle against them. Just like Peng, Liu, and Deng, Lin would be the next victim of one of Mao's brutal political movements. Lin's son, Lin Liguo, planned to assassinate Mao on the latter's way back from Shanghai; however, Mao realized the danger and returned early to Beijing from Hangzhou on September 12, thereby dooming Lin Liguo's plot. Lin had taken a fatal step from which there was no return. On September 13, 1971, at the urging of his wife and son, Lin fled. He commandeered a plane at the Shanhaiguan Airport, and it flew north, heading for the Soviet Union. For unknown reasons, the plane crashed in Mongolia.[23] Lin, his family, crew members and others on board, eight in total, were killed in the crash.

The Lin incident was the most jolting political event since the inception of the Cultural Revolution. Five days after the plane crash, the Central Committee, with the approval of Mao, notified its members of Lin's treasonous flight. Ten days later, the committee informed military officers and commanders at divisional and above levels. In late September, it dismissed all key members of Lin's group from their positions. The following day, Mao chaired the first meeting of the new office. The chairman said that Lin had controlled the armed forces for more than ten years and that many problems existed in the military; the PLA must be unified and prepared for war.[24] On October 6 the Central Committee issued a report regarding the "criminal activities of the Lin Biao clique." Lin was accused of forming an "anti-revolutionary clique," conducting a military coup, planning the assassination of Mao, and betraying his country.[25]

The Sino-Soviet border conflict (1969)

The hostility between China and the Soviet Union reached new heights when the Chinese and Soviet armies prepared for border conflict in the North in 1968. The Soviet Union increased its troops by the end of 1968 from seventeen divisions to twenty-seven divisions along the Sino-Soviet border. Beginning in March 1969, border skirmishes erupted along the Sino-Soviet borders at the Zhenbao (Damansky) and Bacha Islands in Heilongjiang (Heilungkiang), Northeast China. For the rest of the year, sporadic fighting continued in many places along the borders, including Taskti and Tieliekti in Xinjiang, Northwest China, and both nations stood on the brink of war. By 1971, the Soviet Union had deployed up to forty-eight divisions, constituting nearly one million troops along the Russian-Chinese border. Reportedly, Moscow's leaders considered using a "preemptive nuclear strike" against China.[26]

The Soviet Union had been the PLA's big headache not only in Vietnam, but also along the Chinese-Russian borders in the late 1960s. Another major change in the 1960s was an important shift of Beijing's defense strategy and national security concern: from the United States to the Soviet Union. As previously mentioned, when Marshal Lin became the defense minister in August 1959, he terminated most of Peng's reform programs and denounced them as part of the "Soviet revisionist military system." Lin and his lieutenants considered the Soviet Union as a more immediate threat to the PRC. They believed that the United States was a declining power because of its failures in Vietnam and serious problems in other parts of the world. As the United States withdrew from Vietnam, the Soviet Union filled in the power vacuum and replaced the United States as a new "imperialist" aggressor. Therefore, China, like other Asian countries, became a target and victim of the new "Soviet socialist imperialist" aggressive policy.[27]

Lin's conception made sense to PLA soldiers and commanders who witnessed increased Soviet hostility as a direct threat to their country. In 1960, the Soviet Union unilaterally ended 600 bilateral contracts and withdrew all Soviet experts from China. In 1961, the Soviets canceled all projects of scientific and technical co-operation, including the joint nuclear programs. Obviously, the Soviet Union did not want to see a strong and prosperous neighbor. In 1962, Soviet agents instigated the migration of tens of thousands of Chinese citizens in Yili Prefecture to the Soviet Union. In 1966, the Soviet government ordered all Chinese students to leave the country within a week. After the Soviet Red Army invaded Czechoslovakia in 1968, its troops broke into the Chinese Embassy and "savagely" beat Chinese diplomats.[28] While tensions mounted, the Soviet Union deployed a large number of Red Army troops along the Soviet-Chinese borders.[29]

Border disputes between China and Russia have a long history back to the eighteenth century. Following China's alliance with the Soviet Union in 1949, both countries accepted the territorial status quo along their 4,150-mile-long border, and signed the 1951 Border Rivers Navigation Agreement. With the emerging Sino-Soviet split in the 1960s, the border issue resurfaced again. China claimed some border territories as its own, and sent PLA troops into these areas. Soviet forces expelled the Chinese, and fighting was usually avoided until the late 1960s. The Soviet Union increased its troops by the end of 1968 from seventeen divisions to twenty-seven divisions along the Sino-Soviet border. In 1968–1969, the PLA was apparently under tremendous pressure and felt directly threatened by the Soviet Union.[30]

In October 1968, Lin warned the army and the country that Soviet forces would soon invade China. Thereafter, the country became militarized and was prepared for an invasion. While planning to defeat the invading troops by a "people's war," Lin instructed the PLA to confront the Soviets wherever an invasion occurred. Beginning in March 1969, small-scale border skirmishes erupted at the Zhen Bao (Damansky) and Bacha Islands in Heilongjiang, Northeast China and at Taskti and Tieliekti in Xinjiang, Northwest China.[31]

In the first clash on March 2, forty Chinese soldiers patrolled Zhen Bao (Damansky) Island, one of the small disputed uninhabited islands (0.74 square miles) in the middle of the Ussuri River. The Soviets dispatched seventy border troops to the island, but the Chinese refused to leave. Both sides blamed the other for opening fire at 9:00am in the morning. With two hundred reinforcements, the Chinese attacked and killed thirty Soviet soldiers, losing only six of their own. After a twelve-day stand-off, on March 15, over one hundred Soviet troops and six tanks counter-attacked. Heavy artillery pieces

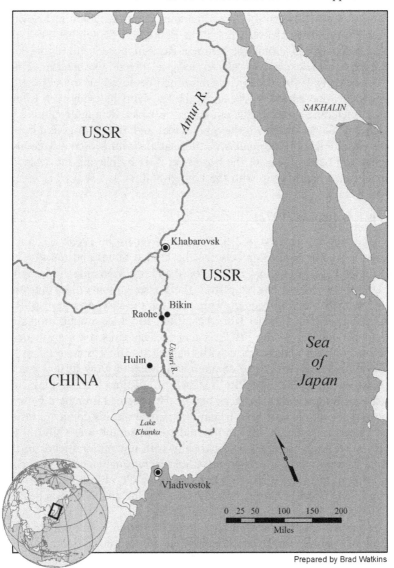

Map 10.1 The Sino-Soviet border conflict

shelled both shores. More than forty Chinese soldiers were killed. The Soviets lost eight men and one T-62 tank that sank in the river when artillery fire shattered the two-meter thick ice cover.[32]

For the rest of the year, sporadic fighting continued in many places along the borders, and both nations stood on the brink of war, with the Soviets threatening nuclear retaliation. Among the border incidents, on June 10, fifty Soviet soldiers attacked the Chinese in Taskti, Xinjiang. On July 8, the fighting in Heilongjiang extended to the Bacha Islands along the Amur River. On August 13, more than three hundred Soviet troops supported by twenty tanks and two helicopters engaged in Tieliekti, Xinjiang, and annihilated all the Chinese troops in the battle. The border conflicts did not escalate into total war between the two communist countries. Zhou met Soviet President of the Ministers Council Aleksei Kosygin in Beijing on September 11, 1969. But the border clashes continued along the Chinese-Russian borders until the late 1970s.[33] Reportedly, Moscow's leaders considered using a "preemptive nuclear strike" against China.[34] By the early 1970s, the Soviet Union had deployed up to forty-eight divisions, constituting nearly one million troops along the Russian-Chinese border. China prepared for total war, including possible Russian nuclear attacks. Beijing demanded a reduction in the number of Soviet troops on the Sino-Soviet and Sino-Mongolian borders as one of the three conditions for a normalization of relations with Moscow. Mao also intended to undermine the rising power of the Soviets in Asia by playing the "American card" and opening a new relationship with the United States.[35]

Nixon's visit to Beijing (1972)

After the United States entered into the Vietnam War in the 1960s, a chance appeared for thawing the frosty relationship between the United States and the PRC. China and the Soviet Union began vying for influence on the North Vietnamese side, and eventually North Vietnam chose to accept help from the Soviet Union rather than the Chinese. This furthered a rift that had been growing between the PRC and the USSR. Earlier in the 1950s, the Soviet Union, under Khrushchev, undertook de-Stalinization and reformist actions that ran counter to the PRC's practices. This caused China to denounce the Soviet Union's policies and, coupled with the rejection of Chinese aid in Vietnam in favor of Soviet aid, caused the two communist powers to grow further apart. In 1969, tensions between the USSR and PRC reached an all-time high as they engaged in a series of clashes along China's northern border. War seemed imminent between the two nuclear powers for a time and Mao began to worry about his country's future security. The Asian Communist nation, also in the midst of its tumultuous Cultural Revolution, found itself increasingly isolated diplomatically with few major friends in the international arena. Compounding the situation, China increasingly faced a major threat from the Soviet Union, formerly their strongest supporter. The PRC began to take steps to shore up its own position internationally, and by the late 1960s appeared open to approaching its old bitter enemy, the United States.

Under previous US administrations, a uniform foreign policy was in place to deal with communist nations, under the theory that all communist states were the same. This theory proved to be untrue, as the split between the PRC and USSR illustrated. Under the Nixon administration, national security advisor and future secretary of state Henry Kissinger proposed the idea that the United States could deal with China differently, and that the United States had an opportunity to unbalance its key enemy, the Soviet Union.

With tensions rising between the two major communist powers, Premier Zhou Enlai, under blessings from Mao Zedong, agreed to speak with his American counterparts in an effort to negotiate a better relationship. A period known as Rapprochement began, with both sides considering the possibilities of establishing bilateral relations with one another. Relations continued to improve with the accidental actions of an American ping-pong player and his rival team from the PRC.

In April 1971, Japan played host to an international ping-pong tournament. The Chinese, in an effort to engage other nations of the world, participated in the sporting event. Glen Cowan, a member of the American ping-pong team, was practicing in

Nagoya and inadvertently stepped onto the Chinese team's bus when practices were over. One of the Chinese players, Zhuang Zedong, realized Glen's mistake and helped him to get back to his own team. The American player was treated with hospitality during his ride with the opposing players, and he formed a friendship with them. The Chinese team invited him to visit the PRC as a token of goodwill and when the Communist government got wind of this, they used it as a diplomatic maneuver and extended an official invitation to the American team to tour China. With relations becoming increasingly amicable, the time was rapidly approaching for an official diplomatic visit between the two nations.

In July 1971, Kissinger was on a diplomatic trip to Pakistan. During the night he slipped out on a secret mission to the PRC. The mission was actually an attempt to open relations between the two governments, and Kissinger engaged in discussions with his Chinese counterpart, Premier Zhou. The two came to an agreement and on July 15, President Nixon stated that he had formally been invited to the PRC.

On February 21, 1972, Nixon, accompanied by Kissinger and several other advisors, made his way to China and held high-level meetings with Mao and Zhou. The meetings were fruitful, and on February 28, the two parties released the Shanghai Communiqué. This Communiqué, authored by both the United States and the PRC, endorsed further contact between the two nations in the form of diplomatic and cultural exchanges, with both sides disavowing the pursuit of hegemony in the Asian-Pacific region. The PRC also outlined several of its positions in the Communiqué. Namely, the reinforcement of the "one China policy," stating that Taiwan was a province of China and that the government of the PRC was the sole government of China. The question of liberation of Taiwan was an internal affair of China and wasn't to be interfered with The Communiqué also stated that all US military installations and forces must be withdrawn from Taiwan. The United States responded to this in the Communiqué by saying that a peaceful settlement between Taiwan and China must be reached by the Chinese themselves, and affirmed its commitment to reduction and eventual withdrawal of US forces from Taiwan. Both sides expressed interest in conducting bilateral trade and remained committed to keeping in contact with each other via the sending of officials.

Relations continued to improve between the two nations, with an official liaison office set up in both America and the PRC in 1973. In 1978, under the advice of National Security Advisor Zbigniew Brzezinski, President Jimmy Carter (1924–) sought full diplomatic relations with the PRC. A joint communiqué was released on December 15, 1978, whereby the United States and the PRC agreed to formally recognize each other on January 1, 1979 and to establish formal diplomatic relations. The United States also agreed to recognize the Communist government as the sole government of China, and formally adopted the "one China policy." Additionally, both sides reaffirmed their belief that the normalization of relations between the two countries would be in the best interests of both the Chinese and American peoples, and would lead to peace in Asia and the world.

On January 1, 1979, Vice Premier Deng Xiaoping went to Washington to attend a special ceremony where the government of the United States officially recognized the PRC. What followed was an unprecedented increase in trade relations, and further diplomatic contact between the two nations. The strategy of Rapprochement appeared successful, and the USSR became agitated over the two enemies coming together. The Soviets then engaged the United States in several treaties, namely the SALT (Strategic Arms Limitation Talks) treaties, to encourage peaceful limitations and disarmament of strategic weapons, in an effort to reduce military tensions. Overtures to the PRC also had an impact on the Republic of China when, in 1971, the United Nations decided to revoke Taiwan's membership in favor of the PRC. Relations between the United States and PRC improved throughout the 1980s, but encountered a serious problem in 1989 with Deng Xiaoping's heavy-handed response to the Tiananmen Square protests. In 1991, the USSR collapsed and relations changed to a more cautious approach. With no single enemy to unite against, and with the PRC emerging as a major economic power, relations between the US and China continue to play an important part of global foreign policy.

Mao's Death and the Gang of Four (1976)

After Lin's death, Mao launched a nationwide movement to "Criticize Lin and Confucius," (*pilin pikong*) and labeled Lin as a "closet Confucianist," "Bourgeois careerist," conspirator, and "ultra-rightist." Historians are surprised to see that "These obviously contradictory criticisms were heaped on a man who had been a brilliant general and one of Mao's closest friends." June Grasso, Jay Corrin, and Michael Kort state that "Lin Biao was blamed for nearly everything that went wrong in China during the late 1960s."[36] Since Lin promoted the Mao cult and the Cultural Revolution, his death brought great joy to China's millions. But close scrutiny also revealed that the Cultural Revolution was open to serious question about its entire course of action, orientation, and policy. Mao himself certainly knew better. A person who worked closely beside him later recalled: "After Lin Biao crashed, the Chairman became very ill. Lin's betrayal had a serious effect on his health."[37]

As it was in the past, Mao's political criticism was followed by another top-down purge and shakeup in the military. During the movement to "Criticize Lin and Confucius," most of Lin's generals were expunged, and his military programs were terminated. By January 1973, the CMC had completed its thorough replacement and reorganization of all services and departments before the year's end. It ordered all chiefs of eight regional commands to exchange positions within ten days. Thereafter, Marshal Ye Jianying took charge of the PLA daily affairs with the consultation of Premier Zhou Enlai. This Zhou-Ye system replaced the Lin-Jiang system that had dominated the years from 1966 to 1971. A new power struggle soon began between Zhou-Ye and Jiang Qing, who continued to control the media and to preach class struggle. The Great Cultural Revolution lasted until Mao's death in September 1976.[38]

After Lin's death in 1971, continuing threats from the Soviet Union, together with the fading status of Mao's "continuous revolution" at home, created motives on Beijing's part to pursue a rapprochement with the United States. Both President Richard Nixon and his national security advisor Henry Kissinger saw an improvement in the relationship with China as beneficial to the United States since it would, in the short run, help extricate the United States from the Vietnam War, and in the long term would dramatically enhance Washington's strategic position in a global confrontation vis-à-vis the Soviet Union.[39] All this paved the way for Nixon's historic visit to China in February 1972. In the meantime, a political power group rose at the Party Centre: "the Gang of Four."

The Gang of Four was the name given to a radical leftist political group composed of four CCP bureaucrats led by Mao's wife Jiang Qing. They became notorious due to the Cultural Revolution. Aside from Jiang, the group included Wang Hongwen (a former factory worker), Yao Wenyuan (a polemicist), and Zhang Chunqiao (a propaganda expert), all three of whom were party leaders in Shanghai and had played foremost roles in taking over that city for Mao during the Cultural Revolution.

Jiang Qing became China's first lady after the founding of the PRC in 1949. She served as director of film in the Department of Central Propaganda of the CCP and also as a member of the Ministry of Culture steering committee for film production. After being condemned by other CCP high-ranking officials for the failure of the Great Leap Forward, Mao turned to Jiang. Powered by her husband, Jiang made the best use of her advantage to carry out the reform of the Chinese theatre. Mao's support made it possible for Jiang to be assigned the position of deputy director of the Central Cultural Revolution Group.

Jiang gained actual power within Chinese politics for the first time and became one of the architects of the Cultural Revolution. During this time she played a progressively vigorous political role, participating in principal CCP and state activities. Her position was cemented by her membership in the all-powerful Politburo in 1969, when she had already created a particularly strong relationship with what was eventually recognized as the Gang of Four. After 1973, these four radicals held unlimited control over all national institutions in practice limited by Mao and to a lesser extent by Zhou Enlai, and occupied influential positions in the Politburo. The Gang of Four effectively dominated the power organs of the Communist Party of China through the latter stages of the Cultural Revolution. However, it remains unclear which major decisions were made by Mao and which were the result of the Gang of Four's own arrangement.

Jiang and Lin worked together at the beginning of the Cultural Revolution, but after Lin's death in 1971, Jiang turned against him publicly in the Condemning Lin and Confucius Movement. During the mid-1970s, Jiang directed her crusade against Deng Xiaoping. At that time, the Chinese people became vehemently dissatisfied with her and chose to blame her when the entire Gang of Four was working hard to take advantage of Mao's declining health and power.

Jiang vigorously championed her husband's political ideas, and her status as the chairman's wife seemed to make her untouchable. Mao's favourite was Wang Hongwen, one of the radicals who seemed poised to become Zhou Enlai's successor, but Mao knew that Wang was not up to the task and feared that the Gang of Four would plunge the country into renewed chaos with their revolutionary zeal. Nearing the end of his life, Mao turned against Jiang Qing and her associates, leading to the rise of Hua Guofeng.

On September 9, 1976, Mao died. The power struggle in the party between the Maoists, or the Gang of Four, including Jiang Qing, Zhang Chunqiao, Yao Wenyuan, and Wang Hongwen, and the old guard, including Chen Yun, Xu Xiangqian, Ye, Nie Rongzhen, and Wang Zhen surfaced. Real control, however, remained in the hands of Ye, who was vice chairman of the CCP Central Committee, a member of the Standing Committee of the Politburo, vice chairman of the CMC, and minister of defense. On October 6, Ye ordered security troops to arrest the Gang of Four and Mao Yuanxin, Mao Zedong's cousin.[40] The CCP leadership survived the Cultural Revolution in 1966–1976.

After the demise of the Gang of Four, Deng Xiaoping staged his third comeback in 1977. He won an intense struggle in the post-Mao succession by removing the Maoists and having a firm control of Beijing. He then ended the Cultural Revolution and led China from a period of political turmoil to one of economic development by denying the need for any continuous domestic class struggle, the underlying impulse of Mao's Cultural Revolution. In 1978, he emerged as the new paramount leader and launched new reform policies, opening China up to the outside world. Meanwhile, he represented a new generation of Chinese leadership.[41] The CCP experience between 1949 and 1979 indicated that the party could learn, not only from its successes, but also its failures. "The party of learning" determined its political nature of flexibility, adaptation to new circumstances, and readiness for change.

Notes

1 David Shambaugh, *China's Communist Party: Atrophy and Adaptation* (Berkeley: University of California Press, 2008), 7.
2 For more discussions from Chinese perspective, see: Gong Li. *Kuayue honggou: 1969–1979 nian zhongmei guanxi de yanbian* [Bridging the Chasm: The Evolution of Sino-American Relations, 1969–1979] (Zhengzhou: Henan renmin [Henan People's Press], 1992), 106–108; Wang, ed., *Zhonghua renmin gongheguo waijiaoshi* [Diplomatic History of the People's Republic of China], 345, 346–348.
3 Thomas A. Bailey, *A Diplomatic History of the American People*, 10th ed. (Englewood Cliffs, NJ: Prentice-Hall, 1980), 928.
4 Chen and Li, "China and the End of the Cold War," 120.
5 The quote of the "May 16 Circular" is from Fang Zhu, *Gun Barrel Politics: Party-Army Relations in Mao's China* (Boulder, CO: Westview Press, 1998), 116.
6 Zhu, *ibid.*, 117.
7 CCP Party History Research Division, *Zhongguo gongchandang lishi dashiji, 1919–1987* [Major Historical Events of the CCP, 1919–1987] (Beijing: Renmin [People's Press], 1989), 283.
8 Mao's letter is quoted in Deng Rong, *Deng Xiaoping and the Cultural Revolution – A Daughter Recalls the Critical Years*, trans. Sidney Shapiro (Beijing: Foreign Languages Press, 2002), 17.
9 Mao's quote in Deng, *ibid.*, 20.
10 Spence, *The Search for Modern China*, 545.
11 For more discussions on the Great Cultural Revolution, see: Li and Hao, *Wenhua dageming zhong de renmin jiefangjun* [The PLA during the Cultural Revolution]; Maurice Meisner, *Mao's China: A History of the People's Republic* (New York: The Free Press, 1977), chapters 18–20.
12 Joffe, *The Chinese Army after Mao*, 2.
13 Meisner, *Mao's China,* 318.
14 Mao approved most of Lin's requests. See Mao's instructions and approvals in *Mao's Manuscripts since 1949*, 12: 201, 209, 218, 226–268, 380, 383.
15 Lushun Naval Command, "Collective Documents on Lin Biao and Li Zuopeng's Criminal Activities of Attacking the Party and Betraying the PLA," in *Lushun Naval Base Archives (PLAN)*, 1972, Lushun, Liaoning, 56.
16 Military History Research Division, CAMS, *Zhongguo renmin jiefangjun de 70 nian* [Seventy Years of the PLA], 559.
17 Capt. Zhou Baoshan, interview by the author, Harbin, Heilongjiang, April 2000. See also Zhou, "China's Crouching Dragon," in *Voices from the Korean War: Personal Stories of American, Korean, and Chinese Soldiers* by Richard Peters and Xiaobing Li (Lexington: University Press of Kentucky, 2004), 93.
18 Han, *Dangdai zhongguo jundui de junshi gongzuo* [Military Affairs of Contemporary China's Armed Forces], 1: 62; Military History Research Division, CAMS, *Zhongguo renmin jiefangjun de qishinian* [Seventy Years of the PLA], 563–564.
19 Li, *The Private Life of Chairman Mao*, 512.
20 Among the publications on Marshal Lin Biao in English are Michael Y. M. Kau, ed. *The Lin Biao Affair: Power Politics and Military Coup* (White Plains, NY: International Arts and Science Press, 1975); Martin Ebon, *Lin Piao: The Life and Writings of China's New Ruler* (New York: Stein and Day Publishers, 1970).

21 CCP Party History Research Division, *Zhongguo gongchandang lishi dashiji* [Major Historical Events of the CCP], 305–308; Military History Research Division, CAMS, *Zhongguo renmin jiefangjun de qishinian* [Seventy Years of the PLA], 564–565.

22 Military History Research Division, CAMS, *ibid.*

23 There have been several speculations about the crash of Lin's plane, including a Chinese missile attack, running out of fuel, or simply an accident. See: Gao Wenqian, *Wannian Zhou Enlai* [Zhou Enlai's Later Years] (Hong Kong: Mingjing [Bright Mirror Publishing], 2003), 350–355; Huang Yao and Yan Jingtang. *Lin Biao yisheng* [Lin Biao's Life] (Beijing: Jiefangjun wenyi [PLA Literature Press], 2004), 490–507; Ye Yonglie, *Gaoceng jiaoliang* [Power Struggle at the Top] (Urumqi: Xinjiang renmin [Xinjiang People's Press], 2004), 369–376.

24 Military History Research Division, CAMS, *Zhongguo renmin jiefangjun de 70 nian* [Seventy years of the PLA], 566.

25 CCP Party History Research Division, *Zhongguo gongchandang lishi dashiji, 1919–1987* [Major Historical Events of the CCP, 1919–1987] (Beijing: Renmin [People's Press], 1989), 309.

26 Yang Kuisong, "From the Zhenbao Island Incident to Sino-American Rapprochement," *Dangshi yanjiu ziliao* [Party History Research Materials] no. 12 (1997), 7–8; Thomas Robinson, "The Sino-Soviet Border Conflicts of 1969," in Ryan, Finkelstein, and McDevitt, eds., *Chinese Warfighting*, 198–216.

27 For example, Premier Zhou said on April 29, 1968 that the Soviet Union [like America] was apparently circulating and containing China. Li Danhui, "Conflicts between China and the Soviet Union in Their Efforts to Aid Vietnam and Resist America," in Zhang and Niu, eds., *Lengzhan yu zhongguo* (The Cold War and China) 373n1.

28 Xinhua News Agency, *China's Foreign Relations: A Chronology of Events, 1949–88*, 461–467.

29 After the Soviet invasion of Czechoslovakia in 1968, Moscow reinforced its border forces from seventeen divisions to twenty-seven divisions in 1969 along the Russo-Chinese borders. See: Xiaobing Li, "Sino-Soviet Border Disputes," in *MaGill's Guide to Military History*, ed. John Powell (Pasadena, CA: Salem Press, 2001), 4: 1423.

30 Among the recent publications on the rise and demise of the Sino-Soviet alliance in English are Odd Arne Westad, ed., *Brothers in Arms;* and Gordon H. Chang, *Friends and Enemies.*

31 Xiaobing Li, "Sino-Soviet Border Disputes," in *MaGill's Guide to Military History*, 4: 1424.

32 Han, *Dangdai zhongguo jundui de junshi gongzuo* [Military Affairs of Contemporary China's Armed Forces], 1: 639–642; CAMS, *Zhongguo renmin jiefangjun de qishinian* [Seventy Years of the PLA], 580–581.

33 Han, *ibid.*, 1: 643–644; CAMS, *ibid.*, 582.

34 Yang Kuisong, "From the Zhenboa Island Incident to Sino-American Rapprochement," *Dangshi yanjiu ziliao* [Party History Research Materials] no. 12 (1997), 7–8; Thomas Robinson, "The Sino-Soviet Border Conflicts of 1969: New Evidence Three Decades Later," in *Chinese Warfighting*, Ryan, Finkelstein, and McDevitt, eds. 198–216.

35 Chen and Li, "China and the End of the Cold War," 124.

36 June Grasso, Jay Corrin, and Michael Kort, *Modernization and Revolution in China: From the Opium Wars to World Power*, 3rd ed. (Armonk, NY: M. E. Sharpe, 2004), 234.

37 Deng, *Deng Xiaoping and the Cultural Revolution*, 189.

38 For the last phase of the Cultural Revolution, see: Gao Meng and Yan Jiaqi, *Wenhua dageming shi nian shi* [Ten Years of the Cultural Revolution] (Tianjin: Tianjin renmin [Tianjin People's Publishing], 1986), chapters 6–7; Li and Hao, *Wenhua dageming zhong de renmin jiefangjun* [The PLA during the Cultural Revolution]; Meisner, *Mao's China*, chapter 20.

39 Richard Nixon, *The Memoirs of Richard Nixon* (New York: Grosset & Dunlap, 1978), 390; Charles Freeman, Jr., "The Process of Rapprochement: Achievements and Problems," in *Sino-American Normalization and Its Policy Implications,* eds. Gene T. Hsiao and Michael Witunsky (New York: Praeger, 1983): 2–3, 10–14.

40 For the details of arresting the "Gang of Four," see Deng, *Deng Xiaoping and the Cultural Revolution*, chapter 55, "Thoroughly Smash the Gang of Four," 436–443.

41 Deng became the second generation of the CCP political and military leadership. Li, *China's Leaders*, 7–9.

11 China's reforming movement (1978–1989)

After Mao's death in 1976 and on his third return, Deng Xiaoping and the reformers launched an unprecedented seismic reform in 1978 and opened China to the outside world in order to bring the "Four Modernizations," including defense modernization, to the country. The latter, who were in such large numbers with popular support, soon overthrew the Maoists. Consequently, a new crucial feature in the Cold War in East Asia as well as in the world emerged – international politics became dominated by a specific "triangular structure."[1] Taking the "Soviet threat" as an overriding concern, Beijing and Washington established a "quasi strategic partnership."[2] Toward such crises as Vietnam's invasion of Cambodia in 1979 and the Soviet invasion of Afghanistan in 1980, Beijing's and Washington's reactions were compatible – they both condemned Hanoi and Moscow. Both also emphasized the inner-connectivity between the events in Cambodia and Afghanistan, and both provided various support to resistance movements in these two countries.[3] Eventually, in February 1979, China invaded Vietnam with 200,000 PLA troops.

Deng Xiaoping, as the leading figure of the second generation leadership (1978–1989), took control and launched a wave of tremendous change, particularly in the evolution from a centrally planned communist economy to a free-market system seeking global inclusion and meeting an increasingly popular demand for modernization along with improvement in the standard of living. Deng adapted to changing circumstances and prevented the CCP and the PRC from bankruptcy, as happened in the Soviet Union a few years later. The economic reforms in the 1980s were, in Deng's words, comparable to "crossing the river by feeling the stepping stones."[4] These reforms successfully transformed China from an agricultural economy to one of booming industry, which in turn brought transformation from a communistic totalitarian government to an authoritarian one.

Even though the Cultural Revolution was said to have "crucially weakened the CCP's efficiency and morale," the Party survived after Mao's death in 1976.[5] Jonathan D. Spence points out that in the 1980s, "With the suppression of the broad-based pleas for greater democratic participation, the party reconsolidated its power." Richard McGregor attributes the Party's survival to leaders who had been able "to maintain the political institutions and authoritarian powers of old-style communism, while dumping the ideological straitjacket that inspired them."[6] According to Patrick Fuliang Shan's argument, the Party's association with Chinese grassroots society "in a total native social setting" guaranteed its flexibility and adaptation to the ever-changing China during the continuing revolution.[7] The findings suggest that the CCP had grown beyond the Leninist party system which depended on secrecy and institutional control and had developed a self-improvement mechanism and functionality which could adapt

to a new environment and allow changes within the Party. David Shambaugh concludes: "The CCP has exhibited many classic symptoms of an atrophying and decaying
Leninist party – but, at the same time, it is also showing itself capable of significant
adaptation and reform in a number of key areas."[8]

These changes were not without challenges, and more often than not the reforms
contained issues of contradiction, uncertainty, and clashes that are inherent in the
intermingling of tradition and modernity. Deng was required to make many promises
by revising the constitution for more civil rights, institutionalizing the bureaucracy, and
establishing the checks and balances by giving more power to the National People's
Congress (NPC). Deng was determined to ensure a smooth political succession in the
wake of the failures of his two previously appointed successors. However, unable to
solve some of the economic and social problems, and unwilling to carry the reform into
the political arena, Deng and his generation found themselves challenged by
pro-democracy demonstrations during the spring of 1989.

Between 1986 and 1991, most communist countries, including the Soviet Union,
underwent political reforms and economic transformation. The epochal developments
were spurred by Gorbachev's bold reform programs, *glasnost* and *perestroika*, which
helped to release the Eastern bloc countries from the long Kremlin control. It was an
open admission that economic stagnation in the communist camp had reached a point
where it threatened national survival itself. In turn, freed former Soviet satellite countries
in Eastern Europe adopted various political measures pursuing society-wide democratization and institutional pluralism. This effectively terminated not only the Soviet-led
Communist movement in the world, but also the traditional East-West rivalry. China,
Vietnam, and North Korea faced similar challenges and made their own choices during
the worldwide communist crisis.

Deng's returns and economic reform

During the Cultural Revolution, Deng was purged along with Liu Shaoqi as the head
of the "bourgeoisie headquarters within the Party" and ousted from the CCP and PRC
hierarchy in 1966. Thereafter, Deng and his wife were placed under house arrest in
Beijing for two years before being sent to Jiangxi to work at a tractor-repair factory
in 1969.[9] Rehabilitated by Mao, Deng was appointed as a member of the Central
Committee in 1973 and then chief of PLA General Staff, vice chairman of the CMC,
vice chairman of the Central Committee, and a member of the Politburo Standing
Committee in 1975.[10] Maoists, including Mao's wife, Jiang Qing, criticized Deng's
reforms arguing that they were restoring old bourgeoisie lines, and turning back
(*fan'an*) to the rightist ways. In 1976, Mao and leftists accused Deng of criticizing the
Cultural Revolution and Jiang Qing and dismissed him from the government in April.
The new reform movement seemed over before it even started.

After the demise of the Gang of Four, Deng staged his third comeback in 1977. He
won an intense struggle in the post-Mao succession by removing the Maoists and
having a firm control of Beijing. Then, he ended the Cultural Revolution and led China
from a period of political turmoil to one of economic development by denying the need
for any continuous domestic class struggle, the underlying impulse of Mao's Cultural
Revolution. In 1978, he emerged as the new paramount leader and launched new
reform policies, opening China up to the outside world. Meanwhile, he represented a
new generation of the Chinese leadership.[11]

In 1978, Deng made his historic speech, "Emancipate the Mind," at the Third Plenary Session of the CCP Eleventh Party Central Committee. His speech declared an unprecedented seismic reform that would bring the "Four Modernizations" to China, including industry, agriculture, science and technology, and national defense.[12] He told a press delegation from the Federal Republic of Germany that:

> Due to the interference of Lin Biao and the Gang of Four, China's development was held up for ten years. In the early 1960s, we were behind the developed countries in science and technology, but the gap was not so wide. However, over the past dozen years, the gap has widened because the world has been developing with tremendous speed. Compared with developed countries, China's economy has fallen behind at least ten years, perhaps 20, 30, or even 50 years in some areas.[13]

Deng was determined to lead China onto the road of economic prosperity by deprogramming Mao's system and convincing people that reality was the only criterion for judging whether a theory represented the truth. Deng stressed that Marxism was a century-old theory imported from the West. To expect Marxism to reflect China's reality in the twentieth century would simply be unrealistic. Deng defended the market economy, as having no contradiction with socialism, because the market system is simply an economic tool that may serve any ideological cause, including socialism.[14] In Deng's system, Marxism and Mao's Thought became means to support the reform rather than ends that the party must abide by.

The market economy changed the structure of Chinese society dramatically, especially rural society. After 1978, the concept of Mao's people's communes weakened considerably. Deng was the first Communist leader to encourage people to get rich. With his slogan "To be rich is glorious," Deng won the people's endorsement, especially among peasants. Small Chinese farmers were determined to improve their living standard, and they succeeded, leading directly to the collapse of the entire commune system. The state retreated substantially from grassroots rural society.[15]

Long-dissatisfied peasants started to redistribute the land to households on the condition that each household would submit a certain amount of output to the government. This practice achieved great success immediately because once again individual farmsteads gained complete control of their inputs and outputs. The practice was also officially accepted nationwide after a short pioneer experiment in some areas and then was promoted as the "household production responsibility system" (HPRS) in 1979. The production contracting system simply gave villagers control rights to production. The redistribution or the fear of redistribution prevented peasants from leaving their village, resulting in a decline of interest in serving the military. A peasant family needed as many household members as possible in order to receive a larger piece of land. The parents also wanted to keep their sons on the farm to succeed in competitive market farming.

In 1985, each HPRS contract specified a quota output to sell to the government, but the rest of the output could be consumed or sold to markets. The markets for agricultural products were the first free markets in Deng's reform that eventually opened up almost all markets in China. This practice achieved great success immediately because, once again, individual farmsteads gained complete control of their inputs and outputs. In the 1980s, with sizable land and able hands, some of the peasants in the southern provinces got rich quick and became "*wanyuanhu*" (10,000 yuan family) with an annual income of about $3,000, compared to a national peasant average income of 200 yuan RMB ($60) a year.

For the first time, peasants needed to produce their own leadership, win the election against corrupted cadres, and carry out their own policy to benefit their village. Villagers had long been dissatisfied with the parasitic nature of local cadres, or what they called "eat a lot, take a lot" behavior. This dissatisfaction was the core motivation behind many villagers leaving their homes during the Maoist period. Now the successful peasants wanted to work in their villages rather than serve in the military. As a result, peasants gained control rights over production, the opportunity for social mobility, and the power to participate in village governance. Peasants now had their own choices: farm to improve their living, or leave for new opportunities.[16] Labor migration from rural to urban areas had emerged as a nationwide phenomenon since the mid-1980s. Before then, the household registration system had successfully confined the population to the place of birth. Rural to urban migration only occurred on an extremely small scale under the government auspices, including the veteran administrative arrangement. Since the late 1970s, economic reforms improved food supply to the cities and abolished food rationing (or quota) systems for urban residents. As the old apparatuses of migration control became less effective, rural people began spontaneously to migrate to urban areas without obtaining government approval. In the mid-1980s, a large number of migrants successfully entered cities without official approval; by the late 1990s, an estimated total was about twelve million. This caused problems with employment, housing, public education, healthcare, transportation, and law enforcement in the cities, whose governments continued to deny permanent residency to rural people. The urban-rural segregation caused serious concerns and hostility between the government and migrants.[17]

Deng introduced capitalist management by establishing the "special economic zones" (SEZs) in 1979. In the early 1980s, four SEZs were set up, including Shenzhen across the border from Hong Kong. Fourteen coastal cities were soon open for international trade and for investment with special tax breaks and incentives to promote China's exports and to lure foreign capital and technology. He later expanded the experience to the rest of the country. Deng did not intend to send socialism to Mao's bier. Deng believed that socialism and the CCP were incompatible with the market economy. Both planned and market economies were ways to "liberate productivity."

In January 1980, while speaking at a CCP leaders' meeting, Deng emphasized economic development as the pivot:

> Any deviation from this pivotal task endangers our material base. All other tasks must revolve around the pivot and must absolutely not interfere with or upset it. In the 20-odd years since 1957 we have learned bitter lessons in this respect.[18]

He considered the reforming movement a revolution, or the second revolution of the country, comparable to the founding of the PRC in 1949: "China is now carrying out a reform. I am all in favor of that. There is no other solution for us."[19] In a 1987 speech given to high-level officials, Deng pointed out that both planned and market mechanisms were instruments to serve economic growth. He believed it best for China to develop a "socialist market economy," rather than a capitalist market economy. Deng explained that unlike the capitalist society, where individualism prevails, the socialist market economy leads to common prosperity. Although some individuals or regions get rich ahead of others this would not lead to polarization, because the socialist system has the strength of working effectively for common prosperity.[20]

Deng terminated the central planning in the early 1980s by giving autonomy to state-owned enterprises (SOEs) and by experimenting with remuneration to performance. Many SOEs were key national enterprises of leading industries such as energy, steel and iron, defense, automobiles, high tech, and transportation, all under control of the central government. Other medium-sized SOEs were machinery, manufacturing, textile, construction, retails, medicine, mass media, entertainment, and service under the provincial, municipal, and county-level governments. The collectively or publicly owned enterprises included local factories and small business such as hotels, restaurants, and stores. By the mid-1960s, the state and the public owned 94–96 percent of business, and privately owned enterprises (POE) were almost non-existent. To increase SOE productivity, Deng instituted a "two-track system," in which SOEs first fulfilled the production quota and could then produce beyond the quota and sell at market (usually higher) prices. A direct outcome of this change was that the privately owned enterprises (POEs) pushed the SOEs to become more competitive. The SOEs either had to shake off inertia or disintegrate into privately owned companies. By 2000, private enterprise accounted for roughly 40 percent of the economy.

In 1987, Deng laid out three stages for China's modernization: sufficiency, relative affluence, and reaching the living standard of a medium-level developed country. In terms of income figures, the first step was to reach a per capita GDP of $500 by 1990, doubling the 1980 figure of $250. The second step was to reach a per capita GDP of $1,000 and achieve "relative comfort" (*xiaokang*) by the turn of the century. The third step was to quadruple the $1,000 figure of the year 2000 within thirty to fifty years.[21]

Market economy and opening to the West

As a traditional agrarian country since ancient times, agriculture played a crucial role in China's economy and its social stability. Its current agriculture must meet the food needs of 1.3 billion people, over 20 percent of the world's total population. Small farmers were determined to improve their living standard, and they succeeded, leading directly to the collapse of the entire People's Commune system in the 1980s. The redistribution or the fear of redistribution prevented peasants from leaving their village.

The crops had 87.5 percent of total farming acreage in 1949, but only 80 percent in 1978. The grain crops included wheat, corn (maize), soybean, millet, and tubers. They were about 83 percent of the gross value of the total agricultural outputs in 1949, 64 percent in 1978, and 51 percent in 1999. China's most important grain is rice, about 20 percent of total crop farming acreage in 1949 and 23.8 percent in 1978. The total outputs of rice were 48.6 million tons in 1949 and 135 million tons in 1978; about 43 percent of the total grain outputs in 1949 and 45 percent in 1978. The rural sideline products accounted for 4.3 percent of total agricultural output value in 1949, and increased to 17.1 percent in 1980. Village- and town-run enterprises include medical herb farms, botanical gardens, silkworm and mulberry farms, and food processing. Over 1.48 million rural sideline enterprises hired more than thirty million workers in 1980. The state supported the growth of the sideline enterprises in its rural areas.

The service industry, or tertiary industries, such as real estate, financial, insurance, accounting, legal service, tourism, entertainment, public transportation, post, commerce, and telecom services, has had a significant growth in China since the 1980s. The market-oriented economic reform, which began in 1978, focused on an open-trade and consumer-oriented growth strategy that encouraged service sectors with favorable policy support. From 1978 to 1988, the Chinese government invested $175.9 billion in capital construction of basic infrastructure, more than 1.5 times of the total investment in the previous twenty-five years, from 1952 to 1977. As a result, the service industry grew much faster than the whole economy from 1979–1991, when the GDP grew 7–9.4 percent annually, and the service sectors grew in double digits, per annum. In August 1986, the Shenyang Trust and Investment Company first began with over-the-counter trading, then the Shanghai Stock Exchange (SSE) opened in December 1990, and the Shenzhen Stock Exchange (SZSE) opened in July 1991, creating a bond market to generate new financial resources.

Deng claimed that China had opened its door, and would never close it again. The heart of the pragmatist program was a priority commitment to economic development. After his economic reform movement, beginning in 1978, Deng Xiaoping gave greater play to market forces and encouraged foreign trade with, and investment in, China. The open door foreign economic policy reflected a fundamental change in China's developmental strategy from the isolationist policy of previous Chinese leaders such as Mao Zedong.

A pragmatist rather than an ideologue, Deng tried to bring China back into the international system to seek maximum opportunities for its economic and technological development. He signed numerous treaties with Western governments and joined many international organizations.[22] He met presidents Ronald Reagan and George H. W. Bush in Beijing during their state visits to China. Deng also began negotiations with the British to resume Chinese sovereignty over Hong Kong, and with the Portuguese for Macau's return to China. He developed a theory of "one country, two systems" to apply to these territories, as well as Taiwan, for peaceful national reunification. Soon a rapid increase of cross-strait trade, visits, and exchanges occurred, and multilevel official negotiations began between Beijing and Taipei in the 1980s.[23]

The open door economic policy reflected a fundamental change in China's developmental strategy. The desire to get greater access to US economic assistance and technology provided impetus for Beijing to work for improved relations with Washington. From 1978 to 1981, a drive to improve relations with the United States was an important component of China's opening to the outside world. Beijing wanted broad and generous US support for the Four Modernizations and moved to improve relations with the United States to achieve this.[24] The normalization of Sino-US relations on January 1, 1979, led to the rapid creation of an institutional and legal framework for expanded economic co-operation. These efforts paid off; the United States granted "Most Favored Nation" trading status to China in July 1979 and gradually loosened trade restrictions, shifting the PRC to the category of "friendly, non-allied" country in May 1983. The improved relationship was seen in the Sino-US Communiqué of August 17, 1982, signed by Reagan during his visit to China.[25]

Low labor costs made China one of the major sources for low-priced manufactured products in the world in general, and in the United States in particular, during the 1980s. The new international trade policies were extraordinarily successful in transforming China from a closed economy to a major trading nation in a relatively short time. In 1987, China resumed its status as a member of the General Agreement on Tariffs and Trade (GATT). China's total foreign trade rose from $21 billion in 1978 to over $80 billion in 1988, an increase of four times within ten years. China's exports to the US and other countries significantly increased in the 1990s, and included miscellaneous manufactured articles such as toys, games, clothing and apparel, as well as footwear and domestic products. Since the 1990s, China has expanded exports and moved far beyond cheap manufacturing by including petrochemicals, fertilizers, polymers, machine tools, shipping, and electric appliances in their exports.

From 1980 to 1985, restrictions on the type, size, and operations of foreign investment were progressively relaxed. The permissible forms of foreign investment eventually included compensatory trade, processing of materials, assembly, joint ventures, and complete foreign ownership. The cheap labor force, low-cost facilities, and huge domestic markets became attractive to foreign investors. They began their investment in processing manufacturing by processing imported materials or components into exports. China's export-oriented manufacturing strategy encouraged foreign-invested enterprises (FIEs) to engage in processing trade. In the early 1990s, the FIEs (mainly from Hong Kong and Taiwan) manufactured more than 58 percent of China's exported goods.

From 1979–1982, Deng established four SEZs, including Shenzhen across the border from Hong Kong, Zhuhai opposite Macau, and Xiamen across from Taiwan, as "open cities" in order to lure foreign capital. The joint ventures soon became practical for foreign investors in the SEZs, looking for a Chinese partner, setting up a joint company or a project through agreements, and then carrying out operations by both parties. In Shenzhen, the manufacturing factories increased from twenty-six in 1980 to five hundred in 1984. In that year, this previously underdeveloped Chinese town had fulfilled over three thousand business agreements with foreign investors from fifty countries, with a total value of $2.3 billion. In 1991, the four SEZ cities accounted for 14.32 percent of the national export value. In the 1980s, Deng opened fourteen more cities along China's coast for foreign investments and joint ventures. SEZs were so successful that they became an economic reform engine and played an instrumental role in integrating China into the global economy.

China's fast economic development was premised on a stable international environment. Reducing tension was part of Deng's endeavor to construct such an environment. In other words, peace and development were consistent with Deng's foreign policy, which emphasized a non-confrontational approach toward the West in general, and the United States in particular, and good relations with China's neighbors, including Taiwan.[26] Deng adopted a low-profile foreign-policy posture in order to buy time for China's economic take-off and military upgrading. He summarized the foreign-policy guideline as:

> observe patiently, respond sensibly, consolidate our own footing, be skillful in hiding one's capacities and biding one's time, be good at the tactics of low profile diplomacy, never take the lead, and take proper initiatives.[27]

Deng's reform movement brought tremendous changes to China; a "second revolution" comparable to Mao's 1949 revolution. For the first time in history the country began to establish a market economy and participate in the international community. Compared with Mao, who led China's military and political rise, Deng put China on track for its economic growth. Described in the West as a "mountain mover," Deng was one of a very few world leaders to be named *Time Magazine*'s "Man of the Year" twice (in 1978 and 1985). Jing Luo, however, points out that: "Without Mao's systematic failure, there would not have been Deng's systematic reform. In reality, Deng's reform may be understood as following Mao's blueprint in the opposite direction."[28] In 1987, he refused to become the chairman of the CCP, premier of the State Council, or president of the PRC, resigning from the Central Committee along with conservative senior party members to ensure continuity of his reform policies. Though officially retired, Deng remained at the center of China's reforms in the late 1980s and early 1990s, when the third generation of Chinese leaders came to power.[29]

The PRC government began negotiations with the United Kingdom in the early 1980s for the return of Hong Kong to China. Hong Kong is a southern peninsula that is connected to Guangdong province in the north, and surrounded by the South China Sea on three sides. It consists of many islands, a portion of the mainland, and a considerable expanse of water surface. Its deep-water harbors made Hong Kong the shipping hub of Southeast Asia. Hong Kong has a total population of seven million, 95 percent of whom are Chinese. After the Qing Dynasty lost the First Opium War to Great Britain, the Chinese government ceded Hong Kong to the British, in perpetuity, in the Treaty of Nanjing. After the Second Opium War in the 1850s, the British acquired Kowloon in 1860 and the New Territories in 1898, as part of a ninety-nine-year lease. In the 1970s, Hong Kong's economy took off with an annual growth rate between 6 and 8 percent. In the 1980s, its exports reached $73 billion. Deng Xiaoping developed a theory of "one country, two systems" to apply to the territories under European colonial administrations. In 1984, the PRC and UK governments signed an agreement for China to resume the sovereignty of Hong Kong. On July 1, 1997, Britain returned Hong Kong to China and Beijing established an autonomous government of the Hong Kong Special Administrative Region (HKSAR). Chee-hwa Tung was elected as the first Hong Kong chief executive in July 1997. Its GDP per capita totaled $19,000 in 1993, increased to $23,000 in 1996, and then to $42,000 in 2007. Hong Kong's GDP per capita reached $50,900 in 2012, comparing to $9,100 in China, $35,900 in Japan, and $51,700 in the United States that year. Its GDP totaled $365.6 billion in 2012.

Deng Xiaoping was in the middle of normalizing relations with the United States and did not want its strategic position in the communist world challenged by Soviet Satellites. He sought to contain the Vietnamese, calling them "the Cubans of the Orient." If the Vietnamese were not taught "some necessary lessons," Deng said at a press conference in Washington, "their provocations will increase."[30] He attacked Vietnamese towns on the Vietnam-China border in February–March 1979. The result was a massively destructive war that left chaos and suffering in its wake but was ultimately inconclusive. (For more details of the war, see the next chapter.) Chinese troops were forced to retreat, but not before decimating Vietnamese towns near the Chinese border.[31]

The brief 1979 war was a grievous misfortune for both China and Vietnam, not only because of the material and human losses suffered by both nations, but also because it brought years of earlier co-operation to such a dispiriting conclusion. The war showed that American concerns about the domino theory were misplaced, since two communist countries, one of which had just attained national liberation, were now in conflict with each other. Each valued its own national interests much more than the common communist ideology. On February 27, 1979, Deng told American journalists in Beijing that:

> Vietnam claims itself as the third military superpower in the world. We are eliminating this myth. That's all we want, no other purpose. We don't want their territory. We make them to understand that they can't do whatever they want to all the time.[32]

The 1989 Tiananmen Square Event

The economic and military reforms in the 1980s were, in Deng's words, comparable to "crossing the river by feeling the stones." Unfortunately, the economic growth neither significantly contributed to China's democratic transformation nor to its social stability. Arguably, economic development and modernization may have led to political instability.[33] The magnitude of China's social transformation carried within itself seeds of social instability. During the 1980s, new problems emerged. Official corruption, power abuses, and theft of public property were rampant, in spite of the government's efforts to control them. It accelerated the sharp disparities that existed between rich and poor. In addition, the relatively slow growth of economic change for farmers and millions of layoffs in urban areas made the traditional pillar classes feel deprived by the change. Deng's reform strategy contrasted starkly with that of Mikhail Gorbachev's Soviet Union by focusing primarily on liberal economic reform while discouraging and even stifling political reform.[34] To ensure stability, Deng insisted on the "Four Cardinal Principles," that included keeping to the socialist road, upholding the people's democratic dictatorship, sticking to the CCP's leadership, and adhering to Marxism-Leninism and Maoist Thought. Deng believed that, while China must keep its door open to the world, stability must be stressed; to guarantee stability, the Party must be in control.[35]

The government had little tolerance for criticism or calls for greater transparency and accountability, and instead emphasized political control and social stability by employing the law enforcement and legal system to suppress political dissent. The Criminal Law adopted by the National People's Congress (NPC) in 1979, and amended in 1997, provided a category of "counterrevolutionary offenses," such as anti-government propaganda or other acts that "endanger the PRC" and are "committed to the goal of overthrowing the political power of the dictatorship of the proletariat and the socialist system." Therefore, these political dissenters or the counterrevolutionaries would face punishment, including property seizures, deportation, imprisonment, tortures, and the death penalty.

Wei Jingsheng, an electrician working at the Beijing Metropolitan Zoo, posted a critique of Deng Xiaoping's Four Modernizations in 1978, calling for a "fifth modernization": democracy. He was arrested in 1979 and was sentenced to fifteen years in jail. After his release in 1993, Wei was jailed again until 1997, when he was released and deported to the United States. In September 1982, Deng called for "constructing a socialist country with Chinese characteristics" at the Opening Ceremony of the CCP Twelfth National Congress, which was held in Beijing, representing thirty-nine million members.[36] Then, the Fifth NPC was held in November–December 1982, and adopted the current constitution, keeping the same law that China was under CCP leadership. Nevertheless, the 1982 Constitution reinstalled the presidency with Li Xiannian serving from 1983–1988 and Yang Shangkun in 1988–1993. Both were vice chairman of the CCP. The CCP Central Committee now reserves the post of president for its current secretary general.

Increasing political dissatisfaction, highlighted by anti-government minority revolts, pro-democracy student activities, and widespread complaints of corruption among party and government officials threatened stability.[37] Unable to solve some of the economic and social problems and unwilling to carry the reform into political aspect, Deng and other Chinese leaders found themselves challenged by pro-democracy student demonstrations during the spring of 1989.

After Hu Yaobang, the former CCP chairman, died on April 15, student mourning activities in the Beijing campus soon became a city-wide and then a nationwide pro-democracy demonstration asking for political reforms across the country and protesting against corruption and power abuse. Deng denounced the movement later that month.[38] The negative attitude and harsh judgment of the government caused more dissatisfaction, not only among students but among citizens as well. In May, hundreds of thousands of students and citizens joined together and continued their demonstrations at the Tiananmen Square (Beijing's Washington Mall). The demonstrations spread to 116 cities across the country. On May 6–16, the Beijing students encamped at the Tiananmen Square and began their hunger strike to show their determination to promote democracy and to root out corruption.[39]

In the afternoon of May 19, the CCP enforced the "Martial Law" in Beijing and ordered a large number of the PLA troops to move into the capital city. Most generals did not know anything about it, and the announcement came as a total surprise. Some of them felt "varying degrees of sympathy for the students" and some felt "the measure might be too drastic, and besides their views had not been solicited."[40] On May 20, a group of generals signed a letter addressed to Deng Xiaoping and the CMC: "We request that troops not enter the city and that martial law not be carried out in Beijing."[41] Among the others were Generals Ye Fei, Zhang Aiping, Xiao Ke, and Yang Dezhi. After Deng sent top military leaders to visit these generals, and Yang Shangkun, PRC president, made some phone calls, as Zhang Liang points out, "eventually the mini-revolt was pacified."[42]

In the meantime, troops from twenty-two divisions of thirteen PLA armies moved toward Beijing under the "Martial Law Troop Command." The deployment reflected the uncertainty and anxiety of the Party Elders about each army's loyalty and connection to the Party Center which had been divided. Moreover, many troops were stopped in the suburbs or blocked in city streets by the crowds and failed to reach their destinations.[43]

Thus, martial law was not effective at all. The students remained in the Tiananmen Square and the demonstration on May 23 was the largest since the declaration of martial law. On May 24, the CMC held an enlarged meeting, attended by all the top military commanders and political commissars, at Deng's behest to make sure that the top officers were unified in their thinking in support of the Party Center. Yang Shangkun explained Deng's views on the political crisis and ordered the senior commanders to their units to unify their understanding of the Party's position. After the meeting, all PLA general departments, service arms, and the military regional commands, expressed their support publicly for Party Central's decisions to end the turmoil and to restore order. They expressed "total loyalty and submission to the authority of the CMC under the leadership of Deng and Yang."[44]

By the end of May, the Party prepared for a final "crackdown." On June 2, Party Elders Deng, Li Xiannian, Peng, Yang, Bo Yibo, and Wang Zhen met with the Standing Committee of the Politburo. They decided to "put a quick end to the turmoil and restore order in the capital." That meant to clear Tiananmen Square. After initial clashes between the troops and citizens in Beijing, on June 3, the leaders called an emergency meeting and further decided that they confronted a "counterrevolutionary riot" that would have to be put down by force. Even though Deng did not attend the meeting, he agreed that PLA soldiers should open fire on the protesting students.[45]

The emergency meeting issued orders to the PLA martial law troops that they begin to put down the "counterrevolutionary riot" in Beijing at 9:00pm on June 3. By

1:00am on June 4, they should arrive at the Tiananmen Square and clear the square by 6:00am.[46] The troops forced their way through the streets in the late evening on the 3rd, followed by tanks and armored vehicles. They clashed with some of the citizens and students who tried to stop the troops from entering central Beijing. At least seven hundred civilians were killed, and the troops also had some casualties after the bloody clashes.[47] The next morning, the troops successfully ended both the protest and the occupation of the Tiananmen Square. Some soldiers refused to fire upon the unarmed students and civilians. Some dropped their weapons and deserted. Some of the high-ranking military officials only reluctantly followed their orders. General Xu Qinxian, for example, feigned illness to avoid commanding his troops against the demonstrators in Beijing.[48]

The Tiananmen Incident was a major setback of China's reforming movement. Viewed from this perspective, the political crisis in 1989 can be understood as a conflict between the inherent totalitarian tendency within a one party controlled-state and the need to recognize the indispensable roles played by various functional groups in achieving economic growth and modernization of society.

Tiananmen Square had a negative impact on military reforms. Throughout the rest of 1989, no one in the military could voice any disagreement against the Party. According to the PLA documents, as many as 3,500 PLA commanders were investigated after the Tiananmen Incident. Many of them were newly promoted officers, products of the 1980s reforms. The Party believed its investigations and punishments necessary because 111 PLA officers had "breached discipline in a serious way," and 1,400 soldiers "shed their weapons and ran away."[49] The majority of them were reprimanded or charged thereafter. High-level military officials who lost their positions in the aftermath included Generals Hong Xuezhi, deputy secretary general of the CMC; Guo Linxiang, deputy director of the General Political Department; Li Desheng, political commissar of the National Defense University; and Li Yaowen, political commissar of the Navy. The most important of these was General Xu Qinxian, who was court-martialed and imprisoned. From 1989 to 1993, the penetration of politics into the military broke through all non-party barriers. The political restraints and suppression significantly slowed down the military reforms. The relationship and inter-dependencies between the military reforms and social changes were by no means new. But whether the new leadership is interested in the military reform or not is the most important factor between the military and society, and will play the most effective role in a long-term perspective.

After Tiananmen Square, Western countries joined an all-out demonstration against Beijing's military suppression of the student-led movement. The American people supported the George H. W. Bush administration's policies, which suspended all official bilateral exchanges with Beijing and joined international economic sanctions imposed on China by Western industrial countries. Deng, however, continued his economic reform with a new theory of "building socialism with Chinese characteristics."[50] Health problems soon reduced his active political role, as Parkinson's disease, lung ailments, and other problems eventually made him almost blind and deaf by the mid-1990s. Deng died in Beijing on February 28, 1997.[51]

One scholar points out that:

> If Mao Zedong is remembered as the founder of the People's Republic of China, as well as the source of wave after wave of nerve-wracking political campaigns, Deng

Xiaoping is remembered for deprogramming Mao's system and for leading China onto the road of economic prosperity.[52]

Deng proved that market economy and new technology worked in China, and that Chinese people needed a better materialistic life. His reforms, however, succeeded at a high cost of loss of political control by the Party, decentralizing the government, increasing stratification and inequalities in society, and declining status of the military. With their loyalty and patience, the military had been waiting for their turn as Deng promised. After Deng Xiaoping, they were expecting a big pay-back from Jiang Zemin, new leader in Beijing, the third generation of the Chinese Communist leadership.

Notes

1 Bailey, *A Diplomatic History of the American People*, 928.
2 Chen and Li, "China and the End of the Cold War," 120–133.
3 The strategic/geopolitical interpretation has prevailed among scholars and policy practitioners both in China and in the United States. See, for example: Gong Li, *Mao Zedong waijiao fengyunlu* [A Historical Record of Mao Zedong's Diplomacy] (Zhengzhou, Henan: Zhongyuan nongmin [Central China's Peasant Publishing], 1996), 195–206; Qian Jiang, *Ping pong waijiao muhou* [Behind the Ping-Pong Diplomacy] (Beijing: Dongfang [Oriental Press], 1997), chapter 8; Robert Ross, *Negotiating Cooperation: The United States and China: 1969–1989* (Stanford, CA: Stanford University Press, 1995), chapter 1; John W. Garver, *Foreign Relations of the People's Republic of China* (Englewood Cliffs, NJ: Prentice-Hall, 1993), 74–81.
4 Jingyi Song, "Personality and Politics: Deng Xiaoping's Return," in *Evolution of Power: China's Struggle, Survival, and Success*, eds. Xiaobing Li and Xiansheng Tian (Lanham, MD: Lexington Books, 2014), 79.
5 Spence, *The Search for Modern China*, 551.
6 Richard McGregor, *The Party: The Secret World of China's Communist Rulers* (New York: Harper/Perennial, 2012), 26.
7 Fuliang Shan, "Local Revolution, Grassroots Mobilization and Wartime Power Shift to the Rise of Communism," chapter 1.
8 Shambaugh, *China's Communist Party*, 5.
9 For more details of Deng Xiaoping's life during the Cultural Revolution, see Deng, *Deng Xiaoping and the Cultural Revolution*, chapters 17 and 18.
10 Ding Wei, "The 1975 CMC Enlarged Meeting," in *Junqi piaopiao: xinzhongguo 50 nian junshi dashi shushi* [PLA Flag Fluttering: Facts of China's Major Military Events in the Past Fifty Years], ed. Military History Research Division, China Academy of Military Science (CAMS) (Beijing: Jiefangjun [PLA Press], 1999), 2: 591; Merle Goldman and Roderick MacFarquhar, "Dynamic Economy, Declining Party-State," in *The Paradox of China's Post-Mao Reforms*, eds. Goldman and MacFarquhar (Cambridge, MA: Harvard University Press, 1999), 4.
11 Deng became the second generation of the CCP political and military leadership. See: Li, *China's Leaders*, 7–9.
12 Deng, "Emancipate the Mind, Seek Truth from Facts, and Unite as One in Looking to the Future, December 13, 1978," speech as the closing session of the CCP Central Conference. This speech was prepared for the Third Plenary Session of the CCP Eleventh Central Committee. In fact, this speech served as the keynote address for the Third Plenary Session. See Deng, *Selected Works of Deng Xiaoping* (Beijing: Foreign Languages Press, 1994), 2: 150–163; CCP Central Committee, "Communiqué of the Third Plenary Session of the CCP Eleventh Central Committee," adopted on December 22, 1978. The Party document is included in Research Department of Party Papers, *Major Documents of the People's Republic of China – Selected Important Documents since the Third Plenary Session of the Eleventh CCP Central Committee* ed. CCP Central Committee (Beijing: Foreign Languages Press, 1991), 20–22.
13 Deng, "Carry out the Policy of Opening to the Outside World and Learn Advanced Science and Technology from Other Countries, October 10, 1978," *Selected Works of Deng Xiaoping*, 2: 143.

14 Jing Luo argues that "Deng's challenge to what had been the sacred principles opened up people's views, instilled confidence, and gave rise to a broad-based economic recovery." Luo, "Reform of Deng Xiaoping," in *China Today* (Westport, CT: Greenwood Press, 2005), 1: 119.

15 Goldman and MacFarquhar, "Dynamic Economy, Declining Party-State," 8.

16 Dorothy J. Solinger, "China's Floating Population," in *The Paradox of China's Post-Mao Reforms*, eds. Goldman and MacFarquhar, 223–224.

17 Solinger, *ibid.*, 228–229.

18 Deng, "The Present Situation and the Tasks Before Us, January 16, 1980," a speech at a meeting of cadres called by the CCP Central Committee, in *Selected Works of Deng Xiaoping*, 2: 251.

19 Deng, "We Shall Speed up Reform," a talk with Stefan Korosec, member of the Presidium of the Central Committee of the League of Communists of Yugoslavia, *ibid.*, 3: 235.

20 Deng, "Planning and the Market Are Both Means of Developing the Productive Forces, February 6, 1987," excerpt from a talk with leading members of the CCP Central Committee in Beijing, *ibid.*, 3: 203–204.

21 Deng's conversation with Masayoshi Ohira, Prime Minister of Japan, on December 6, 1979, collected as Deng, "China's Goal is to Achieve Comparative Prosperity by the End of the Century," *Selected Works of Deng Xiaoping*, 2: 240.

22 For more details on Deng's reform movement, see: Goldman and MacFarquhar, ed., *The Paradox of China's Post-Mao Reforms*; Orville Schell and David Shambaugh eds., *The China Reader: The Reform Era* (New York: Vintage Books, 1999); Willem Van Kemenade, *China, Hong Kong, Taiwan, Inc.* (New York: Vintage Books, 1997).

23 Xiaobing Li, "New War of Nerves: Mao's Legacy in Beijing's Policy toward Taiwan Strait," *Journal of Chinese Political Science* 3, no. 1 (Summer 1997), 65.

24 Among the recent publications in English on the Sino-American rapprochement are: William Burr, ed., *The Kissinger Transcripts: The Top-Secret Talks with Beijing and Moscow* (New York: New Press, 1999); Jim Mann, *About Face: A History of America's Curious Relationship with China, from Nixon to Clinton* (New York: Knopf, 1999); Rosemary Foot, *The Practice of Power: U.S. Relations with China since 1949* (Oxford, UK: Oxford University Press, 1995); Ross, *Negotiating Cooperation*.

25 Warren I. Cohen, *America's Response to China: A History of Sino-American Relations*, 4th ed. (New York: Columbia University Press, 2000), 206–207.

26 You Ji, "Meeting the Challenge of Multi-Polarity: China's Foreign Policy toward Post-Cold War Asia and the Pacific," in *Asian-Pacific Collective Security in the Post-Cold war Era*, ed. Hung-mao Tien (Taipei: National Policy Institute, 1996), 233–273.

27 Qu Xing, "China's Foreign Policy since the Radical Changes in Eastern Europe and the Disintegration of the USSR," *Waijiao Xueyuan Xuekan* [Journal of Foreign Affairs Collage] 4 (1994), 19–22.

28 Jing Luo, "Deng Xiaoping's Reforms," in *China Today*, ed. Luo, 1: 121.

29 David S. G. Goodman, "Introduction: The Authoritarian Outlook," in *China in the Nineties: Crisis Management and Beyond*, eds. David S. G. Goodman and Gerald Segal (Oxford, UK: Oxford University Press, 1991), 3–5.

30 Quoted in Nayan Chanda, *Brother Enemy: The War after the War* (New York: Harcourt Brace Jovanovich, 1986), 354.

31 *Ibid.*, 357–358.

32 Deng's conversation was quoted from Tian Fuzi, *Zhongyeu zhanzheng jishilu* [Factual Records of the Sino-Vietnam War] (Beijing: Jiefangjun wenyi [PLA Literature Press], 2004), 25.

33 Charles Tilly, "Does Modernization Breed Revolution?" *Comparative Politics* 5, no. 3 (1973), 425–447.

34 Xiaosi Yang, "Politics of Deng Xiaoping," in *China Today*, ed. Luo, 115.

35 Anita Chan, "The Social Origins and Consequences of the Tiananmen Crisis," in *China in the Nineties*, eds. Goodman and Segal, 105.

36 Hu Yaobang, "Create a New Situation in All Fields of Socialist Modernization, September 1, 1982," in *Major Documents of the People's Republic of China – Selected Important Documents since the Third Plenary Session of the Eleventh CCP Central Committee*, ed. Research Department of Party Documents, CCP Central Committee, 267–328.

37 Xiaobing Li, "Introduction: Social-Economic Transition and Cultural Reconstruction in China," in *Social Transition in China*, eds. Jie Zhang and Xiaobing Li (Lanham, MD: University Press of America, 1998), 1–18.

38 Deng's views were reflected in an April 26, 1989 editorial in the *Renmin ribao* (People's Daily). See: Zhang Liang, ed. *The Tiananmen Papers: The Chinese Leadership's Decision to Use Force against Their Own People—in Their Own Words* (New York: Public Affairs, 2001), 71–75.

39 Zhang, ed., *ibid.*, 121–122.

40 Zhang, ed., *ibid.*, 265.

41 Zhang Liang's book listed eight generals, while the others had different numbers. For example, seven generals were mentioned in an essay collection edited by Suzanne Ogden, Kathleen Hartford, Lawrence Sullivan, and David Zweig, *China's Search for Democracy: The Student and the Mass Movement of 1989* (Armonk, NY: M. E. Sharpe, 1992), 292.

42 Zhang, ed., *The Tiananmen Papers*, 265.

43 Martial Law Troop Command, "Martial Law Situation Report, no. 3, May 19," in Zhang, ed., *ibid.*, 227.

44 Zhang, ed., *ibid.*, 287–288, 302–303.

45 For more details on the Tiananmen Incident, see: Zhang, ed., *ibid*; Goodman and Segal, ed., *China in the Nineties*.

46 Party Central Office Secretariat, "Minutes of the Politburo Standing Committee Meeting, June 3, 1989," in Zhang, ed., *ibid.*, 368–370.

47 The official statistics listed 264 deaths, including twenty-three college students and twenty PLA soldiers and officers. The Beijing Red Cross estimated 2,600 deaths, and China Radio International reported in Beijing on June 4 that "several thousand people, mostly innocent citizens" had been killed by "heavily armed soldiers." Zhang, ed., *ibid.*, 385, 389.

48 Harlan Jencks, "Civil-Military Relations in China: Tiananmen and After," *Problems of Communism* 40 (May–June 1991), 22.

49 Extracts from military security report are included in a CMC document, dated December 29, 1989.

50 Deng, "Build Socialism with Chinese Characteristics," conversations with the Japanese delegation to the second session of the Council of Sino-Japanese Non-governmental Figures on June 30, 1984, in Research Department of Party Literature, CCP Central Committee, *Major Documents of the People's Republic of China – Selected Important Documents since the Third Plenary Session of the Eleventh CCP Central Committee*, 1–5.

51 Xiaobing Li, "Reforming the People's Army: Military Modernization in China," *Journal of Southwest Conference on Asian Studies* 5 (2005), 17.

52 Jing Luo, "Reform of Deng Xiaoping," in *China Today*, ed. Luo, 1: 121.

12 Two Koreas and the Sino-Vietnamese Border War

President Nixon's "Vietnamization" initiative, which he laid out in 1969, gave America's East Asian allies a strong impression that the United States was getting out of East Asia. The Nixon administration's assertion that the United States would maintain its nuclear deterrent in the region did not calm the nerves of East Asian allies. The Nixon Doctrine was born against the backdrop of political uncertainty in East Asia. By then the United States was not expected to achieve a clear victory in Vietnam. The nation with the most modern weaponry and tactics but which was politically divided and unsure of its mission in the region, failed to subjugate the ill-equipped but determined Vietnamese guerrilla force. Confronted by the prospect of a long military stalemate and worsening anti-war sentiments at home, Washington was anxious to end the war by withdrawing its forces.

The fact that the new initiative reflected the Nixon administration's strong interest in improving its relations with Communist China further perturbed US allies in East Asia. They suspected that Washington was making a dangerous gesture – a drastic reduction in its security commitment in the region – to pursue the opening of the People's Republic of China (PRC). There was even a fear among Koreans, Japanese, and Taiwanese that the United States might use them as a bargaining chip for a Sino-American rapprochement.

The election of President Ronald Reagan in 1981 was heartily welcomed in East Asia. The governments, including Beijing and Hanoi, expected the conservative president to be more supportive of their cause than President Jimmy Carter. Having endured Carter's policy, which was generally identified with unremitting human rights campaigns, Japan, South Korea, and China welcomed Reagan's steadfast stand against the Soviet Union as an evil empire. Nevertheless, the opposition's contention that the United States had exercised an enormous political influence over East Asian affairs had some valid reference. From the rising radical view that American political interests in East Asia were contradictory to the peoples' wishes, anti-American sentiments continued, especially with the student activists and liberal intellectuals.

During 1986–1991, most communist countries, including the Soviet Union, underwent political reforms and economic transformation. The epochal developments were spurred by Gorbachev's bold reform programs, *glasnost* and *perestroika*, which helped to release the Eastern bloc countries from the long Kremlin control. It was an open admission that economic stagnation in the communist camp had reached a point where it threatened national survival itself. In turn, freed former Soviet satellite countries in Eastern Europe adopted various political measures pursuing society-wide democratization and institutional pluralism. This effectively terminated not only the Soviet-led

Communist movement in the world, but also the traditional East-West rivalry. China, Vietnam, and North Korea faced similar challenges and made their own choices during the worldwide communist crisis.

North Korea: The Kim Dynasty (1972–1994)

When Vietnam and China underwent revolutionary reforms and transformations, Kim Il-sung's North Korea greeted the emerging political reality in the socialist and communist world with typical disdain. Naturally, the dictatorial regime, which had pursued the highly unrealistic dream of building a Socialist paradise with the self-sufficient *Juche* idea, saw the revolutions in Eastern European countries as more of a threat than a benevolent transformation. Having enforced rigid political regimentation for most of the post-Korean War period, the Kim regime harbored an intense fear of reforms that might eventually cause its own demise. Categorically rejecting the seemingly irresistible currency of wholesale reforms in the communist camp, the North Korean leadership elected to continue the course maintained for decades, namely its own brand of isolated Socialism. It showed no inclination of modifying its dictatorial leadership, which was characterized by the intense personality cult of Kim Il-sung and his family.

Nothing is more characteristic of Kim's old-fashioned politics than his succession scheme. Since the early 1970s Kim had undertaken various political maneuvers to gain a legal as well as political sanction to designate his son Kim Jong-il, a man with limited experience and unknown leadership quality, as his successor. The elder Kim's archaic succession scheme, deftly packaged on the pretext of "carrying through the revolution generation after generation," was to ensure the survival of his political legacy. His scheme to perpetuate his family's political monopoly encountered little domestic resistance, at least in public. Kim's brutal politics in treating potential opponents may have been the primary reason for this apparent acquiescence.

As early as 1974 North Korea's Kim Dynasty was already operational; Kim Jong-il took over the daily operation of the Workers' Party, but under his father's close supervision. Nevertheless, the elder Kim continued a relentless, highly organized campaign to consolidate his son's political power throughout the 1970s. By the time the Sixth Congress of the North Korean Workers' Party was held in 1980, Kim had clearly obtained the political support needed to openly force through his anachronistic undertaking. Shortly, the elder Kim made his son the second most powerful man in the nation by naming the younger Kim as secretary of the party's secretariat, the fourth highest position in the Politburo. Kim also appointed his heir-apparent to the third highest position in the party's military commission.[1]

By the early 1980s the North Korean press began to acclaim the younger Kim as the "great thinker and theoretician, outstanding genius of leadership, boundlessly benevolent teacher of the people, and the great leader of the century,"[2] clearly indicating that the systematic transfer of the Pyongyang regime's leadership was under way. The elder Kim turned the political spotlight toward his son, gradually transferring more authority for affairs of the state and the Party to his son. The elder Kim's succession plot was nearly completed by 1993 when young Kim assumed the nation's highest military positions, chairman of the military commission of the party, and commander-in-chief of armed forces.

Kim Il-sung, the only leader North Korea ever knew, died in July 1994, leaving behind even more questions about the secretive regime. The world knew little about

Kim, and even less about the inner workings of the Pyongyang government. Still, North Korea without Kim Il-sung was expected to be quite different, yet what his sudden death meant to intra-Korean relations remained unclear. Consequently, the question of whether Kim Jong-il could someday gain the power and prestige his father had monopolized in North Korea was unanswered for a while.

Gradually, Kim Jong-il succeeded his father to the leadership of North Korea. His ascendancy, although he was unable to claim the presidency outright, was greatly benefitted by the fact that there is no political faction in North Korea capable of foiling the succession scheme the two Kims worked so long and hard for. Kim Jong-il in the North-South equation presented a dimension that was quite different from the one his father represented. He lacked the charisma and revolutionary credentials his father had and used so effectively. On the other hand, he was not burdened by the lofty reputation of his father so there was the possibility he might be able to exercise more flexibility and be open to new approaches.

South Korea: Industrialization and democratization (1963–1996)

After General Park Chung-hee was elected as the fifth president of the ROK (Republic of Korea) in 1963, the political tasks facing the nation were formidable even for the highly dedicated and energetic president. In addition to the nation's faltering economy, which demanded not only immediate but also comprehensive attention, the new administration had to confront several major tasks in both domestic and international areas. Foremost, it had to devise a long-term strategy for the ever-present military threat of North Korea. In foreign relations, it had to revise its relations with the United States to fit the evolving international political climate. The new government faced such intimidating problems without matching national strength. Moreover, it could expect no outpouring of international goodwill from the Western community, to which South Korea remained a hermit kingdom representing nothing but bitter memories of the war and poverty.

First of all, as discussed in Chapter 6, the Park administration normalized its relations with Japan in 1965. One of the most compelling factors that helped complete the normalization of the Japan-Korea relationship was the strong political pressure exerted by the United States. In the meantime, Seoul also answered the Johnson administration's call for a military coalition in Vietnam and sent two infantry divisions and one marine brigade, the second largest foreign force among those participating in the coalition, to the Vietnam War in 1965. Nevertheless, Park's priority went to building an industrial infrastructure for a self-sustained, growth-oriented economy. His plan called for extensive utilization of foreign input, including capital, raw materials, and technology. To facilitate the free movement of capital and technology, he initiated many new fiscal policies, including participation in GATT and the adjustment of exchange rates. The government was mobilizing every available resource to accelerate the nation's economic revitalization. South Korea's economy entered its taking-off stage by the late 1960s. Led by Park's focused leadership, it undertook a rapid import-substitution drive as its export-led industrial expansion was shaping up. During this period, multinational corporations started to enter the South Korean market, providing the domestic economy with a growing influx of foreign capital and technology transfer. The nation's industrial development proceeded at such a rate and scope that it even changed the people's pessimistic attitude. The new promising chapter of a modern, industrial Korea was beginning to unfold. By the 1970s, the South Korean export economy had passed its incubation period and entered the world market, concentrating on its strategic sector of labor-intensive, low technology products.

The close US-South Korea collaboration in Vietnam and warm bilateral relations encountered a sudden chill in 1971 with the Nixon's Doctrine, which included the withdrawal of the remaining US ground forces from South Korea. The full implementation of the doctrine meant that the US East Asian policy was undergoing a fundamental shift; no longer could any nation expect a full and automatic intervention by US forces against Communist aggression in the region. Under the framework of "Asian defense by Asian forces," the Nixon administration was willing to offer its Asian allies only logistical support. South Koreans had not expected the American forces to become a permanent fixture of the Korean landscape. Yet they earnestly wished the US military to remain until the ROK military completed an extensive modernization program, which was needed to strengthen its still inadequately equipped forces to a level at which they could face the North's forces alone. The modernization of ROK forces, a pledge that the Johnson administration made in 1965, had not progressed much by 1969.

Despite Seoul's protest, Washington withdrew its 20,000 American combat troops from South Korea by early 1971. The withdrawal forced the ROK army to assume the defense of the entire Western front along the DMZ, thus making almost a complete front defense by South Korea itself. The United States left one last combat division as a symbol of its security commitment over the peninsula.

In many ways, the 1971 presidential election was an epochal point in South Korea's political maturity. For the first time in history, the government permitted open political forums, although in a limited fashion. It even engaged in a public discussion of the merits of nationalistic unification, the notion that the nation should undertake steps toward the unification process unfettered by political ideology. The new approach represented a radical departure from the stereotypical ideological unification in each side's image. The main opposition candidate, Kim Dae-jung, insisted that national unification was feasible not by military means but by the political guarantee of the four powers, namely China, Japan, the United States, and the Soviet Union. Kim's bold idea was, in spirit, compatible with Nixon's East Asian approach, which argued that the justified interests of the four powers be respected. Although his progressive proposal was largely election material, such a revolutionary idea surfacing in a nation where extreme rightists prevailed was a significant development.

On July 4, 1972, the governments in Seoul and Pyongyang simultaneously issued an extraordinary joint communiqué. In it both governments declared that they would seek national unification in a spirit of independence, peaceful unification, and greater national unity. However, intermittent talks that followed the joint communiqué produced no tangible results. Neither the North nor the South was ready to negotiate anything of substantial value. Talks did not even contribute to the stability of the peninsula's military confrontation. Dialogue served the political purpose of the dictatorial regimes on both sides of the DMZ. President Park's most profound contribution to his country was his successful expansion and upgrading of the nation's defense industry before he was assassinated by his security chief on October 26, 1979.

After the assassination of the president, South Korea experienced the installation of the Yushin Constitution, the Kwangju uprising of 1980, and General Chun Doo-hwan's election of 1981. Walter B. Jung states that:

General Chun added another sad chapter to South Korea's already tainted history of political transition, one that had earned the hermit kingdom a much disparaged reputation in the eyes of the world community.[3]

Like General Park, President Chun exploited the public's fear of weakening national defense and their desire to continue the nation's economic expansion. These two overriding concerns still remained decisive, although it was debatable whether they were sufficient to give Chun an excuse for dashing the nation's long-standing desire to move toward the democratization of political process. Contrary to its generally negative political image, the Chun administration provided focused leadership in the nation's drive for economic development. During President Chun's tenure the nation experienced its first true economic buoyancy, illustrated in the milestone of its first current account surplus in 1986. Under the guidance of the Chun regime the exuberant export sector spearheaded the nation's hyperactive economic expansion. On December 16, 1987, South Korea held its first direct presidential election in sixteen years. Then, in 1992, the nation elected Kim Young-sam as its president, the first non-military president in three decades.

By the mid-1980s, South Korea had made further adjustment in its export economy. It reduced its heavy export dependence on predominantly low-technology, labor-intensive products by expanding the strategic export sectors to medium-technology, capital-intensive products, including automobiles, electronics, and supertankers. The country recorded its first trade surplus in 1986–1988 when its exports grew at a phenomenal rate of 26 percent per year. Its total export reached $60 billion with a positive trade balance of over $11 billion in 1988. In the meantime, it also reduced its export dependency on the US market from 35 percent of its total international trade in 1988 to 30 percent in 1990. Its stable export performance during the 1980s and early 1990s was largely responsible for the nation reaching its economic objectives: a high growth rate with price stability, and a current account surplus. It also secured a coveted place among a small bank of nations by being recognized as one of the newly industrialized countries and one of four of Asia's economic "tigers" (Hong Kong, Taiwan, and Singapore were the others).

The IOC (International Olympic Committee) decision to award the 1988 Summer Olympic Games to Seoul galvanized South Koreans. The Seoul Olympics helped elevate the prestige of industrial South Korea worldwide. The government and Korean people were eager to show their progress and success to the international community. They were sanguine about their accomplishment of conquering age-old poverty and rebuilding the nation over devastated war ruins in less than three decades. They were proud of their "Miracle of the Han River." The games were overwhelmed by the far-reaching political ramifications of the participation of the People's Republic of China, which sent a large delegation to Seoul unhampered by the lack of diplomatic relations between the two nations. It was the Communist giant's first open indication that it was serious in upgrading its relations with South Korea. The Chinese participation totally eclipsed North Korea's absence from the games and was the first tangible success for South Korea's persistent pursuit of non-political contacts with China.

Entering the 1990s, South Korea's export economy was performing at a pace that should have enabled the hermit kingdom to achieve the desired status of a mature industrial power.[4] In the late 1980s, South Korea agreed to accommodate the increasingly vocal demands of its major trading partners. As a step toward free trade, it reduced the rate of import protection by 95 percent in 1988, and 98 percent by 1990, to open domestic markets to foreign goods. The Uruguay Round and the GATT negotiation of 1994 opened the nation's strategic domestic market to foreign products. Another historic shift in the international arena, inaugurated by China's experimentation with a market economy, and a bold initiative of Soviet President Gorbachev, provided further momentum to South Korea's drive. In 1990 South Korea's two-way trade with the Eastern bloc countries and China reached $5 billion, recording a yearly growth rate of over 23 percent. Its trade with China had grown to $10 billion by 1994, making China South Korea's third largest trading partner.

The Sino-Vietnamese conflict in the 1970s

Despite Chinese-North Vietnamese cooperation in the First Indochina War of 1946–1954 and Vietnam War of 1963–1973, there existed a number of serious differences between the two communist parties.[5] In the early 1960s, the growing rift between China and the Soviet Union put North Vietnam in an awkward position. The Vietnamese had to move carefully between their patrons to avoid offending either of them. The Chinese became less willing to facilitate the transport of Soviet aid across China. A Soviet proposal in 1965 to establish an air corridor over China was abruptly refused by Mao, who considered it a pretext for Soviet intrusion. Instead, China permitted a railway corridor for the delivery of Soviet supplies, but the Vietnamese saw this as less advantageous to their national liberation struggle. From 1965 to 1968, China pressured North Vietnam to fight on instead of holding peace talks generating further differences with the Vietnamese. In 1968, North Vietnam entered into negotiations with the United States without first consulting China.

After Ho's death in 1969, North Vietnam moved closer to the Soviet Union, which further provoked Beijing. Although China continued to provide support, relations with Vietnam worsened. Hanoi considered the marked improvement of relations between China and the United States in 1972 in the wake of Nixon's visit as tantamount to betrayal on China's part. Leaders in Beijing, from geopolitical considerations, had decided that they could not stand by while Vietnam was engaged in a war that might endanger Chinese security. The Chinese "tightened their belts" to contribute to North Vietnam's survival. Their continuing military, economic, and diplomatic aid was crucial to the victory won by the North.[6]

As the American menace receded after 1973, border disputes and differences over Indochina caused a rapid deterioration in the Vietnam-China relationship. In the Chinese view, North Vietnam was an ingrate challenging China under Soviet protection. China lamented the loss of Chinese lives and the expenditure of so many resources for so little in return. For the Vietnamese, the Chinese "Northern threat," replaced America as the enemy. The Vietnamese charged that China intended to keep Vietnam in the war in order to exhaust the United States by bleeding Vietnam.

In 1975–1976, the Hanoi government's main priority was to rebuild the newly united country. They had to assert their unquestioned will over political affairs. In agricultural policy, Hanoi sought a quick transformation of Southern lands. Party leaders believed that it was imperative to remove all vestiges of feudal land ownership from the Mekong Delta and other southern areas. Therefore, by 1976, the party embarked upon a bold strategy of collectivization. This process differed markedly from land reform, in which farmers would be categorized and land redistributed based on wealth. Instead, under collectivization, lands were immediately taken by the state in order to create advantageous economies of scale. Party leaders assumed that collectivization would help align Southern peasants with communism. That effort did not succeed. Gadkar-Wilcox argues that first, perhaps Southern Vietnamese farmers were unwilling to cede property control to the state as obediently as their Northern counterparts had. Second, the Southern economy had already been decimated by the pre-1975 inflation. It had lost a substantial portion of its population as refugees fled. Finally, since Northern cadres were responsible for the collectivization efforts, some Southern farmers saw their organizing efforts as a kind of carpet-bagging.[7]

On November 15, 1976, Pham Van Dung, Vietnam's premier, asked for more economic assistance from China. On February 24, 1977, Li Xiannian, the PRC president, declined the Vietnamese request when Nguyen Tien, vice foreign minister, visited Beijing. Premier Pham was not happy when Nguyen told him of the Chinese rejection on March 17. References to Chinese aid have disappeared from Vietnamese historic writing, and China is now portrayed as having been an impediment to the reunification. One of the Vietnamese party leaders told a Swedish reporter that:"Vietnam borders China in the north, which is a powerful country. This neighboring relationship has both positive and negative impact. By any means, the political and cultural pressures from the north must be eliminated."[8] The deteriorating relationship, along with Vietnam's persecution of its ethnic Chinese, the border conflict, and its invasion of Cambodia in late 1978, induced China to take military action in 1979.

Since 1974, the border conflicts began and tension mounted between the countries. At least one hundred border skirmishes occurred in 1974 alone. In 1978, Chinese sources reported 1,100 border incidents, in which about three hundred Chinese troops and civilians were killed or wounded. That same year, the PLA reinforced the border with twenty infantry divisions.[9]

In Cambodia, Pol Pot (1925–1998) became the leader of the Communist Party of Kampuchea (CPK), better known by their informal name, the Khmer Rouge. From the 1960s, the Khmer Rouge was committed to a Maoist version of communism based on the Cultural Revolution. They aimed to eliminate bourgeois and colonialist elements of Cambodian society to return the land to Khmer (ethnically Cambodian) farmers. A central point of their ideology was the restoration of the greatness of Cambodia as it existed during the powerful classical Angkor Empire (802–1431). Though a number of other Cambodian politicians shared this goal, including Lon Nol, only Pol Pot's Communist Party wished to accomplish it by attacking Vietnamese areas that had formerly been Cambodian and cleansing them of their non-Khmer population.[10]

In late April 1975, in the context of the destabilization of Indochina and the impending North Vietnamese conquest of the South, Pol Pot arrived in Phnom Penh with Khmer Rouge forces. By May 1975, the Khmer Rouge had created an eight-point plan of action that called for the evacuation of major cities; the abolition of markets; the withholding of all currency; the defrocking of monks, who were to be put to work growing rice; the execution of all leaders associated with the Lon Nol regime; the establishment of cooperative farming throughout the country, along with communal eating; the expulsion of Vietnamese from the country; and the amassing of troops at the Vietnamese border.[11]

Pol Pot followed up on this plan by stationing massive numbers of troops at the Vietnamese border by 1977. In response, in July 1977, Le Duan made an attempt to stage a pro-Vietnamese coup within the CPK that failed.[12] He ordered Vietnamese troops to amass at the Cambodian border. They began fighting skirmishes on the

Cambodian side. In response to these decisions, the PRC made clear that it would support the Pol Pot regime against what it perceived to be the aggressions of the Soviet-backed Le Duan regime in Vietnam. A clandestine war broke out and continued through 1978 on the Cambodian-Vietnamese border. This war burst into the open in December 1978, when the Vietnamese launched a massive counterattack into Cambodia. By January 1979, the Vietnamese had established a pro-Vietnamese and pro-Soviet People's Republic of Kampuchea, under the *de facto* leadership of Hun Sen (1952–), who is today Cambodia's prime minister.

Then, both the international and internal factors played an important role in the changes of China's security concerns. After Mao's death in 1976, the new Chinese leadership's world view had changed and it had different concerns regarding the country's security. Deng intended to stabilize China's relations in Southeast Asia and create a "peaceful international environment" in order to focus on his 1978 economic reform at home and opening up to the Western world. When Vietnam challenged China's goal by sending troops to Cambodia and clashing with the PLA along the Chinese-Vietnamese borders, Deng decided to punish Vietnam as a warning to some neighboring countries, while pleasing others like Thailand, which was worried about Vietnam's aggressive foreign policy. China's invasion of Vietnam in 1979 and several major attacks along the Sino-Vietnamese borders in 1981 and 1984 also expressed Beijing's concerns on other issues such as Vietnam's expelling some 200,000 Chinese-Vietnamese refugees into China and challenging China's claims of the South China Sea Islands.[13]

China's attack on Vietnam (1979)

On December 20, 1977, Vietnam sent 200,000 troops into Cambodia. Joining the international community and the United States, Beijing denounced the invasion and asked for an immediate and full withdrawal of the Vietnamese troops from Cambodia. On December 25, China closed the border. The next day, the PLA began to deploy 220,000 troops along the Vietnamese border. In the east, along the Guangxi-Guangdong borders, about 110,000 troops, including five armies, moved into their positions under command of General Xu Shiyou. In the west, along the Yunnan borders, more than 100,000 men were deployed under the command of General Yang Dezhi. On July 8, 1978, the PAVN Political Bureau issued the "Outline of the New Tasks of the PAVN," which warned of a possible invasion by "a foreign country" while its troops fought in Cambodia. The Vietnamese military intelligence was accurate. By November 20, the Chinese troops from the Guangzhou Regional Command were combat ready. On December 8, the CMC issued an order of deployment and re-formation. On the December 13, the CMC ordered the troops to move into the border areas. By the end of the month, all the Chinese troops had moved into their positions along the borders. On January 8, 1979, the PAVN occupied Phnom Penh, the capital city of Cambodia.[14]

China saw a good opportunity, not only because of Vietnam's weakened national defense, but also because of a moral justification for invasion. On January 28, Deng Xiaoping paid a state visit to America. He told President Jimmy Carter at Washington that Asia "is very unstable." At the meeting with the Senate Foreign Affairs Committee on January 30, a senator asked if China would attack Vietnam since the Beijing-supported government in Cambodia was overthrown and the country was in a serious crisis. Deng answered that "We will not allow Vietnam to make so many troubles [in Asia]. In order to protect our country and world peace, we probably have to do something that we don't want to."[15] In early February, on his way back to China, Deng told the Japanese prime minister in Tokyo that "To deal with the Vietnamese, it seems no effect by any other means than a necessary lesson." Deng wanted to teach Vietnam "a lesson."[16] Chen points out that "Beijing's leaders used force only when they believed that they were in a position to justify it in a 'moral' sense."[17]

On February 17, 1979, the CMC ordered the attack. Deng set up three principles for the Chinese invasion: a limited attack, quick victory, and avoid "mission creep." The Chinese operation can be divided into three phases. The first phase was an attack on all fronts from February 17 to 26 in two major directions. In the east, the Guangxi troops, five armies, more than 100,000 men, under the command of General Xu crossed the borders in fourteen places. On February 20, his troops encircled Cao Bang, defended by the PAVN 346th Division. The PLA Fifty-fifth Army took the city on February 25, but the Vietnamese division HQs had escaped. Xu was upset and yielded to Bian Guixiang, commander of the Fifty-fifth Army. Serious communication problems arose due to poorly manufactured equipment or untrained operators. Xu's "attack order" to the Sixty-seventh Regiment, for example, somehow changed to a "hold and defense" when it passed through the army and division headquarters. The regiment never joined the general attack against Long Son.[18] In the west, the Yunnan troops, five armies, about 100,000 men, under the command of General Yang concentrated on the Lao Cai region by crossing the Red River in six different places. By February 20, the Yunnan troops took over Lao Cai with strong artillery support. Then, they moved further south toward Gan Tang, a major mining city in the North. The Vietnamese troops reinforced Gan Tang. On February 25, the Yunnan troops captured the city and its mines.[19]

The second phase, from February 27 to March 5, was a focused attack on Long Son, one of the major cities in the North. Long Son, the provincial capital, was well

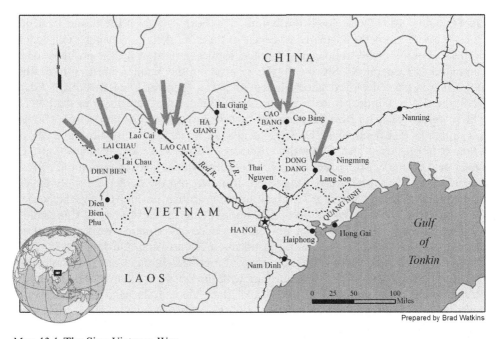

Prepared by Brad Watkins

Map 12.1 The Sino-Vietnam War

connected by railroads, highways, and rivers and defended by a large number of the Vietnamese troops. On February 27, the Guangxi troops attacked the city's defenses. Xu concentrated more than three hundred artillery pieces and issued orders that, "No house stands in Long Son."[20] At about 7:50am, the Chinese bombardment began. Having failed to stop the Chinese attack, the PAVN 308th Division withdrew from Long Son. By March 2, the Chinese troops occupied the northern part of the city. By March 4, they took over the city and threatened Hanoi, only eighty miles away. The Vietnamese government gathered troops for the defense of its capital. The Chinese invaders, however, did not press on and stopped at Long Son.[21]

The third phase was the Chinese withdrawal from Vietnam on March 6–16. The CMC ordered all the troops to move out of Vietnam on March 5. On their way back, Chinese troops looted North Vietnam, removing industrial machinery, equipment, and governmental properties, and destroying the remainders. Many artillery and tank units fired indiscriminately at Vietnamese towns. Some units who suffered heavy casualties retaliated by burning villages, bridges, and anything they could ignite.

Some Chinese soldiers called it a "painful, little war." Vietnamese troops avoided battle and instead harassed PLA forces. Some Chinese officers described it as a "ghost war" since the enemy troops were almost invisible; or a "shadow war," fighting against your own shadow. The Vietnamese troops employed the same tactics, made the same moves, and used the same weapons as the Chinese. They knew exactly what the Chinese were trying to do. They exploited almost every problem and weakness the Chinese had. The Chinese troops had to fight their own problems before they could fight the Vietnamese. Deng's border war taught the PLA a lesson in a hard way.[22]

Many of the PLA's commanding officers were shocked by poor discipline, low morale, combat ineffectiveness, and the high casualties in the 1979 Sino-Vietnam War. During the nineteen days of the first two phases, the PLA suffered 26,000 casualties, about 1,350 per day.[23] Gerald Segal points out that:

> in contrast to Korea, Chinese troops performed poorly. In Korea, they adequately defended North Korea, but in 1979 they failed to punish Vietnam. China's Cambodian allies were relegated to a sideshow along the Thai frontier, and China was unable to help them break out.[24]

During the war, 37,300 Vietnamese troops were killed, and 2,300 were captured. The Soviet Union surprised the Vietnamese by their non-involvement during the conflict. On February 18, Moscow denounced China's aggression and promised that the Soviet Union would keep its commitments according to the Soviet-Vietnam co-operation and friendship treaties. Then, however, the Soviet Union did not make any major moves. The Russian military intelligence increased their reconnaissance planes and ships in the South China Sea and along the Vietnamese coast after China's invasion. On February 24, two Russian transport planes landed at Hanoi and unloaded some military equipment. Most countries maintained a neutral position during the Sino-Vietnamese War in 1979.[25]

The Chinese withdrawal from Vietnam in March 1979 did not end the border conflict. For the next decade, PAVN units, along with a rearmed and retrained militia, maintained as many as 800,000 troops in Northern Vietnam. Across their northern borders, more than 200,000 Chinese troops faced them. In May–June 1981, the PLA attacked Vietnam again after many small border conflicts. The Chinese troops occupied and defended several hills.[26]

The largest offensive campaign after 1979 took place in April–May 1984, when the PLA overran PAVN positions in the Lao Son mountains. The attack began on April 2 when the Chinese artillery heavily shelled the Vietnamese positions in the area. The bombardment continued until April 27. On April 28, the infantry troops from Yunnan Province charged the Vietnamese defense positions at Lao Son, including hills 395, 423, and 662. The Chinese forces eliminated two Vietnamese companies of the 122nd Regiment, PAVN 313th Division, and occupied hill 662, the highest position on the top of the Lao Son mountains. Within a few days, the Chinese troops controlled most of the mountain, and had eliminated about 2,000 Vietnamese troops.[27] Then, the Chinese forces attacked the Vietnamese positions on Yen Son Mountain on April 30. By May 15, the Chinese occupied most of the positions on the two mountains and built defensive works against the PAVN counterattacks. During this five-week offensive campaign, there were 939 Chinese soldiers killed in action, plus another sixty-four Chinese laborers.[28]

From July 12, the Vietnamese launched counterattacks. The Chinese troops held the position for three years until April 1987.

By 1986, Vietnam was at a turning point. The collectivization of the South had not been successful since the Vietnam War ended in 1975. After 1976, the newly established government of the Socialist Republic of Vietnam (SRV) terminated all contracts and leases signed between the GVN and foreign companies by confiscating their assets in the South, including the oil fields owned and operated by US Standard Oil Company. In 1979, Hanoi signed the Soviet-Vietnam Friendship Alliance, and Mutual Assistance Treaty, with Moscow. From 1979 to 1988, the Russian corporations monopolized the energy and other heavy industries in Vietnam. Today, the largest petroleum company, Vietsovpetro (VSP), is a joint venture of PetroVietnam and Zarubezhneft from Russia. It produces 57 percent of the national total of crude oil.

In July 1986, Le Duan died. He had been firmly at the helm in the early 1960s, and had been the major obstacle to a more flexible economic policy before 1986. When political and economic discontent reached its height in 1982, it was Le Duan who sent investigative teams to the South to shut it down. His death allowed other party leaders to pursue reform. The opportunity for such reform was the Sixth Party Congress in December 1986. At that event, the Party decided on a radical new direction. The Sixth Party Congress set into motion a series of new policies to be implemented by the end of the 1980s. Together, these reforms were known as *doi moi*, or renovation. In 1987, for example, Hanoi issued a new economic policy, allowing foreign companies to invest, operate, and produce in Vietnam, and offering favorable foreign investment acts. Then, the government published the Law of the Industries, including manufacturing, textile, petroleum, electricity, transportation, communication, and construction, to guarantee the interests, rights, and benefits of foreign companies in the country.

By the late 1980s, numerous reform measures had been implemented. These included allowing the payment of wages and salaries in cash; allowing the operation of small private companies; the abolition of internal checkpoints between provinces; a revision of the foreign investment laws to allow non-Vietnamese companies to invest in joint ventures with Vietnamese firms; the *de facto* de-collectivization of agriculture; the elimination of most price controls, to allow foreign participation in banking; and the creation of special "Export Processing Zones" on the model of the Special Economic Zones (SEZs) in China, in which 100 percent foreign-owned enterprises would be allowed to do business. Together, these policy changes represented a "dramatic shift toward a market economy."[29]

In 1987, the CMC reduced the scale of their operations in Vietnam, though the Chinese maintained routine patrols at Lao Son and Yen Son. From April 1987 to October 1989, there were only eleven attacks, most of them simply artillery bombardments. In order to gain combat experience, the CMC began to rotate the troops at the Lao Son and Yen Son areas. Many PLA units, including infantry, artillery, anti-aircraft units, and reconnaissance troops, moved into Vietnam from Guangxi and Yunnan provinces. Deng said once that "Let all of our field armies touch the tiger's butt."[30] By the end of the 1980s, China and Vietnam normalized their diplomatic relationship. In 1992, all the Chinese troops withdrew from the Lao Son and Yen Son areas and returned back to China. In order to develop the border trade between the two countries, the PLA troops in Guangxi and Yunnan began their large scale mine clearing operations along the Chinese-Vietnamese borders in 1993.

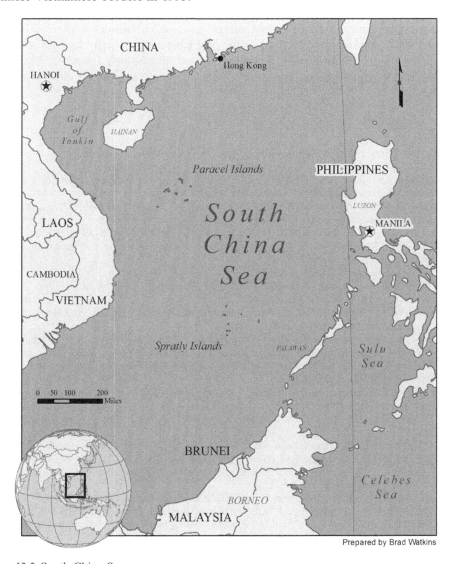

Prepared by Brad Watkins

Map 12.2 South China Sea

By 1995, twenty years after the fall of Saigon, the United States and Vietnam established normal diplomatic relations. Realizing the economic power of remittances sent from refugees abroad, the Vietnamese government encouraged them to re-establish ties with their home country, and to visit or even return to Vietnam. One aspect of renovation policy which tended to repair those relationships, particularly among families in the South, was that the government, under certain circumstances, allowed former owners of businesses in the South that were nationalized after 1975 to re-gain their property. More American companies began to invest and join ventures in Vietnam after 1995, including energy corporations. They recently discovered several oil fields as well as gas fields including Dai Hung, Rang Dong, Ruby, and Lan Do. The annual crude oil production in 2011 was approximately 1.5 million tons, with natural gas at about 6.8 billion cubic meters, which mainly came from seven offshore oil fields in the South China Sea. At that time, Vietnam's proven oil reserve totaled 603 million tons, a six-time increase since 2001. Its proven natural gas reserve had increased to 700 billion cubic meters, three times the increase in the past ten years. Vietnam disputes sovereign rights over several island groups, including Paracel and Spratly Islands in the South China Sea, and against China and the Philippines because of possible offshore oil and gas deposits.

Notes

1 Suh Dae Sook, *Korean Communism, 1945–1980* (Honolulu: University of Hawaii Press, 1981), 281.
2 Bertil Lintner, *Great Leader, Dear Leader: Demystifying North Korea under the Kim Clan* (Muang, Thailand: Silkworm Books, 2005), 76–80.
3 Walter B. Jung, *Nation Building: The Geopolitical History of Korea* (Lanham, MD: University Press of America, 1998), 319.
4 The state-run Korea Institute for International Economic Policy (KIEP) reported that by 1996, South Korea's total trade had reached $240 billion, making the nation one of the world's top ten trade nations.
5 Zhai, *China and the Vietnam Wars*, 152–153.
6 Military History Research Division, CAMS, *Zhongguo renmin jiefangjun de qishinian* [Seventy Years of the PLA], 586–587.
7 Gadkar-Wilcox, writing sections in "East Asia and the West," by Li, Sun, and Gadkar-Wilcox (unpublished manuscript), chapter 8.
8 Haong Sun's conversation with Eric Pier, a Swedish reporter, in 1976. Haong was member of the VWP Central Committee and editor of the party newspaper. Tian Fuzi, *Zhongyeu zhanzheng jishilu* [Factual Records of the Sino-Vietnam War] (Beijing: jiefangjun wenyi [PLA Literature Publishing], 2004), 9–10.
9 Han, *Dangdai zhongguo jundui de junshi gongzuo* [Military Affairs of Contemporary China's Armed Forces], 1: 659–660.
10 Wilfred G. Burchett, *The Cambodia-China-Vietnam Triangle* (Chicago, IL: Vanguard Books, 1981), 58.
11 Ben Kiernan, *The Pol Pot Regime: Race, Power, and Genocide in Cambodia under the Khmer Rouge, 1975–79*. Revised Edition. (New Haven, CT: Yale University Press, 2014), 55.
12 King C. Chen, *China's War with Vietnam, 1979: Issues, Decisions, and Implications* (Stanford, CA: Hoover Institution Press, 1987), 34.
13 Xie Guojun, "The Sino-Vietnamese Border War of Self-defense and Counter-offense," in *Junqi piaopiao* [PLA Flag Fluttering], ed. Military History Research Division, CAMS, 2: 624–625.
14 Military History Research Division, CAMS, *Zhongguo renmin jiefangjun de qishinian* [Seventy Years of the PLA], 609–610.
15 Deng's conversations are quoted from Tian, *Zhongyeu zhanzheng jishilu* [Factual Records of the Sino-Vietnam War], 16–18.

16 Tian, *ibid.*, 18.
17 Chen, *Mao's China and the Cold War*, 14.
18 Tian, *Zhongyeu zhanzheng jishilu* [Factual Records of the Sino-Vietnam War], 42.
19 Tian, *ibid.*, 43.
20 *Ibid.*, 43.
21 Xie, "The Sino-Vietnamese Border War of Self-defense and Counter-offense," 2: 629–630.
22 Tian, *Zhongyeu zhanzheng jishilu* [Factual Records of the Sino-Vietnam War], 327–328.
23 Tian, *ibid.*, 92, 328.
24 Gerald Segal, "Foreign Policy," in *China in the Nineties,* ed. Goodman and Segal, 173.
25 Tian, *Zhongyeu zhanzheng jishilu* [Factual Records of the Sino-Vietnam War], 92, 26–27.
26 For more details of these battles between 1979 and 1984, see: Han, *Dangdai Zhongguo jundui de junshi gongzuo* [Military Affairs of Contemporary China's Armed Forces], 1: 679–682.
27 Tian, *Zhongyeu zhanzheng jishilu* [Factual Records of the Sino-Vietnam War], 72–73.
28 Tian, *ibid.*, 403.
29 William S. Turley and Mark Selden, eds., *Reinventing Vietnamese Socialism: Doi Moi in Comparative Perspective* (Boulder, CO: Westview, 1993), 7.
30 Deng's talks at a 1986 CMC meeting in Tian, *Zhongyeu zhanzheng jishilu* [Factual Records of the Sino-Vietnam War], 55.

13 Surviving the Cold War: China's globalization

The year 1991 witnessed the collapse of the Soviet Union and the end of the global Cold War. Nevertheless, China stayed on its causes by continuing to promote the Party's modernization policy and agenda through the last decade of the twentieth century. In this chapter, the Chinese Communist Party (CCP) is examined not only as a political institution, but also as a social institution, which endorses many social values and popular ideas, such as nationalism. Chinese nationalism, which is deeply rooted in the heart of several generations, has risen significantly since the 1990s as a result of explosive growth. In these years, adopting a pragmatic nationalism has allowed the CCP's national leadership to improve its position in Chinese society. This government has promoted nationalism to emphasize China's unity, strength, prosperity, and dignity over the core values of human rights and democracy. This kind of nationalism emphasizes the loyalty of the community to the state rather than holding human rights as its fundamental value and democracy as its desired result. Oftentimes the government has even called on individuals to sacrifice personal rights for the national interest.

The political survival of the CCP government through its transformation or evolution during the industrialization of the 1990s and urbanization of the 2000s reveals that China's modernization has unique characteristics, transforming not only the country, but also the CCP, from a rural-based totalitarian party to a city-centered authoritarian party, from a people's party to a power-interest group's party. This chapter focuses on how the Party restructured its relationship to a changing society and reacted to political, economic, legal, and social issues such as urban construction, housing expansion, and the rights of citizens.[1] It intended to lead the urban movement by making new policies, empowering pro-party interest groups, controlling the legal system, and putting more pressure on the middle class, which was campaigning for civil liberties, freedom, and democracy.

The unprecedented historical transition of the CCP after 1989 has also drawn attention from other political scientists and legal scholars. In 2000, Bruce Dickson offered "a useful framework for analyzing CCP's policies of co-opting new elites and forging links with non-party organizations, as well as understanding the problems that have arisen as a consequence."[2] After Deng Xiaoping's tenure (1978–1989), both Jiang Zemin (1990–2002) and Hu Jintao (2002–2012) were willing to share power. They provided moderate leadership of the new generations. In other words, the new leaders in Beijing were able to share their governance with the executive, legislative, and judicial branches by empowering congressional committees, ministries of the State Council, courts, and law enforcement. Their practical and inclusive politics reflect the shift of the Party's ideology and political goals from radical communism to moderate nationalism. Dickson, however, concludes in his 2008 book that to share the economic benefits, the private entrepreneurs support the Party's agenda rather than promoting democratization in China.[3] He then predicts that if the CCP succeeds, it may be able to "preempt or postpone" political reforms.[4]

Jiang's struggle for CCP survival

When Deng retired, the Party faced the consequence of the bloody show-down at the Tiananmen Square in June 1989, which convinced both reformers and conservatives that neither could win without a national disaster. They agreed to a continuation of reform as long as it proceeded more slowly and was approved by Deng's choice of successor, Jiang Zemin (1926–), who supported reforms but also stressed Deng's Four Cardinal Principles.[5] The Party saw new hope when Jiang shared power and provided moderate leadership of the third generation. Educated and pragmatic, Jiang led the Party, the government, and the military through a bureaucratic institution of collective leadership, which was not a monolithic group of elites. In other words, Jiang was willing to share his governance with the executive, legislative, and judicial branches in Beijing by empowering congressional committees, ministries of the State Council, and court and law enforcement. Jiang understood that the political survival of the CCP was the most important consideration for his third generation of new leaders.

Jiang Zemin, as a technocratic leader, became the first planner of Shenzhen, China's first special economic zone (SEZ). His successful reform led to him being a member of the Twelfth CCP Central Committee in 1982 and becoming mayor of Shanghai in 1985. Jiang became a member of the Politburo at the First Plenary Session of the Thirteenth Central Committee. In June 1989, at the Fourth Plenary Session of the Thirteenth Central Committee, Jiang was elected a member of the Standing Committee of the Politburo and general secretary of the CCP Central Committee. In November, he became chairman of the CMC at the Fifth Plenary Session of the Thirteenth Central Committee.[6]

At the Eighth NPC held in March 1993, Jiang was elected president of the PRC and chairman of the government's CMC. By 1997, Jiang had established an unprecedented institutionalized authority that enabled him to preside over a vast central bureaucracy encompassing the Party, state, and military. In the 1990s, Jiang gradually shifted the Party's ideology and political goals from radical communism to moderate nationalism as an ideology to unite China, resulting in one more source of legitimacy for the CCP as the country's ruling party. Jiang developed his own theoretical principles of the "Three Represents." These principles specified that the CCP should represent "the development of China's advanced productive forces, the orientation of the development of China's advanced culture, and the fundamental interests of the broadest masses of the Chinese people." The "Three Represents" became the most essential requirements for officials and officers to fulfill their obligations and duties during Jiang's era from 1990 to 2004 as his legacy. As Jiang gradually shifted the Party's ideology and political goals, he faced new challenges such as increasing demands for improvement of the country's human rights, civil liberties, and relations with Tibet and Taiwan. Jiang reached his limits and took tougher positions on the Falun Gong and in the 1995–1996 Taiwan Strait missile crises.

To survive urbanization, the Party leadership became more flexible and was able to adapt to economic and social changes. The CCP governments in the cities responded to the rising demands and expectations of Chinese society. They were willing and able to cope with the middle class by making a few compromises and following certain legal procedures in exchange for continuing political support. These practical compromises characterized a new political culture in PRC history since 1949. The CCP adapted to the changing economic and social environment and was able to control the growing cities through power-sharing among competing political interest groups. This sharing of power entailed a more dynamic and localized political institute, including some urban interest groups taking part in the decision-making processes, but excluding the middle class, who had demanded a representative government, civil society, and democracy in China.

The Party created its new political power bases in the cities during urbanization from the 1990s to the 2010s. The recently established urban power-interest groups consist of the second generation of the revolutionary veterans, pro-CCP entrepreneurs, as well as returning intellectuals sent by the government for Western degrees and overseas training, and bureaucrats, who are mostly CCP members. With political support, special treatment, privileges, and protection, this group has controlled the city governments and has taken advantage of urbanization to generate considerable capital. In return, the urban power-interest groups support the CCP and carry out its policy through the legal system by controlling the "hilt of the knife" (*daobazi*), while ignoring the benefits and rights of professionals and private business owners. The court works for the Party as well as the government. Therefore, most of the metropolitan governments are the Party-governments, and today's China remains a party-state. The Ministry of Justice has been re-established under the State Council, and in public discourse slogans such as "rule the country by law" and "rule the country according to law" have increasingly been used. After 1982, the constitution has had important changes and revisions in 1988, 1993, 1999, and 2004. Even though some civil rights and legal codes were provided by the constitution, many have not been enacted until recent years.

In 1995, the Supreme Court issued its first five-year plan for reforming the country's courts. It addressed problems such as competence, fairness, judicial training, and regularity in court procedures. The plan embraced some important reforms such as the creation of rules regarding the use of evidence and the separation of cases from adjudication, and adjudication from enforcement. Since then, the legal profession has become increasingly institutionalized, marked by an expansion in legal education and an increasing awareness on the part of the citizenry as to their rights under the law.

China has one of the largest law enforcement bodies in the world. As a general rule, police officers in China do not perform static guard duty, but are tasked with controlling the population, fighting crime, and maintaining safety. Police officers patrol on foot, in vehicles, and often operate out of small, interconnected command boxes on city streets. Some urban centers have anti-riot units equipped with a few armored cars. Previously, those involved in law enforcement went unarmed, but since late 1994, circumstances have required them to carry side arms more often. The official Chinese newspaper reported that more than 500 police officers have been killed each year since 1993.[7] In January 1996, new rules were issued concerning the use of batons, tear gas, handcuffs, water cannons, firearms, and explosives. These regulations updated the 1980 guidelines and were a response to the rise in crime. Despite these new adjustments, police forces are not considered part of the armed forces of China as defined by the National Security Law.

Continuing economic reform

Jiang's reform privatized state-owned enterprises (SOEs), decentralized state control, solicited foreign investment, and applied capitalist technology. In the 1990s, more than 80 percent of small- and medium-sized SOEs completed their transformation by 2000 through ownership diversification, which included restructuring, mergers, leasing, contracting, joint-stock companies, and bankruptcies. To clear the entanglement of poorly performing SOEs and inefficient debt-ridden state banks, in 1999 Jiang set up four state asset management agencies to purchase, manage, and dispose of the bad loans of state banks. Instead of paying banks interest, the debtor SOEs paid dividends to the asset agency. Those loans were then sold as initial public offerings or transfers of ownership. By 2000, privately owned enterprises (POEs) accounted for roughly 40 percent of the economy. A direct outcome of this change is that POEs pushed SOEs to become more competitive. SOEs could either shake off inertia or disintegrate into POEs.

As a result, the share of government-invested enterprises produced by SOEs has decreased from 77.6 percent in 1966 to 17.5 percent in 2010, while the number of large-sized SOEs declined from 118,000 in 1995 to 46,800 in 2010. In the 2000s, SOEs faced even greater challenges to their survival because of fierce competition from both domestic POEs and from foreign firms. Many entry barriers to previously state-monopolized industries such as telecommunication, banking, automobiles, insurance, and public utilities have been broken following China's entry into the WTO (World Trade Organization).

From 1991 to 1997, China's GDP rose an average 11 percent annually. After 1992, state enterprises were given greater autonomy to cope with capitalist markets at home and abroad and to issue stocks that could be bought and sold on stock exchanges that were set up in Shenzhen and Shanghai. In the early 1990s, most foreign investment had come from overseas via Hong Kong and Taiwan, but by late in the decade multi-national groups, including Japanese and US corporations, began to surpass the earlier investors. Foreign investment was a central component of Jiang's policy. In the 1990s, China ranked with the United States as one of the two largest recipients of direct foreign investment.

In 1994, a new state budget law separated the banking system from the government by establishing bank autonomy, prohibiting government offices from borrowing from the banks. The major banks were then responsible for their own profits and losses. In 1995, the government issued the Commercial Bank Law, allowing state-owned banks to be commercialized, and commercial banks were established. Many much smaller, local banks had been established, and stock-market trading was booming. More private-sector firms had access to commercial loans and to domestic stock markets. In 1997, the CCP Fifteenth National Congress announced an initiative that provided for the sale of most of the SOEs. Two years later, four national financial asset management companies, China Cinda, Oriental, Great Wall, and Huarong, were established to purchase and manage bad loans from the state banks. CCB (China's Construction Bank) had the lowest ratio of nonperforming loans, of 18.14 percent in 2001, while ICBC (Industrial and Commercial Bank of China) had the highest ratio of 29.78 percent. The state-owned asset companies intended to strengthen the banks' balance sheets while also reducing the state enterprises' debts burden. These companies had disposed of 509.4 billion yuan RMB ($84.9 billion)'s worth of nonperforming loans at the end of 2003, with a cash recovery rate of 19.5 percent. By that time, however, total nonperforming loans at the four major banks totaled 2.44 trillion yuan RMB ($406.7 billion), an amount equal to 28 percent of China's 2003 GDP. The average ratio of nonperforming loans of the major banks had been reduced to 15.59 percent by 2004. In the first years of the new century, while countries around the world entered hard economic times, China still prospered. In 2000 and 2001, the GDP rose 8 and 7.3 percent.[8]

The foreign investment accelerated rural industrialization by establishing various industries in the countryside that absorbed a large proportion of the low-waged rural labor force. The industrialization generated a substantial portion of capital needed for construction of urban projects and stimulated local policy-makers to devote great efforts to planning and building modern cities. Foreign investors also had directly contributed to the building of new urban centers by getting involved in the development of the real estate sector and of urban infrastructure. China experienced rapid urbanization in the 1990s as a process in which the rural landscape (characterized by farmland and scattered villages) had changed into an urban one (characterized by factory compounds and commercial, financial as well as technological facilities). The number of Chinese cities increased from 223 in 1981 to 663 by the end of 2000.[9] China's rural population shifted from agricultural production to non-agricultural economic activities, thereby acquiring the urban way of life including the use of modern utilities.

China's decision to participate in the global market has had a demonstrably powerful effect on domestic administrative structures, economic institutions, and legal norms. For example, once the decision to open up was made, administrative decentralization, enterprise reform, and the creation of a legal framework to protect commercial transactions and property rights were needed to enhance China's competitiveness in the world market. The realization that rapid economic development and technological modernization would require large infusions of foreign capital similarly meant that the new leadership in Beijing had to pay greater attention to foreign concerns, in particular to ways of improving the local investment climate. Under such conditions, they had little choice but to undertake a liberalization of prevailing commercial norms and practices.

Jiang Zemin expanded China's foreign trade by adopting new policies to promote international economic relations such as the Maritime Commerce Law enacted in 1993, Anti-Subsidy Rules issued in 1997, and a revised Foreign Investment Law in 2001. Hong Kong then became part of China, and Taiwan developed extensive trade relations with the mainland. China's total foreign trade had risen from $80 billion in 1988 to $300 billion by 1997; an increase of more than three times in less than ten years. China's entry to WTO in 2001 further promoted its international trade. By 2002, China's exports to the United States exceeded that of Japan. China's total foreign trade rose from $300 million in 1997 to $620 billion in 2002, more than doubling in five years. In 2002 the ranking of China in the world's trading nations jumped from thirty-second to sixth.

China's GDP was only $559 billion in 1994, but it doubled five years later, reaching $1,083 billion in 1999, and it increased to $1.9 trillion in 2004. Its GDP per capita was only $469 in 1994, but it almost doubled, reaching $865 in 1999, and increasing to $1,490 in 2004. The leading industrial outputs are from manufacturing, energy industry, transportation, telecommunication, and digital products. During the late 1990s and early 2000s, the country had become one of the global manufacturing centers, due to its cost production and participation in international trade organizations, such as the

WTO. China's manufacturing includes metallurgy, machinery, transportation, petro-chemical, defense, electronics, and textile industries. It also can be divided into heavy industry such as steel, machinery, automobile, and shipbuilding, and light industry such as electronics, instrument, tools, and consumer products.

Its steel outputs increased from 64.3 million tons in 1980, to 140 million tons in 2000, and 419 million tons in 2006. Low labor costs have made China one of the major sources for low-priced manufactured products in the world, in general, and in the US, in particular, during the 1980s. China's exports to the United States and other countries significantly increased in the 1990s. Automobiles, locomotives, ship-building, and aircraft industries also play a pivotal role in China's economy. Auto-mobile manufacturing increased from 443,400 in 1985, to 1.1 million in 1992, to 2.3 million in 2001, and 4.44 million in 2003. China's industrialization in the 1980s–1990s was based partly on low-cost production, including low wages paid to workers and minimum workplace safety. Many full-time, part-time, and rural migrant workers con-tinue to confront safety problems such as dangerous working conditions, toxic envir-onments, lack of protection and safety education, as well as forced and uncompensated overtime.

Hu's China: Economic superpower

After Jiang retired, Hu Jintao became the Party chairman and the country's president in 2003, and the chairman of the CMC in 2004. He and his generals emerged through a protracted service within the government or military. From 1975 to 1980, he was promoted to deputy director of the committee and later secretary of the Gansu Provincial Committee of CCYL. During the Eleventh CCYL National Congress in 1982, Hu was elected member of the Secretariat of the CCYL Central Committee, president of the All-China Youth Federation, and then the first secretary of the Secretariat of the CCYL. In 1985, at forty-three, Hu was appointed CCP secretary of Guizhou province, youngest of his rank across the country. In 1988, he became party secretary of Tibet. During his four years there, Hu sent the PLA troops to the Tibetan streets to crush the independence movement and Buddhist rebellions. At fifty, when he entered the Standing Committee of the Politburo of the Fourteenth CCP Central Committee in 1992, Hu was the youngest member in this top decision-making body. He was re-elected to the Standing Committee of the Politburo and as a member of the Central Committee's Secretariat in 1997. In November 2002, when Jiang retired, Hu became chairman of the CCP at the Sixteenth CCP National Congress. In March 2003, Hu was elected the president of the PRC at the Sixth NPC.

Even though Hu and Jiang had many disputes over specific issues, they reached a consensus on the key objective: China's economic growth and social stability. Hu designed his "scientific development" concept, entrenching it in the Party's constitution as an official guiding ideology. Hu emphasized political and social harmony by nurturing good relations with central and local governments as well as supporting the growing professionalism and interest groups inside and outside the government. To deal with the problems left behind by Jiang, Hu made certain important changes in China's economic, military, social, and political policies. He strategically shifted China's eco-nomic development from a global oriented policy to a more regionally balanced one. Hu and Wen Jiabao (1942–), new premier of the PRC, employed the macroeconomic control policies over the rapidly growing economy. In the first decade of the twenty-first century, while countries around the world entered hard economic times, China still prospered. In 2002–2012, the country's GDP rose between 7 and 9.4 percent each year.

Foreign investment was a central component of China's continuing economic growth. After China joined the WTO in 2001, the government reduced certain investment measures and opened up more sectors that had previously been closed to foreign companies. The Hu-Wen administration (2002–2012) continued to support the joint ventures and to encourage foreign investment. By 2003, the government had approved establishment of 500,000 joint ventures. In 2004, the United States had 45,000 joint ventures in China with a total investment of $48 billion. Among the major American companies in China today are Boeing, General Motors, ExxonMobil, Chevron, ConocoPhillips, IBM, and General Electricity. As a result of the development of joint ventures, China and the outside world have become truly interdependent.

Foreign investment accelerated China's industrialization in the 2000s by establishing various industries that absorbed a large proportion of the low-wage rural labor force. Foreign investors also directly contributed to the urbanization in the 2010s by getting directly involved in the development of the real estate sector and urban infrastructure. In 2002, China became the world's top recipient of foreign direct investment (FDI). In 2005 China received $80 billion FDI and $69.5 billion FDI in 2006. Foreign banks were allowed to purchase minority stakes in local banks. By 2004, the foreign financial assets in China reached $47 billion. Sixty-two foreign banks from nineteen countries set up 191 business institutions in China, and 211 foreign bank branches operated in China.

In 2007, the Shanghai Stock Exchange (SSE) had 904 stock listings with a market value of $4.5 trillion, and annual turnover value of $5.08 trillion. The total market value of the mainland's stock exchanges in 2007 made China the third largest stock market in Asia, after Japan and Hong Kong. By December 2011, SSE became the sixth largest stock market in the world by market capitalization of $2.3 trillion. The Shenzhen Stock Exchange (SZSE) had an annual turnover value of $2.7 trillion in 2009, and market capitalization of $1 trillion by 2011. In September 2013, China established the Shanghai Free Trade Zone as a new effort to attract more foreign investment, which now has access to almost all sectors in the metropolitan economy.

During the 2000s, the country became one of the global manufacturing centers, due to its cost production and participation in international trade organizations such as the WTO. In 2010, China had 19.8 percent of the world's total manufacturing output and became the largest manufacturer in the world. Its manufacturing accounted for 31.6 percent of China's GDP in 2013, an increase of 7.6 percent from 2012, and it is the largest GDP contributor in the country. It hired more than 400 million manufacturing workers, about 52.3 percent of the labor force in the industries. As the largest steel supplier in the world, China was producing 45 percent of the world's steel in 2011. As the top exporter of steel in the world, China exported 59.2 million tons of steel in 2008, an increase of 5.5 percent from the previous year. By 2006, China had become the third largest automotive manufacturer (after the United States and Japan), and the second largest vehicle consumer (only after the United States) in the world. In 2006, a total of 7.22 million automobiles were sold in China. Automobile production continued to grow, from 8.88 million in 2007, to 9.35 million in 2008, and to 13.83 million in 2009, when China became the largest automobile maker in the world. By 2010, China had also become the largest vehicle consumer in the world when 18 million new cars were sold that year. After 2000, China began exporting cars and auto parts. Its vehicle and component export reached $70 billion in 2010.

Since 2002, the Hu-Wen government expanded the exports and moved far beyond cheap manufacturing such as toys, games, shoes, and cloth by adding petrochemicals, fertilizers, polymers, machine tools, shipping, and electric appliances in their exports. By 2005, China replaced the United States as Japan's main trading partner. In the following year, China's total international trade reached $1.4 trillion, of which $762 billion was with the United States. The leading export partners are currently the United States (20 percent), Hong Kong (12 percent), Japan (9 percent), and South Korea (8 percent). China imported electrical machinery, optical and medical equipment, organic chemicals, telecommunications and sound equipment, as well as oil and mineral fuels. The leading import partners are Japan (16 percent), Hong Kong (12 percent), South Korea (12 percent), the United States (9 percent), and Taiwan (8 percent). China's total foreign trade rose from $1.15 trillion in 2004, to $2.17 trillion in 2007, to $3.64 trillion in 2011, and to $4.16 trillion in 2013, more than tripling in less than ten years.

After 2002, China's foreign exchange reserves increased significantly from $0.8 billion in 1979 to $165.6 billion in 2000, and reached $346.5 billion by 2003, when its reserves were higher than its outstanding debt ($182.6 billion). Its surplus on trade had significantly contributed to the increase of its foreign exchange reserves. China's foreign exchange reserves reached $470.6 billion in mid-2004, and continued to increase to $711 billion in 2005, $941.1 billion in 2006, $1,332.6 billion in 2007, and $1,808.8 billion by June 2008, making it the highest foreign exchange reserve in the world.

From August 8–24, 2008, the Games of the XXIX Olympiad (or the 2008 Summer Olympic Games) were held in Beijing. Beijing won the bid at the IOC meeting in Moscow in July 2001, winning over other applicants on the final list, which included Toronto, Paris, Istanbul, and Osaka. It was the first time for China to host the Olympics and the third time for Asian countries to hold the Summer Olympics; Japan held it at Tokyo in 1964, and Korea at Seoul in 1988. China became the eighteenth nation to host a Summer Olympic Games, and twenty-second to hold the Olympic Games. More than 11,400 athletes, including 4,637 women and 6,305 men, from 204 countries and regions which had National Olympic Committees, traveled to Beijing and competed in 28 sports and 302 events, more than those for the 2004 Games. More than 100 heads of states from all over the world attended the Opening Ceremony and the Games in Beijing, including US President George W. Bush and the first lady. The reported total costs of the 2008 Olympics were between $40 billion and $44 billion, vastly more than the total costs of $15 billion for the 2004 Olympics at Athens.

China is rising in the twenty-first century and became the second largest economy in the world by 2011, following only the United States, and for the first time in its history exceeded Japan. Its GDP increased from $1 trillion in 1999 to $8.2 trillion in 2008 with an average annual growth rate over 13 percent; then $9 trillion in 2009 to $10 trillion in 2010 with a growth rate of 10.4 percent; and from $11.3 trillion in 2011 to $12.6 trillion in 2012 with 7.8 percent growth. Its GDP consists of 10.1 percent of agriculture, 45.3 percent of industry, and 44.6 percent of services. Its GDP per capita increased from $2,172 in 1999 to $6,201 in 2008 with an average annual growth rate over 9 percent; then $6,798 in 2009 to $7,571 in 2010 with a growth rate of 9.9 percent; and from $8,411 in 2011 to $9,185 in 2012 with 7.2 percent growth. The Chinese labor force totals 798.5 million, the largest labor force in the world.

As a new member of the global community, however, the PRC has not always followed every international standard, but has adapted the regulations selectively. While Hu Jintao, head of the CCP's fourth generation of leadership, was cooperative on certain issues, his government did not always agree with the West, especially not with the United States. President George W. Bush, trying to include China in the "War on Terror" after September 11, 2001, as well as coordinate responses to the crises with North Korea, asked China to be a "responsible stakeholder" in multilateral national efforts. Beijing considers many matters, including human rights and civil liberties, as domestic problems, and believes that no foreign government or organization should interfere in its internal affairs. The West believes in natural rights that cannot be taken nor given away, but the Chinese government looks at these same rights as privileges granted by the state.

Social problems, corruption, and civil rights

China became industrialized in the late 1980s, and the new industrial mode of production in the 1990s changed China forever. This change has come through the creation of factory jobs, manufactured goods, and new international markets. China's industrialization, however, has been partly based on low production cost, including low wages paid to workers and minimum workplace safety. Low labor costs have made China one of the major sources for low-priced manufactured products in the world in general, and in the United States in particular. China's export-oriented manufacturing has included miscellaneous manufactured articles such as toys, games, clothing and apparel, footwear, and plastic products in the 1990s. China's entry to the WTO in 2001 further promoted its international trade and its exports to the world. By 2002, China's exports to the US exceeded that of Japan. Many workers were paid below the minimum wage, worked seven days a week, and often twelve to thirteen hours a day. Some workers did not have even one day off during the entire month. Both full-time and part-time workers continue to confront dangerous working conditions, toxic environments, a lack of protection and training, employer violations of minimum wage rules, unpaid pensions and wages, child labor, and forced and uncompensated overtime, especially migrant workers and female workers. Approximately 74 percent of migrant laborers earn 580–1,400 yuan RMB (between $80 and $200) a month. Many of them have no legal rights to housing, school, and health care in the cities.

A rapid expansion of free enterprises demanded more free labor. As the result, a free labor market opened up to both urban and rural labors in the 1980s. As many as 70 million rural laborers migrated to the cities and coastal areas seeking work in cities and coastal areas in the 1990s. In Beijing, Shanghai, Guangzhou, and Tianjin, between one and two million transients camped in railway stations and other public places. Some official estimates suggested that more than 100 million peasants may have left the countryside by 2000, still leaving behind at least an equal number of peasants under-employed in their home rural communities.[10] Since many peasants who moved into urban areas could not find jobs, they become mobile or "floating" populations. Tianjin, for example, had a large number of "floating" populations; about one million around the city. It was estimated twenty-seven million across the country.[11]

The reform movement since the 1980s has not yet contributed significantly to the country's democratic transformation or to its social stability. The new leaders in the 1990s focused on liberal economic reform while discouraging and even stifling political reform. As a result, economic interest groups successfully established an alliance with CCP officials to effectively control economic policy-making and to share political governance. More and more CCP members have increased the private enterprise sector from 12 percent of the total party membership in 1993, to 17 percent in 1997, and more than

20 percent in 2002. The entrenchment of the power-capital establishment institutiona-lizes corruption as a logical consequence of China's economic development. In the 2000s, corruption became one of the key elements of the power-capital institution with three ways of connecting politics and business: making money through abusing power, seeking power through paying bribery, and pursuing power and/or money by pawning intellectual capital.

The officials who controlled the resources, public land management, limited quotas of materials, and other valuable assets constituted one of the major power-interest groups. Benefitting from the monopolization of land, resources, and bank notes, their way of transferring their power to capital was to take bribery and rent-seeking. For instance, in 2000, due to bribery and embezzlement, China lost as much as 3.7 billion yuan RMB (about $610 million) in revenue. The growth of "gray" income represents the extensive scope of corruption in China. The power-interest groups have gradually spread from the upper class to the middle class, demonstrated by the gray income of 6.2 trillion yuan (about $1 trillion), which was 12 percent of the GDP in 2011. Instead of reinvesting profits in domestic enterprises, the assets under the power-capital economy are usually transferred overseas. The transferred resources are seldom invested in over-seas enterprises but rather, they have been placed in an individual's savings accounts, or used for the purpose of facilitating immigration of family members, education of their children or relatives, purchase of houses, etc., because owners of these assets know that most of their income is illegally obtained. The amount of cash that flowed overseas from China increased from $48 billion in 2000 to $65 billion in 2011, and China had become the fourth largest country in the world in regards to outflow of capital. The People's Bank of China (PBC, China's central bank) reported that more than 18,000 government officials and state-owned enterprise CEOs escaped from China in 2008, taking 800 billion yuan (about $133 billion) in cash to foreign countries since the mid-1990s.[12]

Hu paid special attention to political scandals, corruption, and mismanagement in the government and in the Party. Many cases involved the collection of bribes for the procurement of licenses or the manipulation of regulations. In 2005–2006, more than 6,000 officials were investigated, detailed, and sentenced by prosecutors. Hu fought back against the "Shanghai Gang" first in 2006–2008 by arresting and sentencing Chen Liangyu (1946–), mayor and Party Committee secretary of Shanghai and CCP Politburo member, to eighteen years in jail. Chen was charged with corruption and misuse of the city's pension fund. He was responsible for siphoning off 3.45 billion yuan ($439.4 million) from the Shanghai Social Security Pension Fund for illicit loans and investments.[13] Then, Hu arrested Bo Xilai, mayor and Party Committee secretary of Chongqing and CCP Politburo member, in 2012.[14] Hu's victories over Chen and Bo protected his power base through his tenure.

Although the judicial reform continued through Hu's years of power from 2002–2012, the Chinese legal system has not yet been able to protect individual rights and civil liberties rather than enforcing punitive measures as the core purpose of law. Authorities' attempts to expand the scale of capital punishment reflect the government's concerns over the increasing crime rate. This is inconsistent with the global trend of seeking to reduce or eliminate the death sentence altogether, despite China signing two key inter-national human rights treaties in the 2000s that included articles against the sentence.[15] China accounts for over 70 percent of criminals executed in the world per year, and some international human rights organizations put the number at between 10,000 and

15,000 a year, or around twenty to thirty per day, more than the rest of the world combined.[16] The Supreme Court only regained the right to review all death penalty decisions on January 1, 2007. Even though a debate continues concerning the death sentence, and criticism has increased within the legal circle, there is no plan to abolish the practice. The ultra-emphasis on punishment reflects China's legal tradition that the core purpose of law is to enforce punitive measures, rather than the protection of rights. This also reflects the traditional view that the state's authority to maintain social order, wherein all people can benefit, should always be preserved. The extensive use of capital punishment clearly represents the government's intent to maintain political stability and social order. Guided by legal instrumentalism, China has perpetuated the tradition that the nation's collective interests transcend individual rights.

Defendants in criminal proceedings were executed following convictions that sometimes took place under circumstances involving major lack of due process, as well as inadequate channels for appeal. In 2004, Xu Shuangfu, leader of an underground church known as the Three Grades of Servants, was arrested. Some Westerners consider it to be an orthodox Christian house church network, which is an unofficial church based in China's northeast and claims millions of followers. In July 2006, the Heilongjiang Provincial High Court sentenced Xu to death and immediately executed him.[17] In 2005, Wu Weihan was arrested and charged with conducting espionage for Taiwan. At the time of his arrest, he had received his PhD in Germany in the 1990s and worked in an Austrian bio-medical company as a researcher. Dr. Wu was sentenced to death in May 2007 by Beijing's court. No appeals and no family visits were allowed by the court during his entire prison time. One day before his execution, the court gave special permission for his daughter's visit. On November 28, 2008, Wu was executed by gunshot. In July 2009, tens of thousands of Uyghur demonstrators gathered at Urumqi, the capital of Xinjiang, protesting the government's handling of the deaths of two Uyghur workers and demanding a full investigation of the killings. After confrontations with police, the peaceful demonstration escalated into riots on July 5. The official confirmed that on July 18 more than 1,500 Uyghurs were arrested. By December 2009, authorities had sentenced twenty-two Uyghurs to death for their participation in the July 5 religious and ethnic rioting.[18]

Although the constitution recognizes that worship is part of a citizen's rights, it requires respect for those who do not have a religious belief. Since the ruling that CCP is an atheistic party, it must protect its political base. The government maintains control of religious exercises through a registration process and national organizations. In Tibet, authorities continue to control Buddhist activities, and repression of religious freedom remains commonplace. In March 2008, a Buddhist demonstration took place and turned violent on the March 14. By March 28, the government confirmed that twenty-eight civilians and one police officer were dead; 325 civilians were injured, fifty-eight of them critically, along with 241 police officers. The India-based Tibetan government-in-exile reported more than 220 Tibetans were killed in the crackdown. After March 14, the Chinese government arrested 7,000 Tibetans from various parts of Tibet. In Xinjiang, most of the eight million Uyghurs are Muslims, who face harsh religious policies. In June 2007, for example, during the traditional period for a pilgrimage to visit Mecca, Xinjiang authorities collected the passports of all Muslims to prevent any non-state-approved pilgrimage. In early July 2009, as mentioned previously, tens of thousands of Uyghur demonstrators gathered at Urumqi, and confronted police. Then, the peaceful demonstration escalated into riots from July 5–7. The government reported that 197 people were killed and 1,721 others were injured during the two-day riot.[19] The World Uyghur Congress reported a much higher tally, at approximately 600 deaths.

The freedoms of speech, political expression, the press, association, assembly, and peaceful demonstrations are all limited in China. Beijing continues to restrict some of its citizens' fundamental rights by targeting unregistered organizations and unauthorized activities. Chinese journalists, lawyers, intellectuals, and activists who raise issues of official corruption, public health, and environmental crises face persecution, prosecution, harassment, detention, torture, and imprisonment. Liu Xiaobo (1955–), professor of Beijing Normal University with a PhD in literature (1988), served as president (2003–2007) of the Independent Chinese PEN Society. In 2008, he co-authored the *Charter 08* manifesto and posted it online, calling for increased political freedoms and human rights in China. He was arrested in 2009 and sentenced to eleven years of imprisonment on December 23, 2009, for "the crime of inciting subversion of state power." Due to the nature of the charges, Liu is described as a political prisoner. In October 2010, Liu was awarded the Nobel Peace Prize for his "long and non-violent struggle for fundamental human rights in China."[20] The Nobel Committee is still waiting for him to collect his medal, pick up his prize money, and give his Nobel lecture. Liu, however, will remain in jail until 2020. In 2013, the US Department of State issued its annual report on Chinese people's rights and stated that the condition of civil rights in China "remained poor."[21]

Notes

1 For more details on the Cultural Revolution, see Sun and Li, "Mao Zedong and the CCP: Adaptation, Centralization, and Success," 46–55.
2 Bruce J. Dickson, "Cooptation and Corporatism in China: The Logic of Party Adaptation," *Political Science Quarterly* 115, no. 4 (2000): 517–543.
3 Bruce J. Dickson, *Wealth into Power: The Communist Party's Embrace of China's Private Sector* (Cambridge, UK: Cambridge University Press, 2008), Introduction.
4 Bruce J. Dickson, "Updating the China Model," *The Washington Quarterly* 34, no. 4 (Fall 2011): 39–58.
5 To ensure stability, Deng insisted on the "Four Cardinal Principles" that included keeping to the Socialist road, upholding the people's democratic dictatorship, sticking to the CCP's leadership, and adhering to Marxism-Leninism and Maoist Thought. Anita Chan, "The Social Origins and Consequences of the Tiananmen Crisis," in *China in the Nineties*, ed. Goodman and Segal, 105.
6 *Selected Documents of the Fifteenth CCP National Congress* (Beijing: New Star, 1997), 104–106.
7 Headquarters of the People's Armed Police (PAP), *Wujing Tongxun* [The PAP News], August 16, 1999, 11.
8 Patricia B. Ebrey and Anne Walthall, *Modern East Asia from 1600: A Cultural, Social, and Political History* (Boston, MA: Houghton Mifflin, 2006), 2: 581–582.
9 Bureau of National Statistics, PRC State Council, *Zhongguo chengshi jingji shehui nianjian,* 1985 [Almanac of Chinese Urban Economy and Society, 1985] (Beijing: Zhongguo tongji [China Statistics Press], 1986), 39; and *ibid., Zhongguo chengshi tongji nianjian,* 2000 [China's Urban Statistical Yearbook, 2000] (Beijing: Zhongguo tongji [China Statistics Press], 2001), 3.
10 Xiaobing Li, "Social Changes in China and Implications for the PLA," paper at the "International Conference on the Civil-Military Issues in Today's China," the CNA Corporation, Alexandria, VA, March 21–23, 2004, 12.
11 Tianjin Garrison Command HQ, "Information System: Key for National Defense," in Editorial Department of *National Defense Journal, Weile daying mingtian de zhanzheng* (To Win the Future War) (Beijing: Guofand daxue [National Defense University Press], 1999), 47.
12 Andrew Wedeman, *Double Paradox: Rapid Growth and Rising Corruption in China* (Ithaca, NY: Cornell University Press, 2012), introduction and chapter 4.

13 Shambaugh, *China's Communist Party*, 154.
14 Rowan Callick, *The Party Forever: Inside China's Modern Communist Elite* (London: Palgrave Macmillan, 2013), chapters 1 and 5.
15 The two key international rights organizations are Amnesty International (www.amnesty.org) and Human Rights Watch (www.hrw.org).
16 In March 2005, a senior member of the NPC announced that China executes approximately 10,000 people per year.
17 The Heilongjiang Provincial High Court also gave death sentences to three other church leaders, and eleven church members received various sentences from three to fifteen years in prison.
18 Information Office, State Council of the PRC, "Development and Progress in Xinjiang, 2009," in *White Papers of the Chinese Government, 2009–2011*, ed. Information Office, State Council of the PRC (Beijing: Foreign Languages Press, 2012), 177.
19 Information Office, State Council of the PRC, "Development and Progress in Xinjiang," 177.
20 Jean-Philippe Beja, Fu Hualing, and Eva Pils, *Liu Xiaobo, Charter 08 and the Challenges of Political Reform in China* (Hong Kong: Hong Kong University Press, 2012), 2–4.
21 US Department of State, *China (Tibet, Hong Kong, Macau): Human Rights, 2013* (Washington, DC: Government Printing Office, 2014), 2.

Conclusion

East Asia in the twenty-first century

In the new century, East Asia is a powerhouse of dynamic growth, and the region is playing a crucial role in the recovery and development of global economy. Sustainable development in China, Korea, and Japan is improving security and stability in post-Cold War East Asia. The region drawn growing attention since it has showcased the diversity of world civilizations and development patterns as an intersection of interests of major powers. The security and development of East Asia has captured the interests of the world. Major countries shifted their focuses toward East Asia and the Pacific with juxtaposition of co-operation and competition among them. In the meantime, however, East Asians are still troubled by complex and sensitive issues from the past, the rampant spread of terrorism at present, and a grim prospect of non-proliferation. Historical factors and present disputes appear to be mutually reinforcing. Currently, therefore, traditional hot spots remain active and escalation of sovereign or maritime disputes have clear signs, all posing new security challenges. It is a region where historical unsettlement and current disagreement interweave.

The destabilizing factors in the region largely came from the East Asian countries themselves. First, China's political situation and reform have produced uncertainties and instability. The PRC today has little in common with the Cold War China of 1949 to 1979. The government has brought back Confucianism and nationalism – subjects that had been destroyed during the revolution of the CCP in the 1950s–1970s – as ruling philosophies and ideologies. Randall Peerenboom considers this development as China's path forward rather than as a problem, "or at least that it is too early to tell."[1] He believes that "China is now following the path of other East Asian countries that have achieved sustained economic growth, established the rule of law, and developed constitutional or rights-based democracies, albeit not necessarily liberal rights-based democracies."[2] Nevertheless, China's policy toward East Asia allows for a plurality of political systems and swift adjustments to changes in the international context. The drawback to this type of order is that it does not involve clarifying Beijing's long-term objectives. Insofar as China achieves full-blown global great power status, we still do not know what kind of global power China will be. Many strategic calculations and predictions depend on the CCP's current agenda to maintain economic growth and social stability.

The political conflict and social instability, and the need for a stronger government during the urbanization, scuttled many Chinese efforts to construct the rule of law. In many cases, however, the law was reduced further as a political tool of the ruling party, and the law's political status remained largely unaltered through the first decade of the twenty-first century. The CCP generated urban capitals and created political power bases in these cities while ignoring the benefits and rights of urban residents and private business owners.[3] The city governments carried out the Party's policy through law enforcement. Meanwhile, middle class and small business owners not only struggled to survive, but also to make themselves heard through the legal process, to avert being victimized. Whenever citizens had a problem, or even sued the city government, the powerful have always prevailed. The contemporary Chinese legal system in which the judiciary is part of the CCP control has been labeled as the rule *by* law. As Margret Y. K. Woo defines, "rule by law is an instrumentalist view of law meaning to govern by the use of laws."[4] In the PRC, the CCP uses the law to rule but its discretionary power does not subject to the law.[5]

In 2014, Xi Jinping (1953–), chairman of the CCP and president of the PRC in 2012–2017 (and probably in 2017–2022), gave a seemingly contradictory talk about the relations between the CCP and the law, speaking at a top executive conference of politics and judiciary. Invoking former President Jiang Zemin's talk at the CCP Fifteenth National Congress in 1997, Xi remarked that both CCP policies and state laws mirrored the fundamental interests of the people and thus there was no difference between them. "The Party leads the people to enact and enforce the constitution and laws," Xi said, "[the CCP] must lead the legislation, guarantee the law enforcement, and become the leader in conforming the law." Here, Xi seemed to stress the rule of law again. But he then shifted his topic to the Party's leadership of the judiciary. He told political and legal officials (i.e., judges, procurators, and police) that they had to adhere to the Party's leadership. "The leadership of the Party is in tune with the leadership of the people," he said.[6]

The rule *by* law, therefore, is just one of the relations between law and power in China. In fact, the relations between law and power are quite complicated. On the one hand, law and power are different and in many respects contradict each other; on the other hand, law and power have close relations and at times are interactive and intertwined. According to Sinkwan Cheng, there are two kinds of law: law in books and law in action. The first one is "often associated with justice," while the second one "reveals the operation" of power. While it may not be correct all the time, law and justice, in theory, are often said to be inseparable.[7] Neither justice nor law can be disconnected from power. As Dorwin Cartwright argues, power "reveals both the oppressive and benevolent faces of the law. Only through power can law act as an oppressive and benevolent apparatus."[8] The corruption of power can be reduced and alleviated by institutional constructions and mechanisms, but the corruption that comes from capital will never be alleviated or stopped by any means, due to the core of capital, pursuing benefits at all costs.

Understanding China's political and legal systems and the new challenges the government faces is one of the country's most significant goals of the twenty-first century. Even though the new leadership will work to maintain economic growth at home while seeking a growing role on the global political stage in 2014–2022, China is not yet a country ruled by law. While it practices power-sharing through checks and balances, competing political groups may entail a more dynamic and institutionalized decision-making process and may develop better policies, China must solve its own problems consisting of, but not limited to, corruption, power abuse, human rights violations, and urban mismanagement. These factors all delay China's growth and impede improvement of the Sino-US relationship. If the American government works with China on developing shared political, social, and judicial objectives, it may succeed in drawing China further into the international system. China must live up to its international obligations and global standards of civil and human rights while it prepares to host the new US president to visit Beijing in 2018. The leaders of these two economic powers agree that the US-China relationship is the most important international relationship in the twenty-first century. IMF and *Oxford Economics* project the annual economic growth rates of the PRC to be about 6.9 to 7.4 percent in 2016, 6.8 percent in 2017, and 7.2 to 8 percent in 2018.

Japan's policies are swerving strongly since Japan's conservative parties are on the rise with their representation making use of the disputed Senkaku Islands (or Diaoyu Islands in Chinese) to set off a new nationalist wave against China. In 2010, Japan began taking a tougher position against China in the East China Sea, not only politically, but also militarily. In that September, the Japanese Coast Guard changed its routine to chase the Chinese fishing boats away from the Diaoyu/Senkaku Islands, and arrested the Chinese captain. After the ship-collision incident near these islands in 2010, Japan put forward a new version of the National Defense Program Guideline, which links island disputes with military strategy for the first time. After the cataclysmic earthquake and subsequent nuclear disaster, under political pressure, the Japanese government had to purchase a batch of US F-35 fighters in 2012 and presses on with the building of various warships. In that October, the Japanese cabinet decided to appropriate 16.9 billion yen to purchase patrol ships, helicopters, and other equipment for the Japanese Coast Guard.

Moreover, the Chinese government was shocked in September 2012 when the Japanese government purchased three of the disputed islands from a private owner. Considering the purchase as nationalizing seven out of the eight islands, Chinese citizens went on the streets and gathered at the front of the Japanese Embassy in Beijing, holding large-scale protests across the country. In 2013, *The New York Times* reported that the massive Chinese protests seemed "semi-official" since "almost all the voices in China pressing the Okinawa issues are affiliated in some way with the government."[9] With popular support, both governments sent more naval and coast guard vessels to the disputed areas in the East China Sea. BBC reported in early 2013 that the situation had become "the most serious for Sino-Japanese relations in the post-war period in terms of the risk of militarized conflict."[10] In November 2013, Beijing announced its establishment of the Air Defense Identification Zone (ADIZ).[11] In early 2014, the PLA Air Force (PLAAF) began dispatching aircrafts to patrol the ADIZ to identify foreign aircrafts, shadow planes to "collect evidence," and to administer warnings.

In November 2012, a US congressional amendment to the National Defense Act included possible defense of the disputed islands in the East China Sea in the event of armed attacks.[12] In 2013, Secretary John Kerry further warned Beijing that, although the United States does not take a position on the ultimate sovereignty of the islands, the White House acknowledges they are under the administration of Japan and the American government opposes any unilateral actions that would seek to undermine Japanese administration.[13] China seems precautionary about any possible military conflict with the US armed forces in the East China Sea. On November 26, 2013, for example, three days after Beijing's announcement regarding the establishment of ADIZ, two US military warplanes flew into the zone without informing China. Although the PLA did not respond either militarily or politically, Steve Warren,

spokesman of the US Department of Defense, said that "We have conducted operations in the area of the Senkakus. We have continued to follow our normal procedures,
which include not filing flight plans, not radioing ahead and not registering our
frequencies."[14] On April 23–25, 2014, President Barack Obama reconfirmed US commitments to the safety and security of Japan and the Senkaku/Diaoyu Islands through
a joint press conference and joint statement with Prime Minister Abe. He is the first
US president who mentioned these disputed islands under Article V of the US-Japanese
Treaty of Mutual Cooperation and Security.

In 2016, the territorial conflict escalated to military confrontation involving naval
vessels, coast guard gunboats, and fighters in the disputed areas. The recent confrontation between Chinese and Japanese navies in the East China Sea has aroused
serious concerns in the international community regarding security and stability in the
Asia-Pacific region. The East China Sea has become one of the most worrisome flash
points in Asia, an important source of insecurity in the Western Pacific, and a possible
place to involve US armed forces against the PLA in East Asia. The US Air Force
continues to fly military aircrafts in the ADIZ without informing China, defying
China's declaration that the region falls into a Chinese airspace defense zone. Public
debates and strategic research in America focus on what these events may mean to the
United States, and how to best deal with the PLAN (PLA Navy) in case of crisis or
even a war in the Pacific. Moreover, President Donald Trump has promised to commit
US forces for the defense of Japan and South Korea.

Last but not least, the confrontation on the Korean Peninsula, along with North
Korea's nuclear threats and missile testing, may lead to a new crisis and armed
conflict.[15] The Korean Peninsula is the only place in the world where the Cold War
framework still exists. After Kim Jong-il died in December 2011, his third son, Kim
Jong-un, succeeded him, continuing the policy of his father. The situation on the
Korean Peninsula remains the most dangerous potential flashpoint in East Asia. The
border between the two Koreas remains one of the world's most militarized. Diplomatic
means for resolving Pyongyang's nuclear program are not producing results. Within the
past few years, there have been significant breaches of the peace – incidents such as
missile testing and the North's bombardment of the islands in the South. Both Seoul
and Pyongyang clearly have survival-level national security interests hanging in the
balance. Moreover, both the United States and China have major national security
interests at stake. But their security calculus of the regime in Pyongyang in particular is
nearly unfathomable, and it is not entirely clear that the United States and China are
discussing peninsular issues in anything but the most minimalist manner. Moreover,
there is the nuclear factor. Finkelstein warns that:

> For these and many other reasons, we can never discount or ignore this situation.
> It is one that casts a large shadow over the entire region. Like a volcano – some-
> times dormant and sometimes active – it always possesses high potential for major
> destruction and disruption.[16]

Although East Asia faces many challenges, the integration of national interests among
all countries continues to deepen, and most countries have steadily passed their economic
transformation and social transition. While the center of world economies is moving
toward the East Asia-Pacific, stability and prosperity of the region are of great significance to maintaining world peace and development, and are in the best interests of

all East Asian countries as well. We should treasure the favorable and hard-won environment and momentum for growth, establish a new concept of common security, and on the basis of mutual trust, work to build a new type of East Asian security relationship featuring mutual trust, co-operation, mutual benefit, democracy, and equality. The building of strategic mutual trust should follow East Asia's unique characteristics and its own rules of development, adhere to innovation, and actively learn from the experience of other regions. Then, based upon the mutual trust, East Asian countries may develop their own security organization or mechanism in the Asia-Pacific to build and maintain the regional peace and stability. East Asian peoples have been historically able to grasp the opportunities, join hands, forge ahead, and achieve sound and sustainable development.

Notes

1 Randall Peerenboom, "Law and Development of Constitutional Democracy: Is China a Problem Case?" *The Annals of the American Academy, AAPSS* 603 (January 2006): 192.
2 Peerenboom, *ibid.*, 193.
3 Xiaobing Li and Qiang Fang, "Legal Reforms in Twentieth-Century China," in *Modern Chinese Legal Reform: New Perspectives*, eds. Xiaobing Li and Qiang Fang (Lexington: University Press of Kentucky, 2013), 19–20.
4 Margaret Y. K. Woo, "Law and Discretion in Contemporary Chinese Courts" in *The Limits of the Rule of Law in China*, eds. Karen G. Turner, James V. Feinerman, and R. Kent Guy (Seattle: University of Washington Press, 2000), 163, 165.
5 Randle Peerenboom, *China's Long March Toward Rule of Law* (Cambridge: Cambridge University Press, 2002), 27–54.
6 Yang Weihan, "Xi Jinping chuxi zhongyang zhengfa gongzuo huiyi [Xi Jinping Attended the Central Work Meeting of the Politics and Law]" in *Xinhuanet*, January 8, 2014.
7 Sinkwan Cheng, "Introduction" in *Law, Justice, and Power: Between Reason and Will*, ed. Sinkwan Cheng (Stanford, CA: Stanford University Press, 2004): 3.
8 Cited in Cheng, *ibid.*, Introduction.
9 J. Perlez, "Sentiment Builds in China to Press Claim for Okinawa," *The New York Times*, June 13, 2013. Available at: http://www.nytimes.com/2013/06/14/world/asia.html [Accessed on March 11, 2015]
10 BBC, "Viewpoints: How Serious are China-Japan Tensions?" in *BBC Chinese (UK)*, February 8, 2013. Available at: http://news.bbc.co.uk/chinese/trad/hi/newsid_7450000.stm [Accessed on August 19, 2016]
11 You Ji, *China's Military Transformation: Politics and War Preparation* (Cambridge, UK: Polity Press, 2016), 10, 72, 77–78.
12 US Senate, *National Defense Authorization Act for Fiscal Year 2013, H.R. 4310* (Washington, DC: US Government Printing Office, 2013), Sec. 1251.
13 K. Mori, "*Kerry Spells out Policy on Senkaku Islands,*" *UPI*, April 15, 2013. Available at: www.upi.com/Top_News/World-News/2013/04/15 [Accessed on April 20, 2016].
14 Reuters, "Japan Refuses China Demand for Apology in Boat Row," in *Reuters*, September 25, 2010. Available at: www.reuters.com/article/us-japan-china-defense-idUSKCN [Accessed on November 10, 2015].
15 Xia Liping, "The Korean Factor in China's Policy toward East Asia and the United States," *American Foreign Policy Interests* 27, no. 4 (August 2005): 241–258.
16 David M. Finkelstein, "Three Key Issues Affecting Security in the Asia-Pacific Region," in *Asia-Pacific Security: New Issues and New Ideas*, compiled by International Military Committee, China Association for Military Science (Beijing: Military Science Publishing House, 2014), 113.

Bibliography

Primary sources: Documents, papers, and memoirs

Acheson, Dean and John C. Vincent, "China Memo, Top-Secret," September 6, 1945, US State Department Records of the Office of Chinese Affairs, 1945–1955. National Archives, Washington, DC. Digitized by Gale, Archives Unbound Collection. Available at: http://go.galegroup.com. vortex3. [Accessed May 5, 2017].

Air Pouch 181. October 14, 1954, "794a, 5-MSP/1054, RG," National Archives, Washington DC.

Bureau of Foreign Economy and Liaison, "Report on the Current Foreign Aid and Proposal for the Future Tasks," September 1, 1961.

Burr, William, ed. *The Kissinger Transcripts: The Top-Secret Talks with Beijing and Moscow.* New York: New Press, 1999.

CCP Central Archives comps. *Zhonggong zhongyang wenjian xuanji, 1921–1949* [*Selected Documents of the CCP Central Committee, 1921–1949*]. Beijing: Zhonggong zhongyang dangxiao [CCP Central Party Academy Press], 1989–1992.

CCP Party History Research Division. *Zhongguo gongchandang lishi dashiji, 1919–1987* [*Major Historical Events of the CCP, 1919–1987*]. Beijing: Renmin [People's Press], 1989.

Chen Pai. *Yuezhan qinliji* [*My Personal Experience in the Vietnam War*]. Zhengzhou: Henan renmin [Henan People's Press], 1997.

CIA. "Report on the Chinese Offshore Islands Situation, September 9, 1954," CIA Official File, 50318-Formosa (1), box 9, International Series, Dwight D. Eisenhower Papers. Abilene, KA: Dwight D. Eisenhower Library.

Deng Xiaoping. *Selected Works of Deng Xiaoping.* Beijing: Foreign Languages Press, 1994.

Eisenhower, Dwight. *Dwight D. Eisenhower Papers.* Abilene, KA: Dwight D. Eisenhower Library.

Giap, Vo Nguyen. *The Military Art of People's War: Selected Writings of Vo Nguyen Giap.* New York: New York University Press, 1970.

Giap, Vo Nguyen. *People's War, People's Army: The Viet Cong Insurrection Manual for Underdeveloped Countries.* New York: Praeger, 1968.

History Compilation and Translation Bureau, ROC Defense Ministry, ed. *8–23 Paozhan shengli 30 zhounian jinian wenji* [*Recollection for the 30th Anniversary of the Victorious August 23 Artillery Battle*]. Taiwan: Guofangbu yinzhichang [Defense Ministry Printing Office], 1989.

Hurley, Patrick. "Aide Memoirs," September 25, 1944; and his letter to President Roosevelt accompanying the memoirs, September 25, 1944, Ambassador Patrick Hurley Papers, Norman, OK: University of Oklahoma Library.

Information Office, State Council of the PRC. "Development and Progress in Xinjiang, 2009." In *White Papers of the Chinese Government, 2009–2011.* Beijing: Foreign Languages Press, 2012.

Kissinger, Henry. *White House Years.* New York: Little, Brown, 1978.

Le Duan. "Document: Comrade B on the Plot of the Reactionary Chinese Clique against Vietnam." In *Behind the Bamboo Curtain: China, Vietnam, and the World beyond Asia*. Priscilla Roberts, ed. 467–486. Stanford, CA: Stanford University Press, 2006.

Liu Shaoqi. *Jianguo yilai Liu Shaoqi wengao, 1949–1957* [*Liu Shaoqi's Manuscripts since the Founding of the State, 1949–1957*]. Beijing: Zhongyang wenxian [CCP Central Archival and Manuscript Press], 2005–2013.

Luo Guibo. "An Exceptional Model of Proletarian Internationalism: Remember Mao Zedong and the Assistance of Vietnam and Resistance against France." In *Zhongguo junshi guwentuan yuanyue kangfa shilu: dangshiren de huiyi* [*The Records of the Chinese Military Advisory Group (CMAG) in Assisting Vietnam and Resisting France: Personal Accounts of the Veterans*]. Compilation Team, ed. 1–16. Beijing: Zhonggong dangshi [CCP Party History Press], 2002.

Lushun Naval Command. "Collective Documents on Lin Biao and Li Zuopeng's Criminal Activities of Attacking the Party and Betraying the PLA." *Lushun Naval Base Archives (PLAN)*, 1972, Lushun, Liaoning.

Mao Zedong. *Selected Works of Mao Tse-tung*. Beijing: Foreign Languages Press, 1977.

Mao Zedong. *Jianguo yilai Mao Zedong wengao* [*Mao Zedong's Manuscripts since the Founding of the State*]. Beijing: Zhongyang wenxian [CCP Central Archival and Manuscript Press], 1989.

Mao Zedong. *Mao Zedong xuanji* [*Selected Works of Mao Zedong*]. Beijing: Renmin [People's Press], 1991.

Mao Zedong. *Mao Zedong waijiao wenxuan* [*Selected Diplomatic Papers of Mao Zedong*]. Beijing: Zhongyang wenxian [CCP Central Archival and Manuscript Press], 1994.

Mao Zedong. *Jianguo yilai Mao Zedong junshi wengao* [*Mao Zedong's Military Manuscripts since the Founding of the PRC*] (Beijing: Junshi kexue [Military Science Press] and Zhongyang wenxian [CCP Central Archival and Manuscript Press), 2010.

Ministry of Foreign Affairs, People's Republic of China. PRC Foreign Ministry Archives. Beijing, China.

Nhieu, Nguyen. "Electronic Reconnaissance vs. Guerrillas." In *Voices from the Vietnam War: Stories from American, Asian, and Russian Veterans*. Xiaobing Li, ed. 31–38. Lexington: University Press of Kentucky, 2010.

Nie Rongzhen. *Nie Rongzhen huiyilu* [*Memoir of Nie Rongzhen*]. Two volumes. Beijing: Jiefangjun [PLA Press], 1984.

Nixon, Richard. *The Memoirs of Richard Nixon*. New York: Grosset & Dunlap, 1978.

Peng Dehuai. *Peng Dehuai junshi wenxuan* [*Selected Military Papers of Peng Dehuai*]. Beijing: Zhongyang wenxian [CCP Central Archival and Manuscript Press], 1988.

PLA Navy History Compilation Committee, ed. *Haijun: huiyi shiliao* [*The Navy: Memoirs and History Records*]. Beijing: Haichao [Ocean Wave Publishing], 1994

Quang, Mai Ly, ed. *Chuyen ke: cua nhung nguoi giup viec Bac Ho* [*Personal Recollections: Years Working and Living with Uncle Ho*]. Hanoi: The Goi [World Publishing], 2004.

Rankin, Karl Lott. *China Assignment*. Seattle, WA: University of Washington Press, 1964.

Research Department of Party Papers, CCP Central Committee, ed. *Major Documents of the People's Republic of China –Selected Important Documents since the Third Plenary Session of the Eleventh CCP Central Committee*. Beijing: Foreign Languages Press, 1991.

"Selected Conversations of Asian Communist Leaders on Indochina." In *Behind the Bamboo Curtain; China, Vietnam, and the World beyond Asia*. Priscilla Roberts, ed. 487–534. Stanford, CA: Stanford University Press, 2006.

Selected Documents of the Fifteenth CCP National Congress. Beijing: New Star, 1997.

The Tai, Phung. *Remembering Uncle Ho: Memories in War Years*. Hanoi: Gioi Publishers, 2005.

Truman, Harry S. *Memoirs: Years of Trial and Hope*. Garden City, NY: Doubleday, 1956.

Truman, Harry S. *Papers of Harry S. Truman*. Independence, MO: Truman Library and Museum.

US Department of State. *Confidential History of the China Aid Program; Office of Chinese Affairs, 1945–1955*. National Archives: Washington, DC. Digitized by Gale, Archives Unbound Collection, 8.

US Department of State. *Records of the Office of Chinese Affairs, 1945–1955*. National Archives, Washington, DC. Digitized by Gale, *Archives Unbound Collection*, available at http://go.ga legroup.com.vortex3.

US Department of State. *State Department Bulletin*, xii–xxii (1949–1951).

US Department of State. *United States Relations with China: With Special Reference to the Period 1944–1949 (China White Paper)*. Washington, DC: Government Printing Office, 1949.

US Department of State. "Military Situation in the Far East: Policy Memorandum of Formosa, December 23, 1949." *Hearings before the Committees on Armed Services and on Foreign Relations*, Senate, 82nd Congress, First Session. Washington, DC: Government Printing Office, 1951.

US Department of State. *Foreign Relations of the United States*. Washington, DC: Government Printing Office, 1976–1988.

US Department of State, FRUS. "NSC Document, No. 68, 1950." In *US Department of State, FRUS, National Security Affairs: Foreign Economic Policy*. Washington, DC: Government Printing Office, 1977.

US Department of State. *China (Tibet, Hong Kong, Macau): Human Rights, 2013*. Washington, DC: Government Printing Office, 2014.

US Senate. *National Defense Authorization Act for Fiscal Year 2013, H.R. 4310: Sec. 1251.* Washington, DC: US Government Printing Office, 2013. Van Thai, Hoang. *How South Viet Nam Was Liberated*. Hanoi: Gioi Publishers, 2005.

Van, Dinh Thi. *I Engaged in Intelligence Work*. Hanoi: Gioi Publishers, 2006

Vincent, John C. "Memorandum by the Director of the Office of Far Eastern Affairs (Vincent) to the Secretary of State," February 5, 1947, in *FRUS*, 1947, 7: 787.

Xiao Jinguang. *Xiao Jinguang huiyilu* [*Memoirs of Xiao Jinguang*] (Beijing: Jiefangjun [PLA Press]), 1988.

Xuan, Nguyen Yen. "Surviving the Bloody Jungle." In *Voices from the Vietnam War: Stories from American, Asian, and Russian Veterans*. Xiaobing Li, ed. 23–30. Lexington: University Press of Kentucky, 2010.

Xu Xiangqian. "The Purchase of Arms from Moscow." In *Mao's Generals Remember Korea*. Xiaobing Li, Allan R. Millett, and Bin Yu, trans and ed. 139–146. Lawrence: University Press of Kansas, 2000.

Ye Fei. *Ye Fei huiyilu* [*Memoirs of Ye Fei*]. Beijing: Jiefangjun [PLA Press], 1988.

Zhang Guanghua. "The Secret Records of China's Important Decisions to Assist Vietnam and Resist France." In *Zhongguo junshi guwentuan yuanyue kangfa shilu: dangshiren de huiyi* [*The Records of the Chinese Military Advisory Group (CMAG) in Assisting Vietnam and Resisting France: Personal Accounts of the Veterans*]. Compilation Team, ed. 17–31. Beijing: Zhonggong dangshi [CCP Party History Press], 2002.

Zhang Zeshi, ed. *Meijun jizhongying qinliji* [*Personal Stories of the CPVF POWs in UN/U.S. Camps*]. Beijing: Zhongguo wenshi [China History and Literature Publishing], 1996.

Zhou Baoshan. "China's Crouching Dragon." In *Voices from the Korean War: Personal Stories of American, Korean, and Chinese Soldiers*. Richard Peters and Xiaobing Li, eds. 85–96. Lexington: University Press of Kentucky, 2004.

Zhou Enlai. *Junshi wenxuan* [*Selected Military Works of Zhou Enlai*], vols. 1–4. Beijing: Renmin [People's Press], 1997.

Zhou Enlai. *Waijiao wenxuan* [*Selected Diplomatic Papers of Zhou Enlai*]. Beijing: Zhongyang wenxian [CCP Central Archival and Manuscript Press], 1990.

Secondary sources: Books and articles

Alexander, Bevin. *Korea: The First War We Lost*. Revised edition. New York: Hippocrene Books, 1998.

Ambrose, Stephen E. "Bombing Hanoi, Mining Haiphong, and the Moscow Summit." In *Light at the End of the Tunnel: A Vietnam War Anthology.* Andrew Jon Rotter, ed. 123–139. Wilmington, DL: SR Books, 1999.

Ambrose, Stephen E. and Douglas G. Brinkley. *Rise to Globalism: American Foreign Policy since 1938.* New York: Penguin, 1997.

Andressen, Curtis. *A Short History of Japan: From Samurai to Sony.* Canberra, Australia: Allen and Unwin, 2002.

Appleman, Roy E. *South to the Naktong, North to the Yalu (June–November 1950), US Army in the Korean War.* Washington, DC: Office of the Chief of Military History and US Government Printing Office, 1961.

Appy, Christian G. *Patriots: The Vietnam War Remembered from All Sides.* New York: Viking, 2003.

Asselin, Pierre. *Hanoi's Road to the Vietnam War, 1954–1965.* Berkeley: University of California Press, 2013.

Bailey, Thomas A. *A Diplomatic History of the American People.* Tenth edition. Englewood Cliffs, NJ: Prentice-Hall, 1980.

Baozhong, Li. *Zhongwei junshi zhidu bijiao [Comparative Study of Chinese Military System]* Beijing: Shangwu yinshuguan [Shangwu Press], 2003.

Barnett, Doak. *China and the Major Powers in East Asia.* Washington, DC: Brookings Institute, 1977.

BBC. "Viewpoints: How serious are China-Japan Tensions?" In *BBC Chinese (UK),* February 8, 2013. Available at: http://news.bbc.co.uk/chinese/trad/hi/newsid_7450000.stm. [Accessed August 19, 2016].

Beasley, W. G. *The Rise of Modern Japan: Political, Economic and Social Change since 1850.* Revised edition. New York: St. Martin's Press, 2000.

Beja, Jean-Philippe, Fu Hualing, and Eva Pils. *Liu Xiaobo, Charter 08 and the Challenges of Political Reform in China.* Hong Kong: Hong Kong University Press, 2012.

Belair, Felix, Jr. "New Policy Set Up: President Blunt in Plea to Combat 'Coercion as World Peril," *New York Times,* March 13, 1947, 1.

Bergreen, Laurence. *Marco Polo: From Venice to Xanadu.* New York: Vintage, 2008.

Bernstein, Thomas P. and Hua-Yu Li, eds. *China Learns from the Soviet Union, 1949–Present.* Lanham, MD: Lexington Books, 2011.

Black, Jeremy. *The Cold War: A Military History.* London: Bloomsbury Academic, 2015.

Bowers, William T., ed. *Striking Back: Combat in Korea, March–April 1951.* Lexington, KY: University Press of Kentucky, 2010.

Bradley, Mark Philip. *Imagining Vietnam & America: The Making of Postcolonial Vietnam, 1919–1950.* Chapel Hill: University of North Carolina Press, 2000.

Brigham, Robert K. *ARVN: Life and Death in the South Vietnamese Army.* Lawrence, KS: University Press of Kansas, 2006.

Brocheux, Pierre. *Ho Chi Minh: A Biography.* New York: Cambridge University Press, 2007.

Burchett, Wilfred G. *The Cambodia-China-Vietnam Triangle.* Chicago: Vanguard Books, 1981.

Bureau of National Statistics, PRC State Council. *Zhongguo chengshi jingji shehui nianjian, 1985 [Almanac of Chinese Urban Economy and Society, 1985].* Beijing: Zhongguo tongji [China Statistics Press], 1986.

Bureau of National Statistics, PRC State Council. *Zhongguo chengshi tongji nianjian, 2000 [China's Urban Statistical Yearbook, 2000].* Beijing: Zhongguo tongji [China Statistics Press], 2001.

Buzzanco, Robert. "Military Dissent and the Legacy of the Vietnam War." In *The War that Never Ends: New Perspectives on the Vietnam War.* David L. Anderson and John Ernst, eds. 181–207. Lexington, KY: University Press of Kentucky, 2007.

Callick, Rowan. *The Party Forever: Inside China's Modern Communist Elite.* London: Palgrave Macmillan, 2013.

Carter, James M. *Inventing Vietnam: The United States and State Building, 1954–1968.* New York: Cambridge University Press, 2008.

Catton, Philip. *Diem's Final Failure: Prelude to America's War in Vietnam*. Lawrence, KS: University Press of Kansas, 2002.

Chan, Anita. "The Social Origins and Consequences of the Tiananmen Crisis." In *China in the Nineties: Crisis Management and Beyond*. David S. G. Goodman and Gerald Segal, eds. Oxford, UK: Oxford University Press, 1991.

Chan, Sucheng. *The Vietnamese American 1.5 Generation: Stories of War, Revolution, Flight, and New Beginnings*. Philadelphia, PA: Temple University Press, 2006.

Chanda, Nayan. *Brother Enemy: The War after the War*. New York: Harcourt Brace Jovanovich, 1986.

Chandler, David. *A History of Cambodia*. Boulder, CO: Westview, 1992.

Chang, Gordon H. *Friends and Enemies: The United States, China, and the Soviet Union*. Stanford, CA: Stanford University Press, 1990.

Chang, Gordon H. "To the Nuclear Brink: Eisenhower, Dulles, and the Quemoy-Matsu Crisis." *International Security* 12(4) (Spring 1988): 102–116.

Chang, Iris. *The Rape of Nanking; The Forgotten Holocaust of World War II*. New York: Basic Books, 1997.

Chang, Jung and Jon Halliday. *Mao: The Unknown Story*. New York: Knopf, 2005.

Chao, Linda and Ramon H. Myers. *The First Chinese Democracy: Political Life in the Republic of China on Taiwan*. Baltimore, DE: The Johns Hopkins University Press, 1998.

Chapman, Jessica. *Cauldron of Resistance: Ngo Dinh Diem, the United States, and 1950s Southern Vietnam*. Ithaca, NY: Cornell University Press 2013.

Chen, Jian. *China's Road to the Korean War: The Making of the Sino-American Confrontation*. New York: Columbia University Press, 1994.

Chen, Jian. *Mao's China and the Cold War*. Chapel Hill: University of North Carolina Press, 2001.

Chen, Jian and Xiaobing Li. "China and the End of the Global Cold War." In *From Détente to the Soviet Collapse: The Cold War from 1975 to 1991*. Malcolm Muir, Jr., ed. 120–132. Lexington, KY: Virginia Military Institute Press, 2006.

Chen, King C. *China's War with Vietnam, 1979: Issues, Decisions, and Implications*. Stanford, CA: Hoover Institution Press, 1987.

Cheng, Sinkwan, ed. *Law, Justice, and Power: Between Reason and Will*. Stanford, CA: Stanford University Press, 2004.

Chi, Hoang Van. *From Colonialism to Communism: A Case History of North Vietnam*. New York: Praeger, 1964.

Chieu, Vu Ngu. "The Other Side of the 1945 Vietnamese Revolution: The Empire of Viet-Nam (March–August 1945)." *Journal of Asian Studies* 45(2) (February 1986): 287–308.

China Academy of Military Science (CAMS). *Zhongguo gongchandang zhengzhi gongzuo 70 nian* [*The Seventy Years of the CCP Political Tasks*]. Beijing: Jiefangjun [PLA Press], 1992.

Chongji, Jin. "Shanyu duli sikao de zhanlujia he lilunjia" [A Great Strategist and Theorist with His Own Thoughts], keynote speech at the opening ceremony of the Conference on the Liu Shaoqi Studies, Chuzhou, Anhui Province, October 29, 1996. In *Liu Shaoqi yanjiu pingshu* [*On the Studies of Liu Shaoqi*]. Chen Shaotao, ed. 3–6. Beijing: Zhongyang wenxian [CCP Central Archival and Manuscript Press], 1997.

Christensen, Thomas J. *Useful Adversaries: Grand Strategy, Domestic Mobilization, and Sino-American Conflict, 1947–1958*. Princeton, NJ: Princeton University Press, 1996.

Clyde, Paul H. and Burton F. Beers. *A History of Western Impacts and Eastern Responses, 1830–1975*. Sixth edition. Prospect Heights, IL: Waveland, 1975.

CMAG History Compilation Team. *Zhongguo junshi guwentuan yuanyue kangfa douzheng shishi* [*Historical Facts of the Chinese Military Advisory Group (CMAG) in the War to Resist France and Aid Vietnam*]. Beijing: Jiefangjun [PLA Press], 1990.

Cohen, Jerome B. *Japan's Economy in War and Reconstruction*. Minneapolis: University of Minnesota Press, 1949.

Cohen, Warren I. *America's Response to China: A History of Sino-American Relations.* Fifth edition. New York: Columbia University Press, 2010.

Compilation Committee of ROC History. *A Pictorial History of the Republic of China.* Taipei, Taiwan: Modern China Press, 1981.

Conboy, Kenneth and James Morrison. *The CIA's Secret War in Tibet.* Lawrence, KS: University Press of Kansas, 2002.

Copper, John F. *Taiwan: Nation-State or Province?* Fourth edition. Boulder, CO: Westview, 2003.

Cumings, Bruce. *Korea's Place in the Sun: A Modern History.* New York: Norton, 1997.

Cumo, Christopher. "1979 Energy Crisis." In *Oil: A Cultural and Geographic Encyclopedia of Black Gold.* Xiaobing Li and Michael Molina, eds. 1: 216–220. Santa Barbara, CA: ABC-CLIO, 2014.

Cuong, Nguyen Duc. "Building a Market Economy during Wartime." In *Voices from the Second Republic of South Vietnam (1967–1975).* Keith W. Taylor, ed. 96–122. Ithaca, NY: Cornell University Southeast Asia Program Publications, 2014.

Da Ying. *Zhiyuanjun zhanfu jishi; xuji* [*Voices from the CPVF POWs (continued)*]. Beijing: Zhongguo qingnian [China's Youth Press], 1993.

Deng Rong. *Deng Xiaoping and the Cultural Revolution – A Daughter Recalls the Critical Years.* Sidney Shapiro. trans. Beijing: Foreign Languages Press, 2002.

Dickson, Bruce J. "Cooptation and Corporatism in China: The Logic of Party Adaptation." *Political Science Quarterly* 115(4) (2000): 517–543.

Dickson, Bruce J. "Updating the China Model." *The Washington Quarterly* 34(4) (Fall 2011): 39–58.

Dickson, Bruce J. *Wealth into Power: The Communist Party's Embrace of China's Private Sector.* Cambridge, UK: Cambridge University Press, 2008.

Diem, Bui with David Chanoff. *In the Jaws of History.* Bloomington: Indiana University Press, 1987.

Dikotter, Frank. *Mao's Great Famine: The History of China's Most Devastating Catastrophe, 1958–1962.* New York: Walker, 2010.

Dinglie, Wang *et al.*, *Dongdai Zhongguo kongjun* [*Contemporary Chinese Air Force*]. Beijing: Zhongguo shehui kexue [China's Social Sciences Press], 1989.

Dittmer, Lowell. *Liu Shao-ch'i and the Chinese Cultural Revolution: The Politics of Mass Criticism.* Berkeley: University of California Press, 1974.

Dower, John W. *Embracing Defeat: Japan in the Wake of World War II.* New York: Norton, 1999.

Dreyer, Edward L. *China at War, 1901–1949.* New York: Longman, 1995.

Duc, Nguyen Phu. *The Viet-Nam Peace Negotiations: Saigon's Side of the Story.* Christiansburg, VA: Dalley Book, 2005.

Duiker, William. *Ho Chi Minh: A Life.* New York: Theia, 2000.

Duiker, William. *Sacred War; Nationalism and Revolution in a Divided Vietnam.* Boston, MA: McGraw-Hill, 1995.

Duiker, William. *Vietnam; Revolution in Transition.* Second edition. Boulder, CO: Westview, 1995.

Duiker, William. "Foreword: The History of the People's Army." In *Victory in Vietnam: The Official History of the People's Army of Vietnam, 1954–1975*, Military History Institute of Vietnam. Merle L. Pribbenow, trans. Lawrence, KS: University Press of Kansas, 2002, xi.

Duong, Van Nguyen. *The Tragedy of the Vietnam War: A South Vietnamese Officer's Analysis.* Jefferson, NC: McFarland, 2008.

Ebon, Martin. *Lin Piao: The Life and Writings of China's New Ruler.* New York: Stein and Day Publishers, 1970.

Ebrey, Patricia and Anne Walthall. *Modern East Asia from 1600: A Cultural, Social, and Political History.* Third edition. Boston, MA: Houghton Mifflin, 2006.

Ebrey, Patricia and Anne Walthall. *Pre-Modern East Asia: To 1800.* Third edition. Boston, MA: Wadsworth, 2014.

Elleman, Bruce A. *Modern Chinese Warfare, 1795–1989*. London: Routledge, 2001.

Elliott, Mark C. *The Manchu Way: The Eight Banners and Ethnic Identity in Late Imperial China*. Stanford, CA: Stanford University Press, 2001.

Elliott, David W. P. *Changing Worlds: Vietnam's Transition from Cold War to Globalization*. New York: Oxford University Press, 2012.

Esherick, Joseph W. "Revolution in a Feudal Fortress." *Modern China* 24(4) (October 1998), 370.

Espiritu, Yen Le. *Body Counts: The Vietnam War and Militarized Refugees*. Berkeley: University of California Press, 2014.

Fairbank, John K. and Merle Goldman. *China: A New History*. Enlarged ed. Cambridge, MA: Harvard University Press, 1998.

Fairbank, John K., Edwin O. Reischauer, and Albert M. Craig. *East Asia: Transition and Transformation*. Revised edition. Boston, MA: Houghton Mifflin, 1989.

Feng, Chih. *Behind Enemy Lines*. Beijing: Foreign Languages Press, 1979.

Finkelstein, David M. *Washington's Taiwan Dilemma, 1949–1950: From Abandonment to Salvation*. Fairfax, VA: George Mason University Press, 1993.

Finkelstein, David M. "Three Key Issues Affecting Security in the Asia-Pacific Region." In *Asia-Pacific Security: New Issues and New Ideas*. Compiled by International Military Committee, China Association for Military Science, 109–117. Beijing: Military Science Publishing House, 2014.

Folsom, Ralph. *Law and Politics in the People's Republic of China*. Boulder, CO: Westview, 1992.

Foot, Rosemary. *The Practice of Power: U.S. Relations with China since 1949*. Oxford, UK: Oxford University Press, 1995.

Fried, Richard M. *Nightmare in Red*. New York: Oxford University Press, 1990.

Freeman, Charles, Jr. "The Process of Rapprochement: Achievements and Problems." In *Sino-American Normalization and Its Policy Implications*. Gene T. Hsiao and Michael Witunsky, eds. New York: Praeger, 1983.

Fuzi, Tian. *Zhongyeu zhanzheng jishilu* [*Factual Records of the Sino-Vietnam War*]. Beijing: Jiefangjun wenyi [PLA Literature Press], 2004.

Gaddis, John Lewis. *The United States and the Origins of the Cold War, 1941–1947*. New York: Columbia University Press, 1972.

Gaddis, John Lewis. "Was the Truman Doctrine a Real Turning Point?" *Foreign Affairs* 52(2) (January 1974): 383–396.

Gaddis, John Lewis. *The Long Peace: Inquiries into the History of the Cold War*. New York: Oxford University Press, 1987.

Gaddis, John Lewis. *We Now Know: Rethinking Cold War History*, New York: Oxford University Press, 1997.

Gaddis, John Lewis. *Strategies of Containment: A Critical Appraisal of American National Security Policy during the Cold War*. Revisedand expanded edition. New York: Oxford University Press, 2005.

Gadkar-Wilcox, Wynn. Writing sections in "*East Asia and the West*." Xiaobing Li, Yi Sun, and Wynn Gadkar-Wilcox, eds. Unpublished manuscript.

Gaiduk, Ilya V. *The Soviet Union and the Vietnam War*. Chicago: Ivan Dee, 1996.

Gaiduk, Ilya V. "The Second Front of the Soviet Cold War: Asia in the System of Moscow's Foreign Policy Priorities, 1945–1956." In *The Cold War in East Asia, 1945–1991*. Tsuyoshi Hasegawa, ed. 63–80. Stanford, CA: Stanford University Press, 2011.

Gardner, Daniel K. *Confucianism: A Very Short Introduction*. Oxford, UK: Oxford University Press, 2014.

Garver, John W. *Foreign Relations of the People's Republic of China*. Englewood Cliffs, NJ: Prentice-Hall, 1993.

Gernet, Jacques. *Buddhism in Chinese Society*. New York: Columbia University Press, 1998.

Goldman, Merle and Roderick MacFarquhar, eds. *The Paradox of China's Post-Mao Reforms.* Cambridge, MA: Harvard University Press, 1999.

Gong Li. *Kuayue honggou: 1969–1979 nian zhongmei guanxi de yanbian* [*Bridging the Chasm: The Evolution of Sino-American Relations, 1969–1979*]. Zhengzhou: Henan renmin [Henan People's Press], 1992.

Gong Li. *Mao Zedong waijiao fengyunlu* [*A Historical Record of Mao Zedong's Diplomacy*]. Zhengzhou, Henan: Zhongyuan nongmin [Central China's Peasant Publishing], 1996.

Goodman, David S. G. and Gerald Segal, eds. *China in the Nineties: Crisis Management and Beyond.* Oxford, UK: Oxford University Press, 1991.

Goodman, David S. G. "Introduction: The Authoritarian Outlook." In *China in the Nineties: Crisis Management and Beyond.* David S. G. Goodman and Gerald Segal, eds. Oxford, UK: Oxford University Press, 1991.

Gordon, Andrew. "Society and Politics from Trans-war through Post-war Japan." In *Historical Perspectives on Contemporary East Asia.* Merle Goldman and Andrew Gordon, eds. 272–296. Cambridge, MA: Harvard University Press, 2000.

Grasso, June, Jay Corrin, and Michael Kort, *Modernization and Revolution in China: From the Opium Wars to World Power.* Third edition. Armonk, New York: M.E. Sharpe, 2004.

Guan, Ang Cheng. *The Vietnam War from the Other Side.* New York: Routledge, 2013.

Gunn, Geoffrey. "The Great Vietnamese Famine of 1945 Revised." *Asia-Pacific Journal* 9(5) (January 2011): 1–12.

Guo Ming. *Zhongyue guanxi yanbian sishinian* [*Uncertain Relations between China and Vietnam, 1949–1989*]. Nanning: Guangxi renmin [Guangxi People's Press], 1992.

Guo Zhigang. "A Foreign Military Assistance after the Founding of the New Republic." In *Junqi piaopiao: xinzhongguo 50 nian junshi dashi shushi* [*PLA Flag Fluttering: Facts of China's Major Military Events in the Past Fifty Years of the PRC*]. Military History Research Division, China Academy of Military Science (CAMS), ed. 145–161. Beijing: Jiefangjun [PLA Press], 1999.

Guojun, Xie. "The Sino-Vietnamese Border War of Self-Defense and Counter-Offense." In *Junqi piaopiao* [*PLA Flag Fluttering*], Military History Research Division, CAMS, ed. 2: 624–625. Beijing: Jiefangjun [PLA Press], 1999.

Haihao, Qian. *Jundui zuzhi bianzhixue jiaocheng* [*Graduate Curriculum: Military Organization and Formation*]. Beijing: Junshi kexue [Military Science Press], 2001.

Halberstam, David. *Ho.* New York: Alfred Knopf, 1987.

Hamashita, Takeshi. "Tribute and Treaties: Maritime Asia and Treaty Port Networks in the Era of Negotiation, 1800–1900." In *The Resurgence of East Asia: 500, 150 and 50 year perspectives.* Giovanni Arrighi, Takeshi Hamashita, and Mark Selden, eds. 17–50. London: Routledge, 2003.

Hammer, Ellen. *The Struggle for Indochina.* Stanford, CA: Stanford University Press, 1955.

Hane, Mikiso. *Eastern Phoenix: Japan since 1945.* Boulder, CO: Westview, 1996.

Hane, Mikiso and Louis G. Perez. *Modern Japan: A Historical Survey.* Fourth edition. Boulder, CO: Westview, 2009.

Hasegawa, Tsuyoshi, ed. *The Cold War in East Asia 1945–1991.* Stanford, CA: Stanford University Press, 2011.

Hastings, Max. *The Korean War.* New York: Simon and Schuster, 1987.

Headquarters of the People's Armed Police (PAP). *Wujing Tongxun* [*The PAP News*], 1997–2000.

Hellegers, Dale M. *We, the Japanese People: World War II and the Origins of the Japanese Constitution.* Stanford, CA: Stanford University Press, 2002.

Henshall, Kenneth. *A History of Japan.* Second edition. London: Palgrave, 2004.

Herring, George C. *America's Longest War; the United States and Vietnam, 1950–1975.* Third Edition. New York: McGraw-Hill, 1996.

Hevia, James L. *Cherishing Men from Afar: Qing Guest Ritual and the MaCartney Embassy of 1793.* Durham, NC: Duke University Press, 1995.

Hilsman, Roger. "Foreword." In *People's War, People's Army: The Viet Cong Insurrection Manual for Underdeveloped Countries*, Vo Nguyen Giap. New York: Praeger, 1968, ix–xi.

Hirakawa, Sachiko. "Japan: Living in and with Asia." In *Regional Community Building in East Asia*. Lee Lai To and Zarina Othman, eds. 249–270. London: Routledge, 2017.

History Compilation and Translation Bureau, ROC Defense Ministry. *8-23 Paozhan shengli 30 zhounian jinian wenji* [*Recollection for the 30th Anniversary of the Victorious August 23 Artillery Battle*]. Taipei, Taiwan: Guofangbu yinzhichang [Defense Ministry Printing Office], 1989, 33–34.

Holmes, Richard, ed. *Oxford Companion to Military History*. Oxford, UK: Oxford University Press, 2001.

Hook, Glen D., Julie Gilson, Christopher W. Hughes, and Hugo Dobson. *Japan's International Relations: Politics, Economics, and Security*. Second edition. London: Routledge, 2005.

Hsu, Immanuel C. Y. *The Rise of Modern China*. Sixth edition. Oxford, UK: Oxford University Press, 2000.

Huaizhi, Han. *Dangdai zhongguo jundui de junshi gongzuo* [*Military Affairs of Contemporary China's Armed Forces*]. Beijing: Zhongguo shehui kexue [China's Social Science Press], 1989.

Huang, Ray. *1587, A Year of No Significance: The Ming Dynasty in Decline*. New Haven, CT: Yale University Press, 1981.

Huffman, James L. *Modern Japan: A History in Documents*. New York: Oxford University Press, 2011.

Huiting, Chen. "Establishing a Vietnamese Surface-to-Air Missile Regiment." In *Yuanyue kangmei: zhongguo zhiyuan budui zai yuenan* [*Aid Vietnam and Resist America: China's Supporting Forces in Vietnam*]. Major General Qu Aiguo, Bao Mingrong, and Xiao Zuyue, eds. Beijing: Junshi kexue [Military Science Press], 1995.

Hunt, Richard A. *Pacification: The American Struggle for Vietnam's Hearts and Minds*. Boulder, CO: Westview, 1995.

Iriye, Akira. *Power and Culture: The Japanese-American War, 1941–1945*. Cambridge, MA: Harvard University Press, 1981.

Iriye, Akira. "Review on Hasegawa's Book, The Cold War in East Asia, 1945–1991." *American Historical Review* 117(1) (February 2012): 174–175.

James, Leslie and Elisabeth Leake, eds. *Decolonization and the Cold War: Negotiating Independence*. London: Bloomsbury Academic, 2015.

Jencks, Harlan. "Civil-Military Relations in China: Tiananmen and After." *Problems of Communism* 40 (May–June 1991), 14–29. Jianzhang, Pei. *Zhonghua renmin gongheguo waijiaoshi, 1949–1956* [*Diplomatic History of the People's Republic of China, 1949–1956*]. Beijing: Shijie zhishi [World Knowledge Publishing], 1994.

Joffe, Ellis. *The Chinese Army after Mao*. Cambridge, MA: Harvard University Press, 1987.

Joseph, Sarah. *Blame it on the WTO? A Human Rights Critique*. New York: Oxford University Press, 2011.

Juan, Karin Aguilar-San. *Little Saigons: Staying Vietnamese in America*. Minneapolis: University of Minnesota Press, 2009.

Jung, Walter B. *Nation Building: The Geopolitical History of Korea*. Lanham, MD: University Press of America, 1998.

Kang, David C. *East Asia before the West: Five Centuries of Trade and Tribute*. New York: Columbia University Press, 2012.

Kau, Michael Y. M., ed. *The Lin Biao Affair: Power Politics and Military Coup*. White Plains, NY: International Arts and Science Press, 1975.

Keegan, John. *A History of Warfare*. New York: Knopf, 1993.

Kemenade, Willem Van. *China, Hong Kong, Taiwan, Inc*. New York: Vintage, 1997.

Kennedy, Andrew B. "Military Audacity: Mao Zedong, Liu Shaoqi, and China's Adventure in Korea." In *History and Neorealism*. Ernest May, Richard Rosecrance, and Zara Steiner, eds. Cambridge, UK: Cambridge University Press, 2010.

Kenny, Henry J. "Vietnamese Perceptions of the 1979 War with China." In *Chinese Warfighting: the PLA Experience since 1949*. Mark A. Ryan, David M. Finkelstein, and Michael A. McDevitt, eds. 217–240. New York: M. E. Sharpe, 2003.

Kerkvliet, Benedict J. *The Power of Everyday Politics: How Vietnamese Peasants Transformed National Policy*. Ithaca, NY: Cornell University Press, 2005.

Khanh, Huynh Kim. *Vietnamese Communism, 1925–1945*. Ithaca, NY: Cornell University Press, 1982.

Khoo, Nicholas. *Collateral Damage: Sino-Soviet Rivalry and the Termination of the Sino-Vietnamese Alliance*. New York: Columbia University Press, 2011.

Kiernan, Ben. *How Pol Pot Came to Power: Colonialism, Nationalism, and Communism in Cambodia, 1930–1975*. New Haven, CT: Yale University Press, 2004.

Kiernan, Ben. *The Pol Pot Regime: Race, Power, and Genocide in Cambodia under the Khmer Rouge, 1975–1979*. Revised Edition. New Haven, CT: Yale University Press, 2014.

Kieschnick, John. *The Impact of Buddhism on Chinese Material Culture*. Princeton, NJ: Princeton University Press, 2003.

Klein, Donald W. "Japan and Europe in Chinese Foreign Relations." In *China and the World: Chinese Foreign Policy Faces the New Millennium*. Fourth edition. Samuel S. Kim, ed. 133–150. Boulder, CO: Westview Press, 1998.

Kuisong, Yang. *Zouxiang polie: Mao Zedong yu Moscow de enen yuanyuan* [*Road to the Split: Interests and Conflicts between Mao Zedong and Moscow*]. Hong Kong: Sanlian shudian [Three Joint Publishers], 1999.

Kuisong, Yang. "Mao Zedong and the Indochina Wars." In *Zhongguo yu yindu zhina zhanzheng* [*China and the Indochina Wars*]. Li Danhui, ed. 22–58. Hong Kong: Tiandi Tushu [Heaven and Earth Books], 2000.

Kuniholm, Bruce R. *The Origins of the Cold War in the Near East: Great Power Conflict and Diplomacy in Iran, Turkey, and Greece*. Princeton, NJ: Princeton University Press, 1980.

Kwon, Heonik. *After the Massacre: Commemoration and Consolation in Ha My and My Lai*. Berkeley: University of California Press, 2006.

Ky, Nguyen Cao. *How We Lost the Vietnam War*. Lanham, MD: Rowman and Littlefield, 2002.

Ky-Thoai, Ho van. "Naval Battle of the Paracels." In *Voices from the Second Republic of South Vietnam (1967–1975)*. Keith W. Taylor, ed. 149–171. Ithaca, NY: Cornell University Southeast Asia Program Publications, 2014.

Labbé, Danielle. *Land Politics and Livelihoods on the Margins of Hanoi, 1920–2010*. Vancouver, BC: University of British Columbia Press, 2014.

LaFeber, Walter. *America, Russia, and the Cold War, 1945–2006*. Tenth edition. Boston, MA: McGraw Hill, 2008.

Lanning, Michael and Dan Cragg. *Inside the VC and the NVA*. New York: Ballantine Books, 1992.

Lawrence, Mark Atwood. *The Vietnam War: A Concise International History*. New York: Oxford University Press, 2008.

Lee, Jonathan H. X. *Chinese Americans: The History and Culture of a People*. Santa Barbara, CA: ABC-CLIO, 2015.

Lee Jong Kan. "A North Korean Officer's Story." In *Voices of the Korean War: Personal Stories of American, Korean, and Chinese Soldiers*. Richard Peters and Xiaobing Li, eds. 76–84. Lexington, KY: University Press of Kentucky, 2004.

Lew, Christopher. "Liao-Shen Campaign." In *China at War*. Xiaobing Li, ed. 20–22. Santa Barbara, CA: ABC-CLIO, 2012.

Li, Cheng. *China's Leaders: The New Generation*. Lanham, MD: Rowman & Littlefield, 2001.

Li Danhui, "Conflicts between China and the Soviet Union in Their Efforts to Aid Vietnam and Resist America." In *Lengzhan yu zhongguo* [The Cold War and China]. Zhang Baijia and Niu Jun, eds. Beijing: Shijie zhishi [World Knowledge Publishing], 2002.

Li Danhui. "The Sino-Soviet Dispute over Assistance for Vietnam's Anti-American War, 1965–1972."Available at: http://www.shenzhihua.net/ynzz/000123.htm. [Accessed May 5, 2017].

Li, Jieli. "In Transformation toward Socio-Legality with Chinese Characteristics." In *Modern Chinese Legal Reform: New Perspective.* Xiaobing Li and Qiang Fang, eds. 111–130. Lexington, KY: University Press of Kentucky, 2013.

Li Ke and Hao Shengzhang. *Wenhua dageming zhong de renmin jiefangjun* [*The PLA during the Cultural Revolution*]. Beijing: Zhonggong dangshi ziliao [CCP Party Historical Archives Press], 1989.

Li, Xiaobing. "New War of Nerves: Mao's Legacy in Beijing's Policy toward Taiwan Strait." *Journal of Chinese Political Science* 3(1) (Summer 1997 1997), 65.

Li, Xiaobing. "Introduction: Social-Economic Transition and Cultural Reconstruction in China." In *Social Transition in China.* Jie Zhang and Xiaobing Li, eds. 1–18. Lanham, MD: University Press of America, 1998.

Li, Xiaobing. "PLA Attacks and Amphibious Operations during the Taiwan Straits Crises of 1954–1955 and 1958." In *Chinese Warfighting: the PLA Experience since 1949.* Mark A. Ryan, David M. Finkelstein, and Michael A. McDevitt, eds. 143–172. New York: M. E. Sharpe, 2003.

Li, Xiaobing. "Social Changes in China and Implications for the PLA," paper at the International Conference on the Civil-Military Issues in Today's China, the CNA Corporation, Alexandria, VA, March 21–23, 2004, 12.

Li, Xiaobing. "Reforming the People's Army: Military Modernization in China." *Journal of Southwest Conference on Asian Studies* 5 (2005), 17.

Li, Xiaobing. *A History of the Modern Chinese Army.* Lexington: University of Kentucky Press, 2007.

Li, Xiaobing. *Voices from the Vietnam War: Stories from American, Asian, and Russian Veterans.* Lexington, KY: University Press of Kentucky, 2010.

Li, Xiaobing. *Civil Liberties in China.* Santa Barbara, CA: ABC-CLIO, 2010.

Li, Xiaobing. ed. *China at War.* Santa Barbara, CA: ABC-CLIO, 2012.

Li, Xiaobing. "Chinese Communist Party." In *China at War.* Xiaobing Li, ed. 58–63. Santa Barbara, CA: ABC-CLIO, 2012.

Li, Xiaobing. "Truman and Taiwan: A U.S. Policy Change from Face to Faith." In *Northeast Asia and the Legacy of Harry S. Truman: Japan, China, and the Two Koreas.* James I. Matray, ed. 119–144. Kirksville, MO: Truman State University Press, 2012.

Li, Xiaobing. "The Dragon's Tale: China's Efforts toward the Rule of Law." In *Modern Chinese Legal Reform: New Perspectives.* Xiaobing Li and Qiang Fang, eds. 83–110. Lexington, KY: University Press of Kentucky, 2013.

Li, Xiaobing. "Chapter 29: Military Stalemate." In *Ashgate Research Companion to the Korean War.* James I. Matray and Donald W. Boose, Jr., eds. 383–394. Surrey, UK: Ashgate Publishing, 2014.

Li, Xiaobing. *China's Battle for Korea: The 1951 Spring Offensive.* Bloomington: Indiana University Press, 2014.

Li, Xiaobing. *Modern China: Understanding Modern Nations.* Santa Barbara, CA: ABC-CLIO, 2014.

Li, Xiaobing and Qiang Fang, eds. *Modern Chinese Legal Reform: New Perspectives.* Lexington: University Press of Kentucky, 2013.

Li, Xiaobing and Qiang Fang. "Legal Reforms in Twentieth-Century China." In *Modern Chinese Legal Reform: New Perspectives.* Xiaobing Li and Qiang Fang, eds. 19–20. Lexington, KY: University Press of Kentucky, 2013.

Li, Xiaobing, Allan Millett, and Bin Yu, trans. and eds. *Mao's Generals Remember Korea.* Lawrence, KS: University Press of Kansas, 2000.

Li, Xiaobing. "Sino-Soviet Border Disputes." In *MaGill's Guide to Military History*. John Powell ed. Pasadena, CA: Salem Press, 2001.

Li, Xiaobing and Michael Molina. "Japan," and "Taiwan." In *Oil: A Cultural and Geographic Encyclopedia of Black Gold*. Xiaobing Li and Michael Molina, eds. 2: 563–569 and 671–674. Santa Barbara, CA: ABC-CLIO, 2014.

Li, Xiaobing and Zuohong Pan, eds., *Taiwan in the Twenty-First Century*. New York: University of America Press, 2003, 144.

Li, Xiaobing and Xiansheng Tian, eds. *Evolution of Power: China's Struggle, Survival, and Success*. Lanham, MD: Lexington Books, 2014.

Li, Zhisui. *The Private Life of Chairman Mao: The Memoirs of Mao's Personal Physician*. New York: Random House, 1994.

Liang, Zhang, ed. *The Tiananmen Papers: The Chinese Leadership's Decision to Use Force against Their Own People—in Their Own Words*. New York: Public Affairs, 2001.

Lifang, Deng. "The First Anti-aggression War of the New Republic." In *Junqi piaopiao: xinzhongguo 50 nian junshi dashi shushi* [*PLA Flag Fluttering: Facts of China's Major Military Events in the Past Fifty Years*]. CAMS Military History Research Division, ed. Two volumes. Beijing: Jiefangjun [PLA Press], 1999.

Lintner, Bertil. *Great Leader, Dear Leader: Demystifying North Korea under the Kim Clan*. Muang, Thailand: Silkworm Books, 2005.

Lipton, Edward P. *Religious Freedom in Asia*. Hauppauge, NY: Nova Science, 2002.

Liu, Xiaoyuan. *A Partnership for Disorder: China, the United States, and their Policies for the Postwar Disposition of the Japanese Empire, 1941–1945*. Cambridge, UK: Cambridge University Press, 1996.

Liu, Xiaoyuan. "From Five 'Imperial Domains' to a 'Chinese Nation': A Perceptual and Political Transformation in Recent History." In *Ethnic China: Identity, Assimilation, and Resistance*. Xiaobing Li and Patrick Fuliang Shan, eds. 3–38. Lanham, MD: Lexington Books, 2015.

Lockhart, Bruce McFarland. *The End of the Vietnamese Monarchy*. New Haven, CT: Yale University Southeast Asia Studies, 1993.

Logevall, Fredrik. *Embers of War: The Fall of an Empire and the Making of America's Vietnam*. New York: Random House, 2014.

Luo, Jing, ed. *China Today*. Westport, CT: Greenwood Press, 2005.

Luo, Jing. "Reform of Deng Xiaoping," in *China Today*. Jing Luo, ed. 1: 119. Westport, CT: Greenwood Press, 2005.

Lüthi, Lorenz M., ed. *The Regional Cold Wars in Europe, East Asia, and the Middle East: Crucial Periods and Turning Points*. Stanford, CA: Stanford University Press, 2015.

Lüthi, Lorenz M. *The Sino-Soviet Split: Cold War in the Communist World*. Princeton, NJ: Princeton University Press, 2008.

MacLean, Ken. *The Government of Mistrust: Illegibility and Bureaucratic Power in Socialist Vietnam*. Madison: University of Wisconsin Press, 2013.

Maier, Charles S. "Consigning the Twentieth Century to History: Alternatives for the Modern Era." *American Historical Review* 105(3) (June 2000): 807–831.

Mann, Jim. *About Face: A History of America's Curious Relationship with China, from Nixon to Clinton*. New York: Knopf, 1999.

Marr, David. "Ho Chi Minh's Independence Declaration." In *Essays into Vietnamese Pasts*. K. W. Taylor and John K. Whitmore, 215–234. Ithaca, NY: Cornell Southeast Asia Program, 1995.

Marr, David. *Vietnam 1945: The Quest for Power*. Berkeley: University of California Press, 1995.

Marr, David. *Vietnam: State, War, and Revolution, 1945–1946*. Berkeley: University of California Press, 2013.

Matray, James I. "Opening Remarks" at the International Symposium, "The Legacy of Harry S. Truman in East Asia: Japan, China, and the Two Koreas." Key West, FL, May 14–15, 2010.

Matray, James I and Donald W. Boose, Jr. *Ashgate Research Companion to the Korean War.* Surrey, UK: Ashgate Publishing, 2014.

Maxwell, Neville. *India's China War.* New York: Pantheon Books, 1970.

McClain, James L. *Japan: A Modern History.* New York: Norton, 2002.

McGregor, Richard. *The Party: The Secret World of China's Communist Rulers.* New York: Harper/Perennial, 2012.

McHale, Shawn. "Freedom, Violence, and the Struggle over the Public Arena in the Democratic Republic of Vietnam, 1945–1958." In *Naissance d'un État-Parti/Birth of the Party State: Vietnam since 1945.* Christopher E. Goscha and Benoît de Trégoldé, eds. Paris: Les Indes Savantes, 2004.

McMahon, Robert J., ed. *Major Problems in the History of the Vietnam War: Documents and Essays.* Lexington, MA: Heath, 1995.

Meisner, Maurice. *Mao's China: A History of the People's Republic.* New York: The Free Press, 1977.

Meng, Gao and Yan Jiaqi. *Wenhua dageming shi nian shi* [*Ten Years of the Cultural Revolution*]. Tianjin: Tianjin renmin [Tianjin People's Publishing], 1986.

Meyer, Milton W. *Japan: A Concise History.* Fourth edition. Lanham, MD: Rowman & Littlefield, 2013.

Military History Institute of Vietnam. *Victory in Vietnam: The Official History of the People's Army of Vietnam, 1954–1975.* Merle L. Pribbenow, trans. Lawrence, KS: University Press of Kansas, 2002.

Military History Research Division, China Academy of Military Science (CAMS), ed. *Junqi piaopiao: xinzhongguo 50 nian junshi dashi shushi* [*PLA Flag Fluttering: Facts of China's Major Military Events in the Past Fifty Years*]. Beijing: Jiefangjun [PLA Press], 1999.

Military History Research Division, China Academy of Military Science (CAMS), ed. *Zhongguo renmin jiefangjun quanguo jiefang zhanzhengshi* [*History of the PLA in the Chinese Civil War*]. Beijing: Junshi kexue [Military Science Press], 1997.

Military History Research Division, China Academy of Military Science (CAMS), ed. *Zhongguo renmin jiefangjun de 70 nian, 1927–1997* [*Seventy Years of the PLA, 1927–1997*]. Beijing: Junshi kexue [Military Science Press], 1997.

Miller, Edward. *Misalliance: Ngo Dinh Diem, the United States, and the Fate of South Vietnam.* Cambridge, MA: Harvard University Press, 2013.

Millett, Allan R. *The War for Korea, 1950–1951: They Came from the North.* Lawrence, KS: University Press of Kansas, 2010.

Millward, James. *The Silk Road: A Very Short Introduction.* Oxford, UK: Oxford University Press, 2013.

Minh, Tran Quang. "A Decade of Public Service: Nation-building during the Interregnum and Second Republic." In *Voices from the Second Republic of South Vietnam (1967–1975).* K. W. Taylor, ed. 41–58. Ithaca, NY: Cornell Southeast Asia Program Publications, 2014.

Moise, Edwin E. *Land Reform in China and North Vietnam: Consolidating the Revolution at the Village Level.* Chapel Hill: University of North Carolina Press, 1983.

Morgan, Joseph G. *The Vietnam Lobby: The American Friends of Vietnam, 1955–1975.* Chapel Hill: University of North Carolina Press, 1997.

Mori, K. "*Kerry Spells out Policy on Senkaku Islands.*" In *UPI*, April 15, 2013. Available at: www.upi.com/Top_News/World-News/2013/04/15. [Accessed April 20, 2016].

Moss, George Donelson. *Vietnam: An American Ordeal.* Sixth edition. Upper Saddle River, NJ: Prentice Hall, 2010.

Moyar, Mark. *Triumph Forsaken: The Vietnam War, 1954–1965.* New York: Cambridge University Press, 2006.

Neiberg, Michael S. *Warfare in World History.* London: Routledge, 2001.

New York Times, January 25 and February 7, 1955

Nguyen, Lien-Hang. *Hanoi's War: An International History of the War for Peace in Vietnam.* Chapel Hill: University of North Carolina Press, 2012.

Nguyen, Nathalie Huynh Chau. *Memory is Another Country: Women of the Vietnamese Diaspora.* Santa Barbara, CA: ABC-CLIO, 2009.

Nianlong, Han. *Dangdai zhongguo waijiao [Foreign Affairs of Contemporary China].* Beijing: Zhongguo shehui kexue [China's Social Science Press], 1990.

Ninh, Bao. *The Sorrow of War.* New York: Penguin, 1996.

Ninh, Kim N. B. *A World Transformed: The Politics of Culture in Revolutionary Vietnam, 1945–1965.* Ann Arbor: University of Michigan Press, 2002.

Niu Jun. "Mao Zedong's Crisis Conception and Origins of the Sino-Soviet Alliance's Collapse." In *Lengzhan yu zhongguo [The Cold War and China].* Zhang Baijia and Niu Jun, eds. 273–296. Beijing: Shijie zhishi [World Knowledge Publishing], 2002.

Niu Jun. "The Origins of the Sino-Soviet Alliance." In *Brothers in Arms: The Rise and Fall of the Sino-Soviet Alliance, 1945–1963.* Odd Arne Westad, ed. 47–89. Stanford, CA: Stanford University Press, 1998.

Oliver, Kendrick. *The My Lai Massacre in American History and Memory.* Manchester, UK: Manchester University Press, 2006.

Ogden, Suzanne, Kathleen Hartford, Lawrence Sullivan, and David Zweig. *China's Search for Democracy: The Student and the Mass Movement of 1989.* Armonk, NY: M. E. Sharpe, 1992.

Pan, Zuohong. "Democracy and Economic Growth: A Taiwan Case Study." In *Taiwan in the Twenty-First Century.* Xiaobing Li and Zuohong Pan, eds. 139–166. New York: University of America Press, 2003.

Pantsov, Alexander V. and Steven I. Levine. *Mao: The Real Story.* New York: Simon & Schuster, 2012.

Patti, Archimedes L. A. *Why Viet Nam? Prelude to America's Albatross.* Berkeley: University of California Press, 1980.

Peerenboom, Randall. *China's Long March Toward Rule of Law.* Cambridge, UK: Cambridge University Press, 2002.

Peerenboom, Randall. "Law and development of Constitutional Democracy: Is China a Problem Case?" *The Annals of the American Academy, AAPSS,* 603 (January 2006): 181–197.

Pepper, Suzanne. *Civil War in China: The Political Struggle, 1945–1949.* Berkeley: University of California Press, 1978.

Perlez, J. "Sentiment Builds in China to Press Claim for Okinawa." *The New York Times,* June 13, 2013. Available at: http://www.nytimes.com/2013/06/14/world/asia.html. [Accessed March 11, 2015].

Phan, Peter C. *Mission and Catechesis: Alexandre de Rhodes & Enculturation in Seventeenth-Century Vietnam.* Maryknoll, NY: Orbis Books, 1998.

Pike, Douglas. *PAVN: People's Army of Vietnam.* Novato, CA: Presidio Press, 1986.

Pike, Douglas. *Vietnam and the Soviet Union: Anatomy of an Alliance.* Boulder, CO: Westview Press, 1987.

Pregadio, Fabrizio. *Great Clarity: Daoism and Alchemy in Early Medieval China.* Stanford, CA: Stanford University Press, 2006.

Pribbenow, Merle. "General Vo Nguyen Giap and the Mysterious Evolution of the Plan for the 1968 Tet Offensive." *Journal of Vietnamese Studies* 3(2) (2008): 2–21.

Qian Jiang. *Ping pong waijiao muhou [Behind the Ping-Pong Diplomacy].* Beijing: Dongfang [Oriental Press], 1997.

Qiu, Peipei. *Chinese Comfort Women: Testimonies from Imperial Japan's Sex Slaves.* New York: Oxford University Press, 2013.

Quinn-Judge, Sophie. *Ho Chi Minh: The Missing Years, 1919–1945.* Berkeley: University of California Press, 2002.

Quinn-Judge, Sophie. "History of the Vietnamese Communist Party." In *Rethinking Vietnam.* Duncan McCargo, ed. 26–41. New York: Routledge, 2004.

Qu Xing. "China's Foreign Policy since the Radical Changes in Eastern Europe and the Disintegration of the USSR." *Waijiao Xueyuan Xuekan* [*Journal of Foreign Affairs College*] 4(1994): 16–22.

Randle, Robert F. *Geneva 1954: The Settlement of the Indochinese War.* Princeton, NJ: Princeton University Press, 1969.

Reischauer, Edwin and Albert M. Craig. *Japan: Tradition and Transformation.* Revised edition. Boston, MA: Houghton Mifflin, 1989.

Reuters. "Japan Refuses China Demand for Apology in Boat Row." In *Reuters*, September 25, 2010. Available at: www.reuters.com/article/us-japan-china-defense-idUSKCN. [Accessed November 10, 2015].

Rithmire, Meg E. *Land Bargains and Chinese Capitalism: The Politics of Property Rights under Reform.* New York: Cambridge University Press, 2015.

Robinson, David M. *Empire's Twilight: Northeast Asia under the Mongols.* Cambridge, MA: Harvard University Press, 2009.

Robinson, Thomas. "The Sino-Soviet Border Conflicts of 1969: New Evidence Three Decades Later." *Chinese Warfighting: The PLA Experience since 1949.* Mark A. Ryan, David M. Finkelstein, and Michael A. McDevitt, eds. 198–216. Armonk, NY: M. E. Sharpe, 2003.

Ross, Robert. *Negotiating Cooperation: The United States and China: 1969–1989.* Stanford, CA: Stanford University Press, 1995.

Sakwa, Richard. *The Rise and Fall of the Soviet Union, 1917–1991.* London: Routledge, 1999.

Saull, Richard. *Rethinking Theory and History in the Cold War: The State, Military Power, and Social Revolution.* London: Frank Cass, 2001.

Sawyer, Ralph D., ed. *The Seven Military Classics of Ancient China.* New York: Basic Books, 2007.

Schell, Orville and David Shambaugh, eds. *The China Reader: The Reform Era.* New York: Vintage Books, 1999.

Schonberger, Howard B. *Aftermath of War: Americans and the Remaking of Japan, 1945–1952.* Kent, OH: Kent State University Press, 1989.

Schoppa, R. Keith. *Revolution and Its Past: Identities and Change in Modern Chinese History.* Third edition. New York: Prentice Hall, 2011.

Seth, Michael J. *A Concise History of Korea: From the Neolithic Period through the Nineteenth Century.* Lanham, MD: Rowman & Littlefield, 2006.

Shambaugh, David. *China's Communist Party: Atrophy and Adaptation.* Berkeley: University of California Press, 2008.

Shan, Patrick Fuliang. "Local Revolution, Grassroots Mobilization and Wartime Power Shift to the Rise of Communism." In *Evolution of Power: China's Struggle, Survival, and Success.* Xiaobing Li and Xiansheng Tian, eds. 3–26. Lanham, MD: Lexington Books, 2014.

Shen, Weiping. *8–23 Paoji Jinmen* [*8/23 Bombardment of Jinmen*]. Beijing: Huayi [China Literature Publishing], 1998.

Shen, Zhihua. "China Sends Troops to Korea: Beijing's Policy-making Process." In *China and the United States: A New Cold War History.* Xiaobing Li and Hongshan Li, eds. 13–48. Lanham, MD: University Press of America, 1998.

Shen, Zhihua. *Sulian zhuanjia zai zhongguo, 1948–1960* [*Soviet Experts in China, 1948–1960*]. Beijing: Zhongguo guoji guangbo [China International Broadcasting Publishing House], 2003.

Shen, Zhihua. *Mao Zedong, Sidalin he chaoxian zhanzheng* [*Mao Zedong, Stalin, and the Korean War*]. Guangzhou: Guangdong renmin [Guangdong People's Press], 2004.

Shen, Zhihua and Yafeng Xia. *Mao and the Sino-Soviet Partnership, 1945–1959: A New History.* Lanham, MD: Lexington Books, 2015.

Sheng, Michael M. *Battling Western Imperialism: Mao, Stalin, and the United States.* Princeton, NJ: Princeton University Press, 1997.

Short, Philip. *Mao: A Life.* New York: Henry Holt, 1999.

Simons, Geoff. *Korea: The Search for Sovereignty.* New York: St. Martin's Press, 1995.

Solinger, Dorothy J. "China's Floating Population." In *The Paradox of China's Post-Mao Reforms.* Merle Goldman and Roderick MacFarquhar, eds. 220–240. Cambridge, MA: Harvard University Press, 1999.

Song, Jingyi. "Personality and Politics: Deng Xiaoping's Return." In *Evolution of Power: China's Struggle, Survival, and Success.* Xiaobing Li and Xiansheng Tian, eds. 79–97. Lanham, MD: Lexington Books, 2014.

Sook, Suh Dae. *Korean Communism, 1945–1980.* Honolulu: University of Hawaii Press, 1981.

Spence, Jonathan D. *Mao Zedong.* New York: Viking, 1999.

Spence, Jonathan D. *The Search for Modern China.* Third edition. New York: Norton, 2013.

Standing Committee of the National People's Congress. *The Constitution of the People's Republic of China.* Beijing: Renmin [People's Press], 2004.

Strayer, Robert. *The Communist Experiment: Revolution, Socialism, and Global Conflict in the Twentieth Century.* Boston, MA: McGraw Hill, 2007.

Suh, Dae Sook. *Kim Il Sung: The North Korean Leader.* New York: Columbia University Press, 1988.

Sun, Anna. *Confucianism as a World Religion: Contested Histories and Contemporary Realities.* Princeton, NJ: Princeton University Press, 2013.

Sun, Yi and Xiaobing Li. "Mao Zedong and the CCP: Adaptation, Centralization, and Succession." In *Evolution of Power: China's Struggle, Survival, and Success.* Xiaobing Li and Xiansheng Tian, eds. 27–60. Lanham, MD: Lexington Books, 2014.

Sutter, Robert G. *U.S.-Chinese Relations: Perilous Past, Pragmatic Present.* New York: Rowman & Littlefield, 2010.

Tan, Nguyen Phut. *A Modern History of Viet Nam.* Saigon: Khai Tri, 1964.

Tana, Li. *Nguyễn Cochinchina: South Vietnam in the Seventeenth and Eighteenth Centuries.* Ithaca, NY: Cornell University Southeast Asia Program Publications, 1998.

Tang Xiuying. "A Sword Thrusting the Sky." In *Liangdan yixing; zhongguo hewuqi daodan weixing yu feichuan quanjishi* [*A Complete Record of China's Nuclear Bombs, Missiles, Satellites, and Space Programs*]. Political Department of the PLA General Armaments Department, ed. 361–372. Beijing: Jiuzhou [Jiuzhou Press], 2001.

Tanner, Harold M. *China: A History from the Great Qing Empire through the People's Republic of China.* Indianapolis, IN: Hackett, 2010.

Taylor, Keith W. "China and Vietnam: Looking for a New Version of an Old Relationship." In *The Vietnam War: Vietnamese and American Perspectives.* Jayne Werner and Luu Doan Huynh, eds. 244–291. New York: M. E. Sharpe, 1993.

Taylor, Keith W. "Surface Orientations in Vietnam: Beyond Histories of Nation and Region." *Journal of Asian Studies* 57(4) (November 1998): 962–985.

Taylor, Keith W. *A History of the Vietnamese.* New York: Cambridge University Press, 2013.

Taylor, Sandra C. *Vietnamese Women at War: Fighting for Ho Chi Minh and the Revolution.* Lawrence: University Press of Kansas, 1999.

Terrill, Ross. *Mao: A Biography.* Stanford, CA: Stanford University Press, 1999.

Thanh, Hoang Ngoc and Than Thi Nhan Duc. *Why the Vietnam War? President Ngo Dinh Diem and the U.S.: His Overthrow and Assassination.* Tuan-Yen and Quan-Viet, Vietnam: Mai-Nam Publishers, 2001.

Thong, Huynh Sanh. *To Be Made Over: Tales of Socialist Reeducation in Vietnam.* New Haven, CT: Yale Council on Southeast Asia Studies, 1988.

Tian Fuzi. *Zhongyeu zhanzheng jishilu* [*Factual Records of the Sino-Vietnam War*]. Beijing: jiefangjun wenyi [PLA Literature Press], 2004.

Tianjin Garrison Command HQ, "Information System: Key for National Defense." In *Editorial Department of National Defense Journal, Weile daying mingtian de zhanzheng (To Win the Future War).* Beijing: Guofand daxue [National Defense University Press], 1999.

Tilly, Charles. "Does Modernization Breed Revolution?" *Comparative Politics* 5(3) (1973): 425–447.

Time Magazine, February 18, 1946, 29–30.

Time Magazine. "Foreign Relations: Two Decisions." January 2, 1950, 11–12.

Tønneson, Stein. *The Vietnamese Revolution of 1945: Roosevelt, Ho Chi Minh, and De Gaulle in a World at War*. Oslo: International Peace Institute, 1991.

Tønneson, Stein. *Vietnam 1946: How the War Began*. Berkeley, CA: University of California Press, 2010.

Topmiller, Robert J. *The Lotus Unleashed: The Buddhist Peace Movement in South Vietnam, 1964–1966*. Lexington, KY: University Press of Kentucky, 2002.

Totman, Conrad. *Japan Before Perry: A Short History*. Berkeley: University of California Press, 1981.

Tucker, Nancy Bernkopf. *Strait Talk: United States-Taiwan Relations and the Crisis with China*. Cambridge, MA: Harvard University Press, 2009.

Tucker, Spencer C. *Vietnam*. Lexington, KY: University Press of Kentucky, 1999.

Turley, William S. and Mark Selden, eds. *Reinventing Vietnamese Socialism: Doi Moi in Comparative Perspective*. Boulder, CO: Westview, 1993.

Veith, George J. *Black April: The Fall of South Vietnam, 1973–1975*. New York: Encounter Books, 2012.

Vo, Alex-Thai D. "Nguyen Thi Nam and the Land Reform in North Vietnam, 1953." *Journal of Vietnamese Studies* 10(1) (Winter 2015): 19–25.

Vu, Tuong. "'It's Time for the Indochinese Revolution to Show Its True Colors': The Radical Turn of Vietnamese Politics in 1948." *Journal of Southeast Asian Studies* 40(3) (October 2009): 519–542.

Wakeman, Frederic, Jr. *The Fall of Imperial China*. New York: The Free Press, 1975.

Walthall, Anne *Japan: A Cultural, Social, and Political History*. Boston, MA: Houghton Mifflin, 2006.

Wang Taiping, ed. *Zhonghua renmin gongheguo waijiao shi, 1970–1978* [*Diplomatic History of the People's Republic of China, 1970–1978*]. Beijing: Shijie zhishi [World Knowledge Press], 1998.

Wang Xiangen. *Yuanyue kangmei shilu* [*True Stories of Aiding Vietnam and Resisting the U.S.*]. Beijing: Guoji wenhua [International Culture Publishing], 1990.

War History Division, National Defense University (NDU). *Zhongguo renmin jiefangjun zhanshi jianbian* [*A Brief War-Fighting History of the PLA*]. Beijing: Jiefangjun [PLA Press], 2001.

Wedeman, Andrew. *Double Paradox: Rapid Growth and Rising Corruption in China*. Ithaca, NY: Cornell University Press, 2012.

Wei, Ding. "The 1975 CMC Enlarged Meeting." In *Junqi piaopiao: xinzhongguo 50 nian junshi dashi shushi* [*PLA Flag Fluttering: Facts of China's Major Military Events in the Past Fifty Years*] Military History Research Division, China Academy of Military Science (CAMS), ed. Beijing: Jiefangjun [PLA Press], 1999.

Weihan, Yang. "Xi Jinping chuxi zhongyang zhengfa gongzuo huiyi [Xi Jinping Attended the Central Work Meeting of the Politics and Law]" in *Xinhuanet*, January 8, 2014.

Wells-Dang, Andrew. "The Political Influence of Civil Society in Vietnam." In *Politics in Contemporary Vietnam: Party, State, and Authority Relations*. Jonathan D. London, ed. 154–177. New York: Palgrave Macmillan, 2014.

Wenqian, Gao. *Wannian Zhou Enlai* [*Zhou Enlai's Later Years*]. Hong Kong: Mingjing [Bright Mirror Publishing], 2003.

Westad, Odd Arne, ed. *Brothers in Arms: The Rise and Fall of the Sino-Soviet Alliance, 1945–1963*, Washington, DC and Stanford, CA: Woodrow Wilson Center Press and Stanford University Press, 1998.

Westad, Odd Arne, ed. *Decisive Encounters: The Chinese Civil War, 1946–1950*. Stanford, CA: Stanford University Press, 2003.

Westad, Odd Arne, ed. *The Global Cold War: Third World Interventions and the Making of Our Times*, New York: Cambridge University Press, 2005.

Whiting, Allen S. *The Chinese Calculus of Deterrence: India and Indochina*. Ann Arbor: University of Michigan Press, 1975.

Wiest, Andrew. *Vietnam's Forgotten Army: Heroism and Betrayal in the ARVN*. New York: New York University Press, 2007.

Woo, Margaret Y. K. "Law and Discretion in Contemporary Chinese Courts." In *The Limits of the Rule of Law in China*. Karen G. Turner, James V. Feinerman, and R. Kent Guy, eds. 155–176. Seattle: University of Washington Press, 2000.

Woodhull, Nancy J. and Robert W. Snyder, eds. *Defining Moments in Journalism*. New Brunswick, NJ: Transaction Publishers, 1998.

Worthing, Peter. *Occupation and Revolution: China and the Vietnamese August Revolution of 1945*. Berkeley: University of California Press, 2001.

Xia, Liping. "The Korean Factor in China's Policy toward East Asia and the United States." *American Foreign Policy Interests* 27(4) (August 2005): 241–258.

Xia, Yafeng. *Negotiating with the Enemy: U.S.-China Talks during the Cold War, 1949–1972*. Bloomington: Indiana University Press, 2006.

Xiang, Lanxin. *Recasting the Imperial Far East: Britain and America in China, 1945–1950*. Armonk, NY: M. E. Sharpe, 1995.

Xiangen, Wang. *Zhongguo mimi da fabing: yuanyue kangmei shilu* [*The Secret Dispatch of Chinese Forces: True stories of Aiding Vietnam and Resisting the U.S.*]. Ji'nan: Ji'nan chubanshe [Ji'nan Publishing], 1992.

Xinghuo Liaoyuan Composition Department. *Zhongguo renmin jiefangjun jiangshuai minglu* [*Marshals and Generals of the PLA*]. Three volumes. Beijing: Jiefangjun [PLA Press], 1992.

Xinhua News Agency. *China's Foreign Relations: A Chronology of Events, 1949–1988*. Beijing: Foreign Languages Press, 1989.

Xiong, Guangkai. *International Strategy and Revolution in Military Affairs*. Beijing: Tsinghua University Press, 2003.

Xu, Guangqiu. *Congress and the U.S.-China Relationship, 1949–1979*. Akron, OH: University of Akron Press, 2007

Xu, Guangqiu. "Tributary System." In *China at War*. Xiaobing Li, ed. 463–465. Santa Barbara, CA: ABC-CLIO, 2014.

Xu Yan. "Chinese Forces and Their Casualties in the Korean War." Xiaobing Li, trans. *Chinese Historians* 6(2) (Fall 1993): 45–64.

Xu Yan. *Jinmen zhizhan* [*The Battle of Jinmen*]. Beijing: Zhongguo guangbo dianshi [China Broadcasting and Television Publishing], 1992.

Xu Yan. *Mao Zedong yu kangmei yuanchao zhanzheng* [*Mao Zedong and the War to Resist the US and Aid Korea*]. Second edition. Beijing: Jiefangjun [PLA Press], 2006.

Yao, Huang and Yan Jingtang. *Lin Biao yisheng* [*Lin Biao's Life*]. Beijing: Jiefangjun wenyi [PLA Literature Press], 2004.

Yaobang, Hu. "Create a New Situation in All Fields of Socialist Modernization, September 1, 1982." In *Major Documents of the People's Republic of China – Selected Important Documents since the Third Plenary Session of the Eleventh CCP Central Committee*. Research Department of Party Documents, CCP Central Committee, ed. 267–328. Beijing: Foreign Languages Press, 1991.

Yizhi, Wang. "Huiyi Zhang Tailei" [Recollections of Zhang Tailei]. *Jindaishi yanjiu* [*Journal of the Modern History Studies*] 2 (1983).

Yonglie, Ye. *Gaoceng jiaoliang* [*Power Struggle at the Top*]. Urumqi: Xinjiang renmin [Xinjiang People's Press], 2004.

You, Ji. *China's Military Transformation: Politics and War Preparation*. Cambridge, UK: Polity Press, 2016.

You, Ji. "Meeting the Challenge of Multi-Polarity: China's Foreign Policy toward Post-Cold War Asia and the Pacific." In *Asian-Pacific Collective Security in the Post-Cold War Era*. Hung-mao Tien, ed. 233–273. Taipei: National Policy Institute, 1996.

Young, Marilyn B. *The Vietnam Wars, 1945–1990*. New York: HarperCollins, 1991.

Zarrow, Peter. *China in War and Revolution, 1895–1949.* New York: Routledge, 2005.

Zazloff, Joseph J. "Rural Resettlement in South Vietnam: The Agroville Program." *Pacific Affairs* 35(4) (Winter 1962): 320–337.

Zhai, Qiang. *China and the Vietnam Wars, 1950–1975.* Chapel Hill: University of North Carolina Press, 2000.

Zhang, Aiping. *Zhongguo renmin jiefangjun [The Chinese People's Liberation Army].* Beijing: Dangdai zhongguo [Contemporary China Press], 1994.

Zhang, Dainian and Edmund Ryden. *Key Concepts in Chinese Philosophy.* New Haven, CT: Yale University Press, 2000.

Zhang, Shuguang. *Mao's Military Romanticism: China and the Korean War, 1950–1953.* Lawrence, KS: University Press of Kansas, 1995.

Zhang, Shuguang. "Revolution, Security, and Deterrence: The Origins of Sino-American Relations, 1948–1950." *Chinese Historians* 3(1) (January 1990): 1–26.

Zheng, Huang. *Hu zhimin yu zhong guo [Ho Chi Minh and China].* Beijing: Jiefangjun [PLA Press], 1987.

Zheng, Huang. *Liu Shaoqi yisheng [Life of Liu Shaoqi].* Beijing: Zhongyang wenxian [CCP Central Archival and Manuscript Press], 2003.

Zhu, Fang. *Gun Barrel Politics: Party-Army Relations in Mao's China.* Boulder, CO: Westview Press, 1998.

Zinoman, Peter. "Nhan Van-Giai Pham and Vietnamese 'Reform Communism' in the 1950s: A Revisionist Interpretation." *Journal of Cold War Studies* 13(1) (Winter 2011): 60–64.

Zubok, Vladislav and Constantine Pleshakov. *Inside the Kremlin's Cold War: From Stalin to Khrushchev,* Cambridge, MA: Harvard University Press, 1996.

Index

Made in the USA
Monee, IL
31 August 2021